WHERE THE CLOUDS MEET THE WATER

KIMBERLY E. CONTAG
AND
JAMES A. GRABOWSKA

Copyright © 2004 by Kimberly E. Contag and Jim A. Grabowska

Cover and interior designed by Masha Shubin

All rights reserved. No part of this book may be reproduced or transmitted in any form or by any means whatsoever, including photocopying, recording or by any information storage and retrieval system, without written permission from the publisher and/or author. Contact Inkwater Press at 6750 SW Franklin Street, Suite A, Portland, OR 97223-2542.

www.inkwaterpress.com

ISBN 1-59299-073-8

Publisher: Inkwater Press

Printed in the U.S.A.

TABLE OF CONTENTS

ACKNOWLEDGEMENTS v

PROLOGUE ix

COUNTDOWN FROM FREEDOM'S MOUNT 1

LIFE ON THE PICHINCHA 23

ALL ABOARD AT CHIMBACALLE STATION 52

JOURNEY ON THE HORIZON 79

REPATRIATION SAIL 119

BLOOD AND HONOR 182

AIR RAID! 255

RÉFUGIÉ POLITIQUE 304

LETTERS FROM EIGHTH AND 51ST 347

FOG IN THE QUITUS VALLEY 371

EPILOGUE 417

ACKNOWLEDGEMENTS

There is no greater sign of success for a writer than finding one of your readers totally engaged in something you have written. I asked my eleven-year old son who had just finished reading the *Lord of the Rings* series to read *Where the Clouds Meet the Water*. He agreed when I offered him 10 cents a page. I still wondered if the promise of pay would be enough to get him through even a few chapters. His interest in the book grew and by the time he finished reading chapter three, I couldn't print off copies of chapters fast enough to suit him. One evening, as I passed by his room, I heard him laughing and stopped in to ask what he found so funny in the manuscript. He responded, "I was reading about Karl Heinz and I worried he might be killed and would never be reunited with his family again. Then I realized that I knew the man called Karl Heinz. I forgot that he grew up to be my grandpa." When he finished the entire manuscript he exclaimed, "This book should be on the New York Best Seller List."

Since this was the first time Jim or I had attempted to write a work of narrative history or creative non-fiction, it was important to have outside readers review the work. We would like to recognize the readers who read the manuscript in its many forms and at different stages: Ann and Carlos Contag, Roger Sheffer, Suzanne Bunkers, Helen Grabowska, Bill Droessler, Hermann Detken and members of our faculty writing group at Minnesota State Universiy, Sandra Roe, Melissa Holmberg and Janet Cherrington-Cucore.

The telling of this narrative required the cooperation of many individuals and institutions in Ecuador, Germany, France, the United States, Spain and Portugal. We have listed the individuals we interviewed at the end of the works cited. Many of these individuals shared important personal testimony about the German Ecuadorian experience during World War II and the special relationships they had with the Ernesto Contag family. In addition, they shared parallel life stories that we could not incorporate into this book but are no less significant or amazing. A special debt is owed to the people who assisted us even though they had no direct connection with the family. These unnamed assistants were drawn into the research and simply offered to help find historical documents or took us to visit the places that were named in Ernesto Contag's date book.

We would like to acknowledge our gratitude to Dr. Carlos and Ann Contag, Myriam Maldonado de Contag, Pietro and Beti Tosi, and Hermann Detken, whose friendships and contacts in Ecuador and Germany and whose personal archives of historical documents (photographs, letters, bank books, etc.) made the writing of this book possible. The Pietro Tosi family of Cuenca and Mr. Hermann Detken of Quito, Ecuador, assisted us in all aspects of our dealings with Ecuadorian institutions and particularly in making contacts with German Ecuadorians and sharing important personal historical documents. In the United States we thank the Greenbrier Hotel for giving us permission to use historical documents and photographs. We wish to thank Eckart Contag of Zehlendorf, Germany, who spent hours in local and national archives ferreting out vital information for the chapters that take place in Germany, and who served as our guide in the Mark Brandenburg.

I also acknowledge the support from Minnesota State University, Mankato, for granting me a faculty research grant and sabbatical leave in support of the research and writing of this book. The experience of conducting research in five different countries, interviewing people about their personal life stories in times of war, and having ample time to write about these things has been the most satisfying professional experience I have ever had.

Kimberly Contag

PROLOGUE

MANKATO, MINNESOTA, 2002

On December 7, 1997 I knew the course of this book had changed forever. I stood at the foot of my father's hospital bed and watched in horror as his doctor shouted "Carlos, Carlos," trying to wake him from a stroke-induced slumber. After weeks in intensive care he emerged a survivor, but not without great losses. He lost most of the mobility of his right side. He lost his ability to read and to communicate with words. He had been trilingual, speaking German, Spanish and English with native fluency.

Language was his greatest loss. Raised in Quito, Ecuador, he spoke Spanish with a *Quiteño* accent and often colored his descriptions of growing up on the Pichincha mountain with Quechua words he had learned as a child from his indigenous neighbors. His German reflected an accent from the central part of Germany where he had spent over three years of his adolescence as a political deportee in World War II. After living nearly forty years in New Ulm, Minnesota, he spoke English with just the trace of an accent. My father had a gift for languages and communication, unafraid to attempt a conversation in French, Portuguese or Russian, bits and pieces of which he had learned amongst the refugees in the repatriation camp in Beaune-La Rolande, France in 1946. After six months of recovery he was still unable to narrate his past or even pronounce my name. When he greeted me, he called me Irmgard, the name of his only sister and only surviving sibling. As you can imagine, I nearly abandoned my research for *Where the Clouds Meet the Water*. I had, until December 7, planned to write my father's memoirs.

My father's silences were interrupted by attempts to find words or concepts to represent his thoughts. He wanted me to write the book about the experiences of the German-Ecuadorian deportees in World War II because no one knew very much about them. His struggle to communicate encouraged me to continue searching for answers to a fifty-year old enigma. At the beginning of World War II his widowed father had been blacklisted by the United States' State Department, and on May 8, 1942, the family had been exiled from Ecuador, South America in spite of their birthright as Ecuadorian citizens. When I tell people about the deportation instigated by the U.S. and carried out with the cooperation of the Ecuadorian government, they stare at me in disbelief. I know how they feel. As an adult with young children, I have tried to imagine being deported from my home in the U.S. and to envision some foreign country's state department telling me, my husband, and my three young boys that, because of my German heritage or my grandfather's nationality, we would be arrested and interned or deported to a country at war.

Since early childhood, I had heard the stories about the blacklists, the deportation on crowded ships, the starvation rations in Europe, and the little miracles that allowed for most of my grandfather's family to return home to Ecuador. I only had stories, though, and I needed details and corroboration. No one in my family —except my father— knew very much about the events that led up to the deportation, internment or exchange of Latin Americans for Americans in Axis countries, and, frankly, after some searching on the internet and in the library, I was concerned that the detective work, interviews, and historical research I would have to take on would be more than I could handle. I am not trained as an historian. I am a Spanish professor at a comprehensive state university in rural Minnesota. Still, I had the family connections in Ecuador and Germany, I had the five languages to conduct the research, and I had a sabbatical coming up. The more I thought about abandoning the project, the more I felt I had to take it on.

The doctors encouraged family members to speak to my father in Spanish and German as well as English to see if one language might be more retrievable than the others. To the disappointment of my English-speaking mother, my father communicated best in Spanish. So we began the long process of reconstructing language by trying to reconstruct his past. In this way we both gained: by working on the book he improved his language skills, and our sessions gave me more clues to finding answers for the project. We spent two hours per week on average in our version of speech therapy. The stroke had affected the part of his brain that controlled past tense, so we worked in the past using present tense verbs. I learned to narrate through his silences and he learned to speak through allegory and common denominator language. On occasion, for my mother's sake, I frustrated him with English. For example, one day I asked him what he used to eat in Ecuador besides "fanesca," a traditional Ecuadorian Easter dish. He replied, "purple mice soup." That is what I heard him say. When I reverted to Spanish and said in disbelief, "Are you trying to tell me that you ate *ratoncitos de color morado?*" He laughed out loud. That is when I realized that he meant "blue corn" soup. "Maiz" was the only noun he had left in his working brain for corn.

My father was determined to help me with the research for the book and in one of our sessions he kept repeating his brother's name, "Werner," with difficulty. At my husband's urging I wrote Werner's widow, my Aunt Myriam, and asked her to send any documents or photographs that might jog my father's memory about the time the family had spent in Ecuador, in Europe or the U.S. When the FedEx package arrived a few weeks later, I knew *Where the Clouds Meet the Water* had chosen its author. Amongst my grandfather's effects were two letters to Nixon, several dark family photographs, a red bank book from Nazi Germany and three dog-eared pocket calendars from 1942, 1943 and 1945-6. The first pocket calendar recorded the date the family left Quito on the train for deportation, the date the steamer "Arcadia" left the port of Guayaquil for New Orleans, the day my grandfather's family arrived at the Greenbrier Hotel in White Sulphur Springs in West Virginia as "enemy aliens," and the dates of the exchange in Lisbon and arrival in Germany. My grandfather had recorded names of people, hotels, activities, bombings, business trips, addresses. My God, I had a place to begin.

My parents started hunting up old documents and photographs. I wrote countless letters and emails to anyone who might have information or a connection to someone who knew about the events of the deportation and internment or who might have documents about the exchange or the struggles in Nazi Germany. Being family made it easier to collect documents, but data collection was an emotional rollercoaster for me. There are a few things none of us want to know about the war years. By April 1999 I was holding a copy of the secret U.S. blacklist for Ecuadorians of German, Italian or Japanese heritage. I had also acquired a copy of the names of German internees from the Greenbrier Hotel historian Robert Conte. Art Jacobs, an expert on German-Americans in World War II and a German-American deportee to Germany, sent me a copy of my great uncle's family's registration at the internment camp in Crystal City, Texas. Things started coming together.

In May 1999 my husband and colleague, Dr. Jim Grabowska, and I traveled to Ecuador to meet other Ecuadorians of German heritage who had been affected by the blacklist and to conduct archival research. Archival research meant digging through dusty stacks of Ecuadorian newspapers. We were looking for articles and photographs about the treatment of Germans and heritage Germans in Ecuador and their exile. Before we left for Ecuador we believed the deportation and exchange to be a "national secret." When we started researching we learned that there was no secret at all as far as the Ecuadorian media were concerned. Names of those affected by the blacklist were published in the newspaper. Complaints from businesses were documented and we were able to locate publications of reactions to the restrictions and plight of internationals living in Ecuador. We collected digital photographs of newspaper articles, editorials, photographs, letters, and personal histories associated with the project. The outpouring of assistance from Ecuadorians was amazing, the only impediments to our research being limited time and the economic instability of the country. The newspaper research was exciting and we felt like detectives fitting together puzzle pieces of a crime.

There was nothing more frightening or gratifying than the personal histories we reconstructed through the interviews we conducted in Ecuador. There are two personal histories that you should know about before you read this book. Maria Mikette told us her story at the dinner table in her sister's house in Guayaquil. Maria, a sister, and their brother had traveled to Germany in their ailing father's stead. They were young teenagers and found Germany most inhospitable. Her description of the difficult life circumstances in Germany—forced labor, the refugee camps, forced prostitution of women without passports, the scavenging and hunger— were bone chilling, but it was the recollection of how she gathered her siblings and suffered a hostile homecoming that epitomized for me the tragic impact of her exile. Maria Mikette walked to Leipzig with an injured foot in a shoe with a cardboard sole. She walked for eight days without showering, without changing clothing, and was at the mercy of others for food and drink. A day's walk from Leipzig, she learned the city had been destroyed and fleeing refugees told her to turn back. There was no hope to find her sister there. Maria entered the ruined city in tears. She weaved her way through debris and, to her surprise, found the house where her sister served as a housemaid still standing. Her sister answered the door without recognizing Maria and said in disgust, "Fräulein, you smell awful." Maria was also reunited with her brother who had been left for dead under a heap of dead soldiers before being taken as prisoner. More than a year later, Maria's own father refused to recognize his daughter for three days after she returned to Ecuador. The emotional and physical trauma had changed her forever. Nearly blind and still suffering from ills due to her traumatic years in Germany, she signed the "Voluntary Participant" document I needed for my research and gave us permission to use her story in any way we could.

There were several "Marias" who were willing to talk to us about their experiences. Perhaps that is why we were so surprised to find an elderly gentleman who was still terrified to speak of the war years and the restrictions placed on internationals in Ecuador. When a friend of the family spotted the elderly colleague's name on the blacklist, he called the man on the telephone. More than fifty-five years after the blacklist was published, he was still too afraid to say anything. He wanted nothing to do with the project or with us. There were rumors that he had hidden out, changed his nationality, taken evasive and protective action in those days and he had remained in Ecuador. The man granted us an interview but we left his dusty, run-down workshop empty handed. When Jim asked why I had not given him a copy of the "Voluntary Participation" document to sign, I responded, "He would not have signed it. He does not want his story told." The option to stay in Ecuador at all costs had been an expensive one, and he was still living the restrictions more than a half-century later.

These personal stories and the varied reports of the effects restrictions had on many in Ecuador are peripheral to the story that I wanted to tell. Still, reports of attempted suicide and completed suicide by a German-Jew, for example, are pertinent to understanding the psyche of Ecuadorians with international heritage in 1942. For those who are interested in understanding the historical setting for the relocation of hundreds of Ecuadorians in 1942 and 1943, we plan to publish an historical article that traces the events that led up to the deportation. For those who are interested in the political aspects of the Latin American Deportation program there is Thomas Connell's *America's Japanese Hostages: The World War II Plan for a Japanese Free Latin America* (2002). Connell analyses the case of the Japanese in Peru, but his historical research into policy with Latin America has significant implications for Ecuador as well. Many blacklisted citizens could not avoid "choosing" deportation, as they were restricted economically, harassed, arrested, interned and threatened. Some tried to escape. Some went into hiding. The Ecuadorian media turned on these people who had been considered neighbors, friends, employers or clients and called them "Nazis," "totalitarians," and "enemy aliens." Some were shamed; others left the homeland that rejected them with their heads held high.

After returning from Ecuador, Jim and I realized that the book could not be completed successfully without extensive historical research on the war and the media. In addition to the Ecuadorian newspapers and historical accounts of the war, I read the daily foreign communiqués in the *New York Times* from April 1942 to March 1946 and scanned each daily newspaper for articles and cultural information associated with the project. The communiqués often ran six to twelve pages, thereby forcing articles about the murder of 60,000 Jews, an eyewitness report of lampshades made of human skin, and the U.S. army's starvation of German civilians to page 11 or 13. While not directly associated with my project, I was stunned, angered, and numbed by the general atrocities and pervasive nationalistic attitudes and practices of the war years in all countries. I imagine many contemporary readers in the 1940s simply flipped to the social pages, hunted for cheap apartments, or scanned the obituaries. War times were war times and life went on.

My experience with the *New York Times* 1942-45 made the site visits to Germany and France all the more urgent. Jim and I had conducted significant research on the areas of interest to the book in relation to Germany and France but without experiencing the environment and the locations or interviewing the survivors first-hand, my interpretation—at least as I saw it—would be mostly speculation and invention. In May 2000 I left the United States for Germany with my brother Ted who, along with Mr. Eckart Contag of Berlin, assisted me with interviews, photography and archival research.

For the first time since I had begun researching the topic of exile and survival I realized why my father and his sister remembered many aspects of their years in Germany so fondly and so vividly. The tranquil countryside where they learned to *be Germans* and to hide their Ecuadorianness was isolated and utterly beautiful. The importance of self-sufficiency and the continued isolation of rural Germans perpetuated a sense of tranquility and normalcy in the midst of crisis on the one hand, while disinformation and nationalistic practices and propaganda did a good job of making the individual feel indispensable to the community called Greater Germany, on the other. The result was that these displaced people had to fit in, had to become German, even though in doing so they had to deny their cultural identity, citizenship, their own personal language, history, and perception of self. This is why the writing of a narrative history of the Contag family's experiences of alienation and acceptance in Ecuador, the United States, Portugal, Germany and France is so compelling to me and so unique amongst war narratives. The survivors never considered themselves victims, only survivors who like chameleons, dodged danger by adapting and moving on cautiously.

Many people have commented to me how unfortunate it is that we initiated our research more than fifty years after the end of the war. My response is always that we simply could not have written the same book if our research had been conducted before the fall of the Berlin wall or before we had access to information through the Freedom of Information Act. More importantly, no one was talking about these issues ten years ago. In fact, the families of German-Ecuadorian survivors' know very little about the events that took their parents and grandparents on the journey of a lifetime. So much secrecy has surrounded the U.S. State Departments' involvement in the deportation that some survivors, now in their late sixties and early seventies, still believe the German government to be at the helm of the international exchange. *Where the Clouds Meet the Water* is representative of what happened to many of the ordinary families forced from their homes in Latin America and that is why we are compelled to share its intimacies with you.

WHERE THE CLOUDS MEET THE WATER

CHAPTER 1

COUNTDOWN FROM FREEDOM'S MOUNT

QUITO, ECUADOR, MARCH 1942

Ernst Contag arrived late to the gathering at the Deutsche Haus on the north end of city. Ernst was not usually prompt, unlike other Germans and German Ecuadorians in attendance at the meeting. Ernst had an Ecuadorian sense of time and place. He took things as they came and merely shrugged his shoulders when things did not turn out as expected. Only fools think they can control time, place, and destiny.

Ernst removed his gray felt fedora as he entered the Deutsche Haus, a hall that was part of the German school complex, and greeted with a nod the few men seated who noticed his arrival.[1] His entrance did little to interrupt the attention of most in attendance who had been captivated by the German who stood waving a newspaper article at the front of the hall.

"They want to know, my good friends, on which side of the ocean we stand." *¿Es Usted uno de ellos?* Are you one of *them* or are you one of *us*? The North Americans want you to pledge your allegiance to Ecuador and the Americas and to deny your allegiance to Germany. They want you to join up with their "new world order" and turn your back on the fatherland. And there is more! The North Americans want the Ecuadorian government to restrict our economic activities and turn us out of our homes here. This is madness!"

Ernst shifted his weight uncomfortably in his chair and lit a cigarette. The low wooden chairs weren't made for men his size, and what was more, the pistol in his right pocket pushed uncomfortably against his thigh. He straightened his leg and tugged gently at his trousers until he felt at ease.

Ernst had never been able to decide for himself the question that was now posed to all of them. Ernst was German Ecuadorian, born and raised in Ecuador by German immigrants. He had never had to choose between motherland and fatherland nor did he ever expect he could. What he knew of the German fatherland was what he read in the newspaper or heard on radio. The idea of choosing to pay allegiance to a country he had never even visited was political and he left politics to his older brother, Arturo. Ernst felt a similar disgust for Ecuadorian politics, which he considered scandalous and petty, but he liked some of the politicians and could call a few of them friends. Politics seemed a rather futile endeavor to Ernst. Little changed in Quito no matter how the wind changed politically and people lived as they always had. Life was not easy but it was simple. He got by like everyone else. Politics interested him as a topic for conversation but he was not an activist for any particular cause. Let people get on with their own lives was his motto. It was a good motto to live by.

Ernst turned his attention to an Ecuadorian-born German who stood to speak. "Do you remember that political cartoon in the *Mercurio* newspaper that Hans brought to our last meeting? The U.S. wanted Latin America swept clean of all foreign elements.

Political intrigues swept into a dustpan over the United States. Hogwash! The U.S. blacklist has already caused so much commotion among us that some of my friends have started selling their properties. Our businesses have been shut down. Publicity surrounding the blacklist has turned our community and our lives upside down. The blacklist is even dividing families. What are we going to do about this?"

This cartoon, published in *El Mercurio* February 12, 1942 shortly after the Pan-American conference in Rio de Janeiro, shows an artist's perception of how the "*Americas Clean House*" by sweeping Axis leaders and their intrigues toward the United States.

Ernst raised an eyebrow and grimaced. Since the Pan American Conference in Rio de Janeiro in January, the U.S. government had been pressuring Latin American governments to isolate international elements. Ernst had been skeptical of the Ecuadorian government's interest in acquiescing to such ludicrous restrictions, but expected that, most likely, there was money and power involved. The notion of "international elements" in Ecuador had received a broad, sweeping interpretation, and the U.S. blacklist for Ecuador included businesses that employed or did business with foreigners, foreigners living in Ecuador, individuals whose surname sounded foreign, passport internationals born and raised in Ecuador by immigrant parents, and anyone who had known ties to the Axis countries of Germany, Japan and Italy.

Ernst leaned back further in his chair, stroked his long angular face, and mumbled skeptically to himself about the whole situation. He thought the entire hysteria would pass. Ecuador was a peaceful, quiet place. A few people had been arrested and there were plans to deport others. There was even a camp set up for a few Japanese in Riobamba. He didn't believe he would be swept out of his homeland just because a few Ecuadorian politicians had made a deal with Mr. Undersecretary, a certain U.S. politician by the name of Mr. Sumner Welles.

Ernst was wrong.

Just then a rather stocky man from across the hall called out. "That damned blacklist is bad for business, isn't it Karl. I don't see how your delicious sausages could be prejudicial to the well-being of the American Republics." Laughter and words of disgust commingled and increased Ernst's awareness of his own feelings of ambiguity. All eyes turned to the young butcher who flushed in agreement, "Hear, hear!"

A German schoolteacher stood to speak. He was an extraordinarily tall and corpulent man whose head was disproportionately small. "The agents have been pestering Prexel, the soap maker. He isn't even German. Caper Rotenbach is a Yugoslav, for heaven's sake. They have been after anyone working at the Casa Poppe, German or not, and the security agents are harassing just about anyone with a foreign-sounding name."

A tall blond stood and took his turn in flawless German. "Like many of you I was born in Quito, married here, and I am raising my family here. Like you my heritage is German but my country of origin is Ecuador. My fatherland is Germany. My motherland is Ecuador. I have never lived anywhere but Quito. As far as anyone knows, my name is not on the blacklist yet, but I am afraid of what may happen in the next few weeks or months."

The short, taut-lipped man next to Ernst spoke sternly. "You should be nervous, my friend. Arroyo del Rio's government is so broke they'll do anything the Americans say to get their hands on American money. In February they brokered our rights for improvements in delivery of water, agriculture and health and, at the beginning of this month, Arroyo's government agreed to U.S. bases in Ecuador. That was the same week that Undersecretary Welles spoke about the "new crusade to save humanity" to be led by the United American Republics. Hell, everyone knows the director of this humanitarian crusade is the United States." The man's irony escaped no one.

Ernst listened closely while he scanned the faces of the men gathered at the tables. Some were visibly angry. Others just looked perplexed and concerned. A few shook their heads in disbelief. Others shrugged in apparent resignation. Ernst removed the cigarette from his mouth and bit at his bottom lip as he played with the butt between his fingers. It was an unusual group that surrounded him: engineers, teachers, a baker, a butcher, merchants, a mechanic, and several farmers. German born or Ecuadorian born, they were all Germans in this hall tonight. Ernst felt a sense of kinship with all these men and there was no denying his awareness of his own identity. These men held a common heritage that spanned two continents: Germany and South America. He was indeed one of them. Denying his European heritage or his country of birth was nothing more than denying who he really was.

International pressure had put them all in this uncomfortable position. Diplomats and consuls had been ordered to leave Ecuador voluntarily or by mandate before April 16. Some had already been taken into custody by authorities and plans were in the making for shipping them to the U.S. There was talk of repatriation to Germany but no one was sure what the U.S. would do with these people once they left their duties in Ecuador. As was customary, a list of departing travelers would appear in the newspaper and people would talk. With all the economic restrictions and harassment, immigrants and the children of immigrants who had lived in Ecuador many years or a lifetime were already discussing whether their future might be in Germany.

Ernst's musings were interrupted when the room grew quiet. A stern, tall man spoke with eloquence and statesmanship, "I find this whole situation rather remarkable, gentlemen. The newspapers and government officials have been successful in creating fear and suspicion amongst our neighbors, business partners, our clients and even our families. Our stores and businesses are in jeopardy. The restrictions have affected our school and even though we have begun making arrangements to protect it, many teachers here at the *Deutsche Schule* feel it will be difficult to protect our interests. Many fear they will also be asked to leave on a ship for the United States. The detention of Germans and Ecuadorians of German heritage is a crime! If the current economic restrictions are not lifted we have few options as to which side we can take. We want to feed our families and make a decent living."

The room was quiet for a moment but a soft, low voice rose from the back, "I am proud to be "one of them," and I will hold my head high when I sail to the fatherland." It was the art teacher, Herr Winkler, considered by many to be a bit of an activist.

Ernst had no tolerance for Herr Winkler no matter what his opinion was. Winkler was the teacher who had slapped his son, Heinz, because he did not have a clean handkerchief one day. Ernst considered the man too strict with children. Every time he saw him, he was reminded of the rough portrait of Beethoven that hung above the wood table in his dining room. Beethoven's uncanny eyes, treated by a not-so-skillful artist from the *Deutsche Schule*, scared the children. His evil eyes seemed to follow them as they moved about the dining room and left through the door each morning. "Be careful of the evil eye!" Ernst would spook the children cheerfully, pointing to the portrait before they left for school. It was a reminder to take a handkerchief. Ernst had made light of the teacher's reprimand concerning the handkerchief, but he never forgot how upset and humiliated his son had been. From that day on young Heinz made sure everyone in the family carried a clean handkerchief. *If Elisabeth were here, Heinz would not have had to grow up so fast*, Ernst thought, shaking his head. Ernst was often lost in thought about his wife, Elisabeth Dreier Contag. They had been soul mates. "A love made in heaven," is how the neighbors talked of their seven-year marriage. Her death had devastated him and left his four children without a loving mother.

Bernhardt Beate stood and spoke confidently, interrupting Ernst's thoughts. Bio, as his friends called him, had taken a liking to Ernst's sister, Helene. Lenchen, as Ernst called his sister, made her own choices and listened to no one. Ernst refused to entertain the idea of her marriage. He disliked change. There had been rumors about allowing Germans who married Ecuadorians to stay in Ecuador, but he refused to accept the fact that Bio and Lenchen might marry and shrugged off the thought that nagged him. It really was none of his business. Ernst finally stopped musing and listed to what Bio was saying.

"In February the newspaper reported that all Ecuadorians who are residents in Germany would enjoy complete freedom in the territories of the Reich. The Undersecretary of the Chancellery guaranteed it. What do we have to worry about?"

"I am not so sure we can get there to appreciate that freedom," countered Herr Sacklowski who stood between the *Ortsgruppenleiter*, who represented the Nazi party's interests in Quito, and Walter Diener from the hardware store. "The United States denied safe conduct to German and Italian diplomats from La Paz. How can we be sure that we will ever get to Germany? The Americans may arrest us and put us in camps as they have done with the some of German Mexicans, Bolivians, and Peruvians."

This information did not go over well amongst the men and many raised their voices. Hermann Dreier, also a German by birth, did not need to stand to speak but he rose anyway. His shock of blond hair was the only diminutive thing about his presence in the room. He was a levelheaded man and had a good head for negotiation. "The Consulate insists that the Americans want to exchange Latin American Germans, Austrians and Italians for Americans caught in Axis countries. There is every indication that the exchanges will take place."

Ernst studied his belated wife's brother and wondered if Hermann might be fortunate enough to stay in Quito. Hermann and his wife Anita were set on staying in Quito with their two young daughters, six-year old Helen Hope and two-year old Anna Elisabeth, whom they called Betty. Hermann had no interest or dealings with the Nazi party and he was married to an American citizen. Ernst thought it might be tricky for the U.S. State Department to intern him and his American wife in the United States.

"Why don't they trade their own people? There are Germans, Italians and Japanese living in the United States," sneered a young Ecuadorian-born German loudly enough to be heard. "Maybe they will; they probably are!" piped another. Again the hall was filled with chatter. Ernst understood why the Americans were looking beyond their borders for passport or heritage "diplomats." Both governments won with the exchange. The United States would not have a publicity problem at home. The Ecuadorian government and other cooperating Latin American governments would have access to private businesses and land. Germany gained soldiers and workers. The Germans in Ecuador were merely pawns on an international chessboard.

Ernst ran his hand across his hair and patted it into place. On the one hand, it seemed futile to try to stay in Ecuador. There didn't seem to be a way around being harassed out of his homeland. On the other, Germany was completely foreign to him. He had heard stories about Germany from his parents, his sister and his brother. But he had no stories of his own. He had never even crossed the border out of Ecuador. He stroked his jaw thoughtfully and rested his elbow on the fist of his right hand. This wouldn't be easy. No sir, not for a widower with four young children.

Ernst imagined that his brother Arturo, on the other hand, was looking forward to new opportunities in Germany. Arturo, married to an Ecuadorian woman, was a successful businessman and fiercely pro-German. Arturo's continued success was on the line due to economic restrictions against internationals, but he was certain he could support his family in Germany Arturo and Alcira had already decided to go to Germany, when they had the chance.

If Ernst and Lenchen also chose to leave Ecuador, the family could stay together. No matter how odd it seemed to him, he and his three siblings and their families could live in Germany. His brother Carl had been living and working in Berlin since he left Ecuador in 1936. Lenchen had spent a few childhood years in Germany where she had received expert medical treatment. She was strong of character and very talented. She would also find work in Germany. Still, something did not feel right. "*Alles ist hin,*" he mumbled to himself fatefully. How could he leave everything he and his children had known for what was unknown. *Pobrecitos,* he thought to himself. Ernst did not want his children to suffer.

Ernst was no stranger to suffering. His father had suffered enough for all of them the year before he died. Oscar Contag had spent more than a year in bed enduring gout, asthma and dropsy. He had a big wound in his leg that never healed. The open sore bothered young Ernst so much that at times he had to leave the room where his father lay dying. The four Contag siblings had watched their mother nurse him until his death. Ernst was only ten years old when they buried him.

The family's real suffering began after his father's death. His mother, Gertrude Ziehe, bought the house and property on Rocafuerte Street at public auction with the meager 1500 sucres left to her as a widow. Without money to take her children to Germany after her husband's death, she had cured hams and sold them from their new home in Quito to make ends meet. Although she longed to return to Germany to see her ailing father, her sense of responsibility was clear. Her children came first.

Ernst remembered finding his mother standing near her favorite rose bush. She held a letter in her hands and was weeping. When Ernst asked her what happened, she wiped away her tears and stiffened.

"The letter is from your grandfather, Ernst. He cannot move his hand to write. He is totally paralyzed and had to dictate this letter to his nurse. It makes me sad that I cannot see him again or help him when he is so very sick. Let me show you something." Ernst remembered the colorful and artistic drawings in between the verses of the book she brought from her bedroom. His mother had told him the Contag and Ziehe families were fine families and he should be proud to be of such fine German stock.

"My father, your grandfather, is a very special man, Ernst. He is well read and refined. He is a poet, a philosopher and an artist. Look at the drawings in this book he sent me. The watercolor paintings are so wonderful. Look at these lovely green pines. The forests near my childhood home are so beautiful. The lakes, the countryside . . . I can see them when I close my eyes at night." She had smiled through her pain and the words came faster.

"He writes wonderful poetry. See here in the book. Would you like to hear it?" The poem had cheered his mother and he remembered how tender she looked when she read it to him. He did not remember her being a tender woman otherwise. Most of his memories were of making sausages and making ends meet.

It was only as an adult that Ernst considered how many difficult choices his mother had made after his father's death. She never returned to her homeland or saw her family in Germany again.

Ernst straightened in the chair and stretched his aching back muscles, then shrugged his shoulders and sighed visibly, blowing air noisily through his pursed lips. It seemed that the decision had been made for him and his family. He and the children would have to make the best of it. The schools were good in Germany. At thirty-five he was still young and could adapt, find work, and make a temporary home for his children. When the time came, he and the children would sail for Germany with the others. He would tell them their mother had wished it. *Dearest Elisabeth. Mi querida Isabel. How you would have enjoyed taking this journey with us*, he thought. Ernst had never thought such a trip possible.

The meeting droned on. Ernst suddenly felt exhausted and almost bored by the discussion that ranged from declarations of disbelief to opportunistic anger. He snorted softly and closed his eyes. Germany. His earliest memories were German lullabies that his mother sang to him and his sister and brothers.

The opportunity to brew German beer and a desire for adventure had brought his father to Ecuador. German technology, German radios, and German equipment had become his own livelihood. Certainly compared to Ecuadorian technology and equipment the Germans were way ahead. There would be opportunities for him and his brother and sister in Germany. But he still had reservations. Germany was his father's country, his mother's country and his wife's country. But it was not his.

The men shared useful information about the paperwork that had to be completed at the Ministry and made preliminary decisions about travel arrangements. It had been unlike any other meeting they had held on Sunday afternoons at the Deutsche Haus. Ernst could see how each man struggled with personal, political, economic and family consequences as he made decisions about his own future with the other Germans and Ecuadorian-born Germans in the room. The beer flowed freely and made the meeting tolerable. After the meeting, Ernst stood at the door and shook the hands of friends and compatriots. As these men stepped out on to the corner of Veintemilla and 9 de octubre Streets, their customary farewell, *Auf wiedersehen*, seemed ironic and ominous to Ernst. They might not ever see each other again in Quito or elsewhere, given the volatility of the international sphere and relocation efforts.

When everyone had left, he locked the gate and shivered. The cool night air nipped at his fingers and ears as he returned indoors. He had been put in charge of guarding the school compound until dawn, but he expected no commotion. He relaxed and read the *El Mercurio* newspaper that one of the men had left at the table. He read the first two lines of a short anonymous poem that reminded him of his daughter Irmgard who often sat on the sill of the bedroom window overlooking Rocafuerte

Street. He plaited her hair in two long braids before sending her off to school. He read the poem called "Poemita" aloud to himself:

> On the balcony filled with geraniums
> The young girl braids her hair;
> The morrow is in her eyes,
> And there is so much sun in her hair,
> That although she wears it dark
> It turns a brilliant yellow.
> Bold red geraniums,
> The gray road ahead is painful.
> But in the bright wonder
> Of the clear Autumn morning
> My gaze is caught in its mischief
> On the balcony filled with geraniums
> Where the young girl braids her hair.[3]

Ernst knew that growing up without a mother would be difficult for Irmgard. Women often encouraged him to remarry so Irmgard would have a mother to prepare her for life as a woman. Life for girls was different than for boys on the Pichincha. It wouldn't be easy to raise her alone. Ernst frowned as he let the thoughts of adolescent perils cross his mind. Then, he smiled. Irmgard was a warm, happy child. She was sweet and full of love of the little things in life. Enchanted by wild flowers, she brought him joy every day. Irmgard. Bold geraniums were entirely wrong for her. Too grown up for his Irmgard. Lilacs and tiny pink roses should surround her.

Ernst stepped outside the hall and pulled his collar up against his neck. The sun would rise on the horizon hidden behind the mountains to the east soon, but it would not break over the towering mountain peaks surrounding Quito for some time. The maids would already be at his house stoking the wood stove as usual. His children would be stirring and starting to dress for school. It would be too chilly for little Irmgard to brush her long hair while sitting at an open window in the morning.

What of "the gray painful road ahead?" he asked himself. Was the "Little Poem" an omen? Ernst was somewhat superstitious and decided it was best not to even think such thoughts. He shrugged in disregard, tore the poem from the newspaper and thrust it into his left trouser pocket. He was certain that Irmgard would enjoy hearing the little poem about a girl who brushed and braided her hair as she did.

Before leaving the school grounds Ernst decided to wait to talk to his sister, Lenchen, who had a small apartment on the school grounds. While he waited, he let his mind wander to his own childhood experiences at the German School. He and his brothers were charter students of the first German School in Quito. As young children they walked each morning from La Campana brewery to La Magdalena where the first schoolroom was located, a good half hour walk from the brewery behind his parents' home. He, Arturo, and Carlos had always walked together. His little sister had been too ill to attend school in Quito in those days. Now, here she was a schoolteacher.

Helene Contag appeared at the doorway of the girls' dormitory. She was dressed neatly and wore an unusually cheerful smile. She was thin and tall and looked slightly older than her thirty years. She strode confidently and purposefully toward her brother. The limp she had from childhood seemed to fade as she approached him.

"Ernesto," Helene spoke as she kissed her brother on the right cheek in Ecuadorian fashion. "You need a shave."

"I haven't been home, Lenchen. You know that." Ernst frowned and changed the subject. "Why don't you come by the house on the weekend. I think we need to talk about what we are going to do. Arturo and Alcira will be coming to Quito to get their papers in order and we can talk then."

"All right. I'll come by on Sunday afternoon for a while. I have responsibilities until then. Will Anita and Hermann come over too?"

"I don't know what they are planning to do. I think they want to try to stay in Quito. Hermann's name is also on the blacklist and he has registered with the government, but I think there is a pretty good chance that his marriage to Anita might help them stay in business here. He is on a first name basis with the U.S. agents. Who knows?" Ernst leaned closer to his sister and smiled. "By the way, Bio was in fine form at the meeting. Have you spoken with him?"

"Not since yesterday afternoon *before* the meeting. *Eres un mal pensado,*" she scolded her brother in Spanish as she gave him a gentle push. "You are always pestering me with such dishonorable thoughts. Bio wants to stay in Ecuador, of course. He would not have come here from Germany otherwise. These restrictions could not have come at a worse time."

Helene hesitated but then asked in earnest, "Ernesto, has he spoken to you about anything?"

Ernst responded teasingly. "Well, . . . of course we have spoken, but not about anything important . . . not specifically anyway." Ernst knew what his sister was hinting at, but made no mention that he suspected she and Bio might marry soon. "Besides, what do we have to talk about anyway?"

"Well," she brushed off his sarcasm and continued, "It looks like I will have to pack my things soon in any case. The school is to be run by a Russian fellow and rumor has it that we will all have to leave the school some time next month. There is no word yet, but the other teachers are talking about what they will do. Ernesto, how is it possible that in a little more than three months our entire lives have been so changed?" Ernst did not answer her as the question seemed more a statement of defiant resignation than a real question.

"So, get on home and get those kids ready for school," she paused, "and send twenty *centavos* with Heinz so he doesn't ask me for bus money this afternoon. I won't give it to him. I have to save for my future, too, you know." Helene feigned stiffness but her brother understood her subtle reproach for what she thought were his spendthrift ways.

Before the two parted, Ernst walked with his sister toward the dormitory for girls. Fraülein Contag, as she was known at the school, was in charge of getting her young female charges to the showers and she paused a moment before she went to wake them. "I have to brace myself each day for the morning complaints. Those girls shudder so under the chilly spray in the common shower area. They make quite a scene."

Ernst chuckled. He had heard the boarding students' complaints about the frigid morning shower from Hartch, the teacher in charge of the Munich Dormitory where the young boys bunked. According to his own children, Hartch was gruff and bad-tempered. It was not uncommon for the blue-eyed German to slap a child who was misbehaving. His redeeming quality was that he played the accordion quite well and was also good-natured when he woke the children in their bunks at six in the morning.

Lenchen stopped short of the doorway and said, "Your son Heinz must have been in quite a state last week after eating all those bowls of rhubarb sauce. Heinz had at least ten dishes of sauce in front of him and he smacked his lips enthusiastically while emptying each bowl. He was the only one eating any rhubarb! The other boys just looked on in amazement or sneered at him saying, 'How can you eat that cooked onion, Heinz?'" Ernst laughed and patted his sister on the shoulder. "I bet he spent that whole day in the bathroom, Lenchen!" Ernst turned to leave and headed for home. "See you on Sunday."

Ernst lifted the brim of his hat and nodded at the teachers in the schoolyard while on his way toward the door on 9 de octubre Street. He clapped Gunther Möbius, the physical education teacher at the school, on the back. Gunter was particularly friendly. He had come to Ecuador as a wrestler and gave professional demonstrations before he became a teacher at the school. Ernst wondered to himself where all these teachers, professionals, and tradesmen who left Germany might end up if the international elements were indeed cleansed from the country, and what might happen to business as usual in Ecuador, if they were rounded up and shipped out.

Ernst closed the large school gate behind him. He ran through some of the names of international community members aloud to himself. No one was on the street at that hour and it seemed perfectly logical to speak to himself as though he had a companion. "José Prexel makes soap, but maybe he will go to Europe if he cannot run his business here in Quito. Rotenbach is a Yugoslav. The Yugoslavs have nothing to do with this American exchange thing. He will probably stay. I cannot understand why he was put on the blacklist by the Americans anyway. It must have been a mistake. The baker, Heinz Schulte, is determined to stay in Quito. How they would miss the Mariscal bakery if he left! The hardware store, *La Casa Alemana*, on García Moreno will certainly be lost if the restrictions are not lifted. What a pity."

Ernst decided to walk down García Moreno Street. Although it was a brisk morning, he sauntered pensively, lifting his gaze casually as though he had made this trip down García Moreno Street on many occasions. His lank frame moved easily and gracefully beneath his gray wool suit. He was a tall, light-skinned man, "nearly two meters" some of his friends had said to him jealously. "A meter ninety . . . no more than a meter ninety," he had often answered them, his blue eyes twinkling. He was striking in appearance but not terribly handsome. In his twenties his warm, seductive manner had complemented his looks. Now at 35, it was his charming demeanor and forgiving nature that endeared him to many.

Ernst raised his hat and smoothed the lone, unruly curl that had worked itself onto his forehead back under his hat. The neighborhood had begun to stir and he listened to the familiar domestic noises that accompanied his footsteps on the cobblestones. "I hope Blanca has started a good fire. A cup of hot coffee and milk would warm the marrow in my bones," Ernst mumbled to himself as a shiver ran across his shoulders.

Ernst turned his mind to the businesses on García Moreno Street that were now affected by the restrictions. As he walked past the Temple of San Juan, the Temple of Santa Barbara and the newspaper building, he ran through the names of stores and shops that were in danger due to restrictions: La Casa Wiking, the Griesbach and Roohl business on Pasaje Royal, the Salón Viena on García Moreno, the Casa Poppe run by Pablo Poppe on Colón Avenue. The numbers of businesses affected would be even higher in Manta and Guayaquil where there were greater concentrations of Germans and Italians whose businesses relied on imports and good diplomatic relations with Axis countries. The future of large haciendas in Esmeraldas and Manabí were also at stake according to reports at the Sunday afternoon meeting. He thought of La Casa Tagua in Manabí where craftsmen worked the tagua nut for buttons, games, and so forth. The tagua factory had brought many German craftsmen to work the nut for export. For once he actually considered himself fortunate not to have more to lose.

He crossed Manabí, Olmedo and Mejía Streets before arriving at Independence Square. The square was still quiet, but a few people were already about their business in front of the Cathedral. The larger *torcasa* doves milled about in search of breakfast. A few young, polish-stained shoeshine boys were sitting in the square wiping the sleep from their eyes. They chatted on friendly terms before the daily competition for clients began. Ernst tipped his hat and greeted an elderly woman who approached him on the sidewalk. Her eyes were so sunken that they reminded Ernest of the eyes of the *oso de anteojos*, the "spectacled" bears he had hunted, whose white fur around the eyes made them look like they were wearing eyeglasses. He chuckled to himself. "It is better to look like an *oso de anteojos* than a *guatusa!*"[4]

It was still very cool and he could see his breath in the air as he exhaled. Ernst continued down García Moreno with his hands clasped behind his back and crossed Sucre Street, still deep in thought. He spoke to himself aloud, "If we must leave I could ask the Mikette girl to look after the house." This was a reasonable solution to what now seemed possible, if not inevitable. Young Inés Mikette had returned to Quito from Germany to marry an Ecuadorian and to take care of her infirm and aging father. She and her husband were trustworthy and they were friends of the family. He could ask her to watch over the house.

At the corner of Sucre and Benalcázar Ernst lit another cigarette before he headed into San Francisco Square. The twin steeples atop the San Francisco church shone in the morning sun. As Ernst passed through the square his eye caught the watchful gaze of the statue of Monsignor González Suárez. He paused at the foot of the monument and looked up at the monsignor's outstretched hands and spoke. "In the history of the conquest you defended the Spaniards by calling them their own best enemy. Who will tell of our enemies, monsignor? Will our historian cite Ecuadorian or U.S. authorities as the perpetrators of this international deal? What do you say? You call it a crime? An injustice? Oh no, monsignor. History will not call this a crime." He straightened his hat and shrugged, "This part of history will be swept under the rug." He tipped his hat and smiled. "Have a good day, monsignor!"

Ernst climbed the stone stairway at the far corner of the plaza, crossed Bolivar Street and raised his voice as though making an announcement, "Simón Bolívar, the great liberator... tell me, sir, how do we liberate ourselves from our own heritage?" At the other end of the block he turned on Rocafuerte Street, the street on which he had lived since he was ten years old, and headed up the side of the mountain for home.

Ernst turned his thoughts to practical problems as the incline got steeper on Rocafuerte Street. His office space on Pasaje Pérez was rented and he would sell or distribute what he could if they were forced to leave Quito. He asked himself what he was to do with the plot he had purchased to build a house for himself and his children. The government would probably restrict the purchase as long as diplomatic relations were cut, and the property would certainly be lost if he left the country. Ernst's steps slowed as he tried to find solutions. The more he thought about being forced to leave the country, his country, the more he resisted the idea of leaving. Still, the reality nagged at him. No one had come to the house yet, but he suspected that it was just a matter of time before special agents showed up. The men who had met at the Deutsche Haus had filled his ears with uncertainty and fear.

Just in front of the penitentiary below his house Ernst stopped and turned north, looked across the city, and stamped out his cigarette butt with a twist of his foot. The winged Virgin of Quito at the Incan Shyris Temple of the Sun seemed to be turning her back on *La Cima de la Libertad*, the hill called Freedom's Mount that was not visible from where he stood on Rocafuerte Street. "Is it not ironic that I cannot see Freedom's Mount from here where I stand on Pleasure Hill?" he asked himself before turning to face the slope of El Pichincha that rose before him.[5] "Has the countdown to our departure already begun?"

NOTES TO CHAPTER ONE

[1]The *Deutsche Haus* or German House was a hall at the German School compound in Quito. Meetings and gatherings were often held there on Sunday afternoons. The school children also presented plays and pageants there. The compound included the German House, classrooms, dormitories, bathrooms and common shower rooms for male and female students who lived on campus, apartments for teachers who lived in the compound as housemother or housefather, a cafeteria, and a large open area for outdoor activities and physical activities. A tall wall surrounded the entire school compound. There was a main entrance and a back entrance to the compound. The German school was on the north side of Quito on the outskirts.

[2]Published in *El Mercurio* on March 16, 1942.

[3]"Poemita" was published in Spanish in *El Mercurio* on March 8, 1942 in Spanish.

> *Poemita*
> *En el balcón de geranios*
> *se hace la trenza la niña;*
> *la mañana está en sus ojos,*
> *y hay tanto sol en su pelo*
> *que de obscuro que lo tiene*
> *se va volviendo amarillo.*
> *Rojo fuerte de geranios,*

gris doliente del camino,
y en la clara maravilla
de la mañana de Otoño
se me enreda la mirada,
en el balcón de geranios
donde se peina la niña.

[4] A *guatusa* is a large hairy rodent common to the Andean mountain range in Ecuador. Unlike its relative, the nocturnal *guanta* or *aguti*, *guatusas* traveled in packs during the day. *Guatusas*, foxes, long-eared rabbits, ocelots, pumas, and mountain tapirs, were often hunted in the mountains outside Quito.

[5] The "Loma del Placer" or Pleasure Hill is one of the hills formed centuries ago by lava flows from the Pichincha volcano to the northeast of Quito. The volcano had been inactive for more than 260 years in 1942.

CHAPTER TWO

LIFE ON THE PICHINCHA

QUITO, 1942

Ernstchen was the first one up at the house on Rocafuerte Street. "Papa isn't home yet," he announced to his older brother, Heinz, who rolled over and asked, "How do you know?"

"His bed wasn't slept in and the pistol is missing," Ernstchen reported as he slipped into his trousers by hopping on one foot.

Heinz tossed off the black llama wool blanket and looked out the window. From the bedroom he could see the Capulí tree, the lilac bush and colorful rose bushes that Grandmother Gertrude had planted long before he was born. Doves were milling about on the patio below and he imagined that he would have heard them cooing had he opened the window to let in the morning air. Heinz thought he spotted a yellow *huiracchuro* bird on the wall below.

"Look Ernstchen; there is a yellow *huiracchuro* right there." Heinz spoke just loudly enough to call his brother's attention and pointed across the deep windowsill.

Ernstchen, a curious eight year old, joined his older brother at the window. The whitewashed adobe sill was at least a half meter wide so it was possible to crawl up and sit on it. To see the bird, Ernstchen simply leaned over the sill as his brother had and scanned the area below. "It is a good thing that Blanca hasn't put the clothes out to dry near the open tank of water on the patio this morning. There are lots of birds," Ernstchen snickered slyly before shivering in the cool mountain air and rushing for a sweater.

The adobe house, high above all others on the Pichincha foothills, was a terrific lookout. The temple of San Roque and all of central Quito seemed dwarfed by the Virgin with wings perched atop the odd mound across town called the Panecillo. The sun painted the houses a golden yellow as it began to rise from behind the slope. Heinz yawned and stretched. Even when Rocafuerte Street was bustling with activity near the penitentiary, their house was a haven of tranquility. Sometimes, especially when the morning fog was as thick as potato stew, the boys joked about their home being a castle in the sky.

Ernstchen and Heinz looked out beyond the patio, but there was no sight of their father. There were owl nests in the rock quarry, several hundred meters up the slope across the street. Ernstchen strained to see if he could spot an owl returning after an early morning hunt. Nothing. He shrugged his shoulders and buttoned his sweater.

"Do you want to play *el coco chileno* after school today, Heinz?"[1] "Maybe," Heinz answered after he lay back down in the iron-framed bed and stretched from head to toe. He studied the ceiling made of *carrizo* canes that had grown in the rivers in the mountains. The canes were joined with mud and had been left to be painted later. Shivering, Heinz sat up and grabbed his trousers.

"It must be ten degrees centigrade this morning. *"Achachay,"*[2] he danced, chattering his teeth, "brrrrrrr it is cold." As Heinz hurried into his dark trousers and buttoned his shirt, Ernstchen pretended to taunt him for a boxing match. He danced around on the wooden floor pretending to lick his palms and swat at his brother's face. Ernstchen's antics made dressing a challenge but Heinz smiled at his younger brother, put his hand on Ernstchen's head and held him at bay with his long arms.

"*Bist du böse*, Heinz?" Ernstchen asked tauntingly, "Are you mad, yet?"

"It's too early for this, Ernstchen. Why don't you see if Blanca is fixing breakfast? I'll wake Irmgard." Ernstchen feigned one more friendly swat, turned and left the room. "It'll be warmer in the kitchen anyway," he called as he rushed off.

"I'm awake, Heinz." Irmgard called gently from her bed as she rubbed the sleep from her eyes and brushed a few wisps of hair from her face. "Wernerchen is still asleep, though."

"I am not," the five-year old reported defiantly as he fought to open his eyes. Heinz smiled to himself as Werner pushed his face into his feather pillow. The only time Werner was ever really still was when he was asleep. He was usually on his feet and talking before he had rubbed his eyes completely open.

Werner sat up abruptly and asked, "Where's Papa?"

"He's out," answered Heinz. "Are you ready for breakfast?"

"Not yet," he quipped as he slipped past his brother and entered the dining area, dragging his clothes behind him. "Blanca! Help me get dressed. I'm cold!"

Heinz stretched again and muttered, "I hope we won't have *mashca* today" as he closed the door behind him.[3] He liked the toasted barley flour served with milk, but he hoped his father would stop and buy some fresh rolls on his way home.

Irmgard was the last one in the bedroom. She unfolded her clothes and dressed quietly and quickly. Her thick, long hair tumbled down past her shoulders and she pulled it through the top of her white blouse. She brushed her hair away from her face with her hand, pulled on a dark sweater, and headed for the warmth of the kitchen behind her brothers. *Mashca* with a little *raspadura* was fine with her today.[4] Anything warm would make her happy. After passing her father's empty bed in the back bedroom, she called out in German "Heinz, can you help me braid my hair?" Irmgard was not yet seven years old and she could not manage the braids alone. When her brother did not answer, she pulled her sweater down stiffly and mumbled, "Oh . . . Blanca can do it later."

Blanca called to Werner who was already out behind the house. *"A la mesa niño Werner,* time for breakfast." Blanca had arrived at the house before five as usual, started the wood stove so she could start heating the milk by six o'clock. Blanca was a young, sturdy woman about five feet tall, jet-black hair and caramel skin. Her easy smile and full set of teeth revealed her good nature and general state of health. As usual, she was dressed in clothes that indicated her indigenous tribe and social station. She wore a loose white blouse tucked into an ankle-length black wool skirt that was cinched at her waist and woven *alpargatas* on her feet. Her necklaces glistened underneath the shawl she wrapped around her shoulders against the morning chill and long, heavy braids swung on her back as she worked. Blanca was not a part of the family, but she was an essential person in the Contag children's lives.

"Good morning, Blanca," Heinz said before sitting down at the end of the table across from Irmgard. Heinz was certain that Irmgard could not remember anyone else besides Blanca making them breakfast. Irmgard had been only a toddler when their mother died. He could barely remember his mother at the table. The memories he had of her had already faded into the photographs that his father kept in his room. He could no longer imagine her smile or the warmth of her hugs. It was an absence that could never be filled by Blanca's presence in the house.

"Papa is home," Werner called out so loudly that Blanca could hear him from behind the cement wall in the open-air kitchen. "He is coming up the stairs . . . Morning Papa!" Werner said with excitement. "Where've you been?" He jumped up and down shivering in the crisp morning air. "Did you bring us some warm rolls?"

Not to be left out, Irmgard ran to her father and hugged him.

Ernst swooped down and lifted Werner into the air with a groan. "I have been at school all night," he said jestingly. "I studied so hard I can barely keep my eyes open!"

"Papas don't go to school!" Werner said emphatically. Irmgard laughed.

Blanca started preparing *café con leche* for the patron of the house. She greeted him with humility from the kitchen door, "Good morning, don Ernesto. Breakfast is ready." She poured the warm milk into each coffee cup in silence and stained the milk with a tablespoon or so of coffee. The coffee for don Ernesto was more coffee than milk, but the children's cups were only tinged to a gentle tan color. She put the *mashca* into bowls for the children since don Ernesto had arrived empty-handed. Heinz resigned himself to the breakfast of barley mush and started looking around for the sugar bowl.

"Francisco will bring more firewood this afternoon, señor don Ernesto," she told her tall, lanky employer before returning to the kitchen in silence.

Ernst removed his hat and pistol and came to the table with Werner and Irmgard flanking him on either side. Both were fiercely loyal to their father.

Ernstchen took a seat at the table, too, and Heinz called toward the kitchen, "Blanca. Bring the sugar."

"Right away, niño Heinz." Blanca placed the sugar bowl on the table and returned to the kitchen where she was already busy with the preparations for the evening meal. Heinz sniffed at the air. She was cooking the *chaucha* potatoes and cabbage that she had peeled and washed. Later she would fry a small bit of pork meat and pork bone seasoned with bits of onions and garlic to make *locro de papas*, a thick meat and potato stew.[5] Just before serving the stew she would add crushed roasted peanuts, a little milk, and salt. Heinz liked the stew and it was always very filling.

"Papa," asked Ernstchen mischievously, "did you have to threaten anyone with your pistol?"

Ernst looked at his children's wide eyes and brightened. "Oh yes," he exclaimed shrewdly, tickled to have an opportunity to entertain them. "While I was sitting alone in the Deutsche Haus I heard a mysterious sound from behind the entrance. Kerplop, Kerplop, Kerplop, Kerplop. At first it was very, very quiet, but the noise grew louder and louder." Ernst's deep voice resonated within his chest as he added mystery and volume to his story.

The youngest children were spellbound and Irmgard was noticeably nervous, but Heinz could see through his father's bluff and said flatly, "It must have been Herr Schneider riding Rex into the school!"

Ernstchen laughed out loud and countered, "Maybe it was Herr Sacklowski prancing around like a flamingo and not Herr Schneider and his horse!" Ernstchen stood and circled the table with an exaggerated version of Herr Schneider's stagger. Heinz and Ernstchen laughed out loud. The boys enjoyed making fun of the unusual man and his horse who were frequent visitors to the German School.

"What was it really, Papa? Were you scared?" asked Irmgard innocently.

"I was just joking, Irmgard. Nothing happened at the school. The meeting was fine, and I fell asleep at the table afterward. If you are finished with your breakfast get your brush and I will braid your hair. I brought home a poem about a young girl like you. I will read it to you." Ernst had grown serious and it was clear that he was tired and trying to hurry the children on to school.

Werner was unhappy that the excitement had come to an end so quickly and said aloud, "I thought you were telling the truth, Papa. Bim, bam, boom. I thought you were going to get somebody." Werner stood up, dejected, and walked to the back of the house and out the door to look for his own bogeyman amongst the eucalyptus trees behind the house on the slope while the other children got ready for school. Werner, only five years old, liked to chase the tiny lizards that scurried between the broad-leafed plants and grasses on the slope.

Heinz was the first one to the bathroom after breakfast. The morning chill sent another shiver up his spine as he took the outdoor stairs to the bathroom. He combed his hair mechanically and looked out over the penitentiary built on top of an old quarry a half block down the slope of the mountain. He had heard yelling from the inmates the night before. Now the tranquility that he could see on the roof near the panoptical control center gave the sensation that all was well. He counted five guards strolling on the prison roof. They had called out to each other in a drawn-out howl "Uno . . . dos . . . tres . . . cuatro . . . cinco," at night to make sure everything was in order from each corner of the prison roof. Heinz and Ernstchen often reminded each other aloud that the guards were probably checking to see if the other guards were still alive.

You can see forever from this bathroom window, thought Heinz. *You can see the central part of Quito, the San Francisco cathedral in the colonial area downtown, and in the distance you can see the Panecillo hill on the other side of the city.* He looked toward the San Diego cemetery where his mother was buried. More than four years had passed since her death, but he still thought of her often. "She can see the horizon beyond these mountains because she is in heaven," he assured himself quietly.

The Contag home on Rocafuerte Street in Quito, Ecuador (c. 1930)

Heinz rinsed his mouth and washed his face and hands in the sink. His family had running water and an indoor toilet. The water supply came from the reservoir tanks near a dry lagoon high behind the house on Pleasure Hill. The mountain stream from the Pichincha volcano tumbled over rocks into a lagoon, and his father told him that before the city filled in the gorge behind their house to complete the reservoir tanks there had been a beautiful waterfall. Heinz had learned to swim in the chilly waters of the lagoon. His grandmother had taught his father to swim in the lagoon that had been drained to fill the water tanks.

Most houses in Quito did not have running water. In the city people carried water from public spouts. In rural areas many still used a bucket to bring water up from a well. People relieved themselves wherever and whenever it was convenient. Ernst had told Heinz that Oma Ziehe Contag would have nothing less than the most up-to-date plumbing as she considered the outdoor toilet barbaric and unsanitary. His grandmother insisted that her house have electricity too, although it was cut often enough that both Heinz and his father had to read and write with the light of a kerosene lamp.

It was 7:30 and time to leave for school. Heinz stood at the back door and fitted his belt. Ernstchen was outside and had stopped to visit the goat tied up out behind the house. The goat provided milk for the children, but was much more effective as entertainment for Ernstchen. "Bist du böse?" he would ask the goat, taunting her with silly antics just outside the reach of her tether. Ernstchen loved animals and had a special way with them. He was always pleading with his father for a monkey from the jungles. "When I grow up I am going to buy a monkey from a peddler. You'll see." Heinz knew that someday Ernstchen would have his monkey and probably a whole menagerie of animals.

Ernst had finished plaiting Irmgard's long braids and placed a ribbon at each end. "Time to leave for school," Irmgard reported proudly in German. Blanca, who did not understand German, went on with her business in the kitchen. When she heard the door slam, she called for Werner in Spanish. She would have to keep an eye on him while she worked now. Señor Ernesto would certainly lie down to sleep after being out all night.

Irmgard and Heinz followed Ernstchen down the stone stairway to the large, wooden gate on Rocafuerte Street. When they opened the heavy gate they could see that across the street the cobbler's children were kicking an avocado seed around out in front of their lean-to that served as their home. The public school was closer than the *Deutsche Schule* and they could play quite a while yet. Some of the newcomers to Rocafuerte Street were families of the prisoners held at the penitentiary. It was too costly to travel to and from the penitentiary to homes outside the city, so some families just set up shop outside the prison. People who came to the Contag house to visit often commented that it was a bit strange to have squatters and families of criminals near the extraordinary homes on Rocafuerte and Bolivar Streets. Heinz thought secretly that the squatters made the neighborhood more colorful, although he agreed with the adults whenever they spoke disdainfully about the evolving situation on Rocafuerte Street.

The Arias family lived two houses down the Rocafuerte right on the corner. Everyone knew that señor Arias had been a captain in the Ecuadorian army. The family ran a small shop and, like most shopkeepers, he lived behind the storefront with his family. One day when he was nearly ten years old, Heinz had gone into the small shop to look around. He remembered peering through the open door that was nearly flush with the street. He had seen caramelized popcorn balls in glass containers on the counter. His mouth starting watering as he stared at the caramel balls made of popcorn and *raspadura* that sold for five *centavos*. Seeing no one, he stole one ball and hid it under his jacket. No one ever found out, and he told no one, but Heinz still felt uneasy as he walked in front of the shop each morning. He was always glad when they passed the shop without seeing señor Arias.

As the children passed the penitentiary Heinz told Ernstchen of the rumor another German boy had told him about a tunnel that people said had been built between the Contag house and the penitentiary. According to the boy, the tunnel was dug to rescue an Austrian prince who had been incarcerated there. "Do you really think there is a tunnel, Heinz?" asked Ernstchen incredulously. "Could be," Heinz answered. He wondered aloud if it was gossip or truth and decided that, at the very least, it was a mystery worth thinking about and maybe even investigating some day. Irmgard stopped and spoke up rather anxiously, "I hope there isn't a tunnel. I don't want to wake up with prisoners in the house. That's scary." The two boys laughed at their little sister. "Don't worry, Irmgard. It is just a rumor," Heinz consoled her.

"But sometimes prisoners escape," reported Irmgard. "Remember Papa told us that some prisoners escaped when he was a little boy. The prisoners went right up to the house and demanded towels or sheets and money from Grandmother. I bet she was scared of those prisoners."

"Papa said that Grandmother gave them towels to disguise themselves. I can't figure out how they could have disguised themselves with a few towels," Heinz added.

The three children continued down the Rocafuerte toward central Quito. The German School was several kilometers from their house. Sometimes Heinz, Irmgard and Ernstchen rode the bus to the north end of Quito, but today they walked. As usual, their father had sent them off without any money for the bus. The cobblers, knife makers and other tradesmen on Rocafuerte Street were already at work, and the streets were busy as they neared the city center. Some adults and children greeted them in Spanish as they walked past small shops. If some eyed them with envy or curiosity, the Contag children did not notice. They were *gringos* and they stood out among the Ecuadorians for their European appearance, which contrasted with the shorter, caramel-skinned Ecuadorians. Heinz, Ernstchen and Irmgard had dark blond hair and stood a foot taller than Ecuadorian children their age. When callers came and knocked at the gate on Rocafuerte street, the neighbors often called out from nearby windows or doorways, "*Sí, sí. Ahí viven los gringos.*"

As they neared the center of Quito the children were easily distracted from their thoughts. Indian women and men were carrying their wares to market on their backs, huge loads of anything they thought they could sell. Many of the women also carried their small infants in *chalinas* or shawls they wrapped around themselves. The infants were swathed in such a way that they could nurse even while the mother walked. Young children ran barefoot in the streets and darted in and out of storefronts. When they turned onto García Moreno Street they saw a young woman sweeping the narrow sidewalk in front of a small shop. The children stepped into the street to continue on their way to school. It wasn't dangerous to walk in the streets. In Quito there was never much traffic besides foot traffic. A middle-aged man watched them from a doorway as he brushed his small-brimmed, black hat to clean off the dust from the day before.

Just in front of them a short, sun-dried man led his donkey, laden with large containers of milk, down the cobblestone street. He called out to open windows and customers' ears. "*Leche . . . Leche de vaca.*"[6] The donkey's hoofs pounded the cobblestone street in rhythm with her swaying tail. The farmer halted the donkey at a doorway, and a young servant girl handed the farmer a clean bucket. Irmgard slowed to watch. The farmer's hands surprised her. His fingers were short and thick and she wondered why such a small, thin man would have such stout fingers.

"Come on Irmgard," Heinz urged.

The street was like a long string of miniature open markets. Heinz and Ernstchen liked to go to the outdoor market on market day even if they did not buy anything. Small crop farmers and indigenous women sold everything from *naranjilla* fruits to ceramic pots and rope-woven *alpargatas* or *hoshotas* worn as sandals by the Indians.[7] Almost everything anyone needed was available at the market. There were bananas or *guineos* brought to Quito from beyond the mountains to the west, many varieties of colored rice, furry guinea pigs and rabbits, noisy pigs and sheep, all sorts and sizes of beans and peas, yucca roots, vegetables and potatoes in vibrant colors and different sizes. The market was always a very colorful place. The best part of going to the market involved employing one's olfactory sense. The vendors were always cooking something that smelled delicious. Since the vendors spent their entire day at the market they brought their small children and cooked over open fires for themselves and for anyone who wanted to purchase a small meal.

It was easy to tell where the vendors were from based on their clothing and their specialty items. The Otavalo women were dressed in white, embroidered blouses and long, dark wrap-around skirts. They looked very different from the Indian women from the South who wore a wool, embroidered skirt called a *pollera* that hung in ample, stiff folds from the waist to just below the knee. The yards of gold-beaded necklaces circling the Otavaleñas' necks were distinctive to mountain tribes and called attention to the women from quite a distance. The Otavaleño men wore black or white brimmed hats, three-quarter length white trousers and white, long-sleeved shirts that they cinched at the waist with a woven belt. They wore black, knee-length ponchos for warmth, and, like most Indians in the sierra, went barefoot or wore roped *alpargatas*. The men and women sold fine woven goods, ponchos, tapestries, blankets, and clothing at market. They were expert spinners, weavers, and rope makers. Heinz never understood why they only wore black and white while the merchandise they sold was so colorful.

Every once in a while some Colorado Indian merchants from Santo Domingo de los Colorados, a town in the subtropical forest area west of Quito, could be seen at the outdoor market sporting the traditional *achiote*-tinged red hair that made Heinz think of developing a personal umbrella of his own. The men's black hair was covered in an extract from the *achiote* plant, and combed straight forward and out like a bill over their foreheads.[8] Heinz thought it was a great invention for keeping the sun and rain out of the eyes. Only the Colorado Indian men wore their hair in such a fashion, his father had told him. The women had bangs and long, silken black hair that hung to the middle of their bare backs. Heinz had seen the Colorados for the first time when he went with his father on a hunting trip in the pristine forests at the western foothills of the Andes. He couldn't miss the Colorados with their striped loincloths and the bare breasted women!

Heinz remembered the first time he went with his family to the Sangolquí market in the Valley of Los Chillos to the east of Quito. The crowded, outdoor market was considered one of the best near Quito because vendors came from the east, west, north and south to sell their wares. The family had stopped at Sangolquí on a Sunday outing. His father stood tall above the vendors who surrounded themselves with mounds of potatoes, vegetables, grains, fruits, peanuts, knitted caps, stockings, chickens, guinea pigs, goats, large wooden utensils, and ceramic pottery. He followed his father through the maze of vendors and their bundles and piles of wares. Heinz had also been surprised by the languages he heard in the marketplace. The vendors spoke Spanish to his father but the language sounded strange because it was mixed with indigenous Quechua syntax and pronunciation. When the vendors and their families spoke amongst themselves, Heinz understood very little. After they left the square he had imitated the Sangolquí vendors all day long by answering his father's questions with "Sí, pes. Quis pes?" for "Yes, of course. What is it?"[9]

The German School was practically outside the city limits. When the three children were about three hundred meters from the school, Irmgard spotted some of her classmates just ahead and urged her brothers to walk faster so they could all walk together. About half of the students at the German School were descendants of Germans who had immigrated to Ecuador. The rest were the children of wealthy immigrants who sent their boys to the boarding school. The German School looked like most other buildings in Quito. A whitewashed adobe building with a red-clay tile roof, it was unassuming and did not attract much attention except for the large silver *swastika* medal over the gate. The medal was rather new and when it caught the morning sunlight it attracted the eye.

The children entered the school through the large gate and looked around for their schoolmates. Heinz's best friend, Erika

Giese, waved at him and he walked over to talk to her. Erika's father was a prominent German in the community and her mother worked at the school. Mr. Giese organized many of the Sunday afternoon meetings at the Deutsche Haus located on the German School grounds. Erika and her friend, Hilda, were standing near the Detken children, Hermann and Agnes. Ernstchen and Hermann were good friends since kindergarten and he followed his brother to the group. Irmgard tagged along and joined her schoolmates Agnes Detken and Elsa Sonnabend who were giggling nearby.

Some of the older boys who participated in *armas militares*, required military training for Ecuadorian children in the fifth grade or higher and held at the school on Saturday, were talking near the Munich Dormitory. Heinz waved at Pietro Tosi and his younger brother, Frank, the sons of a successful Italian immigrant who had settled in Cuenca and built up the textile industry there. Pietro had been Heinz's classmate and a boarder at the *German School* from the first grade on. The boys often spoke Spanish on Saturdays during *armas militares*, to the delight of many boys whose second language, not first, was German. Pietro had been Heinz's partner in one of the boys' favorite games on Saturday. Ten boys stood in a line facing another ten boys. Each pair made a box chair with their arms and they took turns passing one boy from "arm" chair to "arm" chair. The perilous ride of the boy was always fodder for laughter.

Herr Carlos Hatson was in the courtyard talking to the two Ecuadorian schoolteachers, Señor Torres and Señor Callecas. Hatson was very animated and Heinz wondered what the teachers might be discussing. Soon the three were joined by the school's director, Wilhelm Sacklowski, whose pronounced limp was always material for jokes by the children at the school. Frau Heintze, a sexagenarian, took her time walking stiffly across the courtyard to join the group as well. Heinz noted that Hans Winkler, Frau

Wiesner and his own aunt were nowhere in sight. He surmised they were still in the cafeteria.

Just then Heinz noticed that Gustavo Schneider walked into the school courtyard. Herr Schneider was famous among the younger boys at the school because he was an expert animal trainer and many of the students at the German School admired his well-trained animals. The young boy from Guayaquil, José Antonio Gómez, was particularly impressed by Schneider's beautiful black horse, Rex, whom Schneider had trained to respond to voice commands, and the German Shepherd dog Schneider had trained to climb trees.[10] José Antonio turned to see if Herr Schneider's dogs followed him in through the doors, but they had not. Herr Schneider joined the lively discussion and José Antonio, disappointed, shrugged at Heinz. "No dogs, today."

They must be talking politics this morning, Heinz thought as he entered the classroom. Politics seemed to get everyone so excited, but he was not the least bit interested. Whenever the adults talked about Ecuadorian politics, they argued about which politician was more corrupt. There was general agreement that nothing really changed quickly in Quito. The German immigrants who taught at the school spoke of the need to improve the water and sewage systems or the medical facilities. The teachers pointed out the great advances in technology in Germany, a new highway system and fantastic airplanes. Heinz liked to watch the *stukas* on the movies, but he couldn't really see an application for such advances in Ecuador. They didn't need warplanes in Ecuador, except perhaps to defend the Peruvian-Ecuadorian border. Even so, the notion of war was as alien to his thinking as a new sewage system for Quito.

At lunch one of the younger boys asked Heinz if he was going to fight the Jew from the *longuitos* school again.[11] "Of course not," Heinz answered quite emphatically. The boy continued, "Why did he want to fight you, Heinz?" Heinz answered with a shrug. "I don't know. I think he was mad because I have shoes and he doesn't. He kept saying something about my shoes. But . . . I don't know why we fought. It just happened. I am not going to fight him again though. He just came at me. I wasn't mad at him or anything. I don't even know who he is." Heinz felt embarrassed by the question and grew quiet. The younger boy gave in and wandered away obviously disappointed that there was not going to be another spectacle after school.

During recess the older children played *vogelball* in the courtyard. It was an exciting game played with a large, red medicine ball. There was not a single schoolmate who did not enjoy the game and there was plenty of energy expended before sitting down to tough subjects.

In the afternoon Heinz paid attention in mathematics because he did not want to get swatted for misbehaving or humiliated for poor performance. He actually liked school except for mathematics, and thoroughly enjoyed English and Spanish classes. He had received a copy of a book about Adolf Hitler's life earlier that year for high academic and athletic achievement. The book was thin, about 30 cm by 40 cm in height and width, and had a few pictures from Germany. It was written in German*schrift,* a very different style of penmanship than he was used to. The book was employed in class to study how to read and write the decorative writing style. He was the only one in his family to have his own book in German, and Heinz was very proud of it.

After school Heinz, Irmgard, and Ernstchen met outside the school gate. Ernstchen stepped off the curb to head for home and Irmgard squealed and tugged at his shirt as a car passed nearby. "Stay on the sidewalk, Ernstchen," she said sternly for a six-year old. She had not yet gotten over being hit by a car a few months earlier. Heinz remembered the driver telling him over her sobbing, "You'll have to carry her. Carry her to the bus and go home." She had been hurt, but since nothing was broken, the three youngsters were sent on. Heinz thought it was strange that a car hit her, since there were so few cars in Quito.

They had only walked a block when Erika, Hilda and several students from the German School called to them. Hilda's mother, who had come to walk the girls home, stood behind them and greeted Heinz with a smile. Hilda and Erika were in Heinz's class; the other three were friends of Ernstchen. Hilda wore a broad smile as Erika spoke enthusiastically and quickly. "Hilda and I were wondering if your father would let you bring your *sapo* to the plaza on Saturday afternoon so we can learn to play the game." The *sapo* was a brass-colored, metal toad with a huge, open mouth and Ecuadorian adults and children enjoyed tossing coins in its mouth for points. The coins fell into compartments of different value in a box below the toad. Heinz promised to ask his father.

Heinz, Ernst and Irmgard headed for home. As they neared Bolívar Street Ernstchen and Heinz talked about after school activities. "Let's stop at the store first and see if we can play there before going home," suggested Ernstchen, "then we can play *el coco chileno*." The children agreed, turned off García Moreno and walked up Bolívar Street. The nicest homes were on Bolívar Street. Heinz liked a young Ecuadorian girl who lived on Bolívar Street and suggested they stop at María's house first.

Ernstchen refused. "You can stop on the way back from Dryco, Heinz. Irmgard and I don't want to see her." Dryco, the company store where their father worked with their Uncle Hermann, was a favorite stop after school. The shop was filled with interesting imports from Europe. The children liked to take turns sitting on the shiny green motorcycle that was the shop's biggest, and most expensive attraction. "I want to sit on the *Wanderer* first!" Irmgard chirped, happy to follow her brothers' lead.

Bolívar Street climbed the Pichincha slope at an extraordinary pitch. The children's maternal grandmother, Oma Dreier, used to complain of it when she had stayed at their home in Quito after the death of their mother in 1937. "It is a tough climb when you are not used to the altitude," she would say in her accented Spanish to the local shopkeepers who greeted her. Heinz could not understand his grandmother's complaints about *soroche,* or altitude sickness, because he had never experienced the aching legs and difficult breathing. They were *quiteños* and they could scamper up the side of the Pichincha as well as anyone.

Oma and Opa Dreier had already left for Germany after living in Ecuador for nearly ten years. Heinz missed them. Opa Dreier had closed the store in Quito because he could not tolerate the high altitude. The store in Guayaquil relied on imports from Germany and when they were no longer able to import German products shortly after his mother's death, the store was lost and they left. Their son, Hermann, still lived in Quito and the children stopped from time to time to visit the family business.

Ernstchen was the first to arrive at the Dryco company storefront. "The door is locked," he said. He peered through the window. "And the green motorcycle is gone," he reported flatly. The motorcycle had been a big draw for passersby and many times they found Ecuadorians outside looking in through the window. The business was completely closed.[12] Ernstchen was surprised and wondered aloud if things had been stolen. His father had not said anything about the business or Uncle Hermann, and Heinz was also surprised to see the business all shut up as though it were closed for good.

Puzzled, the three headed for home. When they were climbing Rocafuerte Street, Heinz's friend Helmut stopped them. Helmut went to the public school even though he was half German. The two boys were good friends and often did things together after school or on Saturday if there were no family plans. Helmut and Heinz had been through thick and thin together. Heinz sent Irmgard and Ernstchen ahead while he spoke to Helmut.

Heinz had not told anyone about the secrets he shared with Helmut. The two boys had gone for target practice one sunny afternoon a few months earlier. Heinz had a rifle his father had given him for his eleventh birthday. Helmut did not have his own rifle, but Heinz always let him take some shots. Sometimes they went out to one of the quarries near the Rocafuerte to shoot, but on that day they had walked through city streets on their way to another area where they liked to shoot at natural targets. Heinz was carrying the rifle so that it hung at his side. Not too far from Colón Avenue Helmut told him to shoot at the ground to see what would happen. Heinz agreed and pulled the trigger shooting three or four times. The shots ricocheted. At once Helmut's face turned pale. "Heinz, did you see that? Let's get out of here." The boy took off like a scared rabbit. When Heinz caught up with him, Helmut explained, "I don't know what happened, but before the gun went off there was a *longo* standing near a building.[13] I saw him fall down after the shot was fired. I think he got hurt. Didn't you see him?"

"No, I did not! . . . *Dios mío!*" Heinz exclaimed.[14]

Helmut added, "I think we should get away from here." Heinz agreed, slipped the gun down the leg of his trousers and walked back home. Helmut laughed most of the way, but Heinz was uncomfortable walking with his "peg leg" and he felt somewhat jumpy. "I'll come back in a half hour or so, Helmut," he said as he continued up the slope to his house. Heinz went upstairs to empty and clean the gun. He put the rifle away, and cleaned himself up somewhat before going back out on the street. Heinz was never sure if Helmut had been telling the truth or just making up the story to scare him. Whatever the case, he was careful not to shoot his rifle again when people were about.

Helmut was also one of the boys who helped Heinz push a large boulder down into a rock quarry near the Rocafuerte. It seemed like fun and a chance to prove their strength at the time, but none of the boys had considered the consequences. When they heard the men working down below yell and saw them run from the boulder, the boys ran away and hid. Heinz did not return to the quarry for a long time fearing that someone might have seen them. It was fun to be with Helmut, but it seemed that whenever they were together, there was trouble.

Today Helmut just wanted to find out what Heinz had planned for the rest of the day.

"I don't know, Helmut. I'll stop by later. Hey, guess what? The *Wandererer* must have sold. It isn't in the shop window and the shop is all closed up! I have to find out who bought it!"

"Wow! The *Wanderer* sold. Maybe someone we know bought it and we can get a ride!" Helmut added. "Let me know when you find out, Heinz. Say, do you want to hunt on the Pichincha on Saturday?"

"Sure!" Heinz answered. "Have you got your own gun yet?"

"Not yet, but I thought we could share."

"Only if you help carry it up the slope," Heinz quipped.

"Yes, of course," Helmut said with enthusiasm. "See you later, Heinz."

When Heinz turned to look up the street, he could see that Irmgard and Ernstchen were still waiting for him to call Miche to open the gate. Heinz was the loudest whistler of the three. When he arrived at the gate he whistled to Miche and she came down the stairs to unlock the wooden gate. They climbed the stone stairs and hurried to the back of the house where they found Werner waiting for them. He was excited and spoke quickly, "Papa said we could take the *bodoquera* up the hill and shoot it if you go along, Heinz." The blowgun was a holdover from Ernst's earlier days when he drove lumber out of Ecuador's jungle area. The older children brightened at the idea of spending the few hours of daylight left playing around the eucalyptus and cypress trees surrounding the gorge out behind the house.

"Where is Papa?" Heinz asked.

"Not here," Werner replied. The four children went behind the house to play and it was not long before Heinz completely forgot about the Wanderer and the shop. They ran, played, shot the blowgun, played make-believe, and came up with a plan to scare the servants.

Just after six o'clock the sun dropped behind the mountains to the west and the children returned for the evening meal. Blanca and Miche were talking near the wood stove and Heinz asked them to put on supper. The children ate their meat and potato stew quietly, eyeing each other mischievously, and went obediently to their bedrooms, where the older boys gave the final touches to their plan. Heinz and Ernstchen were equals in the plot; Irmgard and Werner went along with the plan because their older brothers thought it was a good idea and they were always game for a little mischief.

"Are you ready to throw pebbles and rocks at the kitchen to see what the servants do?" Ernstchen snickered as he asked Werner and Irmgard who nodded affirmatively.

While Blanca and Miche were cleaning in the kitchen, the children, who were supposed to be in bed, tiptoed out the door and found a spot from which the older two boys could take aim and smack the open-air wall of the kitchen.

"Smack . . . smack, smack" they heard the small rocks hit the wall. There was nothing but silence from inside. Werner picked up a bigger rock and tossed it. It missed the kitchen wall by a long shot, but he felt triumphant. Irmgard tossed pebbles and they made a curious sound as they hit the embankment. The children crouched and waited. When no one emerged from the kitchen Ernstchen said in a whisper, "They don't hear us. Heinz, throw a bigger rock. See if you can throw it right over the wall!"

When the rock hit the wall of the kitchen the servants screamed. Not to be outdone, Ernstchen threw another one and accidentally hit the lamp hanging in the kitchen. Everything went black. Startled by the darkness, the children sat motionless. "Oh, oh." Heinz mumbled.

They heard the two young servant girls' feet shuffle quickly out of the kitchen and around to the rock stairway. The girls were pushing each other and when they got to the top of the stairs they started yelling, "The devil! It is the devil!" Irmgard grabbed Heinz's trouser leg in fear. "Heinz, let's go in, I'm frightened." "Don't be silly, bubble brain,"[15] the older boys chimed in unison. Irmgard struck out at her brothers who were laughing nervously at her. "They are just mocking us. Remember when they scared us by throwing rocks at the house a few months ago? That is why they are saying that it is the devil. They know we are the ones throwing the rocks at them."

"Gee, that takes all the fun out of it, doesn't it," Ernstchen added. "Well, maybe it doesn't," he said as he whipped another small rock toward the servants who made out to be scared at the top of the stairway.

"You shouldn't have hit the light bulb," Heinz groaned.

"*Niños,*" the servant girls called out.

"Time to go in to bed," Heinz said to the others with a smirk.

Werner clutched Ernstchen's hand, Heinz held Irmgard's hand, and the children made their way back through the darkness and quickly went to bed. Sheepishly, Heinz crawled under the llama wool blanket and wondered what the servants would tell their father in the morning about the broken light bulb. "Tell Dad we were asleep and didn't hear anything," Heinz whispered loudly enough for the servants to hear, even though he knew they wouldn't hear him.

Ernst was not surprised to find his young children asleep when he arrived near midnight after meeting the Vorbecks at the brewery. After sleeping off the exhaustion from his night as guard at the *Deutsche Haus* he had gone to his office to collect a few things he thought he could sell to his good friend, the son of don Jacobo, the brewmaster. The Vorbecks were Danes and therefore were not subject to the harassment and restrictions that affected those of German heritage. After collecting nearly 100 sucres for the items he took to them, he sat down with a few of the Vorbeck boys at their brewery "La Victoria" on Avenue 24 de mayo and talked about business.[16] While the German businesses were floundering or already liquidating, "La Victoria" was doing very, very well. The company took out large ads in the newspapers to increase visibility. Ernst had not thought it was necessary since their beer business was booming.

"La Victoria" was an appropriate label for the Vorbeck family brewery. "Victory" was associated with celebration, with independence, and with freedom in Quito. The Vorbecks claimed victory over the other brew masters like Ernst's own immigrant father whose "Marca C" brewery had simply dried up while Ernst was still a young child in Cuenca. When the elder Vorbeck joined his sons and Ernst at the table, they talked about "the good old days" that really had been quite difficult for all immigrants but much better than the present time with so many restrictions on imports. The elder Vorbeck asked Ernst what he planned to do now that he had been blacklisted.

Ernst, who had until then joked and laughed with the Vorbecks, replied somberly, "I have four children to feed. Poor things. I will make any decision I have to make to keep them safe and healthy. My brother, Arturo, thinks Hitler will be victorious and that we should all go to Germany where there will be many opportunities for us. My brother, Carl, lives and works in Berlin. He could probably get us settled there . . . if we have to leave." He hesitated a moment longer and then continued with a shrug, "If I had a huge, flourishing business like yours, I might protest the restrictions or make some special arrangements with the government, . . . but, in my situation? I am just one man. If the special agents find their way to my house I'll deal with the consequences accordingly. What else can I do?" The elder Vorbeck nodded. The topic was dropped and the men spent the rest of the evening drinking and laughing.

Ernst arrived home just before dawn. His four children were sleeping peacefully. "*Pobrecitos*," he mumbled under his breath so as not to wake them.[17] He hung his clothes over a chair and curled up under the llama wool blanket. His feet were cold and nothing he did seemed to warm them. *It is an omen*, he thought to himself; *the peaceful life we have led on the Pichincha is about to change.*

NOTES TO CHAPTER TWO

[1] *El coco chileno* or "the Chilean nut" is a game that was played in plazas throughout Quito. The adults and older children used small marble-sized nuts, beans or stones to shoot coins out of a circle drawn in the dirt or sand. Each player contributed a coin to play. Winners kept the coins they knocked out of bounds.

[2] *Achachay* is an indigenous word used to express a chill or a shiver. The stress falls on the final syllable of the word and when spoken, sounds very much like teeth chattering.

[3] *Mascha* or *máshica* is food associated more with rural cuisine than city cuisine in Ecuador. The servants prepared traditional criollo or indigenous food they were accustomed to making since there was no one in the home who spent time teaching them to prepare more criollo or even European food. The toasted barley flour with milk and sugar was served occasionally at the Contag home.

[4] *Raspadura*, which literally translated means "scrape hard," is a brick of unrefined sugar that had to be scraped before being served. *Raspadura* is still common today in Ecuador. Its flavor is similar to brown sugar and molasses.

[5] The *chaucha* potato is one of the many varieties of potatoes in Ecuador. The potatoes used in *locro* or meat and potato stew could be peeled (if large) or added whole with the peel.

⁶Cow's milk.

⁷The markets in Ecuador are known for their diversity of produce from the jungles, the mountain ranges and the coast. The *naranjilla* fruit is usually used in juice, as it does not travel well. The *guineo* or banana and pineapples are raised to the west of Quito in the subtropical areas toward the coast. The Ecuadorians are also famous for their weavers and rope makers. Indians wear sandals called *alpargatas* or *hoshotas* made of braided rope for the sole and dyed woven fibers for the area that covers the top of the foot. The rope sole cushioned the foot against the rocky, mountain footpaths and were sturdy.

⁸*Achiote* powder is also used in cooking as a spice and food coloring. It is rubbed on the skin of the hog, for example, before it is roasted to an unusual yellowish-red color.

⁹"*Sí pes. Quis pes?*" When spoken aloud it almost sounds as though the speaker is whispering single syllable words "seepss, keespss." In common Spanish the expression is a five-syllable expression: "*Sí, pues. ¿Qué es pues?*" The large number of indigenous people in Ecuador and the strength of *Quechua*, a language handed down from the Inca Empire, have influenced greatly the Spanish spoken in the mountains of Ecuador. There are many borrowed terms and structures in both languages. *Manavali*, for example, is the way the Quechua population might say "Es malo, no vale para nada" or "it is worthless."

In Cuenca, where the indigenous population is also very high, there are not only lexical adaptations from Quechua, but also syntactical ones. For example, highly educated Cuencan speakers might say "Dame pasando la agüita, ¿no?" when they ask someone to pass them water at the table. This would be expressed in common Spanish syntax as "Pásame el agua por favor" or "Please pass me the water." The closest translation to the Cuencan expression in English is "Give me passing the water, no?" The use of the diminutive "ita" as in the word "agüita" is also very common in the Andean areas of Ecuador.

[10]Interview with José Antonio Gómez Iturralde. Guayaquil, May 1999. Mr. Gómez Iturralde is Director of the Archivo Histórico de Guayas and attended the German School in Quito in 1941-1942.

[11]The pejorative terms *longuito* and *longo* refer to members of the indigenous population.

[12]Many businesses that employed or were owned by Axis nationals living in Ecuador or by Ecuadorian citizens of German, Italian, and Japanese heritage were blacklisted. The restrictions put on these citizens forced many businesses to close in the spring of 1942. The closings not only affected the blacklisted men and their families. There were serious ramifications for Ecuadorian employees and their families as well. Some business owners protested in April without making any real impact. When the Ecuadorian employees realized how severely they would be affected economically, they also complained. The Ecuadorian government agreed to study the problem. The newspaper accounts were in agreement that it was quite unlikely that anything would or could be done about the many people who found themselves without jobs.

[13]Indian.

[14]"Oh my God!"

[15]*No seas boba, cabeza de bola* or "Don't be silly, ball head" was a mocking statement the boys used to make their sister angry. The

liberal translation of "bubble brain" seems to convey the mockery better than "ball head" in English.

[16] Mr. Jacobo Vorbeck inherited the brewery from Mr. (Heinrich) E. Vorbeck who had replaced Arthur Sahm, the brewery's first brewmaster and a German technician, in 1912 after Mr. Sahm's contract with the brewery's owner, Mr. Mariano Negrete, expired in 1911. The elder Vorbeck, a Dane, was a good friend of Mr. Negrete and had lived in Quito for several years prior to Negrete's departure in 1906. Mr. Vorbeck purchased the brewery in 1917 from Mr. Negrete for 70,000 sucres (three times the original investment by Mr. Negrete). According to the brewery's early accounting books, the business took in only about 3 sucres a day since bottles were scarce and could only be found second hand. In the early years, the beer was often sold by the liter in earthen jars and washbasins.

[17] Poor things.

CHAPTER THREE

ALL ABOARD AT CHIMBACALLE STATION

QUITO, MAY 1942

Ernst and his four children walked down Rocafuerte Street carrying their coats. Each child wore several layers of clothing that would accommodate the disparate climates on the train ride from Quito to Guayaquil. Ernst had taken their luggage, one large suitcase full of clothing, to Chimbacalle train station the day before so it could be loaded on the train along with the other baggage belonging to Germans, Japanese and Italians leaving the country. The newspaper and the radio had warned them that any luggage arriving after four in the afternoon would not be loaded on the train.

The sun would not rise for another hour and a half and the children stumbled along the cobbled street in the dark. Ernst held Werner by the hand. Ernstchen, Irmgard, and Heinz walked together in front of them. They walked in silence for quite a while down the empty street. Eventually Heinz looked overhead and broke the silence by talking to Ernstchen about the clear sky and the constellations he recognized. Ernst pointed out the *oso mayor* and the Southern Cross and said to his children, "When we travel north we will not be able to see the Southern Cross at night. The night sky looks entirely different. My father used to tell me when I was young that he could see the North Star from his home in Numeiten. Soon we will see the North Star he told me about."

Ernst hid his sense of defiance from his children, but he could scarcely believe the events that had led to their present departure from Quito. He bit at his bottom lip as he walked purposefully down the slope of the Pichincha and south across the city toward Chimbacalle train station, silently reviewing the events and policies that strong-armed him and his family into the hands of the Americans.

Soon after the March meeting at the Deutsche Haus the Undersecretary of the Ministry of Foreign Affairs and the Ministers from the United States and England met with the Ecuadorian Chief of National security to begin notification of persons to be deported. Forty-eight of the people on that first blacklist were deported the first week of April, the newspapers said, because of their "dangerous activities against the democracies." It was Holy Week, Good Friday in fact, when Ernst read that the first Ecuadorian contingent would leave the following Tuesday, April 7, on a U.S. ship. On April 9 he read in *El Comercio* a list of people who, according to the press, were on the ship, including names like Berghvetz, Panzer, Gissel, Hirz, Will, Pipotz and Kudajewski. But there were odd names in the German legation like Erwin J. Hood and Federico Ebert, and two members of the Japanese legation who had strange, European-sounding surnames, Koki Gusbiken and Hirojo Sakochaski.

Ernst had read in *El Comercio* that before the people were put on board, an Act had to be signed in triplicate by all the countries involved. The agreement provided the thirty-eight Germans and ten Japanese safe conduct to the United States where they would be interned in camps or exchanged for Americans coming out of Axis countries.

But there were contradictory reports. The newspaper made significant errors in who was on the ship, with no real distinction between who was being deported by the government and who was leaving of their own accord. The newspaper mentioned Gunter Lisken and Wilhelm Kehrer had been arrested, detained, and later freed at a train station in Ambato, halfway to Guayaquil, only to be listed again as members of the second group to leave Ecuador. He learned that Lisken had avoided being sent on the first ship because his deportation was declared a mistake. According to the report he was detained again, and given a second reprieve due to his wife's struggle with typhoid fever before the next ship sailed. It was clear that someone wanted Lisken out of the country. *Lisken will probably be at Chimbacalle this morning,* Ernst thought. *I wonder if he'll find a way out this time.* [1]

The Special Agents who went from house to house arresting and notifying people to leave had no idea how they were tearing families apart. Wives of his friends had to decide whether to stay in Ecuador or to follow their husbands to a country at war with most of Europe. Many had never set foot out of Ecuador. Some older Ecuadorian-born children of German parents were asked to volunteer to repatriate to Germany for an infirm parent too ill to travel. *It was a shame to tear so many families apart. These are good families. These are decent, ordinary people,* thought Ernst, *who have ties, however fragile, to Axis countries.* Families in Ecuador were strong and loyal. The choice to leave was a tremendously difficult and heart-wrenching one for many of the people he knew who had settled in Quito years ago or for those who had grown up in Quito.

After Easter the press reports caused a real frenzy. There had been a leak of information that gave hope to many of the Ecuadorian wives of the blacklisted men. They were led to believe by newspaper reports that since they were married to Ecuadorians and had children born in Ecuador, their husbands and families could stay without reprisal. Many had their hopes dashed as agents arrived at their homes or when announcements to the contrary came over the radio and in the newspapers. Although the newspapers never said so, the very Constitution did not protect these women against extradition; in fact it was the key to their deportation. Lenchen, and Bio had married the very same week that newspaper reports indicated that Germans married to Ecuadorian women would not be required to leave. The day they married, April 9, the Undersecretary of Foreign Affairs announced that the information leaked to the press was false and that more than 150 Germans and Italians had been notified to leave Quito. *What a honeymoon!* thought Ernst. Lenchen lost her job on the ninth, got married, and started making arrangements to leave on a train a week later for the voyage to the United States and an uncertain future.

On April 17 Lenchen and Bio Beate had sailed from Guayaquil with over 200 adults from Ecuador. No account was made in *El Comercio* of the children that may have traveled on the ship with their parents. The publication of so many names on passenger lists plus the increased visibility in the newspaper and on the radio of citizens belonging to Axis countries caused a good deal of pandemonium. The same day the ship sailed with Bio and Lenchen, an ex-patriot German woman, Ida Mussbaun Dnaks, committed suicide in Guayaquil. The newspaper reported that she overdosed on a drug meant to control her pain from an operation that she had undergone in Germany. *The fear that she might be deported to Germany must have driven her to take her own life. It was a terrible shame*, Ernst thought.

By mid-April people who had not left Quito but were on the blacklists were scared. Extended families were angry and it was obvious that some were trying very hard to keep their daughters and grandchildren in the country. *To little avail*, thought Ernst. The press was calling everyone who left on the ships *totalitarians* and *Nazis*. They were asked to register. Then the arrests and harassment began. Every day the headlines in the newspapers had become more and more sensational. To make matters worse, the published versions of names on the blacklists just kept getting longer and longer with the inclusion of more and more individuals and businesses. Some business owners had started liquidating even before they were blacklisted. More and more people were being approved very quickly for deportation. There was even a rumor that the Central and South American governments needed a specific number of people for the exchange in Europe and Japan and each country had to come up with their quota of internationals. Some of his closest friends suspected that Alberto Wright was the man who cut a deal for himself by identifying many for the blacklist.[2] Wright and his wife had attended all the fancy affairs put on by the Germans and their son attended the German school. Wright was British and his wife was Italian. Everyone had considered him a friend. There was no way of proving the rumors and Ernst felt none of the betrayal that others had expressed, but he did wonder if the suspicions and rumors were true.

Ernst guided his children past St. John of the Cross Hospital, where he had almost died four years earlier from typhoid fever. He would gladly have joined his dear wife in death if it had not meant abandoning his small children. The thought had kept him from leaving the hospital in one of the wooden coffins that lined the street in front of the building. The hospital was always a grim reminder of how fragile life was. *I need to try to think positively, . . . for the children's sake*, he cautioned himself silently.

"Should we go down to La Ronda or should we take Maldonado Street?" Heinz asked.

"Maldonado," Ernst answered. "It's shorter and has fewer stairs. I don't want any of you to fall. We'll go past the Ministry of National Defense on Recoleta and cross the bridge over the Machángara River. It is quite a walk, but you can rest a lot today in the train."

Never had the street name *Maldonado* seemed more ironic than today as it led them toward *Chimbacalle* station. Ernst kept his skepticism and sarcasm to himself, but he felt particularly *unfortunate* as they approached "rough road" station. On the surface he hoped that this journey would be a pleasant adventure and a road to a better life. This idea allowed him to smile and stand tall. Deep inside he knew the road ahead was not only uncertain but also dangerous.

Werner stumbled and scraped his knee.

"Did you catch the rabbit?" Ernst asked to distract his son.

"No," groaned Werner. "I just tripped."

Ernst picked him up and carried him for a few blocks while he continued to mull over the events of the past few weeks. Two groups totaling nearly three hundred adults had already left Ecuador on ships. According to the newspapers some of them left willingly. *Of course, they left willingly,* he scoffed to himself, *as willingly as I am leaving. When agents close your business, harass your family and make your neighbors distrust you . . . what option is there?* Ernst ruminated with disgust. The restrictions had given them little choice. He remembered what he had told his brother-in-law, Hermann, sarcastically only ten days earlier. "We have to do as they do in Pomasqui. Nothing grows in Pomasqui. It is arid there. It never rains, . . . but the *algarobo* tree grows and you can burn the tree like coal. We will be like *algarobo* trees that survive in bad economic times. We will go like precious coal to be sold for an international profit. There is nothing left for us to do here in

Quito, Hermann. It is clear that I will have to take the children and hope for the best in Germany." He remembered how he and Hermann had laughed at the comparison with the *algarobo* trees. Shortly after that conversation, his brother-in-law Hermann had to sign papers stating that he would have no further contact with Germans or Germany. It looked like Hermann and Anita would remain in Ecuador but no one had made arrangements to say good-bye.

The agents had come to Ernst's home on April 21. Special armed agents stopped at the gate and two asked to enter the house. Ernst shook their hands in greeting and invited them upstairs. He sent Werner outside with Miche. The agents looked around the house briefly while they waited for the young boy to leave. The taller agent reported flatly, "Señor Contag, you are scheduled to leave Quito by train on April 30, and to sail on a ship from Guayaquil a few days after that." Ernst looked astonished, "But that is only nine days from today." The second agent answered abruptly, "Correct. What is the total number of children that will travel with you?"

Ernst answered the men politely, "Four." He gave their names and ages and birth dates while one of the agents recorded the information on paper. "Karl Heinz is eleven. He was born July 25, 1930. Ernst is eight. His was born August 9, 1933. Irmgard will turn six next month. She was born on May 20, 1935. Werner is five. His birth date is December 10, 1936. They will all travel with me, of course." The agents provided some specific information about the departure and necessary documents, and told Ernst to expect them back when it was closer to the time to leave for Guayaquil. When they left the house Ernst felt relieved that the encounter had been congenial, but he laughed cynically to himself. *So, this is what* volunteering *to leave Ecuador is all about. Cinch my belt so tightly I can barely breathe, and then ask me if I prefer to be kicked out or to leave with what is left of my dignity.* He knew that the only way to make their voyage and future tolerable was to focus on positive elements of their deportation. He would stand tall and guide his children to keep their face to the sunshine. *Mine, too,* he grimaced.

That evening Ernst had gathered his children to announce the news. "We are going on a fantastic adventure," he told them. He was determined to keep the children as innocent of international matters as possible. "In the next few weeks, or sooner, we will take a train to Guayaquil and then a big steam ship to the United States a few days later."

Ernst remembered the initial excitement he saw in Heinz's face as his son realized he would not have to finish his academic year. "No more mathematics! Aiiiiii!" The children had all celebrated the thought of leaving, but as the departure day neared, there had been plenty of confusion and uneasiness. Heinz was worried about his red bike, the Doodlebug scooter, and his gray roller skates. Ernstchen wondered what they should do about the hunting rifle and the blowgun. Irmgard and Werner asked questions incessantly when anything was moved out of the house.

Irmgard had been particularly concerned when Ernst announced that he would be selling the good china dishes and the china cabinet. She was defiant. Tante Lenchen had told her once that the pretty things in the house that belonged to her mother would belong to her some day. When Ernst told her he sold the china and the cabinet, Irmgard had cried. Ernst did not have the time nor the strength to wonder what life would be like for his children in the future, whether they would be comfortable or suffer. He simply moved forward with making arrangements and left the big picture out of his thoughts.

It became clear that selling the household items was going to cause more emotional damage than the items were worth, but it had to be done. When it came time to get rid of the children's things, Ernst simply suggested to the children that they put things away in a secure spot in the house. "I will get someone to look after the house. Don't worry, children. Heinz, why don't you take Ernst, Irmgard and Werner up the hill and visit the reservoir while I finish up here. Irmgard, why don't you pick some flowers? We will go to the cemetery tomorrow." He put the rest of the household items in another room and planned to make arrangements to sell them when the children were not around.

The children had often accompanied Ernst to the cemetery. Heinz was really the only child old enough to remember his mother very well but they visited the cemetery as a family the day before they were to leave for the coast. Irmgard placed flowers on her mother's grave and followed her brothers as they walked around looking at the names on the other graves. Ernst let his eyes follow the children down the walkway between the rows of the dead. *Happy children. They are happy children, Isabel.* He spoke aloud to her, "You can see them, can't you, Isabel? They are so beautiful. Look at Heinz. He is tall and strong. Long legs all of them. They all have long Contag legs. Even Werner! Everyone says Ernstchen looks so much like you . . . but he is mischievous like I am," Ernst said with a grin. "I see your eyes when I look at Irmgard. She is sweet, sweet and gentle like you and when she laughs she makes everyone around her smile. Little Werner has your curiosity. He wants to learn everything so quickly. He is very bright. He asks so many questions that sometimes I don't know what to do with him." Ernst remembered lifting his hand instinctively to touch, ever so gently, the pocket of his suit jacket where he carried a small photograph of Elisabeth, whom he called, adoringly, Isabel. Just then a profound sadness came over him unexpectedly, and he had continued defiantly, "I never believed I would take myself and the children from this valley, Isabel . . . I take you with me in my heart, and I will come back to be near you." In matters of the heart, he was impractical and fiercely loyal.

Near El Tejar church just past La Recoleta square Ernst felt the muscles in his back start to ache and he put Werner down. It was still quite a distance to Chimbacalle station but he was determined to walk these streets and breath the air. It would be their last walk in Quito for a very long time and he wanted to take in the smells of the city. Every place had its own unique smell. He thought that Guayaquil, for example, smelled of ocean air, rotting fish and urine because when he was in Guayaquil, he spent time at the wharf. Of course, Quito had many different smells. It was so familiar, however, it was hard to imagine what the smells were. It smelled like home. You had to go away, to the mountains, to another place and return to recognize home. Today, smoke from burned eucalyptus and quiet dominated the cool morning air of the Valley of the Quitus.[3] Most Quiteños were probably still sound asleep in their beds. Servant women in charge of cooking were probably stoking the fires for breakfast. The birds started to chirp in nearby trees. Ernst stopped and looked back down the street. Quito seemed to be at peace. Ernst felt anxious and confused. To relax he took a deep breath and spoke to his children.

"This is where the Machángara River enters Quito. The cold water comes down from the Pichincha. Do you hear the rush of the river against the rocky river bed?" Ernst asked Werner and Irmgard as he walked them across the bridge. The famous *censo* windmills were nearby on the left, their filthy exteriors barely visible in the early morning darkness. Ernst did not point them out to the children.

When the Contag family arrived at Chimbacalle Station around quarter past five, the train station on the city outskirts was bustling with activity. The Contags were in good company. Ernst spotted a family friend, Dr. Walter Wohlermann, and asked his children to follow him. Dr. Wohlermann and his Ecuadorian wife were high society people, and they had always been warm and kind to Ernst and his wife. When Heinz was born he had asked the Wohlermanns to honor their family by serving as his godparents.

"Good morning, Ernst, . . . children. Your cheeks are flushed, Irmgard. Did you walk all the way this morning?" the doctor asked with a smile.

"Yes, sir," piped Heinz. "We walked the entire way," he added with pride. Ernstchen, Irmgard and Werner were busy watching the many people who were walking on the platform near the train.

Wohlermann continued, "You had better find out which rail car you will travel in, Ernst. We will have to board the train soon. The conductor says we are to leave at half past five."

"I can't imagine they would have assigned us a particular rail car. They'll never get the train loaded with all these people until nearly six. I would wager we will leave later than planned. They can't board the ship without us." Ernst laughed nervously. He never worried about such insignificant things as assigned seats or leaving on time. He had never understood the German's interest in punctuality and in this case, punctuality seemed all the more absurd.

"Well, we had better leave by six, otherwise we'll arrive very late in Guayaquil. I guess they need a few extra minutes to load several people from the internment site at Riobamba, too." Wohlermann leaned toward Ernst and murmured slyly, "The security guards in Riobamba won't appreciate a late arrival. They want to get a few afternoon winks after guarding those *dangerous Nazis* and those *Japanese spies* at the internment camp!" Wohlermann winked at Heinz who had missed the meaning of his statement entirely.

Ernst was surprised at the confidence and ease with which his friend made light of their situation. His playful mockery of the public portrayal of members of the international community in Ecuador was refreshing, however. It was as though they were all on a routine trip to the coast. Each individual handled anger and injustice differently, Ernst supposed. Wohlermann's wife did not look at all happy. Her eyes were red and somewhat swollen. Clearly she had slept little. Ernst understood why. There was some indignity associated with their departure. He had also felt the pangs of injustice when he locked the door to his house and imagined that many immigrants and Ecuadorian-born travelers had suffered the same apprehension, emptiness, and sadness as they locked their own homes that morning. Ernst tapped Wohlermann's shoulder with feigned confidence. "We'll have a good trip," he quipped before tipping his hat to the doctor's wife and heading toward the train to check in with security.

Dozens of children were traveling with their parents. To Heinz, it looked as though they were all traveling to the coast for a vacation. They were, for the most part, well dressed and obedient, and he could see excitement in their faces. Heinz had been to the coast for a vacation with his parents before his mother died and this morning he felt the same sense of excitement he had felt on his first train ride. Heinz kept an eye on Werner, who was fascinated more by the train than by the armed guards on the platform. His little brother studied the mechanisms carefully whenever people moved out of his line of vision. Irmgard held Heinz's hand dutifully. Ernstchen was so excited he could hardly stand still. He paced near his father and bounced playfully on his toes.

The time on the platform passed quickly and at six o'clock the train pulled away from the station just as sunrise began to paint the city and its surrounding mountains in a gray-tone silhouette. The children pressed their faces against the windows in an effort to see beyond the train. Ernst settled down near Willi Schmidt, an engineer in Quito. Willi was about five years older than Ernst, and he and his young wife, Dora, had a four-year-old son, Werner, who joined Ernst's children at the window. The children chatted about the noises they heard and tried to decipher plants and trees that appeared suddenly from areas covered by fog. As the train picked up speed, Ernst saw his children try to follow the vegetation outside the window with their eyes.

As the sun rose, the landscape outside the train window cleared and the children were able to scan the inter-Andean valley for animals, shacks and people as the train headed south. They played games trying to spot the first person, the first sheep, the first llama, the first burro, the first cow, the first *sigse*, the first *penco* plant...[4] They started the game over each time they passed a village or town.

Willi turned to Ernst and asked, "How long has your family been in Quito?" The question caught Ernst off guard, as he was about to dose off after a fitful night. He straightened and spoke in a friendly manner.

"I was born here. My father left Germany before 1900. I am not sure of the date."

Ernst did not mention that his father had sailed around the southern tip of South America and landed in Chile. He had decided to ride a horse up through South America looking for the perfect place for establishing a brewery. He had a photo of his father Oscar Contag with his black horse, Flores Negras, and a hunting dog. In the photograph his father looked like one of those wild adventurers right out of one of Karl May's novels."[5] According to the stories he heard, his grandfather had sold the family farm in Numeiten so they could marry off the Contag daughters. He had been told he should be proud the Contags had an aristocratic bloodline that could be traced back to Charles the Great. In Numeiten, the family raised horses but the family must have lost money after 1860 and thirty years later they were forced to sell the farm. His mother had told him that his father wrote a letter to the man who bought the farm, a Mr. Ziehe, and asked him if he knew a young woman who would be courageous and hardworking enough to work with him as his wife in South America. Mr. Ziehe wrote that he knew of such a woman and made arrangements for his daughter, Gertrude, to marry Oscar Contag.

Ernst remembered thinking it was odd that his mother would marry a man she had never met especially since his father had requested someone who could bake bread and make sausages as well as help out with a brewery he planned to build, when his mother was a nurse who had a job in a town some distance from Numeiten. His mother had told him that she had never imagined leaving her home, but her father had told her the journey to South America was one that would lead to happiness and fortune. It certainly had been an opportunity for her to see more of the world. She told him that his father had arrived with a carriage drawn by six horses. It was quite the spectacle, but no one thought it would be the last time she would walk on European soil.

"Your father was in the brewing business, was he not?" Willi Schmidt asked.

"My father established a brewery in the mountains outside Cuenca near an Indian village called Saiausí. There is a beautiful gorge with a healthy stream there. He thought it was an excellent spot for his brewery. Another man came to help with the brewery but he and my father both died before the brewery could take off. My father also bought property in Cuenca near the land of the wealthy Hortensia Mata, of whom I am sure you have heard. He was forced to sell soon after I was born in 1907. My parents moved the family to Quito in 1910 and in 1912 my father tried to establish a brewery near Rocafuerte Street. He had just gotten started when he fell ill. He was sick and bedridden for a year before he died in 1917. I was ten when he died."

"You did not carry on in the brewery business, then, Ernesto?" Willi asked.

"Before my father died he made all of us promise not to work at a brewery. My brothers, Arturo, Carlos and I knew what a struggle my father had in Cuenca. When we moved to Quito in 1910 things did not get easier and soon my parents had another mouth to feed when my sister was born. My mother made sausages. I guess you could say we were in the sausage business."

Ernst recalled the years before his father's illness. They were difficult times for many, not just the Contag family. Lenchen was born in a house on 10 de agosto Street in 1912. Her birthday was impossible to forget. It was the day men broke into the penitentiary on Rocafuerte Street and killed deposed president Eloy Alfaro and his lieutenants. Alfaro was the one who had the railway continued to the south and even allowed women to work in the mail system. He was forced out of Ecuador during his second administration. Alfaro had gone into exile in Panama for a while but returned to Ecuador. Ernst was a young boy, but he remembered an angry anti-Alfarista group dragging the corpses of Alfaro and his lieutenants through the streets to El Ejido Park to be burned. January 28, 1912 there was quite a commotion in the Contag house and also on the street. Ernst supposed it was a horrible memory to recall but as he remembered it, the cries of the men outside drowned out the tiny cries of his baby sister in the next room.

Ernst relaxed and offered Willi a cigarette. He lit Willi's cigarette before his own and blew smoke toward the ceiling of the train. He enjoyed the sensation smoking gave him. The train rocked back and forth on the rails and Ernst let his mind wander back to his mother.

Gertrude Ziehe was a strong woman, some even considered her harsh. She was well educated and resourceful. How else could she have managed raising the four of them as a widow in a country she barely understood? Her husband left them very little money. She couldn't afford to return to Europe. Her father was very ill in 1917 but she had no option than to stay and raise the family in Quito. Still, she had good connections and many friends. She bought the Rocafuerte house at auction and started raising hogs on the property. As children, they had all helped make sausages and hams to sell. Ernst wondered how closely his life was beginning to parallel the life of his mother.

Willi Schmidt interrupted his thoughts. "It would have been a tough business to run in any case. The "Victoria" brewery would have put up stiff competition for your father's brewery."[6]

Ernst responded with nothing more than a nod. He closed his eyes and rested. When the train pulled into Latacunga around noon, Ernst got off with his children to take care of personal needs and to buy something for them to eat. The children played tag under the watchful eyes of guards and the security officers. The children did not notice them, but he did. Ernst walked past one of the Ecuadorian guards, greeted him in Spanish and resisted the urge to squeeze his fingers over an imaginary object in a gesture that said "Thief." Bribery was not only accepted, but expected of military personnel, and Ernst usually enjoyed making fun of the ritual exchange of words and money that had become commonplace everywhere.

The Latacunga train station was not much to look at but the dock was filled with local vendors of all ages who sold cheese, sweets made from dried fruit, and corn on the cob. Young boys called out at the train windows and some passengers leaned out to buy their wares. Other passengers were standing near the train and the vendors crisscrossed between them asking the passengers to try their homemade tidbits. Some turned their noses up at the offerings; others were comfortable making a purchase. Before leaving, the guards made sure all were accounted for on the train. The conductor announced the train's departure and the whistle blew. Ernst watched some of the vendors jog alongside the train as it pulled out. *Pobrecitos,* he thought.

When they returned to their seats, the youngest Contag children sat on either side of their father. After half an hour they were asleep. Ernst could hear Heinz and Erntschen talking in the seat behind him.

"Why does that boy keep standing up and sitting down? It drives me crazy," Ernstchen told Heinz.

"I don't know. He is in my class at school, but no one talks to him much. He is really amazing at figures. Everything he does in mathematics is *precisely correct*," Heinz enunciated the words clearly and mockingly. "He *always* has the right answers." After a moment he added an afterthought, "He isn't German though. I think his father may be British or something. His mother looks Italian, doesn't she? His last name is Reit… No… I think it is Wright," he said thinking through the spelling of the name he had heard on occasion.

Ernstchen interrupted his reasoning. "Maybe he has an itchy bottom after stopping at the bathroom in Latacunga." Heinz laughed and imitated the boy's fidgeting.

When the joke lost its punch, Ernstchen asked Heinz a question. "Wouldn't it be fun to hunt in the foothills of the Cotopaxi?" The train had passed the Cotopaxi volcano just before entering Latacunga. At more than 6,000 meters high it could be seen from very far away on a clear day. "When we come back to Quito we should ask Papa to take us hunting there."

Ernst smiled and listened to his boys talk. It was reassuring to hear them talk of hunting near the Cotopaxi volcano. God, it was gorgeous there. The volcano was snowcapped and its foothills seemed endless. He let his mind wander as the boys continued their discussion.

"You might have to worry about lava flows, Ernstchen. The Cotopaxi is one of the most active volcanoes in the world! It could erupt at any moment! One of the boys at school said his father took him to the foothills of the Cotopaxi and they saw a huge rock, as big as the Hotel Humboldt, sitting right in the middle of a pasture. His father said the volcano spewed the rock straight out of its cone and it landed there. Just think... you could be walking around looking for animals and chiiiiiiuuuuuu a rock could come flying and squish you right where you stood!"

"I don't care;" reported Ernstchen, " I want to live there someday. I could hunt and do whatever I wanted to do. If there were an eruption with flying rocks I could get away fast. I would get one of those trucks they advertise in the newspaper and *ppsssssss,* I'll be out of there, *zoom*, like lightning."

Heinz laughed at his brother's exaggerations and sound effects. "I'd like to see you *zoom* away from a hot lava flow, Ernstchen. Now be quiet; I am tired." Heinz closed his eyes and pretended he was asleep. He wished there were some music to listen to instead of the humdrum and chugging of the train. It was not long before both boys were resting against each other and moving to the rhythm of the train, deep in sleep.

Willi caught Ernst's eye and asked, "Do you know your family in Europe?"

"No. I have never been to Europe and my grandfather never came to South America. I know very little about him, actually."

"So, if your family is exchanged for Americans, where will you go?" Willi asked.

The question brought Ernst back to the moment and the uncertainty of their future. "I have a brother in Berlin. My brother, Carlos... Carl, lives with his wife, Inge, in Berlin. We will go there ... if we have the opportunity. " Ernst raised his eyebrows and leaned forward "That is if we get out of the United States and across the ocean! Things can happen you know." He was playful, but the essence of his statement was rooted in serious anxiety.

There were two more stops at the towns of Salcedo and Ambato before they would arrive at Riobamba. Ernst had made this trip to Guayaquil many times for business. On its regular route the *mixto* train stopped at every village between Quito and Riobamba to pick up passengers and cargo: Machachi, Lasso near Saquisilí, Salcedo, Ambato, Riobamba. Passengers would mill about and buy the food specialties of the village: leaf-wrapped cheese, cooked beans, little crackers made with lard, roasted guinea pig . . . Ernst had always found the long trip relaxing. There was no way to hurry the *mixto*. On routine trips some passengers going south or north would stay in Riobamba where there were two hotels, the Hotel Ecuador and the Metropolitano, and where a passenger could stay for about 5 sucres. An evening snack and a light breakfast were always included in the price.

Ernst looked out the window at the landscape. It was mid afternoon and he was tired. Willi talked about working as an engineer in Quito and the jobs he thought he could get in Germany. Ernst listened and nodded pleasantly, but he felt burdened by thoughts of making a living in Germany. Things were so uncertain! He just listened, nodded his head, smoked a cigarette, and re-situated his sleeping children as necessary.

Suddenly, Werner woke fitfully. The young boy was completely confused by his surroundings and his arms floundered about as he tried to orient himself.

"I am hungry, Papa. Will we stop again soon?" Ernst's answer was of interest to all the children within earshot. "We will stop in Riobamba. It is not far from here and I will get us something to eat."

Werner went to the window to look out. The sun was already dropping in the west and the highlands looked bleak against the mountainous backdrop. Werner's head bobbed back and forth as he followed the blurred ground rushing alongside the train tracks. Ernst yawned discreetly, patted his son automatically, and relaxed with a newspaper the Schmidts had picked up in Ambato. Heinz moved close to his father and spoke quietly into his ear, "I can't wait to tell Werner about the serpents that climb the houses on stilts in the lowlands near Guayaquil. That will spook him!"

"Ssssssssssss. " Ernst waved his son away playfully. Ernst remembered that Heinz had been fascinated by the small bamboo and wood huts built on stilts to keep the floor dry and the snakes out. Ernst rubbed the stubble of beard on his chin and closed his eyes a moment before reading a few newspaper articles. There was a report from New Orleans, Louisiana, about the invention of an artificial eye that could move with one's own eye muscles. The movie, *Dance with Me*, with the famous American dancers Ginger Rogers and Fred Astair, was in Guayaquil. He focused his attention on a few articles about arrests of foreigners in other countries. *Politics*, he sighed. *Economics*. He let his eyes wander to something that could hold his interest. There was an article about increased military spending in the United States but he found the advertisement for the Philco Radio just as interesting. He skipped the social page and looked out the window. *Why read the social page when none of these people will be important to us in a few days? Better to put them out of mind now.*

The train continued south out of Ambato, a city remembered more for its fruits and flowers than its train station, and wove its way between the Carihuairazo Mountain on the right and the Igualata on the left. Just beyond the Igualata the ominous Tungurahua volcano could be seen in the distance. Ernst had taken his family to Baños, a city that had earned its fame with its healing thermal springs. Ironically, that is where his family had become so ill with typhoid fever that led to his wife's death. The thought gave him a sinking feeling and he looked away from the east to the southwest for glimpses of the impressive Chimborazo. The Chimborazo, whose name in Quechua means Blue Snow, was a visual marvel that rose over 6000 meters into the sky. The snow-covered peaks were forbidding, and the foothills at the base seemed bare of life of any kind. Many had tried to climb its slopes and peaks. Even the renowned liberator Simón Bolívar had made an attempt to scale its peaks over a hundred years earlier.[7] When the Chimborazo was in sight, everyone knew that Riobamba was not much further.

By the time the train pulled up to the station, the children were anxious to get off the train. The boys were at the door of the rail car before Ernst was out of his seat. Ernst stood, stretched, and pressed the wrinkles from his clothing with his hands. Riobamba was cooler than Quito so he put on his suit coat and cocked his hat.

"Go with your brothers, Irmgard. I'll be right behind you." He reached down to smooth her hair and noticed three Japanese men under guard on the station platform. He pointed them out with a nod of his head to Willi and Dora Schmidt. "The Japanese must be from the internment site here in Riobamba. They started interning Japanese, Germans and Italians right after Walter Gissel was deported on the *Airen* steamer in January. Did you know that, Willi? Ecuador had not broken off relations with the Axis yet, but people were being arrested."

Willi nodded, but said nothing in response to Ernst. He helped his wife and young son out of the train and vanished into the crowd of passengers and street peddlers. Ernst stopped at the door of the train and the children ran back to meet him.

"Come on, Papa. We are *dying* of starvation." Werner exaggerated as he pulled his father from the rail car stairs. The passengers were guarded but the National Security agents did not seem to bother anyone very much. The few brief moments at the

Riobamba station were delightful. The sun was still warm and the air was crisp and smelled of cooked onions, garlic and potatoes. At the station Ernst spotted Hans Mittman and his wife, Erna Richter de Mittman and their son. *They must have come up from Loja to meet the train*, he thought. Mittman was a brew master in his late fifties and Ernst had met him earlier when Hans was looking to import beer bottling equipment. He greeted the Mittmans cordially and introduced his children to them. The two families stood together and ate sparingly from the variety of foods they bought from local vendors. There were fruits, roasted guinea pig, potato biscuits, hot stews, coconut candies, jellied fruit, and juices.

Everything smelled delicious but the children begged their father for *cui*. The smell of the guinea pigs that the outdoor vendors had roasted over a flame whetted their appetites. Ernstchen asked his father how the Indians prepared *cui*. Ernst explained that the *cui* were killed instantly by pressing their little noses against a hard surface. Ernstchen laughed at the way his father imitated the sound of the guinea pigs' death knell. "If you apply any pressure at all you hear *grreck*, and it is all over. Then the carcasses are submerged in boiling water, skinned, cleaned and hung. Afterward the meat is seasoned, tied whole to a stick, and roasted over a fire like you see there." Only the immigrants were surprised that nothing except the bones went to waste. Anyone who had grown up in Ecuador considered the dish a delicacy. Some considered the brain the best part and sucked it from the skull. When an Ecuadorian native ate *cui*, the bones were sucked clean and left in a tidy pile.

Ernst spoke to several adults as his children moved about carelessly outside the train station. Heinz leaned forward as though he were taking a deep bow and managed to finish his meal of *cui* without dripping juices on his shirt. Ernstchen imitated his older brother in such an exaggerated fashion that he had to catch his balance by taking three running steps forward to avoid falling. Irmgard laughed at her brothers' silly antics and imitated Ernstchen's stumbles. It became a game and Werner and several other children picked up on it. The children's laughter rang throughout the train yard in stark contrast to the seriousness of the situation. A large man eating just beyond the children brought their impromptu game to a halt. The man was coughing and spitting. His face had turned red.

"Look Papa. He's choking," Ernstchen shouted to his father.

"No he isn't," Ernst said calmly with a bit of a smirk. "I saw him put a little too much *ají* on his food. He will be fine. But right now I bet he'd like to die!" Ernst smiled discreetly. The red, spicy pepper sauce even made his own eyes water when he spiced his food too much. The inhabitants of the sierra liked *ají* and used more than most people could stomach. The Contag children stared at the man and giggled. A grown man looked pretty silly waving his hands up and down like that. His face was beet red and he looked very uncomfortable. A woman, perhaps his wife, came to his rescue with some potato biscuits, but her efforts seemed to irritate him even more. The man coughed and sputtered and made quite a spectacle of himself before pushing through the crowd to the rail car.

Before anyone was ready to return to their seats on the rail car, the guards and the train's conductor ushered them back on board. Ernst followed his reluctant children up the stairs and down the aisle. Everyone seemed much more animated now that they had eaten, but no one was ready for another long ride.

As soon as Ernst had taken his seat, shouts could be heard above the chatter in the rail car. Someone in the next rail car was disgruntled. Ernst looked out the window and saw a German couple being moved from one rail car to another.

"What's that all about?" Ernst asked Willi. Dora was the one who responded, "The Japanese were put in that rail car."

Ernst indicated that he understood with a nod and pursed his lips, swallowing a sigh. In situations like this he felt embarrassed by the whims of those who could not treat others with dignity and respect. This could have been the reason the Japanese traveled in a separate train when the first contingent left in April. These were two fiercely proud cultures. The apparent snub made him uncomfortable. His mother had raised him to be respectful of others. She had friends among the highest in society, but she made no enemies of those who worked at her side. His father had not been so charitable with others of different social castes, and he saw some of his father's pretentiousness in his siblings, and in this couple who refused to ride in the same rail car as the Japanese.

The rail car was noisier than ever with chatter when the train whistle blew and the train jerked forward. Ernst closed the windows near him to prevent the steam engine's ash from entering and covering their clothes. Others followed suit as the train choked and coughed and pulled the cars up the steep incline of the mountain. When the tracks had taken them high above the foothills, the children gasped at the ground below that seemed to have fallen suddenly from underneath the track. Two women moved to the slope side of the train to avoid looking at the foothills that lay hundreds of meters below. Ernst considered this the most spectacular section of the ride from Quito to Guayaquil. It was a cliffhanger ride and Ernst, too, was overcome with excitement, as the tracks seemed to carry them toward the clouds.

Just then Ernst thought of a way to keep his children entertained and interested in the exhilarating sites of the trip ahead. The tracks would take them through the unforgettable Andean cliffs to the steamy, sub-tropical jungle on the western lowlands and he wanted his children to remember this trip. It was the trip of a lifetime, and he did not know when they would have the opportunity to return. He used a spooky voice and glaring eyes to tease his children, "Now we head to the Devil's nose!" He lifted his hands and clutched the air in front of him. "You'll have to hang on for your lives!" The drama in Ernst's voice piqued the children's curiosity and they gathered near him to hear the gripping story.

"The devil's nose? Where?" asked Irmgard innocently. Werner's eyes were open wide with interest and he bobbed up and down next to his father. Ernstchen put his thumb to his nose and stretched out his little finger. He mimicked his father's eerie voice, and repeated, "the devil's nose, the devil's nose, hang on for your lives!" Heinz made an insulting gesture by thumbing his nose and wiggling his fingers. He jeered, "Lange Nase, lange Nase."[8]

Ernst calmed his children down by putting his finger to his lips. The younger children leaned in to hear their father's tale above friendly chatter and the chugging of the train as it inched up the steep Andean mountainside toward perpendicular cliffs. Dora Schmidt kept her son Werner at her side and spoke to him directly, fearing the story might frighten him, but her husband Willi relaxed and nodded approvingly at Ernst to go ahead with the tale.

La nariz del diablo is located between Sibambe and Alausí. Just south of Riobamba the train climbs the Andes to an altitude of over 3600 meters. Just outside Sibambe the train must navigate a perpendicular cliff by carefully traveling back and forth across two impressive switchbacks. The train descends nearly 1100 meters while covering less than thirty kilometers of track. Ernst's story, however, had nothing whatsoever to do with altitude, switchbacks or perpendicular cliffs.

Ernst hunched his shoulders and screwed up his face. His eyes were thin slits as he began, "Not far from here is the treacherous Nose of the Devil . . ."[9]

NOTES TO CHAPTER THREE

[1] The newspaper reports provide a different version of what happened to Gunter Lisken than his own autobiographical book, *Der Zeit Zeuge: Ein Deutsches Schicksal in Südamerika*. Mönchengladback: B. Kühlen Verlags GmbH & Co. KG., 1999. According to Lisken, he was ordered to Cuenca on January 1, 1943 (p.52) to live under surveillance until he was arrested, incarcerated in Guayaquil in December 1943, and processed for deportation by FBI-Chief Mr. Gates. On the eve of the New Year he set sail with others for Panama (p 6). Later on he was reunited with his wife and son and interned at the camp in Crystal City, Texas.

[2] Bruggeman interview. May 30, 1999. "Alberto Wright... el cuchillo era éste." (Alberto Wright... he was the blade.") Bruggeman's father was the German consul in Ecuador.

[3] The Quitus Indians were the people who resided in the area of Quito when the Spaniards arrived.

[4] *Sigse* is a pampas grass native to the mountainous regions of Ecuador. The *penco* plant is a succulent native to the Ecuadorian highlands that has many uses. One of the more unusual is its use in the fermented *chicha* drink that is prepared with fruit juices, sugar cane, white corn, cassava, and the center of the *penco* plant.

[5] Karl May wrote adventure novels in Germany during the last half of the nineteenth century. May never traveled to the Americas,

but his adventure novels set in the Americas were very successful in Europe.

[6]Mr. Enrique (Heinrich) E. Vorbeck replaced Arthur Sahm, the brewery's first brew master and a German technician, in 1912 after Mr. Sham's contract with the brewery's owner, Mr. Mariano Negrete, expired in 1911.

[7]Eichler. *Ecuador*. p. 81.

[8]"Long nose, long nose." The gesture and words are insulting in German.

CHAPTER FOUR

JOURNEY ON THE HORIZON

GUAYAQUIL, MAY 1942

At the Treasury Wharf the wind blew gently at women's dresses while they waved at family members who were being transported to the steam ship Arcadia. Heinz noticed a young girl who clung to her mother's skirt. The mother was wiping her face with a handkerchief and must have been crying.

Werner was not tall enough to see through the crowd so Ernst lifted him to shoulder height at the rail of the launch. Werner called out to onlookers at the wharf, "Look at me. Look at how high I am now." His voice was swept away in the wind but his flailing arms got a response from several people on the wharf. A young boy pulled away from his mother and jumped about in excitement beneath a street lamp. Heinz could here his brother call out that he was going on the Arcadia steamer and this was going to be a really amazing voyage and everyone should be jealous. He was the happiest boy on earth! "If Blanca were here, she would be really jealous. She would think it was unfair that I get to ride on a ship and she didn't, wouldn't she Papa?"

Heinz did not hear his father's answer because he was already lost in thought. He stared at the wake caused by the landing craft and sniffed at the warm, humid breeze that brushed his face as the craft moved toward the steam ship Arcadia. The air was fresher and cleaner than at the Durán station where they got off the train. Ernstchen summed up the miserable experience of the Durán station with a few appropriate words. "This place is hot, humid, stinky, and dirty. Let's get out of here." No one seemed unhappy to leave the depressing Durán station on the ferry ride across the Guayas River to Guayaquil. Many travelers were weary after the long train ride from Quito and the seemingly endless wait at the wharf. Others, who had arrived days before, enjoyed the warm, early morning sunshine on the day of their departure. The sight of the enormous and modern steam ship was enough to boost the spirits and energy of the children. The ship caused mixed emotions for the adults.

The families had spent a good part of the day at the wharf in front of the Government Palace waiting to board the Arcadia. The rank smells at the wharf made Heinz wonder what went on there after dark. The U.S. steamer, anchored in the river, dominated the small Grace Line landing craft that carried passengers and cargo to and from its deck. While on the pier, Heinz had overheard Mr. Heinrich Bloemken tell Willi Schmidt that the steamer had a carrying capacity of 1200 passengers. Heinz wondered how many were already aboard the steamer since there were hundreds of passengers at the pier.

The mountain of luggage that the day laborers had loaded at the Customs Wharf surprised Heinz: baskets and leather suitcases, bundles, and assorted boxes and trunks. He wondered what some of the people were taking on the voyage. He could not even imagine having so many things to take along.

From the landing craft the Arcadia looked like nothing Heinz had ever seen before. "It is a floating hotel!" his father told him as they stood together. There were two large booms on either end of the ship and a smoke stack in the center. The mast at the bow had a crow's nest for observation. The boom at the stern had cordage that seemed to hold the pole aloft at a bit of an angle. Ernst explained what he could of the ship's structure to his children, but he found himself at a loss for words. Just above the keel an enormous banner read "DIPLOMATIC" between quotation marks in large, bold, white letters. At first Heinz had thought "Diplomatic" was the name of the ship, but his father explained that the U.S. ship was labeled "Diplomatic" because it was carrying important passengers during war times. In his mind he prayed that the label would keep them safe.

Heinz laughed at the center smoke stack and pointed it out to his brother Ernstchen, "Look at that huge round pipe in the middle of the ship sticking up between those poles! The steam ship looks like a floating volcano!"

The tiny portholes that dotted the side of the steamer fascinated Ernstchen. He started to count them, but there were too many and he returned his gaze to the bubbling wake behind the landing craft, watching in silence.

Friday, May 8, 1942 was a beautiful day and the excitement now seemed genuine among the passengers on the landing craft. The wait on the wharf had been tiresome and uncomfortable. The travelers from Quito were unaccustomed to the humid air and the hot equatorial sun at the coast. The air seemed heavy and thick compared to the air of Quito.

Every effort had been made to keep the travelers under observation. The presence of military men dressed in uniform made some feel uncomfortable, but they had not affected Ernst. He preoccupied himself with thoughts about his brother, Arturo. Arturo, Alcira, and their children had planned to sail with them on this voyage, but Arturo had fallen ill a few days earlier in Guayaquil. That very morning Dr. Max Meitzner, who was also traveling with his family on the Arcadia, warned Alcira that if Arturo traveled with the group now, she would be widowed and her children left without a father. Arturo had pleurisy or pneumonia according to the doctor, and a bad case of it at that. Alcira and Arturo had decided to wait and leave on the ship at its next sailing in June, but Arturo was still in the custody of National Security agents when it was time to board the landing craft. Arturo had been under close surveillance by investigation agents for months, and Ernst knew that it could be only a matter of time before his brother was arrested or interned if he didn't leave Ecuador. The political climate had turned nasty against anyone associated with Axis countries, and Arturo had connections that might be considered problematic.

Ernst became angry at the wharf when press agents from the *El Universo* newspaper started to harass some of the travelers by taking photographs and asking impertinent questions. They lined up some of the youngest children and took a picture of them with the Arcadia in the background. Two little boys were

El Vapor Arcadia Partió Anoche al Sur Con Nazis Que Salen Voluntariamente

DESPUES DE TOMAR EN CALLAO A OTROS NATURALES DE PAISES DEL EJE, EL BARCO VOLVERA A NUEVA ORLEANS, PUERTO DESDE EL CUAL SEGUIRAN TODOS A LISBOA, PARA SU CANJE CON DIPLOMATICOS Y PARTICULARES DE AMERICA

TAMBIEN DEJAN BRASIL OTROS REPRESENTANTES Y SUBDITOS DE ALEMANIA E ITALIA

Photographs of children that sailed on the steamship Arcadia with the Contag family for a diplomatic exchange. The headline labels them "Nazis" (*El Universo*, May 8, 1942).

dressed as *marineros* in navy jackets with seafaring collars and cuffs outlined in white. The press had been so inconsiderate to this point he half expected them to run a headline calling the tiny tots *Nazi* spies.

No doubt the travelers looked unusual as a group. There were over forty children with their parents, all dressed as Europeans. The little girls wore short-sleeved dresses and white socks and dark shoes. The women wore lightweight dresses and bonnets. A few of the men and older boys at the wharf wore white shirts and slacks, dark jackets and berets as though they had purchased appropriate seafaring clothes. Perhaps they had. Ernst was in the company of many successful businessmen and their families. That was clear. Outside of the Deutsche Haus meetings, he did not remember ever standing among such a large homogeneous group of men, women and children. With the exception of the few Japanese at the wharf, the group of people with strong European ancestry stood in stark contrast to the highly indigenous population they were leaving behind. It was true that few of them looked anything like what others might consider a traditional Ecuadorian.

Ernst wore a white shirt, gray slacks and held his gray, brimmed hat in his hand. It was tremendously warm on the coast and there was no good reason to soil his suit jacket. He lifted his arms away from his ribs a bit and let the breeze dry his shirt as they traveled toward the Arcadia.

At that moment Ernst noticed a disturbance back on shore. Uniformed men started running along the loading dock and security personnel appeared near the water at the pier. "Someone must have escaped or jumped ship," Ernst said aloud as he looked around.

"What do you mean by escaped? Escaped from whom? Are there prisoners on the wharf?" asked Ernstchen.

Ernst had not been aware that his voice had carried, but he leaned close to his son's ear and responded. "Some people do not want to leave Ecuador, Ernstchen," his father replied. It was not a good time to explain the political situation to an eight year old. Ernst looked toward the Arcadia. The water in the Guayas River glistened in the sunshine and the brightness of the sun in the sky nearly blinded him. "Stay near me when we go through the hatchway onto the deck, children. Hold hands so we stay together."

The bulk of the ship was overwhelming for the children, and Ernst had to remind them to watch where they stepped so they would not trip or fall. Irmgard held her father's hand tightly and let him guide her. She could not tear her eyes from the steel fortress that loomed above her. The ship's size fascinated her brothers and they jabbered aloud about the Arcadia, but she felt herself cringe with fear as she stepped onto the deck.

Irmgard followed the passengers dutifully and stood quietly next to her father as he waited in line for his passport to be marked for deportation. She felt her father straighten as he approached Dávalos' security crew. Dávalos, in charge of Ecuadorian national security, had made the newspapers quite often and Ernst felt no kinship with him or his hired help.

Someone behind them announced that the steamer was heading north to the Colombian port city Buenaventura, and then to Panama instead of Callao as some expected. A security agent asked for her father's papers, counted the children, and marked each child's name as Ernst identified them. The Contags were assigned a cabin and an agent waved them on.

Ernst led his children to the balustrade where they could look out at Guayaquil in the dimming light of the western sky. Irmgard shuddered, *"La casa se está moviendo!"* "The *house* is not moving, Irmgard," her father corrected her. "We are on a ship on the water. Look." But she trembled even more as she imagined the depth of the water below. "I want to walk around over there, Papa, near the wall. I don't want to stand here anymore." Her eyes looked away from the river and Ernst knew that his daughter was scared. "Boys! Let's go check out the inside of the ship and our cabin, then we can come back out on deck."

The ship was modern and, to Ernst's surprise, quite comfortable. The dining salon was long and had an air of elegance. Below, the hallways were crowded with passengers looking for their cabins, and Ernst noticed that once they were off the deck, Irmgard relaxed her grip a little. Their cabin was small and had two sets of stacked beds in it. Heinz and Ernstchen selected the upper bunks. Ernst hoped they wouldn't roll out and told Werner and Irmgard they should sleep in the lower bunk. He would take the other bunk. The children agreed reluctantly. There was a sink in the room and he told the children to wash their hands and faces. Ernst hung his suit coat in the small closet and looked in the mirror that was just a bit low for his tall frame. "Well, here we are," he sighed aloud. The children waited in silence for him to continue, but he did not, and there was not another word until Heinz, Ernstchen and Werner announced that they were ready to investigate the ship's treasures and to have dinner.

The sun had set by the time they climbed upstairs to the dining salon. The salon was not full and Ernst was surprised to see how few people were aboard. The few Japanese passengers chose to sit together. The Italians did the same. The Germans were no different. Ernst sat with his children at a table with several couples. Ernst learned from them that the disturbance on shore was indeed the result of an attempted escape. Somewhere between the wharf and the ship four men had escaped and were missing. A man from Guayaquil at the end of the table mentioned two names, but Ernst did not recognize them. After dinner, the passengers were asked to return to their cabins for the evening. Ernstchen and Heinz were disappointed, but they knew they would be up all the earlier the next morning.

———

Morning brought renewed enthusiasm to investigate the ship, so after breakfast the boys headed toward the passenger deck of the steamer.

"Lift me up, Heinz," Werner begged. "I want to see, too." Instinctively Ernst lifted Irmgard up as well but when she saw the ship sailing toward . . . *nothing*, she shrieked and wrapped herself around her father, burying her head in his shoulder. Her voice, muffled by his jacket, was still audible and he heard her say, "There is nothing at the end, Papa. We will fall off! The ship will fall off!"

Ernst was perplexed by his daughter's fear, but comforted her. Soon he realized that Irmgard had never seen the horizon at sea level, and she did not understand oceans or traveling over water to another body of land. He put her down gently and pulled slightly away from her tight grasp, held her with his face inches from hers, and explained, "Out there where the clouds meet the water, Irmgard, is the horizon. You'll see that the water goes for a very long way and it seems like the ship will reach a point where it can go no further. But there is more water and more water after that before we get to land."

Ernst's words terrified Irmgard. She shivered and tried to nuzzle closer.

"Irmgard, you have nothing to be afraid of. We are far from land now, but soon you will see islands or shoreline. The horizon is ever changing and each time you look, even though it looks the same to you, we are moving forward to another place. The ship will not fall off the edge. At some point we will land and you'll get off the ship." Still, his words could not reassure her. His gentle manner and careful explanation did little to put her anxiety to rest.

Ernst lifted his daughter again. She dropped her face into his shoulder. "Look, Irmgard. Look." The six-year old lifted her head cautiously in an attempt to trust her father's words. "The ship pushes forward through the water. Look there. In the water below there are many fish and even plants. If you watch you might see the dolphins try to keep up with the ship. Today or tomorrow you will see the port of Buenaventura. More people will board the ship and we will sail out into the water again. Maybe you will see an island, a small bit of land surrounded by water. Try to imagine all the valleys outside of Quito filled up to the top with water. There would be a lot of room for fish to swim and for sea plants to grow, but it would still take a long time to travel by boat from the top of the Pichincha to the top of the Cotopaxi. The ocean is like where we live in Quito; it is just a big valley full of different kinds of life . . . sea life and lots of water. But we can't fall off."

"But how will the ship know where to go?" Irmgard asked innocently. "Everything looks the same. Won't we get lost in the water?"

Ernst smiled at Irmgard and continued, "The ship's captain has studied the sea and the land. He has special equipment to guide the ship." Ernst hesitated, "Remember our walk to the Chimbacalle train station in Quito?" he asked.

Irmgard, still traumatized, responded with a simple nod. Ernst lifted her chin and pointed to the heavens.

"We looked up at the sky and saw the stars. The ship captain can follow the stars to the north. He can steer the ship by sailing in a direction according to the stars at night and according to the sun during the day."

Irmgard seemed somewhat satisfied and nodded her head. "I am fine now, Papa. You can put me down. We can go look for the fish now, if you want to."

Ernst smiled and stood tall. Irmgard walked dutifully and cautiously toward her brothers who were playing a game of chase on the deck. They watched the game together for a while until Irmgard let go of Ernst's hand and joined her brothers and other children in the game.

During the days of the voyage the children had the run of the ship and they scampered about playing hide and seek and *catch me if you can*. When they ran out of game ideas on deck, they simply looked overboard for playful dolphins in the calm equatorial waters or made up stories about what was out there beyond the horizon. Ernst noticed that the guards smiled at the children on board and there seemed to be no ill will toward the youngsters.

It was mid-afternoon on the third day of the voyage when Dr. Meitzner greeted Ernst on deck. The doctor from Guayaquil was in his early sixties and he was starting to show the usual signs of age.

"We have quite a view, eh, Ernst? You must be enjoying the warmth. This is quite a change in climate from Quito."

Ernst nodded and fumbled for a cigarette. He offered one to the doctor and answered. "The children are happier than ever. Look at them."

"My girls are enjoying the trip as well. But it seems they cannot stop chattering," Meitzner chuckled, "We have pretty close quarters, so I came outside for some air."

"How old are your daughters now?"

"Anita is fifteen, Mathilde is eleven, and Maria is seven. She must be about the age of your daughter."

Ernst nodded again in response. "Yes. Irmgard will turn seven this month . . . on the twentieth."

The doctor's voice changed and he spoke with a much more serious tone. "That so," the doctor added without much thought. "I am glad I ran into you just now. I am concerned about your brother, Ernst. The security people in Guayaquil were not at all pleased when I demanded that Arturo be allowed to recuperate before leaving. Dávalos was there when I insisted he be allowed to remain. I did not like the look on Dávalos' face when I said that Arturo should travel on the next ship. If they arrested Arturo, his health could take a turn for the worse. The conditions of confinement in Guayaquil can be quite uncomfortable, you know."

Ernst spoke reassuringly, "Arturo will be fine. Alcira will see to that. Her mother has connections at the U.S. Embassy. As long as he keeps his nose clean and gets healthy, he will be fine. There is a ship scheduled to arrive in June and he will be on it."

"I know that, Ernst," and the doctor leaned closer. "It is his outspoken manner when it comes to politics that worries me . . . if you know what I mean." The doctor raised his eyebrows as he spoke and the furrows on his forehead deepened.

"I learned early on that my brother could take care of himself, Doctor. Say, what do you know about the Iser situation? What happened? Why did they take his daughters off the ship?"

"It seems that Guillermo's wife came up with divorce papers so the government office in charge of minors decided to have the little girls removed from the ship at the last moment. I guess Guillermo's wife Elsa refused to go with him to Germany so he took the children. The divorce papers were delivered at the last minute."

"His wife is from a good family with connections; isn't that so?" asked Ernst.

"The Ercilla and Bustamante families are Ecuadorian families with connections in high places and with excellent social standing. Guillermo told me the girls will go to his wife's sister in Guayaquil until they can be transported to Quito. He is quite devastated as you can imagine."

"Yes, I am sure." Ernst hesitated a moment. "It is unlikely he will ever see those girls again!"

The doctor added, "It is hard to blame his wife. She probably feared the same. None of us have any idea whether we will be able to return to see family and friends or not... What a pity."

"Yes, it is." The two men walked in silence. The enormity of the effect on families and the uncertainty of their own future were, at times, overwhelming.

After a while Ernst continued, "My daughter looked out at the ocean this morning and thought the ship would sail right off the edge of the earth."

Meitzner laughed and patted Ernst on the back. "Children are resilient, Ernst. We are the ones who will suffer these enormous changes. We have to shoulder the responsibilities of starting a new life without showing our fears to our wives or our children. I worry about Guillermo Iser. I worry about you. I worry about me ... I am not a young man anymore. I can tell you that I do not look forward to fixing up young boys who have been injured at the front, if that comes to pass. I thank God that I only have daughters, and my wife is young and strong." He paused and chuckled nervously, "I don't think they will send an old man like me to fight ... Say, tomorrow we will go through the Panama Canal! I am looking forward to seeing one of the greatest man-made wonders of the world. A lot of men died building that canal. Malaria got a lot of them."

Werner came running up to the two men and interrupted. "Papa, I saw a fish. Come see!" Dr. Meitzner patted Ernst on the shoulder and the two parted with a nod and a handshake.

―

The voyage continued to be pleasant and relaxing until the morning the ship arrived near Panama. The ship was now bustling with passengers who had boarded in Buenaventura and the dining room was crowded and noisy. Ernst and his children ate a small breakfast when the announcement was made. There were guards stationed throughout the dining area. All the adult male passengers were called by name and they left with several guards. The women and children would be taken to a separate area. No one was to look out of the windows, or even to approach the windows until that evening. A Colombian woman at a nearby table started to cry when her husband was taken away. Several women near her tried to comfort her, but the emotional damage had been done. No one was at ease and their "vacation" seemed to be over. Ernst asked Alicia Detken if he could leave his children with her and she nodded. As he walked toward the guards he thought of Dr. Meitzner who had hoped to see the canal and wondered what could be so secret that he and the rest of the passengers had to be kept under lock and key.

The women and children were sent to a separate holding area deep in the ship's hull. A large empty room below had been summarily transformed into a jail for the South Americans. With so many people in the room there was barely enough space to move around. There was no furniture, so the women stood and small children played or crawled on the floor. For several hours most of the women and children suffered the enclosure with dignity or resignation. The children continued to play games. Ernstchen and Heinz challenged each other to a stare down every so often. Each time as the older boys winced and wiped their stinging, watering eyes, Werner started a giggling fit. Later on, Werner and Irmgard sang songs with a mother who was trying to keep her own children occupied with some organized activities. Alicia Detken combed Irmgard's hair and plaited her braids while her daughter, Agnes, looked on and offered comments.

Spanish was the language of choice in the room since many of the wives did not speak German well. There was some tension based on social class, but the room was very cramped and no one really had any other choice. By noon, however, the room was becoming uncomfortably hot and stuffy. The children were hungry and tired. Infants cried. Mothers did everything to comfort them, but the lunch hour came and went without any indication they would be fed. The longer their confinement, the greater the number of complaints and tears.

"Mama, when are they going to serve us something to eat?" whined a little boy. "I am hungry and my stomach is grumbling."

"I am hungry too, and hot! Why is it so hot in here?" added the boy's sister who was near Irmgard.

Her mother explained in a strained, but calm voice, "We are in the tropics and the sun is very warm here…I know you are hungry. We just have to wait and see when we can leave. We are going through the Panama Canal and once we emerge in the Gulf we will be able to go out again." The mother chose her words carefully. She did not want to demonstrate her anger and frustration to the children, but she was clearly irritated by the confinement. Several mothers set up a circle game and encouraged their children to get involved.

In the holding area for men Ernst stood between Hermann Detken and Hans Mittman, talking about an opinion piece on power and corruption that Mittman had read in the *Mercurio* newspaper a few days earlier. Suddenly a man standing nearby became angry, turned red, and spoke out in a loud voice, "Seven hours. My God, we have been stuffed in here for seven hours." It seemed that he might bully his way toward the door, but others nearby encouraged him to relax. Truly, they insisted, there was nothing that anyone could do and no one wanted a scene.

Ernst looked at his watch. They had been in the crowded room for nearly eight hours, not seven as the angry man thought. Although there had been no misbehavior, the room smelled of human sweat and smoke. Men wiped their foreheads with handkerchiefs that were no longer white or pressed. Ernst's own shirt was damp with sweat and he rubbed the droplets from his face with his hand. Some men had rolled up their sleeves to try to keep cool. Ernst kept his cuffs buttoned to cover his thin arms.

Around six o'clock a guard made the announcement quietly to passengers near the door that their confinement was nearly at an end. They would be allowed to leave in a few minutes and dinner would be served in an hour's time. The news traveled quickly from man to man. Several men near Ernst took deep breaths and sighed, *"Por fin"* or *"Gott sei Dank."*[1]

The rest of the nine-day ocean voyage was less eventful and by the time the ship arrived in New Orleans on May 17 everyone was in relatively good spirits. Ernst was particularly cheerful to learn that he would not be charged for the food served on board. He sighed with relief. Ernst was quite concerned about being able to get a fresh start in Germany with the little money he had. Some of the other passengers seemed to be well off, and he was surprised by the amount of baggage that some of them were transporting. It looked like some families had at least five bags or trunks per person. He had packed only one large suitcase for his family and had left furniture and other belongings behind. He had no idea where they would live during their exile, but he certainly could not understand transporting armloads of baggage and furniture. He could not have carried more and would not have been able to pay for handling in any case. After all, he did expect to return to Ecuador eventually.

The adult passengers, and especially the children, scurried about the deck to see what they imagined would be the sight of their lives: the grand city of New Orleans, Louisiana and the port to the United States of America. Unfortunately, the port was unimpressive and disappointing, certainly less interesting than the modern steamer that had transported them from their homeland. Ernst and his children, along with the Detkens, the Dreschers, the Meitzners, the Platzers, the Schmidts, Hans and Rosa Viemann, and Rudolf and Amanda von Munchhausen were allowed off the steamer with many passengers from Colombia. Armed men who marched them to the train escorted the group. The children were encouraged to walk together holding hands.

Four-year old Maria Platzer stumbled to the ground in front of Irmgard and started to cry. Her six-year old sister, Elisa, tried to get her to stand up and walk, but she refused. Irmgard stooped to help Maria up and held her hand. "You can hold my hand and walk with me," Irmgard told her. "We are going to the train. It is right over there. Don't you want to ride on the train?" Maria nodded and brushed away her tears. She offered her right hand to Irmgard and held out her other hand for her sister. The three girls walked together. Irmgard's braids swayed as she walked and she smiled sweetly at her new charge.

Heinz was busy looking at the men at the port. He studied them and finally realized what seemed odd to him. Many of the men were wearing eyeglasses. He had seen a pair of eyeglasses on a German tourist one day when he was at the Dryco store. Eyeglasses were almost unheard of in Quito. No one wore them. He pointed the oddity out to Ernstchen who shrugged off the news. The ground felt strange under Ernstchen's feet after spending more than a week on the ship. He also felt uneasy with armed guards everywhere, but he did not want anyone to know how he felt. He walked with his eyes to the ground, scanning right or left only when necessary, and only for brief moments.

It was a short walk to the train. When they arrived, they were met by different guards who smiled at the children and handed each child a small gift bag. The children and their parents were startled. One of the guards spoke to the children and told them in German to have a good trip. No one expected such friendliness and generosity from the guards. Ernst was perplexed by a country that created blacklists to round up "dangerous" citizens and then turned around and treated these same people as high-class guests. The contradiction was just too much and he shook his head in confusion.

Ernst was surprised that not everyone had been escorted off the Arcadia to the train. He speculated that perhaps some of the passengers would be sent to different internment sites before their repatriation. It was clear, however, that passengers were no longer making decisions. They were pawns waiting to be placed in a new position to accommodate the major political players. Curiously, he did not feel scared or worried. He would stay alert, but there was no reason to feel overly anxious. He relaxed his shoulders and took a deep breath.

They boarded and when the time came, Ernst led his children to the dining car. The air in the dining car smelled delightful and the children's faces perked up a bit. Ernst's children stared at the waiters who were dressed in white. The children did not say anything; they just stared. Ernst was convinced that they were too overwhelmed with all the changes to do more than absorb information passively. Excitement and some anxiety had returned to their faces as they looked out the windows of the train at the ever-changing terrain. Heinz and Ernstchen were particularly surprised by the sunset. It was not that it was particularly beautiful, but it occurred hours later than it would have in Quito.

"Why does the sun set so late here?" Ernstchen asked his father.

"Near the equator the sun rises and sets around six in the morning and six at night every day of the year. The further you get from the equator the more variation there is."

"So, does the sun set every night at nine o'clock in the United States, Papa?" Ernstchen asked.

"I don't know, Ernstchen. It seems to me that I recall my mother telling me that in the warm months in Germany the sun rises very early and sets very late. In the cold months of the year the sun sets before supper and rises long after eight o'clock in the morning. But I am not sure."

"That will be strange!" said Heinz. "I will not be able to tell what time to go home for supper if the sun does not set at the same time every day! I guess that is why all the workers are wearing watches," he surmised, "You need them here." "Say, Papa, did you see all those people wearing eyeglasses when we got off the ship?"

"Yes. There must be more doctors here swindling money from their clients, telling them that they will see better if they put two pieces of glass in front of their eyes!" Ernst formed his index fingers and thumbs into round circles and peered through them. "Oh my, Werner," he said with a good deal of exaggeration, "you have a thousand eye lashes. Yes, a thousand!" The children giggled at their father and imitated his hand-held eyeglasses.

When the food arrived, the family ate slowly but deliberately. They had learned their lesson in the hull of the ship. You never knew who might make the next decision as to whether you ate or not and they had every intention of cleaning their plates.

As they were finishing their meal, Ludwig and Berta Aubele entered the dining car with their son, Raimund, who was about fourteen year old. Ludwig worked as an electrical engineer in Quito and was a good seven years older than Ernst, but they got along well and had enjoyed a game of chess on occasion. The adults greeted each other and the Aubeles sat down at a nearby table. Berta, who was around forty years old, seemed relieved to be in the dining car. Raimund sat down opposite his mother and glared at Heinz who tried to ignore his frightening stare. Raimund had bullied Heinz at the German school. He threatened him regularly with his clenched fist, but had never actually hit him. Heinz was not sure, but he thought Raimund was using threats to keep him from talking about the odd things he had seen the boy do. As far as Heinz was concerned, the bigger boy was like a dog that snarled and snapped in fear, threatening anyone who got too close. Raimund's presence made Heinz's skin crawl and he hurried to finish the food on his plate.

Karl Guris, his wife Emilie, and their six-year old son, Gunther, also appeared at the door of the dining car. When Karl passed by Ernst, he laid his hand on Ernst's shoulder and said, "This is almost like a reunion in Quito. Good to see you, Ernst. . . Children . . ." He also greeted the Aubeles, "*Guten Apetit.*" He nodded to Frau Aubele and smiled at Raimund.

Ernstchen watched as a young girl at the next table ordered her first Coca-Cola, a dark fizzy liquid that Ernstchen had heard about even before leaving Quito. Ernstchen asked when they might try a Coca-Cola, but Ernst shrugged without saying a word. The girl's father ordered a clear, bubbly drink that Ernstchen later learned was ginger ale. There were many things to learn about the food and drink in the United States.

When Ernst and the children had finished, they left the dining car and headed toward their sleeping quarters. Werner and Irmgard giggled as the train rocked back and forth making it difficult for them to navigate the hallways without falling clumsily against one wall or another. Heinz and Erntschen, who were more sure-footed, imitated them with exaggerated steps that made the older boys look like drunkards making their way home from a tavern. Ernst could not help but laugh at his children.

It was too early to go to bed so Heinz took out his gift bag and started drawing and coloring with the paper and color crayons that the U.S. government had provided for them. The other children did the same. Heinz drew a picture of the Arcadia at sea with jumping dolphins. Ernstchen drew the guards at the port with enormous guns at their side. The guns were quite detailed, and Ernst complimented Ernstchen on the drawings. Irmgard drew flowers and more flowers. She colored them each a different color and beamed with pleasure. When she held the paper up it looked to Werner as though it were raining flowers and Werner told her so. Werner's drawing was harder to gauge until Ernst looked closely and asked some pertinent questions. "You are drawing the train, Werner. I can see it now. Why don't you put some steam coming out of the top to make it look like it is moving?"

"No. I want it to stop so I can get off and run around outside." Werner answered honestly. He drew what looked like a large-headed boy outside the train. The boy had long spindly legs and arms and he wore a jagged line across his face instead of a smile.

"Is that boy you, Werner? He doesn't look very happy to be outside the train. Why don't you put a nice smile on his face?"

"I will put a smile on his face when the train stops." he answered poignantly.

Werner had long forgotten about changing the boy's expression by the time the train stopped in White Sulphur Springs, West Virginia, more than thirty-two hours after departing New Orleans. The families got off the Chesapeake and Ohio Railway line at an unusual stop, not at a station but simply near a road. Under the watchful eyes of armed guards they were led in a large group from the tracks down a highway to the walled area with large gates. A sign marked that they had arrived at the Greenbrier hotel but greenery at the side of the road blocked any view of the hotel. The Latin American travelers, now known only as members of the German and Japanese legations, passed through the secure front gate and by a small guardhouse. They were led down a winding road that skirted flower gardens, a veritable forest on the right, and a lush green lawn on the left. The grassy lawn was impeccably manicured and it startled the adults who walked near Ernst. None had ever seen such a fussed-over lawn in their lives. They had all seen extensive areas of meadow and pasture, but never had they seen such uniformity of color, height and thickness. "It must be a well-trained bunch of sheep that keeps this grass weeded and well cropped," Ernst said loudly enough for several people to hear. His statement was met with silence, as most did not know whether he was being serious or just making a joke.

White puffy clouds floated above the Allegheny mountains in the distance and the rolling bluffs made the Contag children feel more at home. When the group of travelers rounded a corner to the right, the immensity of the building in front of them made them gasp. From a distance the hotel appeared to be at least six stories high and ran a great length on either side of a neoclassical portico with bold, white columns, at the center. Along the base of the building were arches, much like the whitewashed colonial buildings in Quito, Cuenca, and Guayaquil, but that was the only similarity to buildings they had seen before. The building was a virtual palace. Painted in white, The Greenbrier Hotel nearly blinded them in the sunlight.

"It is immense!" a woman said in Spanish, and another agreed in German, "*Ausgezeichnet!*" Ernstchen wondered what kinds of animals roamed the forests that lined the road and in the hills beyond, but it was clear that he would not be roaming and investigating for himself. When he tried to get a better look at the trees, he ventured a bit out of line and a guard called out to him, "You! Stay in the group!" The focus on walking in a group reminded Heinz of some of the military scenes on the news releases he had seen at the cinema in Quito. He nudged Ernstchen, straightened, and pretended to march like the soldiers he had seen on screen. "Linz, zwo, drei, vier," he mumbled in mock seriousness to his younger brother.

There were small guardhouses with armed guards. Still, there was a feeling of freedom and joy associated with this elegant place and Ernst felt happy. Like the orderly plantings in the flower beds, life at the Greenbrier Hotel would be predetermined and regulated but the surrounding beauty would make the stay, no matter how confining, a joy.

The security personnel led some of the families to the main lobby where they waited to be processed and assigned rooms. Ernst and his family were included in the second group to be processed. His four children stood near him holding hands. In the lobby large, stuffed chairs with pleated skirts matched the drapes that were pulled back at the enormous, arched windows.

"Look Papa, the chairs are all dressed up like big, fat ladies with pleated skirts on the bottom!" Irmgard commented on the chairs that were a tremendous change from the simple wooden chairs she was used to. "They are so pretty with garden flowers painted on them!" She stared at the ornate candelabra with tiny lampshades, and wondered why each small light was covered by a tiny shade. When she tired of looking up she bounced softly on her feet and looked at the rug below them. She leaned around her father's leg to see how far the rug ran in one direction. Startled by the enormity of the rug, she looked around her father on the other side, and like a bird peered back and forth between the people standing near her to see if she could see the edge of the rug.

"Look Heinz. The rug is so big you cannot see the end of it!" she stated in amazement. When Irmgard asked her father how anyone could make or clean such an enormous rug, Ernst offered a response "They must have special machines to make such a rug . . . and to clean it too." A woman nearby corrected Ernst and told him this type of rug was called a "carpet" in English. The man standing next to her pointed to a pamphlet on The Greenbrier Hotel and added with astonishment, "and it says here that the hotel has over ten miles of carpet!" "How much is ten miles, Papa?" Irmgard asked. "The carpet would run across most of Quito . . . and back again," Ernst answered somewhat bewildered at the notion of a rug some 15 kilometers long. According to the pamphlet The Greenbrier Hotel had 625 rooms; it had a drug store, a clothing store, a post office, a telegraph office, a laundry, a dry cleaners, and an indoor pool. Tennis and badminton courts and daily movies were available for daily entertainment. *This is a hotel-city*, thought Ernst. *It is just so amazing!*

While they waited in line, Werner thought it might be fun to play hide and seek behind the huge square columns that ran the length of the room at specified intervals, but there was a sense of formality at the hotel that could not go unnoticed even by a five-year old. He stood quietly at his father's side.

When it was Ernst's turn to register, he gave his name, age, profession, and the names and ages of his children. The typist listed his line of work as "merchant." The Contag family was assigned connected rooms 953 and 955 expeditiously, and a helpful staff person nearby explained where the room was located and gave Ernst information about the dining room hours and the restrictions that were required by the hotel. While Ernst had learned some English through business contacts, he was by no means proficient and this was the first time he had had to use it in quite a while. Still he was able to understand the gist of the information because the staff member used pictures and gestures to get his information across. There was no need to wait for his suitcase. Ernst could pick it up later from among the many suitcases, trunks and boxes that would be brought in from the train as soon as they were checked through hotel security. Guests were to remain in the hotel or within the restricted areas surrounding the hotel. Guests could swim in the pool for five cents and shop at the numerous shops on the ground floor of the hotel. Skeet and trap, golf, horseback riding, and polo were not allowed during their stay. A copy of the *New York Times* was available on a daily basis. Motion pictures were shown each evening. Other activities and important information would be announced on the hotel's public address system.

Ernst was astounded by the genuine luxury of the accommodations and thanked the hotel employee for his help. Hundreds of train passengers were in the hotel lobby waiting to register, several hundred more on the lawn outside the hotel. It seemed so unlikely to Ernst that any country could afford to accommodate the relocation of so many people at once, and with such flair!

At that moment Ernst thought to ask about his sister and her new husband who might also have been interned at the hotel. Ernst asked a staff person in his broken English how he might find out if his brother-in-law and sister were in the hotel. The man pointed to a staff member who was flanked by security personnel, agents who were obviously employed by the Federal Bureau of Investigation. The polite staff member informed Ernst that Bernhardt Beate and his wife were in room 752, a corner room at the south end of the fourth floor. Ernst wrote down the number, put it in his pocket, and thanked the man. He was delighted that his sister was also at the Greenbrier Hotel. He would look for Bio and Lenchen when the children were settled in the room.

The journey through the hotel was confusing. They followed the hotel employee to the sixth floor and down an endless hallway to the north end of the southwest section of the hotel. When they arrived at their conjoined rooms Ernst wondered what gratuity he should give the man. *The hotel employees are accustomed to larger gratuities than I am willing to give*, he thought with trepidation. He had no intention of squandering the money he had but did not wish to be rude. He had been pleased that the meals on the Arcadia were not charged to him, but he began to worry about food costs at the hotel. *I'll distract him*, he decided.

The young man opened the door and handed Ernst a key. The children hurried into the room to inspect it. Ernst put his hand in his coat pocket, pulled it out empty and held out his hand to the bellboy to shake it. "Sank you verrry mooch," he said in English with a thick accent. He held the man's hand briefly before turning his head and nodding with a smile to the room's interior, "My cheeldrren. Sank you verrry mooch." With those words he closed the door on the bellboy who was disgusted by yet another guest's verbal generosity at the expense of a good tip.

There was plenty of room for the children to play in the conjoined rooms. One room was nearly five by seven meters. The other was five meters square and had windows on two sides. Both rooms measured 3 meters from floor to ceiling! There were two bathrooms and a small closet. The rooms were wonderfully decorated and plush.

Heinz moved the curtains away from the windows and peered out. The view looked east over the gardens in front of the main entrance, although, since the sixth floor was set back a bit, he could not see the immediate area just below. Irmgard joined him at the window and called out, "Look what you can see from here, Papa!"

Ernstchen called out with excitement from the bathroom, "There are towels in here, toilet paper . . . and soap, too. Does the hotel just leave these things for people?" His question went unanswered. "Look, Papa, the water runs down the drain the wrong way!" Ernstchen exclaimed. Ernst, Werner and Irmgard went into the bathroom to see what Ernstchen was talking about. Ernstchen ran the water again. "It is true, Papa. The water goes down the drain backwards." Ernst thought a moment and attempted an explanation. "Maybe it has to do with where we are located in the northern hemisphere or . . . perhaps it has something to do with the continental divide. I don't know. Good observation, Ernstchen."

That evening they went to the Colonnades Dining Room for dinner. Ernst stopped at the entry, took a look at his children, and took a deep breath. The splendor of the dining room was breathtaking . . . and daunting, with its warm, burgundy carpet, ivory columns, two-tiered crystal chandeliers, and tables covered with white tablecloths laden with elegant dinnerware. The family was seated at a small table and a waiter brought them each a menu. Werner and Irmgard could not hold theirs. Ernstchen and Heinz were uncomfortable trying to decipher page after page of information in English. Ernst had no idea how he would pay for the food they ordered; yet he knew they would have to eat something. *I'll keep it simple*, he thought. Guests near them had ordered beer and a good amount of German-style food. The food smelled and looked delicious.

Heinz and Ernstchen finally put down their menus and looked around at the occupied tables in their vicinity. At one table a man was eating a large portion of potatoes and meat. "He has enough food on his plate for a whole family!" Ernstchen remarked quietly to Heinz. But it was clear that some of the other new arrivals seemed cautious in their food requests. Ernst ordered one full meal that he planned to share, and several bowls of soup for the children. The waiter brought soft rolls that made the children smile and by the end of the meal everyone seemed satisfied and content.

Ernst took a stroll down the corridors with his children before the children's bedtime. Ernst recognized a few faces, but the majority of the people were complete strangers. Still, it was unnerving to see so many people divided into two groups. There were those who looked much like they did, and the rest who looked Japanese.

After the children were settled under the covers Ernst told them the story of when he caught an Indian woman stealing cabbages from their garden behind the house. He had chased after her and lifted her heavy, woolen skirts to spank her. Seeing that her bottom was bare he had sent her running with nothing more than a little verbal abuse.

"I bet she was embarrassed," Irmgard said with a giggle.

"Oh, I doubt that she was embarrassed." Heinz countered. "Lots of Indian women go without anything under their skirts. Blanca says that some Indian women wear all the clothes that they own all the time. That way no one will take anything they own. They just put the cleanest skirt on the outside. Their bundled clothes stick out to here." Heinz used his hands to indicate the thick layers of clothing and the other children laughed.

Ernst finished the story by telling the children that they should not touch or take things that did not belong to them, no matter how insignificant those things might seem. He pulled the drapes closed to darken the room from the bright lights surrounding the hotel.

When the children were asleep, Ernst left the room to see if he could find Lenchen and Bio. He went to their hotel room and knocked, but no one answered. He walked back to the main lobby where he saw Willi Sacklowski and his wife, Erna. Ernst approached them and clapped the former director of the German School in Quito on his back.

"*Guten Abend*," Ernst greeted the couple. The husband and wife returned a warm greeting. Erna asked about his children. "I left them in the room for the evening," Ernst answered. "They think they are in heaven with all this elegance! I still think that my son, Heinz, believes that the Greenbrier Hotel is just a dream."

"It is quite a wonderful place. We arrived just four days ago and I am amazed that the hotel can accommodate so many people so easily! Say, did you know your sister is here?"

"Yes, they informed me at registration. I just came from their room. No one was there."

"No, Ernst, I mean they are *here* just beyond that pillar to the left. I saw her come in after dinner. We all rode on the train from the internment site together. We were in an internment camp until they could make arrangements for the group of us to travel here. The camp was not uncomfortable, but we never imagined the Greenbrier to be like this. Everything is first class! We cannot complain about the accommodations or the service."

"I don't know if we can complain, but the staff might." Ernst winced. "I don't think that the staff will be too happy with a single *sucre* for their attention and service as the servants in Quito are! The price of one meal here is more than I spend on food for an entire month at home."

"Yes, I am sure of that," Erna replied flatly. "We were told that room and board is covered for all of us. We are only responsible for our daily expenses and gratuities. Most of us from South America could not eat otherwise..."

Ernst brightened at the news and showed surprise in his face. "Can this be true?"

"Yes. Heinrich Gissel from Baños spoke with one of the representatives of the State Department the day we arrived. Many of us were concerned about our current finances. Gissel had prepared an entire speech on how Ecuadorians could not be expected to pay for their own internment at such a fancy, first class hotel. I was in the lobby when he approached the representative. Before he could get more than a sentence off, the representative told him that room and board are covered by a special arrangement made between the Greenbrier Hotel and the U.S. State Department. I watched as his ears turned bright red. I don't know if he was ashamed or angry that the man had not let him give his prepared speech," Willi Sacklowski chuckled.

"It seems you sailed with a large group of Colombians, Ernst. We sat next to a number of them at dinner. Our ship carried Ecuadorians, Peruvians and Bolivians, but no Colombians.

I can tell you that fifty-seven of those who left Ecuador on our ship are now at the hotel.[2] Most of the passengers who sailed with us were married couples without children. Willi Shultz was on the ship, and he is here at the hotel with Louisa and their two young boys, Ernst and Otto. I don't know where the other passengers were taken after we left the ship. Many are not here at the Greenbrier. They could be at internment sites somewhere in the United States. I heard something about camps in Texas from others who are also here . . ."[3]

"Well if the camps are half as luxurious as this hotel they do not have much to worry about," Ernst added without admitting his own nagging fears about their deportation and internment. He was sure others shared his anxiety about the future and decided no one was discussing their anxieties out of fear of possible repercussions. Most were acting as though they were simply heading out on a long vacation for which they were ill prepared. Many women were coping by focusing on the minute details of their children's immediate needs.

Sacklowski caught Lenchen Contag de Beate's eye and called her over with his hand. When Lenchen saw Ernst she nudged Bio and they said good-bye to Herbert and Anneliese Backe, a couple from Bolivia they had met on the train to White Sulphur Springs.

"Ernesto! So, you are here!" Lenchen said with an element of amazement in her voice. "Every day is a surprise, isn't that so, Bio?" Her husband nodded and shook Ernst's hand. "Where is Arturo?" he asked blithely.

"In Guayaquil, I suppose." Ernst answered to the surprise of the couple.

"He did not travel with us on the ship. Alcira told me that Arturo fell ill and Dr. Meitzner told him to stay in Ecuador until the next ship stops in Guayaquil in a few weeks. There is another transport ship scheduled to arrive sometime around the first week in June."

"Well," Bio Beate said, "he does not know what he is missing. What do you think of this *humble* hotel?"

Ernst raised his eyebrows briefly, pursed his lips, and shook his head before responding. "I think someone makes too much money in America. This hotel is bigger than the entire San Francisco square in Quito . . . including the surrounding buildings! And the carpeting . . . it seems we could carpet most of central Quito with the rugs they have installed in this hotel. I have never seen anything like this. We should send a cable to our good President Arroyo del Río and tell him what he is missing out on. He should have made reservations for himself instead of for us." Ernst's comment got a laugh from the group.

"Yes, I would like to send security agent Dávalos a copy of the hotel pamphlet I saw downstairs. I would like him to see how much we are suffering now," Bio said.

Willi Sacklowski screwed up his face somewhat and interrupted, "I can see none of you heard about the terrible earthquake in Guayaquil. It was in the news the day we arrived at the Greenbrier. There were more than 100 people killed in Guayaquil and Portoviejo."

"What? More than a hundred dead?" asked Lenchen in disbelief.

Sacklowski continued. "One estimate was 115 dead. It was a two-minute quake. It made the U.S. newspapers because Vice Consul John M. Slaughter of the United States and his wife were killed when their apartment collapsed. I have scoured the papers for more information, but there has not been anything significant since the fifteenth in the *New York Times*. The newspaper report did not say so, but the tracks could be out. With the destruction in Guayaquil I bet they will delay the next deportation. It would not be realistic to expect people to leave now in the middle of a crisis."

"Oh, I don't know," Bio Beate responded. "They'll schedule a ship as long as they can get the people to it. Dávalos feels no obligation toward any of us, you know."

"It is getting late, Willi."

"Of course, dear." Sacklowski and his wife excused themselves and headed toward the center of the lobby and disappeared down a corridor. Ernst had followed Sacklowski's ungainly walk and noticed that two young, attractive women who had also sailed on the Arcadia were walking toward him. Ernst nodded his head out of respect and smiled at them. The women were around twenty years old and from Medellín, Colombia. He had learned in a conversation on the ship that one was Waltraute Dassler who was traveling with her widowed mother. The other was Hannedorle Blass who was traveling with her parents. Fraülein Blass's father was a chemist. The young, well-dressed women held Ernst's interest.

Bio followed Ernst's line of vision and smiled. "Friends of yours from the ship?" he asked Ernst. "I see the Jungnickel girls from Quito arrived with your group as well. You must have had a very *enjoyable* trip! Lots of sight seeing," he snickered.

Lenchen interrupted the awkward exchange between her husband and her brother with a gentle push. "Ernesto, pay attention. This is terrible. An earthquake and Arturo sick? What illness did Arturo have that was serious enough to keep him off the ship?"

"Pneumonia, I think," he responded, taking his eyes off the young women with some reluctance. "But Dr. Meitzner assured me that Arturo would be fine if he took it easy for a while. Why worry about them? There is no way to contact anyone from here."

The three stood in silence for a while. Then Bio changed the subject. "We were told that twenty-two Ecuadorian families were arriving at the Greenbrier Hotel with your group. Who came in with you?" Bio asked.

"It is hard to know, really. We were all mixed up on the ship and on the train, and I am still not certain who made it to the hotel and who did not. Every time I turn around I expect to see someone I know, but I am more often disappointed than not. I have seen the Aubeles, the Detkens with their four children, the Kliers, the Schmidts, the Gurises, and the Jungnickel women from Quito. From Guayaquil... let's see... Edgar and Sigurd Moller, Friedrich and Rosario Schmidt... the Seegers, the Dreschers and their children. I can't remember any more names... but it is just a handful of those who left Guayaquil! Sacklowski and I were just talking about the others. No one knows where the other passengers were sent or how the decision was made to bring us and not the others to the Greenbrier."

"Well I can tell you that the internment sites in New Orleans and in Texas are nothing like this hotel. We spent a short time in New Orleans and I have talked to others from different internment sites who are here now. This hotel holds the prize for comfort and elegance they say. I am certainly not going to complain about being labeled a first class diplomat! There are some nice advantages."

"The word is that the people who are interned at the Greenbrier are to be repatriated to Germany quickly," Lenchen stated rather unemotionally, still troubled by the news about the earthquake and her older brother. "That is what we were told anyway. No one has given us a specific departure date for Germany, but I would not count on being here more than a few weeks before we are sent on the repatriation sail."

Ernst raised his eyebrows and shifted his gaze to his new brother-in-law and smiled. "This is repatriation for you, Bio, but for me..." Ernst hesitated. How could Bio understand his position? Bio was going *home*. Lenchen had spent quite a bit of time in Germany and she looked forward to living in Germany. He, on the other hand, had never sent foot on European soil. He could hardly be *repatriated*. "I am being . . . patriated! Yes, that's the word." Ernst punctuated his words by holding his index finger erect. "I am being given a new *patria* . . . courtesy of the United States . . ." His tone was deliberately playful, but the seriousness of his meaning was not lost. "Patriation according to political need. Now that is a new idea isn't it . . . and with the cooperation of the Ecuadorian government and Hitler's blessing!"

Lenchen scowled at her brother. "You never could have afforded this trip, Ernesto. Look at this as an excellent opportunity! Your children will have a good education and many opportunities in Germany. Stop pointing fingers and go on."

Bio refused to let Ernst's ambiguous statement go unchecked and he set the record straight with his own biting comment. "Hitler counts his blessings in military terms, Ernesto. He is no fool. Just look around you. One soldier . . . two soldiers . . . three soldiers . . . If you take a look at the median age of the new repatriates there will be a good deal of opportunity for training new recruits and putting them to work."

Bio's statement cut Ernst to the quick and he paled somewhat. He respected Germany for its return to economic and political power after the Great War, but he had not planned on serving in the German military. Before leaving Ecuador he had been convinced that Germany would win the war. Now, the slightest doubt sent a cold sensation through his body, and he felt uneasy. The United States was indeed a powerful enemy. England too. If he were forced to serve, his children could be left as orphans . . . in Germany. Who would look out for them? Lenchen? Carl? His mother-in-law? Should the war go on a few years longer it was possible that Heinz and Ernstchen might be recruited. The notion unnerved him. In Ecuador he had some clout and good connections. Germany was a great unknown. *Someday*, he thought, *I'll look back on the summer of 1942 and laugh or cry*. At that moment he had no answers as to what his future would offer.

When Ernst said nothing, Bio continued lightheartedly. "I heard that they show movies here in the evenings, Ernesto. Lenchen and I were just about to check on what is playing. Would you care to join us?"

"No," Ernst responded coldly, "You are on your honeymoon. The movies will be in English anyway. You go ahead. I have some things I have to do. I'll see you later. Tomorrow perhaps."

Ernst went back to the room and hung his clothes on a chair. He scrubbed some clothes for the children with soap, rinsed them, rung them out and patted them flat before hanging them to dry in the bathroom. Some people could afford the laundry services at the Greenbrier Hotel, but he was not one of them. He washed his face and hands before lying down on the large, comfortable bed. He reached for his cigarettes but decided to wait out the craving as he was nearly out of tobacco and the morning cravings would be stronger. It was clear that he would have to make new friends who smoked. As a youth he had carried around an empty pack of cigarettes on occasion and offered the phantom cigarettes to a buddy. When Ernst feigned surprise that his pack was empty, the friend usually offered him a cigarette from his own pack. It was a trick that worked with his buddies in Ecuador. He hoped it might also work with others here.

Ernst slept fitfully and awoke early. He left the room and walked to the lobby. When he returned he found the children awake and dressed. Ernst surprised Irmgard with a small flower he had plucked from a hotel bouquet. "Happy birthday, Irmgard. I have decided that for your birthday you may order your first ginger ale. You are a big girl now! Seven years old!"

Irmgard's eyes grew wide and she hugged her father. "Thank you, Papa."

"It is quite a spectacular place to celebrate Irmgard's birthday, don't you think boys? She is a very lucky seven-year old! After you wash your faces and hands we will go for breakfast. If you like, we can look in the windows of that tiny shop called the Doll House on the grounds outside the hotel. I think I saw some candy there we could break into five pieces."

The morning was full of investigation as they visited different areas of the grand hotel. However, Heinz and Ernstchen soon lost interest in family togetherness when their father stopped to talk to several gentlemen, and Irmgard and Werner sat in the grass to play. The older boys left to play games with the other children of German heritage who were in the unrestricted area just outside the hotel. Some were kicking a ball around. A few Japanese boys joined in the game. In the matter of ten minutes or so Heinz had learned how to count to five in Japanese with one of the Peruvian Japanese boys about his age.

Herr Sacklowski was out walking around the building to get some exercise and Heinz greeted him when he spotted him some twenty feet away. Sacklowski called him over and Heinz approached him with usual amount of respect and trepidation.

"Yes sir." Heinz addressed the school director.

"Heinz, did you know that there is a swimming pool in the hotel?"

"Yes sir. It is a beautiful one tiled in mosaics and it is inside a building! It is even surrounded by columns. I can show you where it is if you would like."

"You have swum in it then?" asked the director.

"No sir," Heinz dropped his gaze. "We saw it when my father took us on a tour of the hotel earlier this morning. I wanted to swim, but they charge money for using the pool." Heinz's voice drooped like his face.

"Have you got a swimming suit?" Sacklowski asked as he placed two coins in Heinz's hand.

"Yes sir. Thank you sir. Thank you very much sir." He darted across the greenery and climbed the steps of the hotel. He was breathless when he arrived at the room on the sixth floor. He hoped there was no time limit on using the pool. He planned to swim until he couldn't move or they kicked him out!

In his haste Heinz had forgotten to tell anyone where he was going and Ernstchen spent most of the afternoon trying to figure out where Heinz had gone. He looked around the hotel grounds where some adults walked and their children were playing, but Heinz was nowhere to be seen. He walked throughout the unrestricted area and counted paces. He walked around the Doll House to inspect the candies and sweets that were on sale there. He imagined what each delicacy must taste like, and he licked his lips as he circled the small building several times. Later he climbed up and down the hotel stairs until that activity held no more interest for him and he returned to the hotel room to see if Heinz was there. The door was locked so he went to the lobby. Still no one. He played with some children outside until he returned to the hotel room and knocked again. When his father opened the door Ernstchen declared, "Heinz has escaped, Papa. I can't find him anywhere!"

"Nonsense, Ernstchen. Why would Heinz leave such a nice place like this? And where would he go?"

"I don't know but I sure can't find him." Dejected and tired Ernstchen sat on the bed and pouted. "He has escaped!"

"Oh I doubt that. Heinz will be back before dinner. Heinz is not one to forget about a meal. You'll see. He will be here in no time. You must have missed him in the crowds. Irmgard and Werner are drawing pictures in the other room. Why don't you see what they are drawing?"

Late in the afternoon Heinz showed up at the hotel room with wet hair and a sheepish grin on his face. "Herr Sacklowski gave me some American money to go swimming," he said under his breath to his father. "I stayed as long as they let me." Heinz half expected a reprimand for disappearing for so long, but his father gave none. Ernst motioned for Heinz to hang his wet things in the bathroom. "Tomorrow you play with Ernstchen."

"Yes sir," Heinz smiled and slipped off to the bathroom.

When the Contag family walked through the lobby after the midday meal on the following day they spotted a young woman walking slowly with some difficulty, and carrying a tiny baby wrapped in a blanket. Ernst remarked out loud with surprise, "That child cannot be more than a week old!"

A woman sitting in an upholstered chair behind them stood and spoke directly to Ernst, "You are correct. That is Margarete Martín and her infant daughter, Gisela. Margarete arrived at the Greenbrier on February 20 from Bogotá. She has probably been here the longest of all the internees and people have been talking about her since we arrived. Her baby was born last week at a hospital in Virginia. She is the only one who has left the hotel. Security took her out on May 14 and brought her back just a while ago. Margarete probably thought that if she left Bogotá soon enough the baby could be born in Germany but the Germans dragged their feet in making the arrangements for the citizen exchange. The internment until May must have been quite unexpected. So, . . . here she is with her infant and her two-year old, waiting to leave for Germany. It is going to be quite a voyage with that little one on board."

"Well, it was better to deliver on land than on sea!" Ernst remarked flippantly. "Where is the proud father?" Ernst asked.

"That is what has caused the stir. Margarete came here pregnant and with her two-year old daughter, Ursulita. There has been a lot of speculation, but no one has asked her about the baby's father. She never mentioned anything to me about him. Perhaps he stayed in Colombia. I did not ask."

Ernst wondered why the woman was so intent on telling him the life story of Margarete Martín of Bogotá, but he suspected that it had something to do with her attitude toward the mother who was traveling without a husband. He felt nothing but compassion for the young woman whose infant and young daughter were political pawns as much as anyone else interned at the hotel.

He changed the topic slightly and asked, "Do you know how many people left with the first group?"

"I heard from Margarete that two groups have left since she arrived in February. The first group was moved to another hotel in North Carolina. I can't remember the name.[4] That was at the beginning of April and there were no Germans or Japanese in that group . . . almost 200 Italians and a few Hungarians and Bulgarians left then, . . . that is what I think she said. Margarete told me that the State Department brought in the Japanese from the Homestead Hotel in Hot Springs, Virginia, right after that. She did not know why the transfer was made but it had something to do with a disagreement between the hotel management and the State Department. Another man told me that it was the Japanese who wanted to move. No one knows for sure. Margarete did tell me that the second group left on May 5 with over four hundred German repatriates. No one knows if Germans or Japanese will be the next to leave. Did you know that there are more than 400 Japanese here and almost 600 Germans?"

"No. I had no idea there were so many people!" There was a lull in the conversation and Ernst took advantage of the opportunity to move on. "It has been a pleasure . . . would you excuse us? The children want to go outside for a walk in the sunshine."

The days that followed became routine for the children at the Greenbrier, and they seemed content to play for long hours in the hotel rooms or in the lobby. The adults seemed to suffer increasing *angst* as they realized they would soon be loaded on to trains and put aboard ships for the final voyage to Europe or Japan. Some adults spoke of hoarding food before the voyage. Those who had money spent it lavishly on goods that could be purchased at the hotel and that might be scarce in Germany or Japan. Others simply waited out the days by getting some exercise and chatting with people they would be unlikely to meet again.

On Wednesday, May 27, nearly a week before the group was set to leave on the train for the repatriation sail, Ernst signed a paper indicating that he would not take up arms against the Allies. Under the bold, underlined words, <u>The United States of America</u> he read the following statement:

> *I solemnly bind myself under obligation of oath not to bear arms for the duration of the present war.*

He signed his name on the line below it. George D. O'Brien, the notary public for the County of Greenbrier in the State of West Virginia, notarized his declaration and dated it.[6]

As he lined up with his children outside the train station at White Sulphur Springs on June 2, he sighed deeply with the hope that he had made the right choice.

NOTES TO CHAPTER FOUR

[1] "Finally" and "Thank God."

[2] The Greenbrier Hotel is a railroad hotel.

[3] On May 19 the following twenty-two families (totaling 81 people) arrived at the Greenbrier from Ecuador: Aubele (3); Bloemken (4); Brandt (5); Contag (5); Detken ((6); Drescher (6); Guris (3); Jungnickel (3); Klier (5); Meitzner (5); Mittman (2); Moller (2); Peters (2); Platzer (5); F. Schmidt (2); W. Schmidt (3); Schonberger (4); Schroeder (4); Swoboda (6); Trenka (2); Viemann (2); von Munchhausen (2). Only fifty-seven of the 138 people who left Ecuador on April 17 were transported to The Greenbrier on May 15. Those families are included here: Beate (2); Bossarek (2); Endemann (2); Erdelen (2); Faustmann (2); Gissel (2); Holldorfer (2); Huttner (2); Nickel (2); Pohlhaus (2); Roseler (3); Sacklowski (2); Scheel (3); Schroder (2); Schultz (4); Schutz (2); Schwalbe (4); Seegers (3); Sonnabend (4); Thom (2); von Baumbach (2); Wanke (2); Will (2); Zweigert (2). The information is taken from registration documents provided by the Greenbrier Hotel. As many as seventy internment sites in the United States have been identified by Arthur Jacobs.

[4] Grove Park Inn, Asheville, North Carolina.

[5] Ernst Contag retained the original, signed document until his death. W. Contag files.

CHAPTER FIVE

REPATRIATION SAIL

NEW JERSEY, 1942

The train arrived in Jersey City before noon on June 4. The air was warm and the sun was already quite high in the sky. Policemen and security agents herded the repatriates and their children to the Drottningholm, a large Swedish steam ship, in the bay in front of them. The ocean liner was painted white from stem to stern but it looked tired and garish with its bright blue and yellow markings and emblems. Ernst guessed that it must have been a turn of the century ship and close to retirement. The words *Drottningholm* and *Sverige* were written in large letters and there was a banner with the word "Diplomat" that ran amidships. One of the men in line behind Ernst said that he had read in the newspaper that the ship was an 11,000 ton liner and that it had 40 reflectors on the outside and was brightly lighted so it could be seen at night. The man also reported to the group that the ship could carry at least 948 passengers because it had done so on its first exchange voyage a month earlier on May 7. Ernst was glad to hear of the visible security measures taken to assure their safety, but he and many others were still quite concerned about the invisible danger of mines and torpedoes at sea.

Family members, friends, newspaper reporters, and curious spectators were obviously absent at the pier. No one was waving at the group as the "diplomats" walked in orderly fashion toward the ship. Ernst wondered how many people boarding today were not Latin Americans. He speculated that there might be some U.S. Germans leaving on the ship too, but there was no way of knowing. The restrictions throughout Latin America had been enforced with determination, but the articles he read in the newspapers in Ecuador and heard about from others who read *The New York Times* at the Greenbrier indicated a strict enforcement of regulations and restrictions in the United States as well. The situation might be worse for North American Germans than it was for the Latin American Germans, he thought. The United States was truly a powerful country. He wondered how many of these people traveling on the ship today would ever find their way back *home*. Much would depend on the outcome of the war and how it affected attitudes and finances.

He wondered if there would be newspaper reports about their *repatriation* sail. It bothered Ernst that the newspapers announcing the repatriation voyage would probably label all the passengers as *Nazis* and *totalitarians*. He was proud of his German heritage and of the advances the Germans had made in many areas, but he felt no particular tie to the Nazi party or to its policies. He really had no idea as to what Germany would be for him and his family. The Germany he envisioned was based on family photos, stories, and the news releases on the radio and at the cinema. A good deal of German pride had been instilled in him since he was a child, but he had no idea of what he might encounter in a Germany that had already been at war for three years.

The United States he envisioned while in Quito had also been based on media reports, but the United States he had encountered was entirely different. He felt no ill will toward the Americans in spite of their role in his so-called *repatriation*. He and his family had been treated very well and the twenty-seven days they had been in the care of the United States' State Department had been pleasant and almost care free. The United States of America was an impressive country with great economic wealth and political clout in the international arena! The country was either to be feared . . . or admired!

"Papa. Where will this ship take us? Will it take us right to Germany?" asked Ernstchen. There was some excitement in his voice as there had been when they were about to leave from Guayaquil.

"The ship will take us across the Atlantic Ocean to Europe," Ernst answered.

"Is Europe a big place like the Greenbrier?" asked Werner. Ernst smiled.

"Europe isn't a hotel," Heinz said with a degree of superiority. "Europe is a continent with lots of countries and lots of cities and hotels . . . the Greenbrier is just one hotel. It is not even a city."

"It sure seemed like a city," his father countered quietly. "Hang on to the rails as you climb the stairs," he warned his children.

Ernst felt a pang of dread as he took the first step onto the ship. "Now we leave the Americas," he mumbled to himself. He recalled the cartoon an Ecuadorian friend had shown him from the *El Mercurio* with the caption, "The Americas Clean House." Hitler, Mussolini and Hirohito looked like naughty little children who, after a good swat, were being swept out with the dirt after strong Mama America cleaned up. He had laughed about the cartoon then. He was living the clean up now, and the future seemed more forbidding than welcoming. *Would Germany be victorious? Would he find employment in Germany? Would he be drafted in spite of his signed declaration? Would he be able to live with his children or would they be taken from him? When would they return home to Quito? Could this exile be permanent? What if Germany* . . . he hesitated to finish the thought. Ernst felt the heat of the sun on his back as he followed his children. He put these uncomfortable thoughts out of his mind by repeating an old German poem to himself.

> Keep the sun in your heart,
> Whether it rains or snows,
> When the heavens are filled with clouds,
> Or the world itself is troubled.
> Keep the sun in your heart.[1]

The eve of that same day the ship headed out into the deep waters of the Atlantic Ocean. Soon the choppy open sea replaced the calm waters of the bay. The morning after the ship sailed Heinz already started to feel quite queasy and generally uncomfortable. Soon after leaving the Greenbrier he felt his sinuses fill and his nose had become stuffy. Heinz and Ernstchen were on the top passenger deck when he started feeling completely congested. In an effort to clear his nasal passage he plugged one nostril with his index finger, leaned over the rail and blew. He followed the flying mucus with his eyes and watched in horror as it was carried by the wind back aboard past four other passengers to the neatly pressed slacks of a tall man a good twenty feet away.

Heinz's eyes grew wide and he froze in panic. He would have laughed at the flying snot, but the look on the man's face kept him from it.

The targeted man yelled at him. "Come here you rascal. Come here. Clean off my pant leg. How disgusting! Clean it off."

Heinz ran over to the man and used his hand to wipe the goo from the man's trousers. He did not have a handkerchief and the man certainly did not offer his own for the clean up.

"Sorry sir" was all he could mutter without laughing. Although the clean up was unpleasant, the mucus had missed its oceanic mark quite spectacularly and he had quite a time maintaining his composure.

Heinz walked away quickly, ignoring the nasty remarks the man was making to nearby passengers. Ernstchen had moved a comfortable distance from the unpleasant, but hilarious scene. He was doubled over in a giggle fit. Ernstchen was still smirking and snickering, and he broke into a loud guffaw when Heinz sallied up to him and said half seriously, *"Como vuelan los mocos!"*[2] "Like a flying torpedo!" Ernstchen chimed in when he could finally breathe.

Heinz found an inconspicuous spot to leave the gooey evidence of his maritime misdemeanor, and the two boys giggled uncontrollably as they each took turns repeating the phrase, *"Como vuelan los mocos,"* accentuating the phrase with hand gestures and laughter.

Heinz and Ernstchen went back to their cabin and Heinz washed up a bit. Before long Heinz started feeling very queasy again. His father suggested they all go up to the dining room but Heinz refused.

"Come on, Heinz. You will feel better if you go up on deck to get some fresh air."

"No, Papa." Heinz held his hand to his mouth as he rushed to the bathroom. No amount of prodding would get Heinz to accompany them, so the family left without him and went to the dining room. They looked around and saw Walter Detken and his son Hermann at a table. "Look Papa, there is Herr Detken and Hermann. Can we see if Agnes is coming up soon?" Irmgard pleaded. Ernst agreed and they went over to greet the two Detkens.

"Guten Apetit," Ernst offered. "How is the food?"

"Nothing like the Greenbrier, but it is fine. Is Heinz seasick too?" Walter Detken asked after seeing Ernst was short one child.

"My wife and the other children are all queasy. Hermann and I are the only ones that have not been affected."

"Yes. He would not even leave the room. I'll take something down later." Ernst and the children sat down at the nearest table.

"Yes, I will do the same…It seems many people are avoiding dinner tonight. The ship does rock and bob quite a bit. This is not like the smooth voyage on the Arcadia."

Irmgard looked disappointed, but she turned her attention to Werner who was fidgeting with the silverware.

"Werner, put those things down." Irmgard said with what seemed to Werner a look that his aunt Lenchen might have given him.

"Why? I am pretending that I am a buccaneer. I need my sword to attack the other pirates on the ship." He wielded his dinner knife and stabbed at the air in front of Ernstchen until his father finally gave him a disciplinary glare. "Pirates don't play with their flatware, Werner. Save your sea-faring games until after dinner."

Werner shrugged and kicked at his chair before offering a nasty face to his sister. Ernst had already turned his attention to Walter Detken.

"Any news, Walter?"

"Oh, I have heard some interesting news today." Detken said teasingly.

"Is that so? What have you heard?" Ernst asked, his interest piqued. "Well, according to rumor there are some interesting passengers aboard this ship . . . "

Ernst looked at his friend sternly and moved his chair closer to Detken. "What are you talking about, Walter?"

Young Hermann Detken moved to sit near the Contag children as he had already finished eating and preferred to talk to the children rather than listen to his father and Herr Contag talk about the latest news.

"Well, according to a fellow passenger who has been reading the *New York Times,* the Drottningholm arrived in Jersey City on Monday with 908 passengers from Lisbon, including nearly 100 who were unscheduled passengers. According to this fellow, the paper called the passengers "an unusual group of 'Americans' . . . some who had never been in the United States of America." Some of these passengers are even being sent back with us to Lisbon!"[3]

"Well, well. So the Americans did not get exactly what they were hoping for? Not all were diplomats of the highest quality?" Ernst was now quite curious and no less playful.

"He said the newspaper described a scene at the pier. Workers from the Travelers Aid Society and other welfare agencies had been on hand to help the new *repatriates*, and the Red Cross served up hot coffee, milk and baskets of sandwiches and cakes, but officials discovered after the warm welcome and a bit of censorship that only four hundred and eighty of the nine hundred passengers were actually United States citizens. Nearly half on board were aliens. Some, I suppose, were headed for Central and South America. Others probably found themselves in the same situation we did and *chose* to leave Germany, with a bit of a push . . . "

"Well that is not so surprising," Ernst offered knowing that Walter Detken was good at creating suspense when he told stories, adding information bit by bit, and letting the listener play the part of the detective.

"I heard a most curious thing today, Ernesto . . . a small group of these aliens, around forty who had been let out of German prison camps, were considered difficult to identify, and the State Department put them right back on board the Drottningholm. They are sailing back to Lisbon with us."

"Well, their fate is sealed," Ernst responded emphatically. He hesitated a moment before he asked, "What do you mean by 'difficult to identify?' It seems unusual that they would be traveling without papers at the expense of the German government."

"That is what I thought so unusual, Ernesto. The newspaper said that they were being sent 'unexpectedly' to Lisbon in what the *Times* called the 'general exodus of Western Hemisphere diplomats and other nationals.'[4] I think it is a sham. America did not want to accept those people as refugees for some reason. If they thought they were spies, though, they would have interned them in the United States instead of returning them to Europe, don't you think?" The two men shrugged and continued with their meals in silence. Both looked somewhat perplexed as though they were trying to unravel a puzzle.

Meals arrived for the Contag family, and the children ate quickly and hungrily. It was obvious that Ernst was more interested in solving a puzzle than in eating. Suddenly Ernst queried, "*Juden?*" Walter Detken spoke again, shaking his head. "No, the United States has a strong Jewish community. I can't imagine they would return Jews to German prisons. They must have considered the people criminals or riffraff. Perhaps they just lacked documentation of who they really were, or maybe they did not have contacts to help them out in their repatriation . . . the officials must have been afraid to admit them. That is the only rational explanation."

"You are probably right," Ernst agreed, "but I can assure you that those people are pretty upset about their future."

"I certainly would not want to walk in their shoes." Walter Detken slid his hand into his suit pocket and leaned toward his friend. "Ernesto, you might find this interesting too. Another passenger translated a report about us in the *New York Times*. He said that the Drottningholm would be involved in more voyages that "would carry 'bargain' nationals" between the United States and Europe. The exact words in the *Times* were, . . ." Detken pronounced the words he had memorized slowly in English with a heavy German accent, "'Bargain' nationals, or those selected by the belligerent nations to be traded, one for the other."[5]

Detken could see that the words troubled Ernst as he tried to process them. "'Bargain' nationals, the man said, could be interpreted as citizens who are part of a bargain . . . or, he explained, they could be considered citizens who are easily expendable for what you want in trade."

Ernst made light of the information with a bit of sarcasm. "Well, we have been called totalitarians, Nazis, important businessmen, internationals, foreigners in our own country, high ranking diplomats, repatriates, and now 'bargain' nationals. I was a legitimate Ecuadorian citizen who became an Axis subject, and in the next breath an enemy alien. Walter, it is a good thing we cannot be offended by being called human goods for an important political trade with international implications. But. . ." Ernst added, "Which are the 'belligerent' nations that the report referred to?"

Walter Detken shrugged. "I just hope none of us have any trouble in Germany." Just then Kurt Thom joined them and the men spoke at length about the Greenbrier experience, their fear of mines at sea, and their concerns about finding work in Germany, but they did not return to the topic of human trade. The adults continued their discussion until the children were visibly tired and started to complain. Kurt Thom left to take some food to his wife who had stayed below. Ernst wrapped some bread in a handkerchief for Heinz, and Walter Detken called Hermann over to help him carry some food back to their cabin.

The voyage did not improve due to rough seas. The two Detkens and the four Contags saw each other off and on in the dining room that, at times, seemed nearly empty in spite of the crowded conditions aboard the Drottningholm. Heinz did not leave the cabin again until days later. Few who had become seasick improved as the seas grew increasingly rougher and the northern air quite cold. The ship had sailed far north and then south along the coastline of Europe over the course of nine days. There had been no real threat of mines or torpedoes, although the anxiety level amongst the passengers and crew was always extremely high. The waters of the North Atlantic were rough and few passengers emerged from their cabins without feeling sick until the ship docked at the pier in Lisbon, Portugal, at eleven o'clock on the morning of Friday, June 12.

When Heinz emerged from the cabin on the lower deck he was feeling weak and his father said it looked as though he had lost 3 kilos, but he was excited that the ship had finally reached its destination. "We are in Portugal," his father had said that morning. "We are free to leave the ship to visit Lisbon. We will come back on board for meals and sleeping, but the officials will let us go into the city and shop or do what we want."

"Freedom!" Heinz called out and he scrambled toward the cabin door.

"We will go into the city as a family first, Heinz. Then you and Ernstchen can go out together or on your own with the other boys if you would like. There are quite a few children on board and I am sure you can find some playmates."

"What about us, Papa?" Werner asked.

"You two will come with me until we find out where things are and what there is to see. You'll be able to run around, too. Don't worry."

There was a great exodus from the Drottningholm and Ernst was more than content to let the two younger children play at the pier while the older boys went down the street with some companions and a few parents in search of fishing line and hooks. The boys were excited at having the opportunity to fish off the side of the ship and a few parents had been enlisted to get them the necessary equipment, a good amount of fishing line, and hooks.

Ernst, Irmgard and Werner walked along the pier toward a large square called the Praça do Comercio or Commerce Square at the entrance to the city. In the middle of the square stood the statue of Don José I upon a horse. Ernst pointed out that the horse looked like it was about to take its next step right off the pedestal. "This reminds me a little bit of the Plaza de San Francisco in Quito, Papa." Irmgard smiled and loosened her grip on her father's hand. Ernst thought the square that was open on the west side toward the river must have been the site of many transactions during the years of commerce with Brazil and Africa. Certainly that must have been how the square got its name.

At the entrance to the city there was a huge, ornately decorated stone archway with a statue that held its arms out as though he were going to invite the sea right on shore, but when they got closer Ernst could see that the statue was holding out a scale in each hand that probably represented fairness in trade.

Irmgard and Werner clung to their father's hands as he walked them from Commerce Square down the wide street to the Praça do Rossio, the Square of the Virgin of the Dew. There were vendors and shops on either side of the street and the family stopped intermittently to look at the merchandise or to listen to someone giving a sales pitch in Portuguese. There were book stands, fruit stands, and stands with general merchandise or imports and unusual objects of exotic origin.

As they were crossing a street just beyond Rossio Square, Werner saw the castle that loomed above them. "Papa, a castle! Look there! A castle!"

"I see it, Werner. It is a castle, and right in the middle of the city!"

"Do a king and queen live in that castle, Papa?" asked Irmgard. "Is there a princess living there?"

"I don't know who lives there. We can ask someone later."

"Can't you ask someone now? Ask that lady right there. She might know." Werner was pointing to a woman who was standing at a storefront. She was of medium height and slender, and wore a red and white polka dot dress that was fitted and buttoned from the bodice to the gently cinched waist. The skirt, worn in gentle folds that moved in the warm, summer breeze, was hemmed neatly just below the knee. A brimmed straw hat with a red scarf kept the sun from her face. When she turned a bit, Ernst noticed that she was stunningly attractive, and he agreed to ask her the question. He approached her and spoke in Spanish.

"*Perdone señora.* Would you be able to tell us the name of the castle on the hill."

The woman, who was in her late twenties, turned and smiled at the tall man and two young children who looked at her with genuine interest.

"*É o castelo de São Jorge,*" she replied in Portuguese and then corrected herself by responding in Spanish with a strong Castilian accent. "That is the castle of Saint George, one of Lisbon's gems. There is a marvelous view of Lisbon and the harbor from up there."

"You speak Spanish... like the priests in Quito!" said Ernst, somewhat surprised.

"I beg your pardon... like the priests in Quito?" She looked stumped.

"*Sí, pues.* Quito, Ecuador. That city is our home," offered Irmgard.

"I would not have guessed it, child, except for your accent." The woman touched Irmgard on the chin. "It is clearly South American."

"Papa. What does she mean? What is an accent?"

"It means, Irmgard, that you speak Spanish like someone from the Andean sierra and this woman speaks Spanish like people from Spain." He directed the rest of his answer to the gentle woman who stood before him and explained. "Spain sends its missionary priests to South America. Some of them sound like you. I suppose I did not expect to hear Castilian Spanish in Lisbon. I had not even given it a thought. I did not mean to seem rude."

"No offense taken." She directed her next questions to the children, "Your name is Irmgard, a German name. And you?"

"My name is Werner. It is a German name, but I am from Quito, too. We came here on a big ship and we will go to Germany soon. Do you want to see the ship? We are on a walk and we could take you there. It is just down that street on the pier and..."

Ernst interrupted Werner with a squeeze of the hand. "Werner,..."

But before Ernst could silence the boy with his gentle reprimand the woman responded, "I would love to see the ship, Werner,... that is if you, Irmgard, and your... father... have time to show me. I am out for a walk and I would be delighted to walk with you to the pier. I would like to see the ship, if you don't think your mother will mind."

"I am here alone with the children. I am a widower." Ernst floundered for words. He felt strange, and wondered why they were still talking to this Portuguese woman in the red and white polka dot dress.

"Oh, I am sorry." She looked at the children and continued. "Werner, my name is Maria. Would you like to introduce me to your father?"

"Sure. Papa, this is Señora Maria. Señora Maria, this is Papa." He declared emphatically.

"Hello, Papa," Maria said with a smile and extended her hand. "It is a pleasure to meet you."

"Ernesto Contag at your service." Ernst bowed over her hand briefly as though kissing it and said, "Indeed, the pleasure of making your acquaintance is mine."

"Would you like to hold my hand, Señora Maria, so you don't get lost?" Werner offered enthusiastically.

"Yes, of course, Werner." Maria replied with a giggle. "But I thought you were interested in the castle."

"Oh yes, of course, but I want you to see the ship first," Werner chirped as he took her hand.

Irmgard watched the exchange with curiosity. She felt a little uncomfortable with the situation that had unfolded so quickly but said nothing.

"Señora, are you sure that you are. . ." Ernst hesitated without finishing his sentence.

"Certainly. It is not often that I am invited by such charming children who have come all the way from Quito, Ecuador to show me their ship! Werner, Irmgard, will you lead the way?"

Ernst enjoyed her playfulness and he agreed with a smile. Maria spoke to Werner and Irmgard as they walked toward Commerce Square hand in hand. Ernst shook his head in pleasant disbelief at his son and daughter who had warmed the heart of this Portuguese woman so quickly. When they arrived at the pier Werner pointed out the ship and talked at length about their voyage.

"My brother, Heinz, spent nine days in the cabin in the ship. He has been very sick. The ship rocked a lot and he got sick in the bathroom all the time. He is better today. He and my brother Ernstchen went with some boys to buy some fishing line. Look, there they are. They are fishing! Papa, can I go up there, too? Señora Maria, you can come, too."

"Oh no, I don't think that they will let me on that big ship, Werner. I will watch you from here. You go ahead, if your father says so."

"You and Irmgard may go together, but please thank . . . Señora Maria before you leave. She has been very kind."

Werner put his face up and Maria leaned over instinctively to say good-bye. The five year old kissed her on the right cheek, as he was accustomed to doing in Ecuador. "Good bye Señora Maria. See you later, Papa. Good bye." Irmgard smiled and kissed Maria as well. "It was nice to meet you. Good bye." She trailed after her brother, her thick braids bouncing at her shoulders. As they ran off Werner called to his brothers who were on the top deck of the passenger ship. "Heinz. . . Heiiiinnnzzz. . . Ernestchennn."

Maria followed them with her eyes and said in Portuguese, "A prince and a princess." She turned and spoke directly to Ernst in Spanish. Ernst could see her eyes for the first time underneath the broad brim of her hat. Maria's eyes were deep brown and her face was cheerful. "I am sorry, I cannot remember your surname. . ."

"Contag, but please call me Ernesto. You have been so kind. It has been a long trip with so many new faces and so many changes. And, well, the children have not been trained in social etiquette. . . You really have been very kind."

Maria put on a playful scowl. "They are precious, Ernesto. Let them be children." She turned and looked at the Drottningholm. "So, . . . you arrived today on this monstrosity of a ship. It is quite a sight! It must be at least thirty years old."

"I think someone said it is more like forty or fifty years old. . . and it is overcrowded, too. We are waiting for the U.S. Legation to arrive for the diplomatic exchange, but no one seems to know when the Legation will arrive."

"If it is like the last exchange, the trains will be on their way from Bad Nauheim and Rome with a stop in Biarritz, France. Last time there were three trains that brought the group to Lisbon. They never publish the travel information beforehand; I think it must have something to do with the safety of the travelers."

"It seems that you have been following events quite closely." Ernst added, somewhat curious about her knowledge about the exchange. "Do you have a special interest in the exchange?"

"People who live in neutral countries should always be aware of what political adversaries are up to within their borders, don't you think?"

"Yes, I suppose so." In any other situation Ernst might have been suspicious of the young woman who had befriended his children and spoke her mind so frankly, but he was completely at ease with Maria and enjoyed her company. He wanted to invite her for a cool drink, but he did not have any Portuguese *escudos*. They stood a moment looking toward the ship without saying anything. Ernst reached in his pocket for his pack of cigarettes, but his hand came out empty.

"I don't smoke, but I always carry a pack. Would you like a cigarette, Ernesto?"

She is amazing, Ernst thought. "Thank you," he responded still in awe of her awareness of him. She smiled broadly and looked into his eyes.

"How long did you live in Ecuador?

"All my life. . . I was born there. Until a month ago I had never taken a step out of Ecuador. Now I have spent two weeks at one of the finest hotels in the United States, I have traveled on a Swedish ocean liner, and I am standing on the shores of the Iberian peninsula speaking to a beautiful . . . but inquisitive Portuguese woman about whom I know absolutely nothing. "

"I was never considered timid by anyone's account, Ernesto. I hope you do not find my questions offensive."

"Of course not. I enjoy your company. . . and your questions."

"Good. I have an appointment this afternoon and evening, but I would enjoy taking you and your children on a short tour of Lisbon tomorrow afternoon, if you would like. . . if this is your first visit to Europe you should see more than the inside of that ship!"

"It would be a pleasure, Maria. You are very kind," Ernst replied, still somewhat perplexed by this strange, exciting turn of events.

"Fabulous. Shall we meet tomorrow. . . at six? Why don't we meet in front of the shop near the Rossio Square where we met today . . . in case Werner and Irmgard want to go up to the castle? Do you think you can find the shop again?"

"Yes, I am sure I can. I look forward to seeing you then." Ernst put his hand out but Maria leaned her head back and allowed him to kiss her on the cheek. His head brushed the brim of her hat as he pulled away and she laughed. "These hats can be dangerous, Ernesto. Especially since you are so tall. See you tomorrow. *Adeus.*"

"*Adiós.*" Ernst felt strangely moved by Maria's carefree demeanor. She was beautiful and so charming. He watched her as she walked away across the pier and disappeared down a narrow street.

That evening at dinner the children talked of nothing but fishing off the deck of the ship. Heinz and Ernstchen were excited about the fish they had caught.

"They were forty centimeters long, Papa, at least forty centimeters. It is too bad that we had to throw them back. We could have had fish for supper. Can we fish with the other boys again tomorrow, too, Papa?" Ernstchen asked.

"Of course." Ernst responded. "Unless you want to take a tour of Lisbon."

"No, we want to fish. Don't we, Ernstchen?" Heinz piped.

"And I thought you would be the first one to want to stay on dry land, Heinz." Ernst laughed, referring to Heinz's seasick days on the Drottningholm.

"I am fine if the ocean doesn't rock the ship and I can be outside. We had fun today with the other boys. Besides, when we went in to get fishing line and hooks we saw part of the city and it just looks like Quito without mountains and slopes... just a lot of churches and narrow streets. Ernstchen and I would rather fish, but you can take Werner and Irmgard," Heinz urged.

"Well, I'll tell you what. You can fish most of the day, but I would like you two to go with me into the city just before six o'clock. Maybe we can get something special, something typically Portuguese, to try."

Heinz and Ernstchen looked at each other and shrugged. "Sure, Papa."

Ernst and the children were standing outside the shop where they had been the day before and it was a few minutes after six o'clock. Ernst had said nothing to the children about the meeting place just in case the rendezvous did not work out. Ernst walked them up and down the street twice but Ernstchen was clever and said, "We've been down this street twice. Are you looking for the place where you wanted to get something special to try?"

"Yes." Ernst answered without revealing his disappointment. "I thought it was here that I had seen it. Just a moment." He walked into the shop to see if Maria had gone inside. Nothing. He had felt sure Maria was sincere when she made plans to meet them, but it seemed he had been wrong. "Let's see if we can find a place around the corner to get something to eat." Ernst found some outdoor seating where they could sit comfortably in the shade. Ernst sat and reached into his pocket for a cigarette, but found nothing there. When the waiter arrived he asked him to bring his children something special, perhaps fruit in season.

"*Cerezas?*" the waiter asked first in Portuguese and then in Castilian Spanish.[6]

Ernst had never heard of "*ther ray thas*," but he agreed.

"What are *therethas,* Papa?"

"You will have to wait and see, Irmgard," Ernst answered, avoiding a description he could not offer.

Some people were out strolling. It was not tremendously hot, but the shaded part of the street was busy. Ernst kept an eye out for Maria although he suspected that it was unlikely he would ever see her again.

When the bowls of cherries arrived the children stared at them. "They look like tiny red and pink apples, but these are so very... pink!" Irmgard said with an air of curiosity in her voice. She picked one up and studied it.

"Try the pink one and see what it tastes like," Ernst encouraged them. He picked one up himself and put it in his mouth. "They are a little squishy and,... oh, be careful, there is a tiny pit in them," he warned after crunching the pit uncomfortably between his dentures.

"This one is really sweet." Heinz said as he sucked the bright pink flesh from the pit.

"Heinz, Werner, don't spit the pit on the plate. Look at me." Ernst passed the pit discreetly into his cupped hand, as though he were coughing, and then let the pit fall inconspicuously on the plate. "It looks better." The children practiced the discreet "pit blowing," but the practicing was accompanied by a good number of giggles and several pits that purposefully *got away*.

After they finished relaxing at the outdoor café Ernst paid the waiter and they decided to walk back to the ship. Ernstchen thought about asking to take a tram ride around to look at the city, but he was pretty sure his father would say no, so he did not ask. Ernst suggested they walk around the city, but the children were less interested in seeing Lisbon than fishing or playing with other children and Ernst decided that he would go out alone.

The next afternoon, the boys went fishing and Werner and Irmgard went to play with several other children. Ernst walked into Lisbon with a few men who were planning to visit Heinz

Jeanroud on the second floor at Sociedad Farmacéutica Street, number 56. Ernst had planned to go along with them, but as the six o'clock hour approached he felt compelled to walk over to the Rossio Square on the chance that Maria might be out for a walk. He knew it was a crazy idea, but he decided to go anyway. He wrote Heinz Jeanroud's address in his pocket calendar and told the others he would meet them later.

The Rossio Square was crowded with families who were out enjoying the afternoon. He walked down the street where he and the children had first met Maria, but even amongst the many it was easy to see that no one was wearing the red and white moon speckled dress he remembered. He walked up and down the street, took another look at the meeting spot and turned the corner. St. George castle loomed above and he decided to climb the hill.

The cobblestone street reminded him of Rocafuerte Street at home and he breathed a deep sigh. All the uncertainty of their future weighed heavily on his shoulders again. Although many reports indicated that Germany would be victorious, he wondered what their personal future in that Germany might be. When Maria had been with them, he had felt lighthearted, even playful, at what their future might bring: new faces, new opportunities. . . but now the cruelty of perpetual departures and good-byes hit its mark. Each step up the steep incline seemed more futile than the one before it and he shrugged his shoulders, clasped his hands behind his back, sighed deeply, and felt older than his thirty-five years.

There were small shops at the outer entrance to the castle wall and he stopped to look over the merchandise somewhat absentmindedly before heading back down the winding cobblestone street he had just negotiated.

"Well, Ernesto, are you going up to look at the view or are you just going to turn around and head back to that ship."

The voice was Maria's and Ernst turned with a start. "Maria?"

"Good afternoon, *Papa*." she said with a bit of *picardía*. "The view from the castle is breathtaking, as I told you. You should not miss it. Shall we continue up to the castle?" Maria said as she took Ernst's arm by the elbow.

"Yes. . . of course, but I did not expect to see you."

"You expected to see me yesterday according to the shopkeeper. I stopped there this morning as soon as I could leave the house. We had a bit of a family emergency and I could not get away until this morning. I am sorry. I suppose the children were with you. Werner and Irmgard must have been disappointed."

"I did not tell them we planned to meet you. I took them out for. . . cherries. They were not disappointed."

"I hoped you might return with them today." When Ernst remained silent she continued. "I was in the Rossio Square when I spotted you walking past the shop. I saw you turn at the corner and I followed you up the hill just now." She giggled, "I was only about twenty steps behind you. You were so deep in thought. I probably could have walked right by you without you noticing me. I thought you were ready to sing *fado*."[7]

Ernst stopped and smiled gently. "I don't know what to say, Maria."

"Good. Then we can walk to the castle and I can show you our beautiful city." She put her hand to his elbow and urged him on. "Lisbon is a city of hand-painted *azulejo* tiles, of wrought-iron verandas, and of tremendous city and river views. Many civilizations have appreciated our spectacular location."

"Maria, you said I was about to sing . . . fado. What is that?" he imitated her words.

"Fado is Portuguese folk music. It is filled with musical cries of pain and suffering." Maria added facial expressions to her words. "Your face looked like you were about to cry out a dismal Portuguese dirge."

Maria's exaggeration was impish and Ernst could see she enjoyed the tease. He laughed out loud and felt the same liberation he had felt before from the worries and fears that plagued him when he was alone.

"If all of Portugal thinks as you do, there is not much to whine and cry about."

"Oh, Portugal has had plenty to cry about, Ernesto. Look where we live! Strategically speaking, every political power in the Mediterranean wanted to get their hands on this part of the peninsula. The Phoenicians used this castle hill as a lookout over the Tejo River. The Romans built below the castle. The Visigoths and the Arabs came and occupied the areas of the streets below here, too. As a maritime port Lisbon has seen many people and their goods come and go. Ships came from Brazil, Africa, England, the United States . . . "

"You speak like a history book," Ernst offered.

She hesitated a moment and then continued. "Of course, but I have just begun the tour. Look, from here you can see much of Lisbon. There are Renaissance palaces, convents belonging to religious orders, market places and beautiful old buildings that speak to you of joys and sorrows written in the history on their worn walls. Invasions, occupations, earthquakes, fires. . . Lisbon and the Tejo River have seen a good deal of history. See, we have had plenty to laugh and to cry about."

Maria stopped speaking and the two simply looked out over the Portuguese city. After a moment she nudged Ernst and pointed to the west. "Look, Ernesto, look at the Tejo river. From here I always feel a sense of tranquility, . . . and hope for the future. Some say that *fado* was a way to suffer the loss of men at sea, but when I look to the sea I marvel at the rich history, the exciting present, and the unknown future it brings us."

Ernst touched Maria's hand and lifted it to his lips and brushed it with a kiss. "*You* bring tranquility and hope to the future." His words were sincere and succinct, and his face was filled with warmth. He was very close to her when he repeated her name, "Maria." Suddenly, he straightened, dropped her hand and backed away from her a good distance. "But I don't know a thing about you!" Ernst spoke defiantly with his hands in the air. "Nothing."

"Well, I have two hands, two feet and . . . " Maria began in jest.

Ernst threw out his hands again in frustration. "No. I don't know *anything about* you. I don't know anything about your family or . . . or . . . who you are or . . . anything."

Maria looked at Ernst for a few moments before speaking. "My family name is Dias. I am a widow. I have some family responsibilities that complicate my life. . . like everyone does. She hesitated as though she were pondering some important matter, and continued with a smile. "I have every reason in the world to be happy. What else can I tell you that could possibly matter to a man from Quito, Ecuador, on his way to Germany?"

"You are an unusual woman, Maria Dias. Thank you for coming to meet me today. You make me feel as though I did not have a care in the world. May I invite you for something to drink?"

"Of course," Maria responded enthusiastically, "but only after our little tour!"

Ernst and Maria spent most of the next four days together, getting to know each other. On Wednesday morning, June 17 Ernst was informed that the Americans to be exchanged had arrived, and that their train for France and Germany would depart Thursday, June 18. On Wednesday afternoon Ernst and Maria met for a final time. She wrote her address in his date book under the German words *Fernsprech-Adressen*. She wrote: Maria Dias d'Almeida, Rua Aquiles Monteverde No 26, *Lisboa* and drew a line above and below her name and address.[8]

She handed Ernst the pocket calendar and he held her hand captive in his. "I am not a complicated man, Maria. I know how I feel about you and the time we have spent together in Lisbon, but my future is uncertain and neither of us has wrestled with our past. . . "

"Ernst, my destiny is to be happy. I have been happy with you this week. That is enough." Maria's words were light-hearted, but her eyes were filled with passion and sorrow. Ernst thought that she looked as though she were ready to sing her own *fado*.

The parting later that evening was bittersweet, and Ernst returned to the ship once again burdened with the worries of the days ahead and with the sorrow of leaving Maria. Before he fell asleep that night he repeated Maria's poignant words, "My destiny is to be happy. . . That is enough." She certainly had conviction. At that moment Ernst knew he would never see her again. He was not ready to take a wife.

The following day the South American German Legation and the American Legation from Europe stood on opposite sides of the avenue that ran along the Tejo River.[9] There they

Ernst Contag, Ernstschen, Irmgard and Werner await the next leg of the journey (1942).

were exchanged one by one. The American Legation boarded the ship for the Americas and the South American Germans boarded the train for the journey to the *Vaterland*.[10]

The train traveled through Portugal and Spain, chugging along much like the train that had carried the passengers from Quito to Durán weeks before. The Spanish Pyrenees Mountains slowed the train down measurably and when it finally stopped at the border towns Irún and Hendaya on Friday, June 19, everyone was tired. The passengers went through customs, and the children received gifts and sweets supplied by the German government before boarding a train that took them through the French Pyrenees to Biarritz, France where they were given accommodations at the Zvarriten Hotel. The Zvarriten was an old hotel, not too far from the beach or the train station. With the arrival of a thousand guests, the hotel was abuzz. The hotel showed signs of decades of wear and the overburdened structure reminded Ernst of an aging grand dame who, after years of widowhood and declining finances, had begun to sag and bulge uncomfortably in all the wrong places.

After the evening meal several South American born Germans remained at the table and talked. When one of the men mentioned that Napoleon and Prince Otto Bismarck had once been guests at the hotel, the conversation moved to the topic of "famous people." Ernst said that while in Lisbon he had learned from Heinz Jeanroud that the American Legation had been kept at Bad Nauheim before their train journey, and that some of the people involved in the exchange were rather famous. He wondered aloud if anyone knew of Bad Nauheim. When no one at his table offered an explanation, he paged through his pocket calendar and said that Heinz Jeanroud had reported that Teddy Lynch, the wife of wealthy Los Angeles oil man, J. Paul Getty, had spent a night in the hotel a month earlier with the first American Legation to be returned to the Americas.[11]

Another man at the table added that according to rumors there were quite a few famous people leaving on the Drottningholm for the Americas as part of the exchange. The fellow scrunched up his nose and stuck his chin out snobbishly when he said that a woman from American high society, some lady called Mrs. Del Drago, had been part of the exchange. Ernst snickered at the exaggerated gesture. He had never heard of Mrs. Del Drago. He had not heard of the American boxer, Nabby Gans, or of the American singer, Elizabeth Lawrence, that the man's wife was talking about either. But Ernst's interest was held captive by the older man at the end of the table who told the story of an American woman named Ruth Mitchell, a leader of the Yugoslav guerrilla band called the *komitaji*, who was freed by the German government for the exchange after being held as a prisoner in the Liebenau Concentration Camp.

The men also talked about Biarritz. Biarritz, located on the Basque coast of the Atlantic Ocean, was known during the nineteenth century as a resort town for the wealthy as well as a spa for the mentally and physically ill. Ernst wondered aloud why the German government had chosen Biarritz for the overnight stay. A woman seated next to the man with the moustache answered, "Why, it is Europe's Greenbrier, of course." Some laughed at her declaration; others nodded in agreement.

At the Zvarriten friends and acquaintances swapped future addresses in Germany in the vague hope that someday they might see each other again. There was a sense of excitement, but also fear and anxiety that swept the dining room filled with South Americans who now had to be considered *Ausländer Deutscher* or foreign-born Germans more than the diplomats they had been labeled as for the international exchange. German was now the preferred language amongst the travelers. It was as though they were getting themselves prepared to take on their new identity. They now had to *act like* and *be Germans*.

On Monday, June 22 the four Contag children enjoyed bread for breakfast. They would have preferred the bread topped with a bit of fresh black cherry jam and locally made cheese spread that they had tried the night before, but they were too busy talking. The hotel personnel seemed pleased that they had something filling to offer the travelers. A good deal of the famous preserves produced in the area had been sent to the troops and milk was already hard to acquire in large amounts. Nevertheless, no one left the hotel hungry.

Ernst said good-bye to the Detkens who were heading to Bad-Neuenahr with their final destination being Bremen, where Walter Detken's parents lived.

"Well, Ernesto. I hope to see you again." Walter said shaking Ernst's hand.

"Yes, I hope so, too." He turned to Mrs. Detken and said in Spanish, "*Espero que nos veamos otra vez en Quito, ¿no?*"

Walter answered, "I expect we'll all see each other again in Quito."

"*Si Dios quiere, don Ernesto.* If God wills it so," Mrs. Detken responded.

At the train station the children smiled when they received small gifts and sweets from the German government before boarding the train. Ernst thought the German government's generosity was a good omen and he boarded the train feeling fortunate and not at all anxious.

The train trip to Stuttgart, the first stop on their way to Berlin, was a pleasant one. The passengers watched the changing terrain, and chatted about their common experiences and diverging future paths. When the train arrived at Stuttgart, a group of them was sent to the Offenhäuser Hotel at Ernst Weinstrasse 35.[12] Ernst and his family settled in. It was cramped, but comfortable.

Three days passed before Ernst could get passage to Berlin. Just before the train was to leave, Ernst telephoned his brother

Carl and sister-in-law Inge to announce their arrival. He dialed the number 6380 and his brother answered. Ernst announced their arrival time and Carl agreed to meet them at the train station in Potsdam. The exchange was brief but animated. There was excitement in Ernst's voice when he told the children that their Uncle Carl and Aunt Inge were looking forward to meeting them.

"We will go directly to your Uncle Carl's home once we get to Berlin." Ernst said with enthusiasm. "You will meet his wife, Tante Inge, tomorrow. They live in Potsdam, just outside Berlin."

The Ernst Contag family boarded the train in Stuttgart on Thursday evening, June 25. On Friday, June 26 they arrived at their final destination that would now be considered their home, their *patria*, their future. This city, these people, this war... were theirs now, too.

Ernst spotted his brother in the distance and raised his hand. Carl was as tall as Ernst and quite slender. His hair was a good deal darker than it had been in Quito and he had a distinguishing quality that attracted attention wherever he went. His broad forehead seemed to overwhelm his unusually narrow jaw line. To Ernst's surprise Carl was smiling from ear to ear and the first words out of Ernst's mouth were, "Your teeth! You have perfect teeth!"

"Yes, perfect, if they were really mine!" Carl joked before he embraced his brother and clapped him on the back. "Ernst! How are you? Welcome to Potsdam. Heinz... you have grown up already! Ernstchen! You were just a runt when I left Quito. Now look at you." Carl greeted the two boys with a handshake and a head rub. The boys responded with big smiles and a loud "Hello, Uncle Carl!"

Heinz only remembered his uncle vaguely, recalling the time he saw him ironing clothes at the back of the house on the Rocafuerte. Heinz had been surprised to see him take a drink of water and spritz it like an expert from his mouth over the clothing before pressing it with the iron. Today his uncle looked completely relaxed and very happy. He was just as tall and slender as Heinz remembered. His uncle had the most triangular face that Heinz remembered seeing and he still wore his hair parted on the left side and combed over neatly as he had years ago. The style accentuated his broad forehead that served as the base of the inverted triangle whose point ended in Uncle Carl's strong but slender jaw. His uncle's smile was endearing and he warmed up right away.

Irmgard and Werner were not as responsive as Heinz or Ernstchen to their Uncle Carl. They certainly did not remember him and they were somewhat cautious at first. When Carl noticed their trepidation he got down on his haunches and looked Irmgard right in the eye. "And you must be Irmgard. What a beautiful young girl you are. You have your mother's smile and your father's eyes." Irmgard smiled from ear to ear with the compliment, threw her arms around her uncle, and gave him a hug.

"I'm Werner," the young man stated rather defiantly. "Do you remember me, Uncle Carl?"

Carl put his cigar back into his mouth for a puff. He looked serious and spoke like a man who had important business to take care of. "So, you are Werner," he said, looking the boy over. "I think the last time I saw you, young man, you were wearing diapers." A smile spread across Uncle Carl's face and the other children laughed.

"Well I don't wear diapers anymore, Uncle Carl. I am five years old! I am growing up. I can even whistle!" Werner made a hissing sound through his teeth.

"You *can* whistle! Well then, you are growing up!' Uncle Carl swept Werner into his arms and lifted him high enough so they were eye to eye. "You are nearly as tall as I am," he said as he stood still holding the five year old in front of him, "and nearly as heavy! Uff!" He put Werner down with a chuckle, and kept hold of his small hand. Carl clapped his brother again on the back before taking his cigar out of his mouth. "It is good to see you Ernst. This way, Werner. Our apartment is on Schützenstrasse, not very far away. From our apartment you can see the entire city of Potsdam!"

The train had arrived on the west side of the train station and they walked around to the east where trains left for Cologne, Kassel and Magdeburg. In front of them was a bridge and what looked like a large island.

"That is the *Freundschafts* Island you see there. In the distance you can see the *Stadtschloss* Castle. It was begun in the middle of the seventeenth century and finished almost a hundred years later in 1751. You can also see the Nicolai Church with the round roof and the tower of City Hall. Now we have to go this way on Alte König Street to get to our apartment."

On the way Ernst told his brother that he was surprised to find Berlin buzzing with so much activity.

"Berlin is a first class city where there are no restrictions on gas and where theater, concert and vaudeville show tickets have to be purchased three weeks in advance. You might be surprised to know that every restaurant in Berlin is full by fifteen minutes after twelve noon."

"Impressive. Just like Quito," Ernst said facetiously. Ecuadorian towns and cities were not renowned for having a plethora of cafés and restaurants.

Carl laughed at the comparison. "Now that you are in Germany, Ernst, you'll miss the fresh, tropical fruits you had in Quito. I'd give my right shoe for a mango or a bunch of bananas. And that would be a huge sacrifice. Shoes are not easily replaced right now in Germany. . . You didn't smuggle any cherimoyas or avocados in your suitcase, did you, Werner?" Uncle Carl asked the boy who walked near his long legs.

Werner looked up at his uncle and shook his head innocently, "We didn't pack any food, Uncle Carl."

Carl stopped short and acted surprised. "What? No food? Well, I guess we'll just have to send you back to get some! I can't imagine traveling without a few *guineos,* some *mote,* two or three dozen *oritos* . . . maybe a *guatusa*...[13]

"You can't put a *guatusa* in a suitcase, Uncle Carl." Ernstchen said defiantly albeit with a smile, "and the bananas and *mote* would get squished!"

"Well then, we will have to live on hard rolls and *apfel strudel* made with apple replacement for a while. They make some delicious modern desserts with chemical products that taste very much like the real thing! Or at least they are supposed to." He turned to Ernst and scrunched his nose a bit. "I am not so fond of them. You are in a modern country now. . . We eat different kinds of food than they eat in Ecuador."

"Do you know what is funny, Ernst? In Ecuador we were resourceful as a matter of course because no one really had anything modern or technical to worry about. We didn't have replacement foods. Here they have an ersatz for just about anything you can imagine. In Quito we just made do with the natural things that we found in our surroundings because all natural things were plentiful. In Europe people have had access to so many imported things for so long that they have nearly forgotten to live from the earth. Now, with the scarcity of some things, the Germans are learning to live from the earth again. They sent the children out to collect linden tree blossoms to make tea this past spring, for instance. When you have access to so many things from around the world you forget the delicacies you have right in your neighborhood."

"I suppose that is true," Ernst agreed.

Carl's next statement caught Ernst off guard.

"You will be surprised to taste the beer, Ernst. All those years while we were growing up we were taught how great

German beer was. Well, the war has improved on that great taste. The beer flows like water, almost tastes like water, and affects you like water." Carl chuckled and winked at Ernst. "You won't have to worry about drinking too much for a while!"

Ernst did not miss his brother's sarcasm.

Carl was a bit thinner than the last time he saw him in Quito, but seemed to be bubbling over with energy and Ernst suspected that things were going quite well with his brother. "*Eres todo un pícaro*, Carlos," Ernst said not twenty centimeters from his brother's ear. "No more a rogue than you," Carl countered with a smile.

"The dentists here must be magicians." Ernst motioned to his own teeth and then pointed to his brother's mouth. "Do you really think they can do something for me and the children?"

"Sure. There is a push to get everyone to look after their teeth. The government paid for my dental work. Pretty nice smile, eh Ernesto?" Carl beamed. "I got a wife out of the deal too! Maybe you can make a similar arrangement." Carl winked at his brother. Ernst knew that Carl and Inge Beutner had met at the hospital where she worked as a nurse and where he had work done on his teeth and gums. Carl lifted his dark eyebrows as he spoke, "You might want to make arrangements for your children to see a German dentist before they have to have all their teeth pulled like you and I did." Ernst frowned at his brother and brushed him off, "Their teeth are fine. Don't start scaring the children with your stories."

Heinz and Ernstchen gave each other an anxious look and chattered their teeth at each other in jest as they had a few months before in a mutual comment about an adventure they had shared in Quito. The two boys had unearthed a single plate of false teeth out in the backyard behind their house. They spent most of the afternoon after they found the false teeth trying to scare people with the ghoulish discovery. They had run across the street and chased a few children with the plate of false teeth before a woman called them over, putting an end to their nasty game.

The woman, who made gunpowder for general use, and blasting powder for the quarry on Rocafuerte Street, had seen them chase the younger children with the false teeth and she had laughed out loud at their shrieks. She stood in front of her small wooden lean-to and said to them through the few yellow teeth that were scattered haphazardly in her mouth, "*Vengan acá, gringuitos.* I see you have found my teeth. Have you found my fingers also?"[14] Heinz and Ernstchen had giggled nervously and ran as she threatened to chase them.

Heinz was not afraid of the leathery woman, although he had cringed at the idea of finding the bones of her two missing fingers that had been blown away in an explosion years earlier.

Heinz and Ernstchen had often tagged along with their neighbor, Adriano, when his mother went to buy gunpowder for the quarry workers from the blasting-powder woman. The three boys, Erntschen, Adriano and Heinz, had watched her mix charcoal, sulphur and potassium nitrate in water on occasion. She ground the mixture into pebbles using rocks, and sold the pebbles a pound or two at a time to Adriano's mother. Adriano's mother would carry a small bundle of blasting-powder pebbles over to the quarry where the workers pounded out an area of rock, dropped in the gunpowder pebbles with a few shreds of cotton rags, whistled loudly, and ran to safety before the explosion.

Heinz was distracted by his thoughts about the adventure with the false teeth and blasting-powder lady when a man who was missing an arm walked right past them on Alte König Street. Heinz noticed the man and nudged Ernstchen. "Look. He must have been working with gun powder, too, like our neighbor lady without her fingers!" But his Uncle Carl corrected him, "No. He was wounded in battle. You must be careful what you say, Heinz. The wounded are considered heroes. Missing parts are worn here like medals! It is an honor to sacrifice something for Greater Germany."

Ernst was about to chide Carl for his remark that cut, like a double-edged sword, between the patriotic and the absurd, but he decided it might be unwise to make any snide remarks in public, and he reserved his comments for a more private moment.

The six Contags climbed the street behind the train station that led up a hill. Every once in a while Ernstchen would turn to look back over the city. He spotted a monument with a man on horseback just beyond a stand of trees. Just then his uncle paused and turned.

"Look over there. Just beyond the Kaiser Wilhelm Bridge is the City Castle. It is the enormous building right there."

"The one that looks like it has hundreds of statues about to jump off the roof?" asked Irmgard.

"Yes. That is the one," Carl said with twinkle in his eye. "And do you see the dome of the Nikolai church beyond it? Yes? And there is the Old Courthouse building. It is the one with the tower."

Ernstchen pointed across the city and asked, "What is that over there, Uncle Carl? It looks like a tiny castle in a huge forest of trees."

"Oh, yes. You can just make the castle out from here, can't you. That is Frederick the Great's castle at Sans Souci."

"We saw a castle in Lisbon when we got off the boat," Werner offered, but we didn't go up to see it. Can we see that castle, Papa?"

"Perhaps," his father answered looking across the city and noticing the waterways that connected to a river that ran throughout Potsdam.

"What is that word you said, Uncle Carl, . . . *sands saucy*?" Ernstchen asked.

"*Sans souci*. That is French. It means "without worries." When we go to Sans Souci you'll see that it is a fairy tale place. It really is a large garden full of palaces, not just the palace that you can see from here. There is the Orangerie, the Neues Palais, the classic ruins. . . . The king wanted to see something different from each window and door, I think. It is a marvelous place. We will have to go before you leave next week, children."

"Next week?" Ernstchen stopped. "But we just got here. I thought we were staying here, Papa. Now where do we have to go?"

"The government offices in Berlin have been working on finding schools for you ever since we had word you were coming," Uncle Carl responded.

"But it is summer, Uncle Carl," Heinz piped. "We don't go to school in the summer months."

"Of course you do! The children in Germany are so fortunate that they get to go year-round! That is why your Papa brought you to Germany. . . to go to school. You didn't think that we have lazy students here like they do in Quito?"

This comment brought scowls and frowns from Heinz and Ernstchen who felt they had the most to lose with year-round classes.

"There is a special orientation program for Heinz and Ernstchen in Hohenelse. It is a school just for boys and girls like you who have come from other countries to live in Germany. It is a bit like the German school in Quito. Some of the children are boarders like the boys in that one wing at the German School, what is it, the Munich Dormitory. . . I can't remember. Anyway, Hohenelse has special classes to prepare you for regular German classes."

"Great," Heinz said without much enthusiasm. "Where is . . . Hohen. . . eh. . . what did you call it?"

"Hohenelse. It is a boarding school complex just outside the town of Rheinsberg here in Mark Brandenburg. There are lots of lakes in that area. Big trees, too. One of the government officials told me that the Rheinsberger Lake has an island in the middle of it! You'll probably go swimming there sometimes. Maybe you can climb a few trees!"

Ernstchen was cheered by these words. "Gee, Uncle Carl, that's terrific. They didn't let us go near the trees at the Greenbrier Hotel in the United States. If there is a lake there, do you think we can go fishing?"

"Probably. Your papa has to get things in order first, Ernstchen. He has a lot of work to do to get you all settled and to find a job. But I bet he will take you boating on a few weekends if the weather is nice. Won't you Ernst?"

"I am going to stay with Papa," Irmgard said defiantly. "Wherever Papa goes, I go."

When Ernst said nothing Carl responded to his seven-year old niece. "But your Oma and Opa Dreier are looking forward to having you and Werner come for a visit! Wouldn't you like to see your Oma and Opa in Hannover?"

"Yes, I suppose, but I want Papa to stay with them, too," Irmgard said as she moved as close as she could to her father without tripping him. She was feeling a little uncomfortable with the idea of her older brothers staying at school and her father living away from her. Werner, on the other hand, took no part in the conversation as he was trying to get out of his brothers' way as they tried to pass him on the hill.

"It is the first street to the right, boys," Carl called after them.

Ernst turned to his brother and said with surprise, "It cost me nearly 115 Reichsmark just for food and drink since Tuesday![15] Do you know how many *sucres* that is, Carl?"

"Don't worry, Ernst, *sans souci*. In Germany there is plenty of money and plenty of jobs to go around for a strong fellow like you. You are in a modern country with modern prices and modern problems. Forget about it. Right now the problem is not money so much, but finding the goods to buy. Some things have become scarce. We'll take care of you and get you started."

Schützenstrasse was located southwest of the Potsdam city railway station, up the hill, and down the street to the right.

"Here we are," said Uncle Carl, "Schutzenstrasse 12. Home."

The *homecoming* for the five Contags was wonderful. If Ernst had been on vacation in Germany, he would not have harbored resentment about being forced from Ecuador. There was an arc of flowers over the doorway. Carl's wife, Inge, met the family at the door holding a bouquet of freshly cut flowers that she gave to Irmgard.

Inge was in her forties, wore her curly, blonde hair parted and pulled back off her forehead. She was a good deal shorter than her tall husband, and although she was nearly eight years older than he was, she looked about the same age.

Ernst bent over her hand and was just about to say, "It is a great pleasure to meet you, dearest Inge," when Carl clapped his debonair brother on the back and said with a wink, "Remember what I said, Inge. This brother of mine is quite the ladies' man. Don't let him get away with anything!"

Ernst stood and said directly to Inge after kissing her on the cheek, "Your husband is a rascal... It makes me very happy to be able to say hello to my sister-in-law."

The apartment was small, but comfortable and clean. Ernst and his children took a few moments to freshen up before retuning to the living room. It was strange being in a home after being on the road and the sea for nearly two months. The children sat quietly as though they were afraid to move.

Carl offered Ernst a cigar that he took gladly, lit, and puffed. The smell of cigar smoke permeated the apartment with a pleasant pungent odor.

Tante Inge wore a green, fitted dress with tiny black dots all over it. It was short-sleeved and had a loose-fitting bodice with a round neck. The skirt was rather straight and hung to mid-calf. After meeting the relatives she excused herself and went to the kitchen where she continued preparing a meal for the family.

Carl told Ernst they had a small vegetable garden that the government encouraged them to cultivate. "A garden just like we had at home, only we don't have any eucalyptus trees overhead," he added as he settled into a chair. "Speaking of home, what's the news?"

"There will be plenty of time for reminiscing, " Inge interrupted. She called the family to the table and offered the children ersatz lemonade, a tangy treat that quenched their thirst. She served a warm vegetable soup with potatoes and crusty, gray rolls for dinner. The meal was tasty, and no one missed a dessert.

When the meal was finished Ernstchen directed a questioning look at his uncle and said, "Uncle Carl, on the way from the train station you said you have something special to show us. What is it?"

"Oh yes." Carl stood and reached for a small box. He sat back down in his chair and called out an afterthought to his wife, "Inge, can you bring in the boxes for the children?" He opened his small rectangular box and pulled out a shiny harmonica. "Irmgard. Come here so I can tell you something. You, boys, sit there." When the children were situated, Uncle Carl tested his harmonica by blowing it from left to right. The children giggled.

"As you know all the lights must be put out a bit before eight-thirty in the evening. We cover the windows and it is pretty dark in the rooms, so your Tante Inge and I thought that you might like to have something to keep you company when you are inside in the evenings. It is something to make a little music so you don't get lonely. I'll show you how the harmonica is played."

Uncle Carl started with *"Mein Hut der hat drei Ecken,"* and ended his demonstration with a version of *"Yo soy el chiquillo quiteño"* which made them all clap.[16]

Tante Inge handed each child a box. The children found a shiny, silver Hohner harmonica inside. It took several demonstrations to show the children how to hold the harmonica and to blow a few notes. Ernst took a turn showing off his inability to produce a tune. Soon Werner was honking noisily on the floor. Irmgard was smiling and laughing at each tiny sound she made, giving each hole a toot before she giggled. The two older boys were actually trying to make up little tunes. Inge looked at her brother-in-law and his children and wondered what she had gotten herself into by marrying into such a family. She shook her head and smiled. What a wonderful day it was.

It was not long before Ernst insisted the children go to sleep in their makeshift beds on the floor. Ernst told his children a story about a boy who found a young donkey and carried him on his shoulders every day for a year. Many people made fun of the boy and told him he was foolish because he was serving the donkey and the donkey was not serving him as it was supposed to. Uncle Carl, who had heard the story himself as a boy, finished it.

"At the end of a year that boy was the strongest boy around. The same people who had once called him a fool now thought he was wise and they talked about him for years and years."

"Is that a true story?" Werner asked.

"It's a good story, Werner. Now, go to sleep." Ernst patted his back and went to the kitchen with his brother. Carl and Ernst talked for quite a while after Inge went to bed. Carl helped Ernst make plans to get the children to Hohenelse and Hannover.

"The trip to Hohenelse will cost you around fifteen Reichsmarks. It will almost cost you double that to take Irmgard and Werner to Hannover. Your mother-in-law has agreed to come and get the children. She thinks they will be better off in Hannover since they are still so young," he added.

After a short hesitation Carl smiled and spoke just above a whisper, "The rumor in the Berlin coffee houses is that there is a secret gentleman's agreement between the German government and the British government. They say the agreement will keep the British from bombing Berlin and the Germans from bombing London. I don't know if there is anything to the rumor, but there hasn't been an air raid since November 7 of last year. We all feel quite safe."

"The *New York Times* did not give any hint of the optimism about such a rumor," Ernst countered quietly.

Carl scoffed, "What do the Americans have to be optimistic about?" He was about to light another cigar when he changed his mind and nudged his brother. "Come outside a moment." The two brothers fumbled their way to the door and down the stairs. It was pitch dark outside, and quiet. All the houses were dark, the street lights out. "Look up." Carl nudged his brother. "I'll bet you have never seen those stars."

Ernst felt completely disoriented by the northern sky but he chided his brother. "Well, they don't look so different from the ones I saw in Stuttgart two nights ago."

"When I first came to Berlin you could barely see the stars at night because of all the lights. When the lights-out order came I used to come outside in the evening and think of the quiet and darkness of the early morning hunt in the jungle areas near Santo Domingo or at the foot of the Cotopaxi. But nothing was really the same. The air here is so different, the people, the landscape, the sandy soil..."

Carl continued hardly above a whisper and switched to Spanish. "*Dios mío, ¡cuánto extraño Quito!* What I wouldn't give for eight weeks in the Andes."

"*Ha cambiado mucho*, eh. They don't like Germans anymore." Ernst grunted.

"I miss the freedom in Quito ¿*sabes*?... the eucalyptus... the air... I miss the simple life. I am not complaining about Potsdam. I am happy here, but I sure wouldn't mind going home for a while."

"Maybe when the war is over. ¿*Quién sabe*?" Ernst was encouraging.

"Who knows?" Carl took a puff on his cigar and changed the subject. "Inge was wonderful with the children today. I bet seeing them will change her mind about taking a trip to Ecuador. She was never too interested in going there, but maybe now that she has seen the children... Perhaps I'll get back home *before* we are old and retired..."

Neither brother said anything for a moment.

Ernst was the first to speak. "Aren't there any schools in Potsdam? I would like to have them nearby. Maybe I could find an apartment... "

"Nearly all the children have been sent out of Berlin. You know, Ernst, three years ago there were more than four million people living in Berlin. Even with the refugees from other cities, the number of people living and working in Berlin has nearly dropped to half. The school in Hohenelse is quite nice, I hear. It is quiet and safe. The children will be happy there."

"I know I have to send the boys away, and I am sure that it must be a nice school for children there in Hohenelse, but... it will be hard for you to understand this, Carl. I am all they have, you know. My children don't know anyone and they won't fit in right away. Heinz and Ernstchen speak more Spanish than German. I feel even worse about Werner and Irmgardchen. They are so young and they don't remember their grandparents. I know my in-laws will do their best for the children. It just breaks my heart to know that I won't be there in the morning to greet them, to help them if something bad happens, to braid Irmgard's hair. The two little ones have never had anyone else to count on. Now they won't be able to count on me either."

"You act like Hohenelse and Hannover are at the edge of the world, Ernst. You can take the train to Rheinsberg every weekend if you want. It can't be more than a few hours away by train. You will stay here with us, of course. I wouldn't have it any other way. Inge agrees. That way you can save some money. We'll help you get to Hannover to see the little ones. Things will work out. You'll see. And, as far as Irmgard and Werner are concerned, it will do them good to have someone else to count on besides you, you softy!"

"I knew you would understand," Ernst added with sarcasm. Carl didn't seem to notice and he spoke with a serious tone.

"I'm glad you are here in any case. Things could change quickly for us, too."

"What do you mean?" Ernst asked, somewhat confused.

"Inge is a proud woman and she expects Germany to be victorious as we all do," Carl said cautiously. "The factory where I work making files . . . well, Inge doesn't think we are doing enough for the war effort. So it looks as though I'll be leaving in a uniform at some point. Not soon, but at some point it could happen."

Ernst grimaced in the darkness. The idea was mad! His brother was no mercenary.

Carl patted his brother on the shoulder and said, "Well? Won't you comment on your Ecuadorian brother heading off to fight with the Germans?" Ernst noted some uneasiness in his brother's voice, but it was too dark to read his brother's face.

Ernst chuckled nervously, "If you can't keep your factory job, at least you are a good marksman. I'd worry more about the other fellow."

"What about you, Ernst? You are a better marksman than I," Carl added.

Ernst leaned against the brick wall and squelched his desire for a cigarette or another cigar. He sighed. "I signed a paper in

West Virginia saying I would not participate in the armed conflict against the Allies." Ernst scratched his head and rubbed his forehead pensively. "I hope the German government will honor the agreement."

"Good. That is what I will tell Inge. She was wondering what your plans were. I am happy for you, Ernst, and for the children. I hope the German government honors the agreement, too. . . you can watch out for things around here when I am called to serve." Ernst thought Carl expressed a sense of relief.

The brothers stood in silence for quite a while. Ernst was keenly aware that his brother was making every effort to stay within prescribed boundaries concerning the perception of being *German* so he spoke first, "Let's go inside. I do have something important to tell you." They climbed the stairs and went back to the kitchen where they spoke softly and in German again. He told Carl about Lenchen's marriage to Bio Beate and seeing them at the Greenbrier. Carl was shocked that they did not arrive in Berlin at the same time.

Ernst explained, "The strangest thing about this exchange program is that no one knows anything about where anyone is going. Everything is so secretive."

"She is planning to come to Berlin, isn't she?" Carl asked of Lenchen.

"Yes, of course. I didn't see them in Lisbon, so they must be coming on another exchange ship. But I am not sure what Bio's plans are." Ernst took out his pocket calendar.

"Did her husband sign a contract in the United States too?" Carl asked.

"I don't know. I only talked to them briefly one evening. There were a thousand people at the hotel. I did not see them again during our entire ten-day stay." Without the comfort of a beer, Ernst decided it was time for bed. There would be plenty of time to talk to Carl. The trip had been exhausting.

On Sunday Carl took the family on an outing to Sans Souci. On their way to the street car, Carl told Ernst that if he had used his given name, Maximillian Victor Ernst, people in Berlin might have taken him for the famous Max Contag, the internationally known architect who designed and built the Teltow canal in 1905.

"If I thought it would get me anywhere I'd use the name, but I can't pass myself off as an architect of anything," Ernst said.

"You can always drop the name at businesses to see if you can get an interview. Who knows? Maybe just being related will help."

"Just speaking German will help, Carl. I have never been so glad as I am now that our mother kept us speaking German. I met a good number of people at the Greenbrier Hotel and on the two ships who did not speak much German. Many of the Ecuadorian and Colombian wives did not speak much German. Their children didn't all speak German, either. Think what it will take for them to adjust to the new surroundings." Ernst scratched his head and waited for Carl to respond, but Carl was already explaining things about Sans Souci to the children.

"The king drew the original floor plan. Can you imagine? Wait until you see the place. The walkways are cobblestone or dirt and they go forever! Wherever you look you will spot something new and different. That is what the king wanted, you know. He did not want to get bored."

The two brothers and the children strolled through the gardens of the palace grounds. The red-leafed buche, sycamore, and horse chestnut trees towered over them and shaded the walkways. It was green everywhere and the flowering plants moved in the summer breeze, attracting the eye almost as much as the unusual palaces at the end of each walkway. In the shaded areas there were all sorts of ferns and wild flowers and Irmgard asked if she could pick them.

"Not here," Carl answered. "But you can smell every blossom if you like. We should leave the flowers for others to see."

"So, what is the hunting like here in Mark Brandenburg?"

"I don't hunt much anymore. There used to be lots of ducks, deer, rabbits, and wild pigs. The wild pig population was so large when I first arrived that people complained because the darned animals ate the flower blossoms at the cemeteries! That was before the wild pigs started to disappear onto the dinner table."

The Contags spent the afternoon at Sans Souci and returned early in the evening for supper at Carl and Inge's apartment on the Brewery hill, named after the Unions Brewery on the Havel river at the foot of the hill across from the Potsdam city train station. The children were exhausted after dinner and fell asleep almost immediately.

On Monday the children followed their father from store to store. Ernst bought a suitcase for about fourteen Reichsmarks in which he planned to pack all of Werner and Irmgard's things. Oma Dreier was scheduled to arrive on Tuesday morning, June 30, and he needed to have everything ready.

For Ernst and his mother-in-law, the reunion in Potsdam would be bittersweet. Oma Dreier was thrilled to see her grandchildren again after having left Ecuador when Werner was barely a year and a half old, but her joy was tempered with personal sorrow because the wound of her daughter's untimely death in Ecuador had never fully healed. Now she had additional worries. Her elderly in-laws in Quickborn were not in good health. Her own husband was ill, and she was taking on another responsibility: two small children who needed, . . . well, . . . proper training.

It was a blessing that her grandchildren were in Germany, but it was a blessing that came with many complications in a country that was running a *blitzkrieg* on many fronts against many countries. The two young children would be a handful for her.

Oma Dreier was brutally honest. Endearing, but brutally honest. Ernst trusted his mother-in-law as he trusted no other woman. She was not overly generous with money that was always tight, but she was extremely generous with her time and genuinely loving without being softhearted. He admired her and appreciated the kindness she had always shown him.

"*Mutter*," he interrupted his own thoughts with a sigh. "Until a few months ago I never imagined I could bring my children to Germany. I know this is what Elisabeth wanted. She wanted the children educated in Germany, but I never imagined I would have the opportunity to do it. Here we are! Of course, now I can't imagine what I would have done if you had not been here to help me again."

Cecilie Dreier shook her head and lifted her eyes to meet Ernst's directly. "I can't imagine what you would have done either. I worry about these children, Ernst. Don't be a fool. While you are here find yourself a nice wife and give these children a mother. You can't raise them alone in Germany. I can't raise them for you. Elisabeth would not have wanted them running around everywhere as you let them do in Quito. Irmgard needs a mother. She is a beautiful girl. In a few years you'll be wondering what to do with her. Girls are different, you know. Girls need a mother and a stern hand, Ernst. The boys need a mother, too. Stop sulking around and get on with it. You are so stubborn sometimes."

Ernst shifted his weight. "Bah! You mean they need a stepmother. They *don't need* a stepmother!" he said emphatically.

Cecilie Dreier responded quickly and sternly, "I'd rather you set an example for them by marrying a decent woman. You are a young man, Ernst, and you can find plenty of women eager to get married. Germany is full of them. Choose one who will love these children. When I left Ecuador in 1938 I expected you to find a good woman to take care of my grandchildren. Stop being so selfish and think about them."

"I *was* thinking about them!" Ernst said with surprise.

"No, you were just thinking of yourself!" His mother-in-law had the last word, and she went to get the children ready for their trip with her to Hannover.

On Wednesday Irmgard and Werner left the Schutzenstrasse apartment in the care of their maternal grandmother. The departure was not painless. When they got to the station, Ernst hugged his young children and told them he would see them in Hannover in nine days.

"I'll bring everything you asked for, Mutter, if I can find it." His mother-in-law had scolded him when she saw the nearly empty suitcase and demanded that he bring them more to wear. "You will have to buy a few things, Ernesto. Here is a list. Get some decent clothing and shoes for yourself as well. You look unfit in that suit. Inge, you'll have to make sure he puts some meat on those bones of his. Get some decent trousers, too," she added.

Irmgard hung on to her father's leg. When he leaned over to kiss her good-bye she threw her arms around his neck. Shyly, she whispered into his ear. "I don't want to go without you, Papa. You must come with us. I'm scared."

Ernst faced his daughter and spoke encouragingly but firmly, "I have to take Heinz and Ernstchen to school, Irmgard. I'll come to see you as soon as I can. Now be good for Oma, before I get in more trouble for not doing what I am supposed to."

Ernst lifted his children onto the train and walked them to their seats. He put the suitcase near his mother-in-law and thanked her. He patted his two children gently on the head and left the train. He stood at the window and waved until he was sure that the children could no longer see him or his sadness. A few hours later he was back at the train station with Ernstchen and Heinz.

"The schoolmaster will be in Rheinsberg to meet you boys. Heinz, keep your eye on your brother. Watch yourselves. I'll be up to visit for your birthday, Heinz. That is less than a month!"

"All right, Papa," Heinz answered with self-confidence. Ernstchen simply wrapped himself around his father. He was not ready to leave.

"Let's get you on the train, boys," Ernst said as a matter-of-fact. "In Germany the trains don't wait for slowpokes."

After the train was out of sight Ernst wandered aimlessly around the downtown area for a while, not ready to go back to the small apartment. He needed time to deal with his sorrow. He had lost his entire family in a matter of hours and felt entirely alone and uncomfortably free. There were no hands grabbing for his, no child asking him a string of questions, no smiles full of trust and love to comfort him.

By morning Ernst had turned sadness and loneliness into a mission. Finding suitable clothing and shoes for himself and the children was not going to be a simple task in Potsdam so Ernst took a trip into Berlin where shopping would be easier. He found a pair of shoes for himself for 15.20 Reichsmark, a suit for 12.55 RM, two dresses, three pairs of stockings, and slippers for Irmgard (31 RM), and six handkerchiefs for 2 RM. Each child would have one handkerchief, and he would reserve two for himself. With the cost of three one-way tickets to Hannover for Oma, Werner and Irmgard, and two one-way trips to Hohenelse for the boys, he had spent a grand total of 255.77 RM in a couple days. It was a bundle of money.

Inge and his mother-in-law had already helped him out a bit financially, and there were funds he had for relocation and repatriation from the sale of their household goods in Quito. Nevertheless, it was a chilly realization of his new position in German society when he was called to pick up his work papers on Wednesday, July 15 and found he was assigned a *Sunderdienst*, or a welfare post, as though he were a delinquent. It was then he thought longingly of his freedom and social position in Quito. "Someday," he promised himself, "I will go home."

The very next evening he started writing letters. First he wrote to Heinz Jeanroud in Lisbon. He asked if another ship had arrived from the United States. He hoped to find out if Lenchen, and perhaps even his brother Arturo and family, would be arriving in Germany soon. Secretly, Ernst hoped that Arturo had remained in Ecuador. This would facilitate their eventual return to Ecuador. In the letter he asked Jeanroud to send word of their arrival in Germany to his brother in Ecuador if he thought he could, but he wrote nothing of his secret desire to Jeanroud. It might prejudice his stay in Germany or Jeanroud's position in Lisbon. He also asked Jeanroud to take a bouquet of flowers to Maria. He enclosed a note in German with her address and a message to be included in the bouquet. It read: I wish you happiness always, my dearest Maria. *Adeus*. He signed the note, "Ernesto."

Ernst felt overwhelmed with his new life, but he took solace in writing his children. After receiving a letter from the director of the Youth Home and School in Hohenelse, he wrote a brief letter to Heinz and put it in a package with overalls, pants and socks and addressed it to his son in the care of Fraülein Cotthaus. The director's letter had outlined the living arrangements for the children and other information he had considered pertinent for a parent. In his letter to Heinz he mentioned that Ernstchen was in the care of Fraülein Neydhart and that, hopefully, the boys would see each other at the school. Ernst kept the letter short, even though he wanted to ask Heinz how things were going under the leadership of headmaster Vagt who, in Ernst's estimation, might be ruthless with the young *foreign-born* boys who had been placed under his watchful eye.

Ernst also wrote a letter to his mother-in-law, Cecilie, with simple, kind messages for his children. He tucked the note gently in the package of clothing and incidentals for Werner and Irmgard. Then he wrote Fraülein Maria Renaud, a woman whose name had been given to him for the care of Irmgard, and perhaps Werner too, when school started. Fraülein Renaud lived in Nuremberg at Velserstrasse 42. He addressed the envelope and stared at it. Nuremberg. He opened his pocket calendar to the list of cities in greater Germany with a population over 100,000 in 1940. He scanned the cities that were listed in order of size. Nuremberg. 423,000. *Was Nuremberg an important industrial city? Would Irmgard be safe there?*

Ernst rested poorly that evening. There were so many decisions to be made and none of them made him feel comfortable or good.

There was no word from Lenchen or Arturo. His children were scattered. Ernst had been in Europe nearly a month and a little more than two months had passed since he had sailed from Guayaquil on the Arcadia. In spite of Inge's exuberant support for modern Germany, Ernst could not get caught up in *the cause*. He felt like an alien in his new country. The topics for small talk were different. The customary daily interaction between people who lived right next door to each other was different. The worst part of it was that he felt like he was a nobody, a man without history. Looking and acting like everyone else just made things worse. He couldn't quite put his finger on what it was, but things had definitely changed. No matter how he tried to direct his thoughts, his silent moments were filled with thoughts of bananas, mangoes, even oranges, or marmalade made with fresh berries or *babaco* fruit. He could put on a good show as a German, but his heart was in Quito.

There was one woman who made him feel at home in Germany. Tante Grete Contag. Tante Grete was beloved by Carl and Inge, and by the majority of Contags who lived in or visited Berlin. She had invited Ernst to have tea with her in the garden behind her house on Sunday, July 19.

"It's nice to meet another Contag nephew," Tante Grete said warmly.

"Are you finally starting to feel at home?"

"A little, Tante Grete, but I am not sure I'll ever feel truly at home. The Mark Brandenburg area is so different from everything I knew growing up in Quito. It is going to take some time."

"I suppose that is so," the middle-aged woman responded before she poured him a cup of berry tea. She hushed her voice before adding, "The Mark Brandenburg is not what it used to be either, Ernst. I have been trying to adjust to all the changes. I can't even go to church anymore. The Führer tells the preachers what to preach. Christian beliefs aren't allowed. I know Christ and I know he isn't there in the church building with those people. So, I go to a church group that meets in a home. We all have to adjust and be patient."

Ernst smiled, but Tante Grete was deadly serious.

"I worked as a maid for a month when I was young. I earned one gold Mark. I thought it was a fortune. I remember having a terrific time in the city with my sister, and we only had 10 pfennig. Now look at what things cost. Everything changes, Ernst. We just have to hold fast to our values and make the necessary adjustments to the insignificant but fast-moving changes all around us. Things will be all right in the end for us if we do that."

Tea or coffee with Tante Grete put things back into balance for Ernst. She was right, of course. Pay attention to the things that matter: family and friends.

Shortly after their visit Ernst heard that Lenchen had arrived and was staying at Gürtelstrasse 14 in Berlin. A day later he got off the tram at Sonntagstrasse and went to meet her at her apartment. The room was small but Lenchen had arranged things and it was rather tidy.

"It looks like you just arrived," Ernst remarked after greeting his sister.

"Yes, on Friday," she answered before offering her brother some water and a simple biscuit-like dessert that he had not seen before.

"You look warm and uncomfortable. I'll open the window a bit more. Bio is already in a meeting with an officer this afternoon. He thinks that he will be sent to the Ukraine. He knows a man there who can employ him, a fellow by the name of Neuendorf, in Berditschef. It is a collection area for metal filings and that sort of thing. It must be like the factory where Carl works, I suppose. Bio is making arrangements." Lenchen spoke rapidly and sternly. Her honeymoon had indeed been short-lived. " I don't know what to think."

Not wanting to set his sister off with excessive sympathy, Ernst hesitated before offering a response. Before he could say anything to her she sat down an arm's length from him and continued with a heavy sigh. She spoke in German.

"*Mein Gott*, it is hot. You know, Ernesto, there were a few days at the beginning of this month when I did not think we would ever get to Berlin. I thought they might keep us in the United States. I even thought our ship might be blown to bits. It was an awful experience."

"Why? What happened?"

Lenchen looked directly at Ernst and said, "Now don't interrupt me. I am only going to say this once. Then I am going to forget all about it." She took a deep breath and began. "After the large group left the Greenbrier Hotel there were just a few hundred of us at the hotel. I kept wondering why we were not sent out on the train like you were. No one gave us any idea why we had to stay even when we had arrived earlier than you. I guess the agents wanted to talk more with some of the people in our group."

"Were you pestered by the agents, too?" Ernst asked, his interest piqued.

"Don't interrupt me, Ernst. I'll tell you. The *New York Times* indicated that the ship that took you to Lisbon, now what was it called?"

"The Drottningholm."

"Yes, we read that the Drottningholm arrived safely in Lisbon, but there was nothing about your group in the newspaper after that. There was information about the ship, and its returning *American* passengers though. One fellow who got on in Lisbon died as soon as he boarded the ship! Heart attack. That was no surprise to those of us still at the Greenbrier Hotel. Every day that passed after all of you left was tense. And things got really nasty once that... Drottningholm... got back to the U.S. harbor. I guess some important people from the Americas were on the ship too, but when it arrived at the port on July 1 they wouldn't let most of the passengers off the ship. The *New York Times* called them "mystery passengers" and hundreds of them were kept like prisoners on the ship. The newspaper said they were under investigation even when we were about to board the *Serpa Pinto* days after the ship had arrived. Those poor people. It must have been dreadfully hot with all those people on the ship."

She paused for a breath and continued, "We left the Greenbrier Hotel on the third of July, but even though the Serpa Pinto was ready to sail on Thursday night, they kept it moored at Pier 8 on a place called Staten Island. No one knew what was holding things up, but it was clear that we were not going anywhere. Agents came aboard and interviewed more passengers. It went on for hours and hours. It was nerve-wracking because someone said that they had read in the *New York Times* . . . I think it was the day we left the Greenbrier Hotel... that Germany had denied safe conduct to any more refugee ships. First I was worried that we might never sail, and then I was even more worried that we might. It was terrible. The ship was hot and nothing was moving. It was just awful."

"Well, you sailed and you are here now," Ernst interrupted, trying to calm her down.

Lenchen continued as if she had not heard him. "People kept talking about the mines in the ocean and how we were sure to sink. Oh yes, then there was that nasty rumor that was published in the newspaper. They said the rumor came from the Polish underground by way of London. The rumor said that there was propaganda urging the Allies to save millions of people's lives by executing Germans living in Allied countries. I couldn't believe it. *Retaliation*, they called it. I'd call it indiscriminate killing! I can't tell you how that made us feel. . . stuck there on the *Serpa Pinto*. *Refugee* ship, indeed. It makes my skin crawl to think of it."

Lenchen tried to work through her mixed feelings. "There was a lot of U.S. war propaganda in that newspaper, the *New York Times*." Lenchen fixed her eyes on her brother. "It is hard to know what to believe, Ernst. Each government tries to save face by printing what makes them look good. Everyone is out to get the other."

Ernst raised an eyebrow and said, "That's nothing new."

"No. I suppose not, but they published the most curious things even about Ecuador, Ernst, not just German victories and enemy losses like you get on the radio here. After three days in Berlin I feel completely isolated from international news. Listen. The U.S. State Department made a new map of the world for the display windows of some big company at Rockefeller Plaza in New York.[17] They made the new world map exactly according to the established borders of 1939 with the exception of one thing."

"What was that?" Ernst was interested but started to feel annoyed. Lenchen had not even asked about the children.

"Can you believe it? The one change they made was the Ecuadorian-Peruvian border. For me, that was the crowning blow. The Americans ignored the strides made in Europe, but they acquiesced to those Peruvian thieves. They have been in cahoots with the Peruvians since that ridiculous border treaty was signed in January."

Ernst felt angry. The Peruvians were thieves. Arroyo del Rio was spineless.

"We won't get any information about Ecuador here I bet, so you had better know the latest. Galo Plaza Lasso is in California. Anti-Axis students attacked Arroyo del Rio's palace and called for his resignation. His brother, Leónidas was accused of leading an anti-Axis demonstration and he has been court-martialed and sentenced to sixteen years in prison!"

"I bet he was just trying to throw Arroyo del Rio out on his ear. Oh, he'll find a way to weasel out of that one," Ernst added with a smile. "He is very clever, and his brother and father will help him out of that predicament." The news was surprising, but Ecuadorian politics always had a way of working out for the big fellows. Leónidas Plaza Lazo was near the top and Ernst was confident that he would find a way to avoid being locked up.[18]

"The United States thinks Clemente Ballén de Guzmán is being used as bait to get Ecuadorian cooperation for Germany. Hundreds of workers in the textile factories in Ambato have protested against the factory owners who have been accused of being accomplices in helping some people get off the American blacklist."[19]

When Ernesto said nothing she lowered her voice to a whisper and went on. "Things at sea are getting really ugly, too. Three Argentinean ships were bombed and it has caused a big stink. According to publicity in the *Times* it is just a question of time before Argentina and Chile turn their backs on the Reich."

Ernst stopped his sister and spoke sternly but quietly. "If I have learned anything in the last month, Lenchen, it is to remain tight-lipped about any negative press about Germany. *En boca cerrada no entra mosca.* Keep a smile on your face and do what is asked of you. Whatever you do, keep your opinions to yourself... y *por Dios*, speak German if anyone else is around."

Lenchen gave her brother a look of superiority. "Did you know that the city of Cologne was bombed?"

"No."

She whispered again. "Of course not. You hear about the destruction of the Soviet army and the capture of prisoners, but you don't hear about German losses. Not everything is as it seems."

Ernst was getting irritated and he tried to change the subject. "Have you heard from Arturo?"

"*Ni una palabra.* I didn't expect to hear anything, though. He didn't know where we were. I am not sure where he is. The *New York Times* had an article about the censorship of letters destined for Latin America. Everybody at the Greenbrier was talking about it. There were excerpts in the paper of a letter returned to the sender. It was ridiculous. It was just a simple personal letter. No political arguments. No worthwhile opinion for or against anyone but it was censored. Oh, that reminds me. I've got a name for you." She pulled out a small sheet of paper. "It is the name of the American in charge of the diplomatic exchange voyages on the Drottningholm and the Gripsholm." Lenchen spelled the name. "J-e-s-s-e S-a-u-g-s-t-a-d... U.S. State Department. His name was in the newspaper the day we left The Greenbrier Hotel. I thought you might like to know."

Ernst smiled and repeated "Saugstad" before writing the name down on a piece of paper that he added to his pocket calendar. Ernst always kept notes, just in case.

"While you have your pocket calendar out I have a few addresses to give you, too. Our good friend Giese is at the Hotel Rheingau on Mittelstrasse. Griesbach is staying in Hermsdorf just outside Berlin on Silvesterweg 6. They have a telephone, 47-43-46. Ernst Moller is in Berlin, too. I don't have an address but his telephone number is 66-74-50.

Ernst scribbled the numbers and names in the back pages of his pocket calendar. When Lenchen sat without speaking Ernst decided it was his turn.

"It looks like I will be working for the government as a translator of some sort. It means I will have to travel a lot, but I've made good arrangements for the children."

"The children! Where are the children?" Lenchen asked throwing up her hands as though she had forgotten all about them.

"I thought you would never ask!" Ernst smiled and relaxed for the first time since meeting his sister at the door and talked at length about the accommodations that had been made for the children. He finished by saying, "the welfare office that oversees schoolchildren for the NSDAP, makes most of the decisions.[20] I don't make the majority of decisions for them anymore."

"Well, it seems you have everything in hand, Ernesto. How are Carl and his wife? When will I see them?"

Ernst smiled broadly. "Carl had his teeth fixed. He has a terrific smile! Carl looks the same, a little thinner perhaps. He wants to keep working at the factory but Inge is trying to persuade him to defend the cause in a more *productive* way."

Lenchen was taken aback, "Do you mean she thinks he should head off to the front?"

"Carl only said she thinks he should do more than he is doing."

"Is he going to go? I can't imagine Carl as a soldier. He is such a . . . free spirit."

Ernst shrugged and rubbed his jaw before responding. "I don't know what to think, and he hasn't made a move one way or the other since we arrived. I don't think he will join until he is forced to."

The rest of the conversation concerned Carl and Inge. Ernst explained that Inge worked long hours at the hospital. All the anesthesia had been sent along with any hard liquor and other essentials to the front. This made her job extremely difficult, but she managed. Ernst reported that some of the food shortages in the area were due to severe frost in the spring that ruined the wheat and rye crops. Carl and Inge cultivated a small garden. Things seemed quite comfortable for them and the two seemed happy.

Ernst and Lenchen spoke for more than two and a half hours, but Bio had not yet returned when Ernst finally got up to leave. Lenchen had Ernst write down the name of a contact, Walter Fessel in Przyfullen, with whom he thought she might find a job. Ernst embraced his sister and left in high spirits for Carl and Inge's apartment in Potsdam. He enjoyed having new information to tell Carl and Inge at supper that evening.

On Saturday morning, July 25, Ernst went to the station in Potsdam to pick up Heinz. It was Heinz's birthday and he had made arrangements with Dr. Kuhlmann to send Heinz to Potsdam. Ernst arrived at the station a few minutes late, as usual, and most of the passengers had already made their way out of the area. *He must be hiding*, Ernst thought, and he put on his disinterested *I'm not concerned look*. He strolled along the platform expecting Heinz to pop out from behind a corner at any moment. Heinz liked a game as much as anyone.

After several minutes Ernst became concerned. Heinz was not anywhere. He started asking questions. "Have you seen a boy, about twelve years old? Did he get off with you?" But to no avail. Ernst decided that something had happened and that Heinz had remained in Hohenelse. *He must be sick*, he thought, *or maybe he missed the train*. Just then a man in uniform approached him, "Herr Contag?"

"Yes?"

"Heil Hitler."

"Heil Hitler."

"I have a message for you from Dr. Kuhlmann in Hohenelse. He asked me to give this to you. When he said it was about your son, I told him I was returning to Rheinsberg-Hohenelse in three days and that I would bring a response if you wanted to send one."

"Thank you." Ernst replied with a look of concern. He took the paper into his hand, unfolded it and read the message.

```
Herr Contag.
    Heinz is in Rheinsberg until
tomorrow. We brought him to the
hospital for a hernia operation
that was successful. He is on his
feet.
    I can make arrangements for him
to visit Potsdam next Saturday.
    Please advise.
                        Dr. Kuhlmann.
```

Ernst took out a pencil and wrote on the back of the note.

Thank you for your note. I will meet Heinz on August 1 in Potsdam. Give him my regards.
Ernst Contag

Ernst handed the uniformed man the slip of paper and thanked him for serving as messenger. He walked back to the apartment.

Heinz. . . in the hospital for surgery! Ernst tried to shrug the news off by arguing with himself that it was a common operation and that Heinz was in good hands. Then something occurred to him that made him cringe. Inge had told him the hospitals and clinics had *no anesthesia.*

NOTES TO CHAPTER FIVE

1

> Hab Sonne im Herzen,
> ob es regnet oder schneit!
> Ob der Himmel voll Wolken.
> die Erde voll Streit!
> Hab Sonne im Herzen.

In a curious turn of events Ernst Contag sent this poem (in German and with his own English translation) in a letter to Richard Nixon dated July 22, 1968, nearly ten years after he shook Nixon's hand at a celebration of Ecuadorian independence in Quito. In his letter Ernst added, "Because of the people, who all wanted to greet you it was not possible to express my thoughts to you, but I do it now during the important political moments around you an[d] my best wishes for you, to be nominated as President of the United States." Richard Nixon answered with a personal letter on August 27, 1968. He wrote, "Mrs. Nixon and I have a deep feeling of friendship toward the people of Ecuador and it was a great honor for us to represent the American people on a visit to your land. Your letter brought back wonderful memories and assures us that there will always be a strong bond of good will and brotherhood between our nations."

Ernst sent the poem again in November 1972 in honor of the president's reelection. Maxwell Chaplin, the Deputy Chief of Mission at the Embassy of the United States of America in

Quito, Ecuador, thanked Ernesto Contag on Nixon's behalf in a letter he wrote on January 4, 1973.

[2]"Wow. Snot really flies!" Translation from Spanish.

[3]*New York Times.* June 2, 1942.

[4]*New York Times.* June 3, 1942. "…members of one group from German prison camps had been difficult to identify, and that they had been sent unexpectedly to Portugal in the general exodus of Western Hemisphere diplomats and other nationals."

[5]*New York Times.* June 2, 1942, p. 5. "subsequent voyages would carry 'bargain' nationals, or those selected by the belligerent nations to be traded, one for the other."

[6]Cherries. The family had never seen cherries, which were unknown in Ecuador.

[7]Fado is melancholy folk music.

[8]E.Contag 1942 pocket calendar.

[9]The word "Legation" is an official word used for people who work as part of the State Department's diplomatic corps. "Legation," in this case, refers to people who make up the group of people being moved by the official legations of each country. The term is used in official and non-official documents and reports in 1942.

[10]Fatherland.

[11]*The New York Times* reported on famous people traveling on the Drottningholm from Lisbon. *New York Times*, June 18 and 19, 1942.

[12] The Ernst-Weinstein-Strasse in downtown Stuttgart only existed until 1945 and was renamed Sophienstrasse after the war. The "Offenhäuser Hotel and Schankwirtschaft" was owned by K. Franck. Several articles about the arrival of the German Americans were published in the newspaper. On Tuesday, June 23. 1942 (p. 2) the *Stuttgarter Neues Tagblatt* reported the "Amerika-Deutsche" who arrived in Stuttgart were met by members of the Overseas Organization, the NSDAP and greeted by the mayor of Stuttgart, Dr. Strölin. It is listed as the second train of exchanged internationals to arrive in Stuttgart.

[13] *Guineos* and *oritos* are different kinds of bananas. The *oritos*, or "gold nuggets," are small, plump, sweet bananas. *Guineos* are common bananas. In Ecuador, bananas were considered "green gold" because the banana export business brought in a good deal of money to the country. *Mote* refers to cooked corn kernels. The *mote* kernel is similar to hominy, and is yellow or white in color. When *mote* is prepared with pork chitlins or fried in pork fat, it is called *mote sucio* or dirtied *mote*. The *guatusa* is a large hairy rodent that is native to South American jungles. Carl and Ernst would have hunted guatusas during their teen years in Ecuador.

[14] C. H. Contag interview. *Gringuitos* was the term commonly used to refer to children of European heritage or appearance.

[15] 1942 Pocket calendar. Reichsmark (RM). Monetary unit.

[16] "My hat has three corners" and "I am a young lad from Quito."

[17] The newly revised world map was made for the windows of the National Cash Register Company at 50 Rockefeller Plaza according to the article on page 29 in the *New York Times* published on June 21, 1942.

[18] Leonidas Plaza Lasso and Luis Felipe Borja del Alcázar were arrested after they stormed the presidencial palace and tried to depose Arroyo del Río on May 28, 1942. Plaza Lasso fled Ecuador with the help of his brothers José María and Galo Plaza Lasso. The three brothers were the sons of diplomat, general, ex-president Leonidas Plaza Gutiérrez and his aristocratic wife, Avelina Lasso de Plaza.

[19] *New York Times*. Friday, July 3, p. 2.

[20] Nationalsocialistische Volkswohlfahrt.

CHAPTER SIX

BLOOD AND HONOR

MARK BRANDENBURG, 1942

Karl-Heinz pulled his handkerchief from his pocket and rubbed the metal face of his belt buckle until its luster glistened in the morning light. *Blut und Ehre.* The two words, blood and honor, and the shiny eagle on his buckle made him feel proud. He was finally a full-fledged German Youth member with medals to prove his abilities. He had excelled in swimming, marksmanship, and even in war game strategies.

Everyone called him Karl-Heinz now, his given name at birth, except for his family, of course, who still called him Heinz. The first few weeks at the training center for foreign-born German youth at Hohenelse had not gone very smoothly, but now, weeks later, he had completed the training in Hohenelse with high marks and felt comfortable around the other *Ausländer* boys who went to class with him. He was used to the three minute drill in the morning, could wash and dress as quickly as anyone, and had swum to the island on Rheinsberger Lake and picked apples with the other good swimmers.

Karl-Heinz had really only made one big mistake since his arrival at Hohenelse. On the second day after he arrived he saw many boys lining up under orders, so he joined them. But the fellow giving orders had yelled at him. Karl-Heinz had not understood that the orders were for boys involved in forced exercise after getting three checks for improper behavior. "You don't belong here! Get out of here!" He had not understood the word "schleifdienst" and had mistakenly joined the boys who were scheduled for their exercise that, in this case, required the perpetrators to do fifty-one push-ups and a few lengthy headstands. The leader's rude treatment left him in tears, but he was glad not to get involved in the other boys' punishment. On that day he determined to learn as much German vocabulary as quickly as he could, and to complete all the necessary requirements without making any mistakes.

Karl-Heinz had turned twelve on July 25, too old for the grade school at Hohenelse-Schlaborn, and therefore, he was scheduled to leave Mark Brandenburg in September. The German Welfare Office, the NSV, had placed him in a school in Kassel that was quite far to the west. He had discovered Kassel's location on a map in the classroom but he really had no sense of where Kassel was or what sort it life he might find there.

Karl-Heinz put his leather briefcase on the bottom bunk in the bedroom he shared with three other foreign-born German boys. He pulled his orientation papers and books out of the briefcase, stuffed in some clothing for his trip to Potsdam to see his father, and secured the leather straps. He combed his hair and carried his baggage down to the entrance of the boarding house where headmaster Kuhlmann was to meet him moments later.

The complex of buildings was called the *Nationalsozialische Reichsjugendheimstätte Jugendorf Hohenelse-Schlaborn*.[1] It was under the direction of the NSDAP's organization as a youth home for foreign-born Germans. The school on the lake had been in operation since 1935 although the buildings had been around since 1905.

It was peaceful and warm in the sun. The long, two-story, red-tiled buildings that made up the school campus surrounded Karl-Heinz. The buildings were a mixture of red brick and whitewash, the roofs gabled and some of the buildings neatly decorated with a half-timbered look and curious, arched windows or an onion-topped turret. He had never seen anything quite like the buildings. What he liked most about the *Jugendorf* was that the campus was right on Rheinsberger Lake surrounded by a thick pine forest. Karl-Heinz kicked at a pinecone while he waited for the headmaster who would take him a few kilometers along the shore to Rheinsberg where he would pick up the train for Berlin.

His enthusiasm for the weekend with his father was tempered only slightly with the anxiety of starting up at a new school in a different city.

"What do you think Kassel will be like, Dr. Kuhlmann?" Karl-Heinz asked somewhat anxiously.

"Oh, you'll get along. Kassel is an industrialized city of about 200,000 people, and I imagine that will make it less inviting than Hohenelse is with its big Rheinsberger Lake and tall trees. But you'll get along just fine." Dr. Kuhlmann slapped Karl-Heinz gently on the shoulder as though he were trying to build confidence. The boy tried not to cringe, but the gentle jolt had caused him to tighten his abdominal muscles, still tender from hernia surgery.

"Your father will meet you at the station in Potsdam. Are you excited about spending the weekend with your father?"

"Yes sir, Dr. Kuhlmann!"

"That's good. And don't you worry about Kassel. I went through Kassel on my way to Luxembourg once. It was a long time ago, but it won't have changed much. You'll like it there once you get used to it. You'll be living in a family too, and joining up with a German Youth program in Kassel, so you'll make some friends."

Karl-Heinz put his hand out to shake Dr. Kuhlmann's hand, but the headmaster clapped him informally on the shoulder instead and turned away. Karl-Heinz once again curled his shoulders to protect his healing abdomen. He was alone and made his way to a seat on the train. It was not long before the train pulled away from Rheinsberg and headed south for the Berlin area. The gentle rocking of the train would have been pleasant except for the pressure it put on his belly and every so often he winced in pain.

About a week before his birthday he had felt a strange sensation on his abdomen near his left pelvic bone. Then, all of a sudden an unusual bulge popped out. The bulge hurt, and it looked strange, so he asked Herr Vagt, the youth leader, to look at it that morning before school. Before he knew what was happening, he was on his way to the clinic in Rheinsberg for surgery!

Karl-Heinz retraced the events that led to the scar that he touched gently through his clothes with his second and third fingers.

"But it doesn't hurt that much," Karl-Heinz had tried to argue to the doctor. "Shouldn't we wait for my father?"

"No."

The doctor had not explained anything to him. "Prepare the boy for surgery," he told the nurse as he walked out of the room. The Rheinsberg clinic was nothing special to look at. It was a sharply gabled, two-story row house that looked just like the rest of the houses attached to it on either side on the main street. It was simply painted a different color and people knew which house was the clinic.

"What is it?" Karl-Heinz had asked the nurse, pointing at the bulge on his abdomen.

"A hernia. Your intestine has bulged out so the doctor has to stitch up the hole in the abdominal wall under your skin. You'll get very sick if he doesn't tuck the intestine back in and stitch it up." She smiled briefly, then her eyes turned colder and she stiffened. "You'll have to be brave, though. All the anesthesia has been sent to the front. The doctor will stitch you up quickly, but you have to hold very still. It will hurt some. If you move, it will hurt more and take longer."

Karl-Heinz's eyes bulged and he swallowed hard. With some trepidation he nodded, "I'll hold still."

It was not easy to think about the surgery even now, weeks later. Karl-Heinz was glad it was easy to forget the pain after some time had passed. He had felt *everything!* Suddenly, he hunched his shoulders and screwed up his face. The moment the doctor forced the tip of the blade into his abdomen . . . that was unforgettable. Karl-Heinz had held his muscles taut. He clenched his teeth and fists allowing his nails to dig into his palm as the doctor drew a painful slit across the tender skin. When the doctor returned to the initial puncture to begin cutting what Karl-Heinz suspected was a lower layer of muscle, he felt tears well up in his eyes and he tried to concentrate on the lesser pain in his palms. Then he felt his calves cramp as he curled his toes under and held himself stiff as a board.

The doctor worked over him seemingly unaffected by the job at hand or by the crippling pain of his patient. From the position on the surgery table Heinz could not see the doctor's ice blue eyes, and he felt that at least he was spared the doctor's cruel stare. He tried to concentrate on the thin strands of hair on the doctor's bald head, but the wisps of hair that, in any other situation, might have made him laugh, could not keep his attention. The nurse had tied him down tightly to the table and soon after the doctor began prodding his abdomen he felt his bound hands and feet get cold and numb from a lack of circulation. He felt a cold shiver run across his belly. It must have been a metal instrument. Then something warm, perhaps his own blood as it soaked through, dripped down toward his navel. He tried to concentrate on the ceiling overhead, but the noises around him distracted him back to the searing pain and the strange prodding and pulling in his abdomen. Then it fell. Clank. Metal on floor. The doctor had dropped an instrument! Heinz was caught off guard by the noise and jerked suddenly. Pain. "Hold still!" the doctor yelled, "or I can't finish this off properly."

Karl-Heinz froze again. He took in a quick breath between his clenched teeth, held it, and stared without blinking at the ceiling. His eyes began to water again, but the smarting made him feel better. The prodding and pulling seemed endless, but finally the doctor finished the stitching and he was rolled back to a room where another patient lay groaning.

The pain was continuous hours after the incision was closed and Karl-Heinz refused to move. When a nurse approached his bed some time later to check the stitches he managed to say, "It hurts."

The nurse touched his head and smiled warmly. "I know."

The sympathy was too much for him and he blinked the tears away, letting them fall to his ears before he wiped them. He was in too much pain to drink or eat . . . and he couldn't imagine moving, or walking again . . . ever! The nurse had forced him to drink and he remembered that he had no kind words or thoughts for her whenever he finally felt the urge to relieve himself. He had determined never to move again of his own free will. He wouldn't sit or stand up. No. Not for anybody. He lay there stiff as a board day after day and, in this way, managed his pain until the surgeon came to the head of his bed four days after the surgery. Heinz froze under the gaze of the man's cold gaze.

"Sit up!" the man barked. Karl-Heinz made an uncommitted effort before returning his head to the pillow. The doctor barked the command again, and shoved his hand behind Heinz's head thrusting him violently to a sitting position. Heinz shrieked.

"See," he said to the nurse snippily. "He can sit up."

The doctor left the room and four days later Heinz was released from the hospital and sent back to Herr Vagt, Fraülein Cotthaus, and headmaster Kuhlmann. What a birthday present that trip to the Rheinsberger clinic had been!

Heinz shook off thoughts of the nightmare at the hospital and mumbled to himself, "Blood and honor. I have medals and a scar to prove I am worthy of the motto and the eagle on my belt buckle!"

During the week that Ernst waited for Heinz to arrive he had managed to keep busy with odd jobs. He filled his days by running necessary errands for himself and his children. One of his first stops was the German National Socialist Workers Party welfare office on Westfahlia Strasse near the Ferberlliner-strasse Square where he had scheduled a meeting with Herr Kraus for Monday, July 27.[2] Ernst was noticeably nervous and found himself scribbling the four items he wanted to discuss with Herr Kraus in the back pages of his pocket calendar as he waited: teeth, housing, furniture, money. It seemed funny that he felt he needed to write the four items down. Surely he would remember them, but when he arrived at the office he was glad he had written in his pocket calendar.

Herr Kraus started with the information concerning the required garments for the children's participation in the German Youth program. All children ages ten to fourteen years of age were required to participate in the German youth. Children over fourteen would be required to join the Hitler Youth. There were special uniforms and the cadets could earn medals through their participation. Herr Kraus provided a list of the requirements and how the items could be located if Ernst did not have everything already. There would be a government stipend for the children in the care of others, he explained. Karl-Heinz was to be transferred to a high school in Kassel. He wrote down the date for his departure on a small sheet of paper.

"Do you have an address for the school, Herr Kraus?" Ernst asked.

"*Nein.* He will be assigned a family as soon as he arrives in Kassel. We don't make these arrangements before the child arrives in the city. Once he is placed in a home we will get you the address, Herr Contag." Herr Kraus was genuinely helpful and Ernst was pleased.

"So, this is not a boarding school for boys?" Ernst inquired.

"*Nein.* It is a high school but the boys are housed in private homes. The name of the school is the Hindenberg School according to the information I have here." Herr Kraus flipped through a few more papers and then told Ernst how to get the necessary ration cards to make purchases. "Don't forget to get them some warm clothes for the winter, Herr Contag. It is warm now, but the winters are cold here . . . in Kassel, too."

"I have heard about the winters from my brother."

When Herr Kraus finished explaining where and how to find clothing, Ernst brought up the matter of dental care. Herr Kraus sent him to speak with a colleague named Schoenemann who helped Ernst make arrangements for family dental care before sending him on to Herr Müller at Westfahlia Strasse 22 to get more specific information about the government stipend for the children and other social matters of concern like finding housing, furniture, and economic help.

Ernst was surprised by the amount of government assistance that accompanied a centralized regime. Still, money went quickly. By the end of July Ernst totaled money spent at 738 Reichsmarks! He had spent 620 on travel, five on laundry, fifteen on cigarettes, sixty on meals, and seven on fun and postage.[3] Ernst registered at the World Mail Association's Foreign Office on Bissingerstrasse in Berlin and filled out an application for a position as a bookkeeper for the Blankenburg and Ziehe Company.

Today, with Heinz, he planned to go shopping for jackets and overcoats. The children would begin their schooling at the end of September and would need a coat for winter weather. It was a priority to get Heinz's clothes in order since he was leaving the area. Ernst hoped to visit the children often, but also needed to plan for the possibility that he might not see them for extended periods of time.

Ernst was so anxious to see Heinz that he actually arrived at the station on time.

"Papa!" Karl-Heinz called out when he finally spotted him.

"Well, it looks as though the doctor did a fine job!" Ernst cajoled his son.

"What do you mean?"

"I can't see any scars!"

"Papa. It was a hernia operation," Karl-Heinz said looking embarrassed, "The scar is *under* my clothing. Right here."

"I see," Ernst said nodding with a roguish expression on his face. "It looks like you came through it all right."

"It was horrible," Karl-Heinz added dramatically with a scowl.

Ernst pulled a pair of socks out of his suit pocket. "I brought you an extra pair. They should almost come up to your knee! Put them in your briefcase for now. We don't need to drop your things off at Carl and Inge's apartment before we go downtown, do we?"

Karl-Heinz shook his head.

"No? Good. This is all you have right here. When we finish shopping we'll eat and then you can tell me all your stories."

Karl-Heinz was all smiles. A day alone with Papa! He opened his briefcase and tucked the socks into the top before pulling the leather straps through the buckle.

"This way!" Ernst said cheerfully.

Potsdam was a city and much larger than the few buildings at Hohenelse. Karl-Heinz thought it would be fun to walk around the city looking at the buildings and the people. The first stop was at the *Stadtschloss* they had seen the day they arrived in Potsdam, a short walk from the train station.

"This castle was designed by the architect Knobelsdorff. It took eighty-seven years to build it!"

"Wow! That is a long time," Karl-Heinz responded. "I like all the statues on the roof, Papa. How did they get them up there?"

"I don't know how they would have done it back then. The castle was begun in 1664. They must have used pulleys to get the sculptures up there, I suppose. They are quite impressive, aren't they?"

"Yes, sir."

"Do you know what? Frederick the Great lived in this palace. King Frederick Wilhelm I and Queen Louise lived here too, I have been told."

Karl-Heinz tried to place faces with the royal names, but couldn't.

"Climb up there and show me how you would act if you were king of the palace, Heinz." Heinz climbed between the two-headed sculpture at the base of a stairway to the palace and Ernst took a picture. Karl-Heinz put on a serious face for the photo. He was warm in his dark sweater. He had overdressed and did not feel anything like a king.

Karl Heinz poses for his father outside Potsdam's town castle (Stadtschloß) before being transferred to Kassel to attend high school. The palace and the sculpture were destroyed by bombing in 1945.

They left the palace courtyard and strolled down Humboldstrasse until they reached the domed Nikolai Church at the other end of the palace.

"I bet the Nikolai Church is fifteen stories high! Wouldn't it be fun to see Potsdam from the top of the dome, Heinz?" Ernst asked.

"Oh, yes, Papa. Can we go up there?"

"No, I don't suppose they let people go up, but they should!"

There were mostly women in the streets, few men, and no children. Karl-Heinz was perplexed at why there were no men or children, so he asked his father to explain.

"Many of the young men are soldiers. The older men and the women have had to take over their jobs. That is why you see so many women working. The children, of course, have been taken out of Potsdam in the event of a bombing."

"So, lots of German boys and girls are separated from their parents just like we are separated from you?"

Ernst nodded. Knowing this did not make either feel better about the separation.

"I'm quite hungry. I did not have breakfast this morning, remember Papa?"

Ernst nodded, "Neither did I. I know a restaurant that serves food at this hour. It is not far from here."

When the bowl of soup Ernst ordered for his son arrived, it smelled strange. Karl-Heinz did not lean over to sniff the vapor that wafted toward his nose, but instead lifted the spoon to his mouth without sniffing and tasted a mouthful. He tried not to make a face, but his father was aware that something was wrong. He squelched a laugh and stated rather dogmatically, "They put castor oil in the soup. It is good for the digestive system."

"But it tastes awful, Papa!" His father remained quiet on the subject so Karl-Heinz lifted the disgusting spoonful to his mouth with reluctance and finished what he knew was going to be his lunch. He would have preferred throwing it down the toilet if he had not been so hungry.

Karl-Heinz leaned over the table and whispered to his father, "The food is a lot better at Hohenelse, Papa! Maybe the teachers will let you come and stay with us! You'll get really skinny on this rancid stuff!"

"Oh, I don't eat this too often, Heinz. The food will probably be better in Kassel. You'll be in a home there."

"Oh, have they told you where I am going in Kassel?" he asked.

"Not yet," Ernst replied.

"It is awfully far away, Papa. I saw where Kassel is on the map. I am not sure I really want to go that far away," Karl-Heinz said with a shrug.

"Well . . . I am looking forward to taking a trip over to see you there in Kassel. How else do you think I am going to get to see different areas of Germany, Heinz? With you in Kassel, Irmgard in Nuremberg, and Werner in Hanover, I'll get to travel cross-country every once in a while. What a great adventure that will be."

"I'll be all alone there, Papa. What if I don't like it there?" Karl-Heinz asked rather sullenly.

"You are growing up, Karl-Heinz. When I was your age I already had a job. Now let's go do our shopping." Ernst stood up and paid the bill.

When the two were alone later on, Karl-Heinz asked his father a question that had been bothering him since their arrival in Berlin five weeks earlier. "Do you remember when we were in Berlin and we saw a Jewish man walk past us really fast?"

"No, I don't think I remember." Ernst looked instinctively to see if they were indeed alone.

"Well, I have been wondering, Papa. We learned in school that the government makes the Jews all wear a star. Why does the government require all the Jews to wear a star?"

Ernst thought a moment before answering. "They wear the Star of David. It is a symbol of their beliefs. The government wants the Jews to wear a star to indicate to others that they practice the Jewish faith."

"The boys at my school wear a uniform to indicate that they are part of the German youth. Is that the same sort of thing?"

"Yes, I suppose so," Ernst said.

"So, it is kind of like the priests wearing a cassock or a Roman collar, right?"

"Yes. Something like that . . . so we know who they are."

Karl-Heinz shrugged. "Well, I don't understand why some of the other boys make such a fuss about the Jewish star then."

"It isn't very popular to be a Jew in Germany, Heinz. That is why the other children say those things. Children repeat what they hear from the adults around them. Don't pay attention to them."

Heinz shrugged in agreement. "I need soap at school, Papa. Could you buy some for me?"

"Let's do that now, then we'll go up to Sans Souci to enjoy the day *without worries*," Ernst suggested.

At Sans Souci they talked about Karl-Heinz's operation and Ernst winced at his son's description of the surgery and recovery. He really did not want to hear any details, but he let his son talk his way through the ordeal.

"Papa. . . Hohenelse is a nice place and, well, I suppose Kassel will be fine, too, but when do you think that we'll go back to Ecuador? Do you think we'll go back in a year or so?" Karl-Heinz asked.

"I don't know, Heinz. I don't know when we'll go back. I don't think we'll know the answer to that question for a long, long time."

The two walked in silence down the sandy walkways of the Sans Souci palace grounds. Every once in a while they stopped to look at an unusual plant or tree or to comment on another unusually beautiful view of a minor palace. The afternoon went by quickly.

By evening it was clear to Ernst that Karl-Heinz was doing well at the school in Hohenelse. His son was proud of his accomplishments at the school. He even enjoyed going out and working in the fields with the other children and competing in swimming races and marksmanship. Ernst noticed that Karl-Heinz's German proficiency had improved considerably in a few short weeks, and he seemed quite sure of himself although every once in a while he stumbled over vocabulary. Ernst was pleased with his son.

When they found themselves saying good-bye the following day at the station in Potsdam, his father was surprised that his son looked so upset.

"I looked in your pocket calendar, Papa. You didn't write down when you are planning to visit. Will you visit me soon, Papa?"

Ernst pulled the calendar from his pocket and thumbed up to the first two weeks of August. The pages were bare. "You are a sneak, Heinz," he said jokingly. "Yes. If you see your brother at the school grounds, tell him I will try to come on Sunday for his birthday."

"Can we go for a boat ride then, Papa?" Karl-Heinz's eyes revealed his excitement and he waited motionless for a response.

"Perhaps," was all Ernst said before Karl-Heinz began a little gallop around him repeating in a singsong voice, "A boat ride, a boat ride."

Ernst was smiling because he felt a bit silly with his son dancing around him but Karl-Heinz soon realized how young his antics must have made him look and he quit.

Ernst explained his reluctance to commit to a date. "It all depends on work that I find, Heinz. But I will come to visit as soon as I can. I am going to make arrangements for Irmgard to come to Rheinsberg before I take her to school in Nuremberg. Then we can all go for a ride in a boat on Rheinsberger Lake if you want."

"What about Werner?" Karl-Heinz asked, surprised at his omission.

"He will stay in Hanover with Oma and Opa. He is too young for boarding school and your grandmother thinks she can still handle him. Well, get aboard now, Heinz."

Karl-Heinz hugged his father and clambered aboard with his briefcase strap over his shoulder. He waved at his father who stood on the platform until the train pulled away. Each was alone again.

Two days later Ernst was called up for an urgent business trip that took him to twelve different cities and villages. While on the business trip, he missed Ernstchen's birthday on August 9, but payment for a completed job meant that he could finally open an account as a businessman. On Thursday, September 3, Ernst opened an account and received his Postparbuch Number 6.949.146.[4] He deposited 300 Reichsmarks on September 3. It felt good to have money in the bank.

Ernst had no contact with his family for weeks. When he arrived at Carl and Inge's home in the second week of September, he learned that he had missed out on many things. His sister, Lenchen, had moved in with the Wosatka family, the repatriated restaurant owner from Quito, who lived on Hohenstanger Strasse in Berlin. She had a room on the third floor of the building and she had a regular job although he did not know what it was. Ernst had also received a letter from the Recruitment Office dated September 10, 1942 that his brother had laid out on the table for him to read.[5] It said:

```
The Recruitment Office-Foreign Com-
mand Division informs you that,
according to the decision of the
Armed Forces High Command, the Ger-
man Reich citizens who were swept
back from America that were re-
quired to pledge under oath not to
bear arms for the duration of the
ongoing war will not be called up
for Military Service. Therefore, —
even if you report as a volunteer—
you will not be called to serve.
Sign and return the enclosed form.
```

Ernst was secretly pleased with this document as he now had ready proof for anyone who demanded that he join the armed forces. He put the letter with his important identification documents and carried them on his person whenever he thought it might be necessary.

The welfare office notified Ernst that Karl-Heinz would be sent to Kassel, the capital of Hessen-Nassau, in September but they still did not have an address or family for him. Ernstchen was also to be moved from the orientation classes for foreign-born Germans held in Hohenelse to regular academic courses. Irmgard was to be placed in Nuremberg.

Ernst organized a well-deserved family picnic with Heinz, Ernstchen, and Irmgard at Rheinsberger Lake on Saturday, September 19.

"Come on, Heinz," Irmgard called to her brother. Let's go in the boat."

"They call me Karl-Heinz now, *Irmgardchen*," he responded with a tone that indicated he was older and much more grown up than his sister.

"Who's that?" she retorted gleefully and chased her brother, Ernstchen, down the green slope to the lake that was filled with reeds.

Karl-Heinz, Irmgard and Ernstchen climbed into an old rowboat near the shore for fun. Karl-Heinz was wearing his new German Youth uniform and he looked proud and happy. Ernstchen kept looking overboard to spot a fish that he might grab with his hands. Irmgard sat daintily in the dress her father had bought for her with some of the money from the sale of her mother's china. It was her favorite dress and she was already growing out of it.

Ernst had borrowed a camera for the outing and snapped a picture of Heinz, Irmgard, and Ernstchen from the shore. The boys and their father took turns rowing the boat. Karl-Heinz and Ernstchen had rowed the boat into some nearby reeds and, for a while, Ernst wondered if he would have to roll up his trousers and wade into the water to get the boat free. With a shove of the oar, Ernstchen freed the boat and rowed into shore. It was a perfectly wonderful afternoon with Papa. Only Irmgard whined about Werner being all alone at Oma and Opa's house in Hanover.

Irmgard had not spent time at Hohenelse even though Schlaborn house for small children was nearby. The tall pine, birch and linden trees towered over her and she enjoyed walking on the forest floor that was covered with pine needles and cones. Except for the grassy area where the Hohenelse school buildings were, little sunlight streaked through the towering branches.

"Papa, are there many kinds of animals in this forest?" she asked.

"I am sure there are deer and wild boar roaming around here." Ernst kicked at the ground as he spoke. "I am surprised that this soil is so sandy around here. It is a wonder that the farmers can grow a good crop of corn, rye or potatoes in this soil!"

"They have apple trees on the island, Papa. We went to pick some after we swam over there a few weeks ago," Ernstchen offered. "Fraülein Cotthaus said that if more of the farmers go to the front we'll get to go out into the fields to help with the harvest. I think I would like that a lot more than sitting around in a classroom spelling words and learning history."

Ernst walked out of the forest to a grassy slope near the lake. His children followed him and sat near his long legs. Ernst closed his eyes and took in a deep breath. The children's happy voices fed his soul. He thought to himself, "I wish you could see us now, Elisabeth, surrounded by whispering pine trees and cool, fresh water. I wish you could see the children, so young, so fresh, so happy . . ."

"Papa," Irmgard interrupted his thoughts, "Why do we have to go far away to school? Why can't we all stay right here? It is wonderful here in Hohenelse. I could live here forever!" She stretched her neck and took in a full breath. "Mmmm. It smells so good!"

Ernst decided not to answer his daughter's question. No explanation was really going to convince anyone of anything. Certainly a seven-year old would not understand the influence of government policy in her life.

That evening Ernst said good-bye to Heinz, who was scheduled to leave for Kassel a few days later, and to Ernstchen, whom he expected to see often in Rheinsberg in the following months, and he boarded the train for Nuremberg with his daughter. It was clear that after Ernst delivered Irmgard to her foster family in Nuremberg every member of his family would be located in a different city. He tried not to dwell on the notion of separation. It was the way things had to be.

When Ernst and Irmgard arrived in Nuremberg it was morning. Ernst took his daughter to the washroom to clean up and then they made their way to Velserstrasse 42. Fräulein Maria Renaud answered the door. She was a young, energetic, and to Ernst's way of thinking, an attractive woman. She was slender, tall, and quite fair. Maria's manner of speaking led Ernst to believe that she was refined and well educated. Her home was clean and stylish. She even had a piano and knew how to play it. Irmgard seemed happy enough to be in her home and she called her new mistress *Tante* Maria.

Ernst spent the day with Irmgard and Maria. He was surprised that Maria made him feel so welcome and he remembered another Maria that had made him feel the same way. By afternoon Ernst felt that the arrangement with Maria would be a very good one for Irmgard, and quite possibly . . . for him. *Perhaps his mother-in-law was right. Maybe he should think of . . . no, his heart always belonged to Elisabeth.*

Irmgard unpacked her things with Maria's help while Ernst smoked a cigarette outside the two-story house. Maria tried to help Irmgard feel comfortable in her new home. Although she talked about all the school children Irmgard would meet and the garden she could help tend, the little girl felt ill at ease, and as soon as she could she went to look for her father.

Irmgard spoke from her heart. "But Papa, you were away a very long time when I was with Oma. Can't you stay here a while longer? We have only had a little time together. I'll be all alone here, Papa. All alone. Please stay," Irmgard pleaded.

"Maria will be with you, and you will be fine."

"I won't be fine. I won't." Irmgard pouted.

"You will," he said encouragingly with a smile.

Irmgard threw her arms around her father's neck and held him fast. "I won't," she said defiantly with a strangle hold on her father. "You'll just have to stay or take me back with you."

"In the last few weeks have you grown any new ribs?" he whispered as he poked her gently in the side. Irmgard shrieked, dropped her arms to protect her ribs, and giggled.

"You're not ticklish, are you? Let's count your ribs! One . . . two . . ." Irmgard squirmed and laughed as he teased and tickled her.

Just then Maria appeared at the door and turned the lights out. It was nearly sundown. "When will you come back to get me, Papa?" she whispered.

Ernst bent down and kissed Irmgard on her forehead. "Very soon, *mihija*."6 Now, go to sleep."

Ernst knew in his heart of hearts that he was telling his daughter a lie.

When Irmgard was asleep he went to say goodbye to Fräulein Renaud. "Thank you, Maria. I will try to come back for a visit in a month or two. It depends on my work schedule. I want to visit Heinz in Kassel, too."

"Your son is in Kassel?" Maria inquired rather surprised. "You have children all over the country, Herr Contag."

"Please call me Ernst, *Tante* Maria," he smiled warmly.

"Yes, Ernst. Please write down my mother's name, Frau Wagner Renaud." Ernst wrote down the name and address she gave him reluctantly. He did not see any reason for keeping Maria's mother's name in his pocket calendar. Maria explained, "She has good connections and could help you if something happens."

"What is going to happen, Maria?" Ernst asked, perplexed.

"Things happen. You never know. It is just a good thing to have contacts right now in Germany. Anyway, you've got her address in your pocket calendar. That is good."

Ernst did not understand the significance of the address and he left the house feeling somewhat confused. *She is an interesting woman, this Maria. Very attractive. Very knowledgeable. Mysterious. Every reason to keep my distance*, he thought.

Ernst returned to Potsdam, but Karl-Heinz did not see his father again before he set off for Kassel a few weeks later. Kassel was one of the best-known railway cities in Europe, he had learned from Dr. Kuhlmann. It was known for the Henschel Gemein train factory, the largest in Europe. Karl-Heinz never thought about the Henschel Gemein factory creating a safety issue for the city, but many others, including Dr. Kuhlmann, had thought about it. Dr. Kuhlmann had wondered how smart it was for the NSV to send the boy to Kassel, but he had not said anything to Karl-Heinz.

After a long train ride Karl-Heinz got off the train in Kassel and a government official from the NSV met him and walked him to a community shelter.

"You will stay here until arrangements can be made with a family," he said rather curtly. "Yes, sir." Karl-Heinz did not even have the courage to look at his face. There were a number of people at the community shelter but Karl-Heinz did not strike up a conversation with anyone. Suddenly he felt very much alone. The minutes dragged on and he wished he could get back on the train and return to the familiar surroundings in Hohenelse. Instead, he rested uncomfortably in a makeshift bed in the community shelter. Three days went by and no one came to take him from the shelter.

On the third day Karl-Heinz did not recognize the official who had brought him to the shelter, but he stood when he saw a man, a woman and a girl approach him and call his name.

"Here he is," he heard the man say. "Karl-Heinz, we have made arrangements for you to live with Frau Rümler." Karl-Heinz shook the hand of the woman in front of him. Frau Rümler seemed pleasant enough. She was a tiny, delicate woman who looked to be a good ten years older than his aunt Lenchen. She wore her hair parted just off-center and pulled it gently to the back of her head. Her hair seemed somewhat severe for her gentle, kind face.

"Hello Karl-Heinz. It is a pleasure to meet you. This is my daughter, Ursula."

Karl-Heinz looked at the daughter who smiled sweetly at Karl-Heinz. And, as far as girls go, she seemed nice enough. He guessed that Ursula was about fifteen years old, about two years older than he was. Karl-Heinz imitated his father's stance when greeting a woman. He leaned over slightly, put out his hand and stated in formal German, "It is a great pleasure to meet you, Frau Rümler. Fraülein." He repeated the formality with her daughter who considered his affected charm a real giggle.

"Excuse me," Karl-Heinz added. "I should get my things."

"Here is the paperwork, Frau Rümler," the NSV official said as he guided her toward a table.

Ursula waited for Karl-Heinz who returned momentarily. When he was standing just a meter from her she said with a smile, "Karl-Heinz, you can call me Uli. All my friends do."

"All right," he responded without emotion.

"Have you been here at the community center very long?"

"*Drei Tage!*" he replied holding up three fingers.

"Three days!" she exclaimed. "I wish my mother had known! We would have come sooner. She saw the announcement only yesterday! Well, we are glad you are coming home with us today. Our house is much more comfortable than the center."

"Thank you."

"My mother said that you are from very far away. . ."

"Well, sort of. I've been at a school for foreign-born German children. The boarding school is in Hohenelse. It is a ways from Berlin. A bit north, I guess. But my home is in Quito."

"Quito?" she repeated with a questioning look.

"Yes, the capital of Ecuador. It is a small South American country right on the equator. . . on the Pacific side."

"That *is* far way!" Uli said with awe. "What brought your family to Germany?"

Karl-Heinz puffed up like a peacock. No one had really asked him about his trip or why his family was in Germany and he was determined to explain how his family was blacklisted and deported, scattered and alone. He summarized briefly and spoke mostly about his family.

Karl-Heinz added an afterthought, "My youngest brother, Werner, is almost six years old and he is staying with my mother's parents in Hanover."

"Is your mother there with him in Hanover, then?" Uli asked.

"No. She contracted typhoid fever when I was seven. It is a common illness in Ecuador. She died in Quito," Karl-Heinz said rather flippantly trying not to encourage any sympathy.

"I'm really sorry about your mother . . . we lost my brother, Martin, a year ago. He was a soldier in the war. He was only nineteen. I really miss him." Uli's tone was sympathetic and it made Karl-Heinz feel uncomfortable that he had been so flippant about his mother's death. He changed the subject. "Do you live very far from here?" he said, looking around.

"No, not far at all," Uli answered with a smile. Her mother called from the doorway to the street, "Come on, you two. Let's go home."

On the way to the house Uli repeated the story that Karl-Heinz had told her about his family.

"What a shame your family is so split up," Frau Rümler shook her head. "It isn't easy for anyone in times like these, is it? It seems to me that the VDA should have been able to find a school somewhat closer to Potsdam. It doesn't seem right for the welfare agency to split up families like this . . . anyway, it is a good thing that you have come to live with us, Karl-Heinz. My husband has military duties and he is away."

"He is an officer," Uli piped up proudly.

"We have plenty of room for you and it will be nice to have a young man like you around the house," Frau Rümler added.

"Thank you, Frau Rümler," Karl-Heinz responded energetically trying to please the small, gentle woman.

"Oh my, Karl-Heinz!" Frau Rümler stopped short. "Frau Rümler sounds so formal! If you are going to be living at our house, you'll have to call me *Mutti* just like Uli does. Do you think you could do that?"

"*Jawohl*, I suppose I can," he responded with a nod. Her warmth was comforting but somewhat unnerving.

"*Gut*. That will be just fine with me. Is that all right with you, Uli?

"Oh yes, Mutti," she responded, but Karl-Heinz wasn't quite sure what to make of the whole exchange. He would have to see how things went around the house before he really would feel comfortable calling this small-statured woman *Mutti*.

The cobblestone streets they walked looked well maintained and quite decorative with interesting designs. They crossed over streetcar tracks that ran in front of the St. Martins Church that Frau Rümler pointed out. The houses along the street were tiled in red and they appeared to be well looked after. Many had chimneys jutting out from the roofs. The area looked remarkably clean and neat. After a short walk they arrived at the edge of the city where there were fewer houses and a lot of greenery. They walked down a small incline that passed a green area that Uli said was a park that had government bunkers buried below seven meters of rock.

"There are three entrances. I'll show you where the steel doors are later. The bunkers are not for us, though. They are for the people who work at the commando building down the street. We will go into the basement if the sirens go off." Uli hesitated before she added, "I can introduce you to the neighbors, too. You'll like them, I think." Uli was very friendly and Karl-Heinz started to feel more at ease.

At the end of the park she pointed to their house on the corner. The house at Trottstrasse 18 was a two-story, whitewashed duplex with a good-sized garden to the right side of the front entrance. There were a few houses nearby, but it was quite obvious that they were at the outskirts of the city.

"The railroad tracks run beyond that house there," Uli pointed straight ahead. Old Grandpa Farber lives over there. You have to watch out for his flying axe."

"Oh, stop your teasing, Uli," Frau Rümler said as she opened the heavy wooden door to the house.

"Well, he did kill a chicken by throwing an axe, Mutti! I saw him do it, Karl-Heinz. It was really tragic!"

Karl-Heinz shrugged. Most chickens died by the axe. This old Grandpa Farber was just a little more creative than most. He snickered through his nose, but didn't say anything.

Frau Rümler changed the subject. "The Strecker family lives five houses down the street just this side of the railroad tracks,

Karl-Heinz. They have a boy about your age. I'll ask if he can go with you to school the first few days until you get your bearings."

"That would be nice, mm . . . *Mutti*," the word felt strange in his mouth and he stammered a bit.

Frau Rümler opened the front door and Karl-Heinz let Uli go in ahead of him. His eyes took a few minutes to adjust to the darkness. The first thing that Karl-Heinz saw when he entered the house was a wooden staircase that went up from the vestibule to the second floor.

"The bedrooms are upstairs and the kitchen and living room are down here on the first floor," Uli said. "There are so many doors in each room that you can go from room to room in a circle on both floors of the house," Uli laughed. Her laugh was contagious and Karl-Heinz smiled. "So, you can't get lost at all!"

Karl-Heinz thought to himself that living in the house might be fun if he could chase his brother, Ernstchen, in circles but he didn't know what to think about Uli. If Ernstchen were here they would slip and slide across the hardwood floors and have a terrific time. Somehow, chasing Uli didn't appeal to him much . . . at least, not yet. Uli did not act at all superior. She was fun-loving and made him feel happy. He was already growing to like her.

Karl-Heinz learned quickly that the kitchen and living room were heated. They were his favorite spaces in the house when it was cold outside. The chilly, upstairs bedrooms reminded him of his own bedroom in Quito. Uli had warned him that the upstairs rooms would be even colder in the winter, and he was not looking forward to those frigid days. There was a bed and a dresser for him to put things in, and for Karl-Heinz, the accommodations seemed quite comfortable.

Frau Rümler and Uli tried to make Karl-Heinz's living situation as normal as possible. They got a government pension to house him but what they wanted most was to be sure he was happy.

Heinz still acted as though he felt very much alone. Everything he did seemed to make him feel alien. In Ecuador he had felt accepted no matter how different he was physically from other Ecuadorians. He always felt "at home" in Quito. He realized now that he had never known anything different. In Kassel his very self seemed to be in sharp contrast to what everyone wanted him to be. He had begun to "look and act" German like everyone else, but it was perhaps this outward similarity that made him feel so much like an outsider.

The two Rümler women asked him many questions about his family and his homeland. They sympathized with his family's situation and this helped to build a stronger bond between the three of them. The women introduced him to the neighbors and made sure that he met Ottokarl Strecker whom he could befriend, if he chose to. They corrected his German when necessary and involved him in their home life as much as possible. Frau Rümler was delighted to have another person in the house to dote on and Uli felt that she had another chance to have a brother to tease and to care about.

Although Frau Rümler was open-minded about most things, she warned Karl-Heinz not to mix languages or talk about growing up in Ecuador when classes began at school. She reminded him that he should only use German in their home, and when she caught him listening to a Spanish language radio program one day she hurried to turn it off. "Under penalty of death," she whispered fervently, "Under penalty of death." Her eyes were fiery and he felt as though he had committed an unforgivable crime.

"There is to be no, absolutely no listening to non-German stations, Karl-Heinz. *Verstehst du?* You could be shot. You could get us in trouble ... terrible trouble!" Karl-Heinz apologized and promised not to repeat the offense, but secretly he wondered what could be so terribly dangerous or criminal about listening to a Spanish radio broadcast.

"It must be that they can't understand it," he mumbled to himself when he was alone. Later that week he learned that the threat to body and limb was real. The first day at the Hindenberg School on Wilhelmshöhe Avenue Karl-Heinz used Spanish to impress some other kids who did not think that he had really come from South America.

"Claro que sí," he said all puffed up with pride. "Soy de Quito, Ecuador."[7]

Before he could translate what he had said, the teacher who was nearby slapped him hard in front of the other kids. "Only German," the teacher yelled at his stinging cheek. "What do you think you are doing, fool?" Karl-Heinz felt humiliated. He learned a painful lesson: nothing foreign is acceptable even if it was a part of who he was. He kept his family history secret and never talked about Ecuador or used Spanish again at school.

All the teachers at Hindenberg High School were male and Heinz learned quickly that because he was an *Ausland Deutscher*[8] the teachers paid special attention to his development. Their plan was to keep him in line and teach him how to act and speak like a *real* German. The second week of school a substitute teacher in Herr Cors' classroom was reading some boring literary piece about a lion. The teacher's inability to read with any expression led to snickers around the room and Karl-Heinz's glee was too obvious for the teacher to ignore. The substitute teacher called him forward and slapped him so hard that Karl-Heinz turned around three times in front of the class before scrambling back to his chair, red-faced and humiliated. The room was silent but the teacher called two other students forward to receive what they already knew was their painful fate. The three boys sat with lowered eyes and a swath of red finger marks on one cheek.

At least Herr Cors was more interesting to look at, but he had a way of making Karl-Heinz feel very uncomfortable. Herr Cors was nearly bald, with just a few wisps of hair circling his shiny head, just above his ears. The baldness made his beady eyes all the more piercing. Karl-Heinz took him for a man in his fifties or sixties like his own grandfather, but that was where the similarity ended. He had been in Herr Cors' classroom for just a few weeks before the man really turned on him. On a cool day the first week of November, Karl-Heinz was called to the front of the room, all eyes on him as he walked toward the teacher.

"*Komm hier*," Herr Cors barked. "Today we will make an example of you, young man."

Karl-Heinz could feel his ears getting red and instinctively started to smile with embarrassment.

Herr Cors shouted out several questions, none of which Karl-Heinz could answer. The first question was about German history. The second was about German geography. The third left Karl-Heinz shaking his head wondering why he was still in front of the class. The words "Ich bin kein Deutscher" ran through his mind, but admitting that he was different would only make things worse for him. He was sure of that.

Karl-Heinz did not know whether it was that he shook his head, or the fact that he had not answered one question correctly, that caused Herr Cors to lose his temper, but it was obvious that he had when the teacher slapped him across the face and yelled, "You have one month to learn these things, Herr Contag. *Ein Monat!*"

Karl-Heinz stood motionless as the color burned into his cheek. Tears welled up, but he blinked them back while he waited to be ordered back to his seat.

"Return to your seat. You see, class, this is what happens when students don't take learning seriously. Greater Germany needs serious students who pay attention and learn, not thugs who don't bother to study." Karl-Heinz turned and walked to his seat unable to look at the students around him. He was the only foreign-born German at the school. It seemed unfair to him that the teachers expected him to know exactly the same things the other students knew. They had grown up in Germany. They did not know anything about *Ecuadorian* history . . . or *Ecuadorian* geography. . . or *Ecuadorian* people. . . like he did. It seemed *so* unfair. He felt tears well up in his eyes.

He left school alone that day, certain that not even Ottokarl Strecker would want to walk home with him. Karl-Heinz felt angry and frustrated and never wanted to go back to that classroom. He was too embarrassed to say anything to Frau Rümler when he arrived at home.

Two days later Karl-Heinz learned that someone had arranged for a tutor for him. His tutor was kind, but firm, and he liked her well enough, glad to have anyone help him avoid another incident at the school. He studied hard and listened closely to everything his teachers said. He still made mistakes, but even Herr Cors seemed more tolerant of him.

In the afternoon sometimes he listened to German music on the radio. When everything else seemed wrong, he would close his eyes and listen to the music. He learned to recognize different pieces and he could identify the composers.

Ottokarl became a good friend. He and Ottokarl were in the same German Youth group as well as the same class. The German Youth groups were organized by age and by section of town. Each group had a leader, a *Gruppenführer*, responsible for teaching them songs, teaching them to march and to obey orders. Most of the boys admired the *Gruppenführer* and followed his lead blindly. Karl-Heinz was skeptical. One Sunday morning the group leader suggested the boys steal sausage. Karl-Heinz could tell being a leader was all about power for them. Some boys stole sausages but Karl-Heinz and Ottokarl couldn't take what was not theirs. Food was scarce, but neither could justify stealing —yet. In general, there was water, some milk, a few vegetables, mostly carrots and cabbage, some cheese and a little meat when they could buy or trade for it. But Karl-Heinz learned that he could not steal. He told his friend, Ottokarl, that he had taken a popcorn ball once from a shop down the street from his house, and that incident still bothered him.

Ottokarl laughed, "I might do it for something sweet like that, too, Karl-Heinz! Yum, a ball of crunchy, sugary, popped corn. But I'm not going to take things just because those bullies tell us to. They are so full of themselves."

He liked Ottokarl. He was an ally and Karl-Heinz needed an ally. Uli Rümler also became something of an ally.

Uli was scandalized to learn that Karl-Heinz not only did not attend church services regularly while he was growing up, but that he did not even know the Lord's Prayer.

"We went to church on Easter Sunday this year," Karl-Heinz offered. "But it was raining and the candied eggs got all wet. The ants ate them. I didn't even get to try them."

"Well, Easter is not just about candied eggs, Karl-Heinz! An Evangelical Lutheran has to know his prayers."

Karl-Heinz shrugged but agreed to make Uli happy. He repeated the prayer dutifully after Uli, "Vater unser . . ." Karl-Heinz learned to pray regularly and eventually took pride in saying the Lord's Prayer. It had come in handy those first few months in Kassel, too. It had been several months since he had seen his father and every night after Christmas he prayed the Lord's Prayer just before asking God for a special gift.

"God bless Irmgard, Ernstchen, Werner, and Papa. Keep them safe. It would be a good thing if Papa came for a visit. Amen."

Ernst Contag came for a visit on February 6, 1943, a Saturday. Karl-Heinz was ecstatic when he saw his father at the doorway. He was just at that awkward age when jumping up and down was embarrassing, so he grabbed his father around the waist and hugged him. The embrace went on so long that his father had to break the hold with his hand. He greeted Frau Rümler by standing stiffly and bending over in a gentleman's bow to kiss her hand. This was not a common greeting and Frau Rümler and Uli were on the verge of giggling. He was invited to take his things to Karl-Heinz's room and come downstairs for something to drink and eat. Ernst looked rather haggard to Frau Rümler, who noticed he was missing a button on his dress shirt.

"If you have any mending Herr Contag, Uli is quite a good seamstress. She would be pleased to sew on a button or two, wouldn't you, Uli?"

"Yes, of course," Uli responded rather unconvincingly. Karl-Heinz saw her chase her mother into the kitchen and he laughed to himself. He did not want to share his Papa, but was proud to show him off to the Rümler women. It pleased him to no end that they were going to dote on his father.

When he was alone in his room his father spoke to him briefly in Spanish. Karl-Heinz faced his father and warned him of the house rules. "Keep the conversation in German," he said wide-eyed. "Under penalty of death!" he quoted Frau Rümler in a pertinent whisper. Ernst chuckled to himself, but he did not break the house rules again.

After a welcome cup of ersatz coffee, some rolls with preserves, and a brief conversation with the Rümler women, Karl-Heinz took his father on a brisk walk to downtown.

"It was nice of the two Rümler women to offer to mend my clothing," Ernst said.

"Oh, they do a lot of sewing and knitting. Mutti . . . Frau Rümler belongs to the *Frauenwerk* group in town. They knit socks for the soldiers and that sort of thing. She doesn't belong to the *Frauenschaft* organization, though. I don't think she is too concerned with government policies and that sort of thing. She is really very nice to me."

"Yes, I see that. And it looks like you are getting plenty to eat," his father added.

"Oh, they have some cherry, pear, and apple preserves in the basement that are really delicious and they share everything with me. You saw the English garden they have beside the house, didn't you, Papa? Well, I helped with the harvest last fall and I'll help with spring planting, too. The best thing about the food at the Rümler's is their tradition of the *Bett Hupfal*. Uli said that having something sweet, especially chocolate, before you go to bed is a tradition in Bayern. So, whenever she can, Frau Rümler gives us a *Bett Hupfal*. I love that!"

"You'll be spoiled, Heinz."

"Papa," Karl-Heinz said with pride, "some of my classmates think I should be an artist when I grow up. I did a drawing of Little Red Riding Hood and everyone, even the teacher, was impressed."

"Is that so?" his father said, sauntering at a comfortable pace.

"They call me Karl-Heinz all the time here, too, Papa. I think I am finally used to the name. One of my schoolmates called me 'Karl' once and I didn't know he was trying to get my attention. And no one says 'Grüss Gott' or 'Guten Morgen.'[9] I walked into a shop the first week I got here and the shopkeeper raised his arm and shouted 'Heil Hitler.' It surprised me because we didn't do that every morning in Hohenelse."

"I am sure it did surprise you. That is the way it is a lot of places now, Heinz." Ernst thought about how absurd it must have been for his son to get used to the patriotic, military side of life in Germany after growing up in Ecuador. No one in Quito could even have imagined saying 'Viva Arroyo del Rio' for any reason at all.[10] Politicians and leaders were always considered crooks in Ecuador. It would have been absurd to put them on any sort of pedestal.

Karl-Heinz continued, "I went in to buy something at the shop because I had some government money from the NSV welfare office. I get some money and candy sometimes. Anyway, the shop was almost bare. There was a big glass jar with pickles in it. That was all there was, so I bought one pickle with my money. It was this big." He used both hands to indicate a pickle at least 35 cm. long. "I ate the whole pickle all by myself, too," Karl-Heinz said somewhat sheepishly, just a little ashamed for not having shared his find with Uli and Frau Rümler or his friend Otto. "I have shared my chocolate with Uli and Ottokarl, but the pickle was so delicious and I really couldn't break it into pieces."

"I bet it was wonderful! I might have gobbled it up myself if I had been there. Mmmm. I can taste it now," Ernst said smacking his lips.

Karl-Heinz giggled. "But Papa, the strangest thing was that, when I was leaving the shop, I met another customer who was coming in. When the shopkeeper called out 'Heil Hitler' to him like he did to me, this guy just mumbled something I couldn't understand. The shopkeeper repeated his greeting, 'Heil Hitler,' but I didn't hear the customer say anything. There is a man in the neighborhood who just tips his hat and says 'Guten Tag' instead of 'Heil Hitler.' His name is Herr Dresen. Some of the other children laugh at him when he says that, but I don't. I think it's normal to say 'Good morning' sometimes."

"I agree with you and Herr Dresen, but the children must just be used to hearing 'Heil Hitler' all the time. When in Rome . . . Say, how are things at school?" Ernst inquired, changing the subject. "That is . . . besides your fantastic art projects, of course."

"Well, the other day there was a boy at school who got into big trouble because he mixed up all the caps and no one could find which one was his." Karl-Heinz laughed loud enough for his father to hear him. "Lots of the other boys got to take a swat at him, and Herr Cors gave him a good one, too." Karl-Heinz lowered his voice a bit. "Herr Cors is famous for swatting at us."

"You speak as though you have had some experience, Heinz," his father added inquisitively.

Karl-Heinz decided not to tell his father about the punishments he had received. "Not really. I have had some trouble with the irregular German verbs, but I guess I am doing fine. The teachers are pretty strict, but I don't have a tutor anymore. I don't need one now. There aren't any other foreign-born German boys at my school so it was kind of tough for me at first. My teacher seems to think I have to know everything right away. I can't talk about Quito or use any Spanish and I am supposed to know all these words in German and how to understand their mathematics system and geography and history and Latin and, oh I don't know . . . I'm supposed to know everything the rest of the boys do, I guess." By the end of his statement Karl-Heinz was showing his frustration.

His father was sympathetic, but did not show any signs of it to his son. "You are a very smart boy, Heinz, and I know that you will study hard and keep up with your learning." They walked a while in silence before Karl-Heinz made an announcement.

"I have a new friend, Papa. His name is Ottokarl. He lives just down the street from the Rümler house. We do some things together. He is in my German Youth group, too. I think you'd like him."

"That's good. Your brother Ernstchen has made friends, too." Ernst smiled and pulled his collar up around his ears. The wind was chilly. He picked up the pace. "Irmgard is staying with a very nice woman in Nuremberg. I think she will make friends at the school there. I will go to Nuremberg to see her after I finish this next interpreting job at Henschel Gemein. I'll go to see

Irmgard next weekend. I am pretty sure I will be working in Danzig the next two months, March and April.[11] I wanted to come and see you before I left."

"Thanks, Papa . . . Is Danzig far away?"

"Well, . . . yes." He blew a bunch of air from his cheeks and the frosty air made it look as though he had just exhaled smoke. He wished he had a cigarette. He curled his hands in his pockets and shivered. "Let me see, how can I explain it without a map. I know . . . it is about as far from Kassel to Berlin as it is from Berlin to Danzig if you keep traveling north and east. The city is located on the Baltic Sea in East Prussia, where the Contag family was from originally.

"Do we have any relatives there?"

"Tante Grete Contag in Berlin gave me the address of a Hermann Contag who lives in Königsberg, a city just north and east a bit of Danzig, but I don't really know anything about him. I think he raises horses. Maybe I'll contact him when I get there."

"Who is Tante Grete?" Karl-Heinz asked, not recognizing the name.

"Tante Grete is a wonderful woman, with a cheerful face, Heinz. She is Onkel Bruno Contag's wife. Onkel Bruno is my grandfather's brother's son. Tante Grete has helped me through a great number of difficulties since we came to the Berlin area. She is a small woman, about the size of Frau Rümler, and she pulls her hair back in the same way, swept to the back of her head and pinned there. She has tiny hands and fine facial features and she serves me tea whenever I go to her house." Ernst leaned over toward his son and said just above a whisper, "She is a good cook, too. She can create great desserts even in difficult circumstances and with sugar so hard to find. She is the kindest and gentlest of all the people I have met in Berlin. I like her very much."[12]

"Oh. She sounds very nice, Papa. What about Werner? Is he still with Oma and Opa in Hanover?"

"Of course. I visited them in November. Oma is fine, but Opa has been a little bit sick. He complains about how cold it is all the time. It is hard for Oma. She tries to keep the house warm, but there isn't a lot of coal to go around."

"He could put on another sweater like I do," Karl-Heinz added.

"If Opa doesn't improve, I'll see if I can move Werner to Maria Renaud's home in Nuremberg. Irmgard is doing very well there and the connections to Nuremberg are better for me. I don't know . . . I think your grandmother needs a rest. Your little brother can sometimes be a wild monkey. He is a lot like you and Ernstchen!"

Karl-Heinz laughed but tried to set the record straight. "I'm not a wild monkey any more, Papa. I'm twelve years old. I am almost old enough to join the army!"

Ernst stopped in his tracks. "You stay in school, Heinz. The army is no place for a boy your age. The army is no place for anyone when there is fighting going on."

Ernst complained of the cold so Karl-Heinz showed him a short-cut to the Rümler house.

"See that park there, Papa? There are three entrances to a bunker underneath that park. There are seven meters of stone over the bunker and then grass. The bunker was built for the military personnel who work in the General Commando building which is right over there." Karl-Heinz pointed to a large building a few blocks away. "Do you know what, Papa? Uli and Frau Rümler packed a suitcase that has a book about their family, their jewelry, and a few other things that they take with them whenever there is an alarm. For now we will have to go to the basement because the bunkers are just for military personnel, but the neighbors think that pretty soon they will open the bunkers to the public. It is sort of scary to think that bomber planes could come here. Do you think they will, Papa?"

Ernst put his hand on his son's shoulder and said, "It could happen and you should be prepared, but it isn't something you should spend a lot of time thinking about, Heinz. Just keep your wits about you and be quick on your feet."

"Do you have a special suitcase with our family's stuff in it, Papa?" Karl-Heinz asked.

"No. I carry my papers on me. You, Ernstchen, Irmgard and Werner are my little treasures. You wouldn't fit very well into a suitcase, would you?" Ernst answered with a laugh. "So, how are you and Uli getting along?"

"Great, I guess. She is a girl, you know," Karl-Heinz said emphatically. "Sometimes she treats me like a younger brother, but for the most part . . . we get along. She is funny and she makes me laugh. One time we played with an old helmet that belongs to her father. It is one of those helmets that have a point on top of it. We laughed so hard we could hardly breathe! Boy, that was fun! Sometimes she says I am 'frösh.' What does she mean by that, Papa?"

"You'll have to ask her," Ernst said with a chuckle. "She probably thinks you try to get away with more than you ought to."

"Uli is famous, Papa! When she was only fourteen years old she competed athletically in Breslau in Silesia! She was one of the ten top athletes in running, throwing, and the long jump."

"Really!" Ernst commented enthusiastically.

"She is a leader of the local BDM and says that the girls yell and scream a lot when they are in formation, but no one dares to box their ears or punish them while they are in uniform. The youth groups get away with a lot of things when they are dressed in uniform!"

"I suppose they do. I bet you get away with plenty, too, Karl-Heinz. I am cold now. Shall we go inside?"

Uli and Frau Rümler listened to news that he shared with them after his travels in Germany. He told stories about Irmgard and Ernstchen over a cup of ersatz coffee and some tasty rolls that the two women had prepared. Ernst promised to visit again when he could. "I hope to come for a visit at least twice a year, if you think it would be all right, Frau Rümler."

"You are always welcome here, Herr Contag."

In private he told Frau Rümler that he hoped to take the children on a family vacation in July. "I'll send news about the details as soon as I can."

"Karl-Heinz would enjoy that very much, Herr Contag."

Ernst Contag spent several hours at Henschel Gemein and left on a train that evening for an interpreting job. The following weekend he visited with Maria Renaud and Irmgard. The visits with Heinz and with Irmgard were over practically before they began. The only time in his life Ernst remembered traveling so much was when he moved lumber for a company in Ecuador in the early twenties. After the visits he was confident that Heinz and Irmgard were in good hands and safe. He started to sleep better.

Just as expected, the Monday after he returned to Potsdam, February 15, Ernst received word from Berlin that his new assignment would be Danzig, at the Sales Department of the Color, Dye and Paint Industry's Shareholders Stock Exchange.[13] On Monday night he left for Danzig.

For more than three months he would spend his days working and his evenings alone in a rented room in Frau Nankel's house. There was no reason to write letters. The German mail system was no longer functioning. His daily routine was simple. Work. Eat. Sleep. Work. At night when there was nothing to do, he would let his imagination take him to thoughts of his children. He started planning a summer vacation, envisioning hills and lakes, long walks, picnics, hugs . . . the thoughts kept him sane. He had no idea what his children were doing or whether they were safe or not. It was better to avoid thinking about it.

Karl-Heinz counted the days after his father's visit until the end of April. For some reason he expected his father to show up in Kassel the first Saturday in May but he did not. He did not visit on the second Saturday in May either. On Monday, May 17, just after midnight, the air raid alarm sounded and Karl-Heinz ran to the bomb shelter with Uli and Frau Rümler. It was dark and everyone kept repeating they had to be quiet. They waited in fear surrounded by a few children who were crying and their mothers who tried to comfort and quiet them. Karl-Heinz heard Uli pray and he imagined Frau Rümler must have been wringing her hands. Karl-Heinz wondered how long they were going to stay in the bunker. The wait seemed endless and they had only been inside a few moments. He was tired but too anxious to sleep.

Uli turned to Karl-Heinz and whispered, "Do you want to pray the *Our Father* with me?"

Karl-Heinz nodded and they began. When the sirens finally sounded the all clear the families made their way back to their homes in the dark. Their house had not been hit and they did not see damage anywhere nearby. But the following Monday, at school, the school children were recruited for clean up. The British had bombed the Sperrmauer Dam and the Eder Lake had flooded the towns and pastures below the dam.

Ottokarl and Karl-Heinz went with the other boys from the school to help in the small towns. The ride in the truck was fun at first until they saw several bloated cows lying in mud, surrounded by broken wood, furniture and more mud. They saw a house that was completely blown away except for two walls that leaned against a tree. There were piles of dirt and rocks, tools, household goods, clothing, and lots of mud. The worst damage, it was rumored, was in the town of Affoldern which had been completely flooded, but they did not hear about how many people were hurt or dead. No one doing clean up asked. None of them really wanted to know.

The two boys climbed out of the truck and unloaded a shovel. Instead of talking about the work at hand Ottokarl asked, "Did your father come on Saturday like you thought he would?"

"No. Maybe my father will come next Saturday," he said with a shrug as though he were not worried. He picked up another piece of broken wood that looked like the leg of a chair and tossed it into the pile. "When he was here in February he said he was going to work in Danzig on the Baltic Sea, but he thought he would finish up in April. He might have gone to see my sister first in Nuremberg. I don't know."

Ottokarl lowered his eyes and his voice. "When I see all this damage I worry about my family, too." He pushed the shovel into the pile of muck and wood, a heavy load for a twelve-year old boy. "So many men have just disappeared, you know. My mother doesn't even talk about getting news anymore. It seems that the news is always bad. So and so gave up his life for Greater Germany. Everyone is afraid to talk about it." No one else was near them, but Ottokarl barely talked above a whisper, "I look at this rubble and I wonder if we'll be here when the men from our area come back or if they'll ever come home. Every day I wonder if I will die."

"Cut that out! Don't think like that, Ottokarl! I wouldn't have anyone to kid around with if you weren't here driving me crazy." Karl-Heinz tried to cheer his friend, but the recent air raid and personal experience with the smelly muck left by the broken dam and damaged towns and farms had made both boys worry about their situation and their families.

In Ernst Contag's case there was little to worry about. At 3:30 in the afternoon on May 17, 1943 Ernst was in good spirits and quite healthy, heading back to Berlin by way of Königsberg. The railway at Danzig was out so he made the final leg of the journey north to Königsberg on horseback with a horse lent to him by his relative, Hermann Contag. He took some pride in being resourceful in difficult travel situations, and he certainly was not afraid to ask for assistance when he needed it. He arrived just in time to take the 10:30 p.m. train out of Königsberg to Berlin.

He was exhausted, but too restless to sleep. This was a happy trip, he thought, very different than the emergency trip he had made a month earlier to Hanover. On April 17 he was notified in Danzig that there had been a death in the family and he was to travel to Hanover immediately. Opa Dreier had died. When he arrived in Hanover on Wednesday, April 21, the day after the celebration of the Führer's birthday, his mother-in-law, whom he had called *Mutter* since his marriage to Elisabeth, was beside herself with grief. She greeted Ernst with a warm embrace and weary smile. "Werner is still asleep. He couldn't sleep last night. Many nights now, Ernst, the boy has nightmares." Oma sighed and rubbed her forehead. "He cries at night, Ernst. I can't take it. He was afraid for months when Opa was so sick. This is too much for a little boy." She wiped the tears from her face and sat down at the table. Ernst followed her and sat without saying a word. "You must take Werner to Nuremberg. He is devastated. I cannot take care of him now. He needs to be in a different home for a while. Maybe later I can do something. I don't know . . ."

"You've done so much already, Mutter. I can't tell you how much I appreciate what you have done. You should have someone come in to help you. Perhaps you can get someone who is doing their required apprenticeship year."

"They are just more work than I can handle, Ernst. It is just like in Ecuador. You have to train them like you have to train the maids. I don't want to train anyone to cook and clean. It is just easier to do things myself."

Ernst reached for his mother-in-law's hand and they sat in silence. After several minutes had passed, Cecilie Dreier looked at her son-in-law and sighed deeply. "You haven't slept either, Ernst. I'll get some breakfast. Then you can make the travel arrangements. No. While I prepare breakfast I want you to go through Opa's clothing." She blinked back tears and continued with a voice that cracked and then grew stronger, "I put some things in a box that you can use. The socks are in there. The rest is on the bed. I couldn't sleep last night either. Take whatever you can use and carry. There is a small straw suitcase in there, too."

Ernst spent two days with his mother-in-law. They both knew it was unlikely he would return to Hanover now until the war ended. He fixed a few things around the house, and had afternoon tea with Oma, Werner, and a few ladies who stopped by to express their condolences. Werner shadowed his father everywhere around the house and outside. The house seemed empty to him without Opa Dreier. Oma helped Ernst pack Werner's things, but she insisted Ernst go through her husband's clothing, shoes, and leather belts alone. At night Ernst slept with Werner curled up at his side. Two days later, on Friday, Ernst and Werner said good-bye to Oma and got on the train for Nuremberg.

Ernst thought about how Werner had clung to his arm when they were on the train. "I am six years old now, Papa."

"Yes, I know. How did you celebrate your birthday with Oma?"

"And Opa." Werner interjected somberly. "Oma made a cake and I got some candy, too. I told Opa I wanted a pocketknife, but he said I had to wait until I was a little older. He was going to teach me how to whittle. Do you think *you* can teach me?"

"Yes, I suppose I can."

"When, Papa? Before I turn seven?" Werner asked excitedly, hoping to get a knife sooner than he expected.

"I think Opa was right. You will have to be a little older."

"Do you know what, Papa?"

"What?"

"I like to fix things. Oma and Opa let me fix all sorts of things around the house. Opa used to say that I was going to be a *genier* when I grow up because I like to take things apart and put them together. Do you think I'll be a *genier*?"

"An engineer? That sounds like a good profession to me."

"Oma said I have to go to a special school to be a . . . gen . . . an engineer."

"Oh yes. There is a special school called *La escuela de artes y oficios* in Quito.[14] That is a good school to learn how to be an engineer."

Werner gave his father a strange look. He could not even repeat the name he heard. *What* in Quito?

It was then that Ernst realized Werner was losing his grasp of the Spanish language. He translated the name of the school for Werner and told him to put his head against his arm. It was going to be a long trip and they needed their rest.

"Why did Opa have to die, Papa?" Werner asked, his eyes filled with pain.

"No one ever knows why someone has to die, Werner. He was sick and old. People die when they get sick and old," Ernst said trying to comfort his son.

"I don't want to get sick and old, Papa. I don't want to die," Werner snuggled under his father's arm.

"I don't want you to die, either, Wernerchen. I want you to grow old so you can take care of me. Do you think you can help your brothers and your sister take care of me when you get bigger?"

"Of course, Papa. And we can take care of Oma, too, can't we?"

"Yes, Wernerchen. We can take care of Oma, too. Now, go to sleep," Ernst said, closing his eyes.

Ernst shifted his weight and tried to relax. It was dark in the rail car and there was absolutely nothing to distract him from his thoughts. His last visit with Maria Renaud in Nuremberg had been delightful and somewhat worrisome. He and Maria had taken Irmgard and Werner to the forest on a Sunday where they enjoyed a picnic and a long, tranquil walk. With each visit he made to Nuremberg, he and Maria had grown fonder of each other. During the two-day April visit she had gotten very close to him physically which made him nervous. It was clear to him that Maria loved Irmgard like a daughter, and she took to Werner as though she had known him all his life. Part of him resented the closeness she had to his children. On the other hand, he thought to himself, she would make a good stepmother for his children. Ernst was well aware that these thoughts had already crossed Maria's mind.

At one point, when they were alone the evening before he was to return to Danzig, she sneaked up behind him and said just above a whisper, "We could raise these children together, Ernst." She was so close to him that he could feel her breath as she spoke. He jumped from the chair. "Maria," he had managed to say before he started an odd dance. He was aware that she watched him move into the next room lifting his legs and arms in the absurd manner he always did when he was uncomfortable in a situation with a woman. He was smacking his thumb against his right hand and making, what seemed to her, a strange hissing sound through his teeth.

"You look absolutely ridiculous, Ernst!" Maria said covering her laughter with her right hand. "What *are* you doing?"

Ernst stopped after a few more exaggerated steps and then stood motionless for a moment before shaking his head.

"It is clear that you have never set foot in Ecuador, Maria. Everyone in Ecuador knows what this hand gesture means. The hissing sound, made by taking in breath through clenched teeth, just adds emphasis. All this means is... is that I am in trouble!" he said while smacking his thumb noisily against his hand. As Maria approached him he make a hilarious face and repeated, "Big trouble!"

"You're not in big trouble," Maria said as she chased him around the room.

"Yes I am, yes I am," he called out just a few steps ahead of her. The two ended up laughing hysterically in the living room, but Ernst made no moves toward getting any closer to Maria that day. He was glad to leave just after midnight for Danzig, via Berlin.

Now, three weeks later he was on his way back to Berlin. The first order of business was to celebrate Irmgard's birthday on Thursday. *An entire year has passed since we were at the Greenbrier Hotel.* He shook his head. *Unbelievable. An entire year!* As he drifted off to sleep in the train one thought perturbed him. He was not concerned about his brother, Arturo, who never arrived in Germany. He was not concerned about Heinz in Kassel. He did not think about his job in Danzig. The only thought that bounced around in his weary mind was *Maria. What was he going to do about Maria?*

On Wednesday, June 2, 1943, the second anniversary of the victory in Crete,[15] Carl Contag left for military duty. Ernst felt uncomfortable staying in the apartment with Inge. It would not have been prudent for him to continue living there. In addition, he was angry that she had encouraged his brother to enlist. *This is not his battle*, he thought. Ernst packed his bag and went to Tante Grete Contag's house on 25 Wilhelm Street in Berlin for a few nights. She had a way with Ernst, and by the time he left for a weekend with Ernstchen in Rheinsberg, he was happy-go-lucky again. He spent two days with Ernstchen and then returned to Potsdam to find a room to rent at 11 Kronprinzen Strasse from Frau von Kauffungen.

While moving things in the apartment he felt a sharp pain in his abdomen. *Could it be possible?* he thought. On June 11 he sent notice to his employer that he was scheduled for a hernia operation. On Sunday he left his apartment for the hospital, and by Wednesday, June 16, he knew exactly how his son, Heinz, had felt on the operating table. What was more, there were complications and a nasty struggle with pneumonia. Coughing affected the stitches and he had to be very careful. He did not get out of bed until June 28 when his lungs finally cleared of fluid. On June 29 Dr. Labenka signed the release from the hospital and issued an order for three weeks of rest and mineral baths at the state-owned spa half way between the Austrian cities of Salzburg and Vienna.[16]

Ernst returned to Frau von Kauffungen's home on Kronprinzen Strasse. He waited four hours, but when Frau von Kauffungen did not return he decided to stay with his sister at her apartment in the Wosatka's home in Berlin. He was exhausted and weak, but secretly delighted with his sister's doting. He also looked forward to the doctor's prescribed treatment. In Quito the doctor would have issued bed rest in the chilly confines of his own home on Rocafuerte Street. Burg Kreuzen sounded much more relaxing and inviting. If he could get the children together, they would thoroughly enjoy the vacation time.

The following week he applied for a new job with the Trans Ocean Packing and Shipping Company in Berlin. Ernst agreed to the interview when the company told him that he would be allowed to take the doctor-ordered cure at Burg Kreuzen. The trip would go on as scheduled if he passed the entrance examination for Trans Ocean Berlin. He passed the entrance exam on July 6 and received a job offer on July 7. He sent the two required photos of himself to the Trans Ocean Packing and Shipping Company on Saturday and spent the next three days in Berlin. Ernst arranged for Heinz to meet the rest of the family in Nuremberg.

Ernst was pleased with himself. He had a new job; he was starting to feel much better, and was scheduled to take a state-ordered vacation. He sat down and wrote a long letter to his brother, Arturo, updating him on their life in Germany. It was easier to write Arturo when he was in a good mood. Ernst sent the letter to a contact in Spain and hoped that Arturo would be in Ecuador when it arrived. They had received no information about Arturo or his family in a year. He wondered, even as he wrote the letter, if Arturo would ever read it.

On Wednesday night, July 14, Ernst and Ernstchen set off for Nuremberg. The train left at 10:14 p.m. from Rheinsberg. They arrived in Nuremberg early Thursday morning and for the first time in a year the entire family was together. They celebrated their good fortune with breakfast, lunch and dinner at Maria's house. The children competed for attention from their father who, still weak, responded to their questions, antics and demonstrations with a nod or a grunt.

"Papa, we are a family again." Irmgard shouted above her brothers' voices with delight.

"Yeah, and listen to Heinz's voice, Papa! He sounds like a bird when his voice does that."

Maria smiled at Heinz and reprimanded Ernstchen gently. "His voice is changing, Ernstchen. Your voice will change too when you turn twelve or thirteen."

"Well, I won't sound like *that!*" He laughed and pointed at his brother.

"At least I don't sound like a girl with a high voice like you have *all the time*!" Heinz said taking great care to keep his voice at one tone without success.

Everyone laughed and Heinz could not resist laughing either. It was wonderful to be surrounded by family again.

"Tomorrow we will go to Burg Kreuzen. It is a small village and we will be able to go on walks and you can play for hours, go swimming, sit in the sun, go mushroom hunting, whatever you want." Ernst did not think it was necessary to add that he was on doctor's orders for a lung condition.

The children's cheers drowned out Ernst's words. When they had settled down a little, Ernst said to Maria, "At least you will get a break from their crazy antics and the noise."

"I *love* their crazy antics," Maria responded poignantly, "but I will enjoy being on my own for a while. Everyone needs a vacation from something." Maria was going to spend some time with her mother, Frau Wagner Renaud. Ernst was glad she had made her own plans. He wanted to spend time alone with his children.

"Let's take a photograph, Ernst," Maria suggested.

"Good idea. Where?" Ernst asked.

"On the stairs, children. Let's sit on the stairs. Irmgard, you sit here. Boys, find a spot." Maria held Irmgard on her lap and the children laughed at their father's attempts to get them to smile all at the same time. He snapped a photo with Maria's camera.

"Ernst, why don't you take my camera with you on holiday. That way I can see where you take the children. I won't feel like I've missed out on as much," Maria added with a smile.

"Thank you, Maria. That is a great idea," Ernst responded with a side hug.

The arrangement with Maria was getting quite complicated and although Ernst enjoyed her company, he started to feel a bit nervous about their budding relationship. On the eve of their departure for Burg Kreuzen Maria joined Ernst in the kitchen after the children had gone to bed.

"Ernst. I want to talk to you about something."

"What is it?"

"First you have to promise me that you won't do that strange little Ecuadorian dance around the room."

Ernst laughed. "I won't dance if you won't make me nervous." Ernst felt the color rise in his cheeks.

The shades in the house were drawn as they were every night to protect the city from bombing. Maria had also turned off most of the lights in the home. She pulled a chair up close to him and spoke in a soft voice. Her eyes were filled with excitement and they sparkled with mischief.

"I am going to talk to my mother next week about getting married."

Ernst put his hands under his legs on the chair. "To whom?" he asked indignantly. His legs started bouncing nervously on the floor and it was clear that he wanted to squirm out of the chair and run. Instinctively, he scratched his head and pulled a tuft of hair onto the middle of his forehead.

"What are you afraid of Ernst? We have known each other long enough. I mean... what will people think. You stay here for days. The neighbors see us with the children. People are starting to talk. I think it is time for you to talk to my mother. Perhaps when you come back from Burg Kreuzen we can all get together." Maria was confident.

Caught completely off guard, Ernst rubbed his chin, his hair, his chin, his forehead. He fidgeted with the tuft of hair that brushed his forehead. He made strange facial contortions by tensing his face and neck muscles, then pursing his lips. He fumbled for a cigarette. He rolled his shoulders back and straightened in his chair. He pressed his hands into his thighs and straightened his back. He took deep breaths, but said nothing. His gut reaction was to say "Bah" and to brush off the entire idea, but for some reason he could not say a word.

"Good." Maria interjected into his restless silence. "I'll talk to mother this week. I will try to convince her to come back here with me so the two of you can talk to each other. She will expect you to talk to her *directly*."

Ernst pursed his lips again and then looked at Maria suddenly free from worry. "I wrote my brother Arturo that I am thinking about returning to Quito."

Although Maria was surprised she was not thwarted. "Fine. I am sure I'll like Quito," and she walked away to her bedroom. "I can learn Spanish, and that little nervous dance, too."

She had had the last word. Ernst was befuddled. He spent a good long time in the chair. Thinking about Maria's suggestion made him feel grumpy. He did not like others making decisions for him. After leaving Quito everyone wanted to make choices for him and his family. Decisions were made in the best interest of everyone else except him. The Ecuadorian government sold them to the United States because it was in their best interest, financially. The U.S. State Department exchanged them for terrorists and passport Americans because it was in the U.S. government's best political interest. The children went to boarding schools in towns far from him because, according to the NSV, it was in their best interest... *to survive*. Maria wanted to get married because she believed it was in her best interest and the best interest of the children. Even his mother-in-law thought he should marry for the sake of the children. "What about my best interests?" he mumbled under his breath before heading to the living room.

He was very fond of Maria, but liked the idea of *Tante Maria* better than Frau Contag. Staying in Germany forever was definitely not in his best interest. The thought made him shiver.

In the morning Maria helped him pack a picnic lunch before the family left for their vacation in Burg Kreuzen. She kissed the children and their father on the cheek, winked boldly at Ernst, and said good-bye.

The summer adventure was on. They took several modes of transportation through the countryside but the children enjoyed the last one the best. Burg Kreuzen was in a remote area of *Donauland* that had belonged to Austria, near the towns of Amstetten and Grein. You could only get to the conservative, Catholic village on horseback or by horse-drawn wagon.

Just outside the village there was a twelfth-century fortress that looked mysterious. In the distance they could see the Alps and the boys marveled at how different the peaks looked from the peaks surrounding Quito. The wagon arrived at Burg Kreuzen at five o'clock in the afternoon. There was one main street in the village; the houses and few buildings were overshadowed by a Roman Catholic church in the center. The children and Ernst felt as though they had arrived in heaven.

As Ernst's condition improved they took longer and longer hikes. One day they stopped at a spectacular waterfall enclosed in lush greenery.

"The waterfall reminds me of *Las tres Marias* on the way to Santo Domingo de los Colorados," Ernst said jubilantly.[17]

"No Spanish, Papa. Remember? *Under penalty of death*." But Ernst ignored his eldest son's admonition and shrugged. "No one can hear us here, Heinz. Let's just have fun."

For eighteen glorious days they were a family. Karl-Heinz was Heinz again. Ernstchen was Ernestito. Irmgard and Werner had older brothers to imitate. And Ernst was just *Papa*. The war, the pressures of school and work seemed far, far away.

Ernst left discipline in Nuremberg with Maria. They slept late, ate when they were hungry, and went to bed when they were tired. There was plenty of good food to eat and *even some beer*. Ernst's health improved markedly.

Irmgard and Werner laughed uproariously at the games their older brothers played on each other. When they were out on walks they stopped to rest and Werner dug for worms and bugs with a stick. Irmgard tied stems and flower-topped weeds into bracelets and hair decorations. Papa rested in the sun on the grass. Ernstchen and Heinz chased each other on the hillsides. They impressed Werner and Irmgard when they whittled with the knife each carried as part of his German Youth uniform. The words 'Blut und Ehre' fascinated Werner, who had begun to learn to read. He pronounced the words each time a knife was taken from its leather sheath. Werner, of course, had to make do with a whittled stick that he called a knife since he was not old enough to carry one of his own. "Here's my blood and honor," he said pulling the whittled stick from his belt, "Look out!"

The Contag children vacation in Burg Kreuzen in 1943 while Ernst recuperates from surgery and a respiratory illness. The family would not be reunited again until March 1946.

They also went on a special mushroom hunting adventure near the Ammergau. They found Eierschwarmm mushrooms, an egg yolk-colored, spongy variety that reminded Ernstchen of yellow trumpets jutting out of the ground. They collected some of the trumpet-shaped mushrooms along with the more common Steinpilz mushrooms that grew in tiny colonies in the grass. When they returned to Burg Kreuzen, Ernst found someone to sautée their finds for a special evening treat.

The lazy summer days were filled with swimming and games of "catch me if you can." On July 25 Karl-Heinz celebrated his thirteenth birthday at Burg Kreuzen. He considered this birthday a far better one than the one he had experienced in the small Rheinsberger hospital the year before.

For nearly three weeks, nothing could interrupt the freedom and delight the Contag family felt in this bucolic place. The holiday at Burg Kreuzen was the gift they all needed to feel whole again. On August 4 they left for Grein and Linz in a horse-drawn wagon. In Linz they boarded a train for Nuremberg. The children chatted about their days in Burg Kreuzen and busied themselves with storytelling and finger games. But Ernst found himself dreading the return to Nuremberg. *What can I do about Maria?*

When the children and Ernst arrived at Maria's house at five o'clock in the afternoon on Thursday, August 5, she welcomed them warmly — and alone! Ernst sighed in relief. Irmgard and Werner rushed to tell her all about their discoveries and adventures on vacation. Heinz and Ernstchen, who felt more like guests than family in Maria's house, busied themselves outside the house until just before suppertime. Maria outlined the nighttime routine for the children. The realization that they were being forced back on a strict schedule made everyone, especially Ernst, a bit edgy.

By the time the children were in bed, Ernst felt quite tired and somewhat grouchy. For three weeks he had felt free. He dreaded the conversation he knew he was about to have with Maria. In addition, on Monday he would be back in Berlin; Heinz would be in Kassel; Ernstchen would return to school in Hohenelse; and Maria, Werner and Irmgard would remain in Nuremberg. He sighed deeply, rubbed his eyes, and rested his weary head in the palm of his hand.

Maria closed the bedroom door where she had tucked in Irmgard and Werner. She looked in on Heinz and Ernstchen who were trying to fall asleep on the floor in the living room.

"*Gute Nacht*. Sleep well," she said closing the door to the kitchen behind her. She untied her apron, hung it on a hook, and sat down at the kitchen table across from Ernst.

She smiled sweetly at him. "I missed the children," she said simply as she settled into a kitchen chair. He made a grunting sound and nodded in agreement without looking up at her. Part of him thought if he kept his eyes downcast and sighed at regular intervals, the fateful, dreaded conversation would not come to pass. Maria reached toward him and put her hand, palm up, right in front of him. He let his right hand drop into her palm and they sat in silence for several minutes.

"I almost expected to see your mother on your doorstep this afternoon." The words had emerged from his mouth without any prompting from his brain, or so he thought. Half-kicking himself for initiating the conversation he sat up straight and looked at Maria. "I'm not sure . . ."

Maria hushed him with a wave of her hand and spoke in a soft voice. "I have thought about nothing but this moment for three weeks, Ernst." She hesitated, "I don't think I can go with you to Ecuador. My mother is getting older and I have a responsibility to her. If you decide to stay in Germany and make your home here, I want to be with you." Maria squeezed his hand. "My heart will always be with you and your children, but the decision to stay or not is yours."

Ernst answered without lifting his eyes from the floor. "You are a wise woman, Maria," he said earnestly, feeling relieved.

Maria must not have gotten the response she had expected. She let go of his hand and straightened forcefully drawing his eyes to her face. "I am a fool. I have fallen in love with a man from a tiny country in South America who jumps around like a bird with a clipped wing every time I try to get close to him. And besides that, he has four children, no home, and no money. Now what can be more fool-hardy than that?" Ernst remained silent and still.

He let his head fall into the palm of his hand and he closed his eyes. In his mind he could see the snow-covered top of the Cotopaxi. He felt the cool air rush across his face as he turned his face into the wind that blew across the inter-Andean valley. He breathed a memory of the unforgettable, relaxing smell of eucalyptus wood burning outdoors behind his house on Rocafuerte Street. He savored the thought of the soft, fleshy wetness of a ripe mango against his lips. *Home.* He opened his eyes, reached across the table and touched Maria's face. Her skin was so fair. So soft. Her eyes so gentle and kind.

When Maria saw that he was not going to react as she had hoped, tears welled up in her eyes, and she bit at her trembling upper lip. Ernst could see that she feared the worst. He did not say anything for a very long time. The words couldn't make their way to his lips. Finally he managed one sentence.

"If I stay in Germany, there is no one I would marry but you."

Maria heaved a huge sigh of relief. She went around the corner of the table, plopped down on his lap, and wrapped her arms around Ernst.

"Careful, Maria. The chair will break!"

Maria shrugged. "I can fix it." She pulled Ernst close to her and held him tightly. She whispered in his ear, "Do you think the children are asleep?"

The next morning Ernstchen and Karl-Heinz woke up before their father who was snoring on the floor next to them. They decided it was a perfect opportunity to play a little trick. "Get your handkerchief, Heinz," Ernstchen whispered. "You hold that side and I'll hold this side. We'll see if Papa can keep the handkerchief in the air when he snores." The two boys snickered quietly but their snickering made their bodies tremble. Karl-Heinz made motions to try to get his brother to stop shaking so he could stop laughing too, but his brother's silly antics just made Ernstchen laugh all the harder. Between the two boys' hisses and their father's snoring, the room was filled with sound. Before the boys could hold the handkerchief over their father's face to test their trick, Papa had opened one eye.

"You look like a lizard, Papa," Ernstchen offered with glee, leaning over his father inches from his face. Ernst grunted, reached out and grabbed at Ernstchen's middle, but the boy moved away too fast. Karl-Heinz started to giggle and the battle to tickle both boys began. Before long the three were wrestling noisily and Maria appeared at the doorway looking rather disheveled.

"Herr Contag," she glowered with a forceful whisper.

The two boys jumped away from their father who curled his shoulders and put his hand to his mouth saying "Sssshhhhh. You two are getting me in trouble with the lady of the house." Karl-Heinz and Ernstchen sat wide-eyed, but with smiles on their faces, waiting to see what would happen.

"Boys," Ernst said, "Get dressed. I am going to take you to see the city today." As he walked past Maria, he added, "Maybe I can stay *out* of trouble if I stay *out* of the house."

Ernst left with the boys soon after they finished breakfast. When Irmgard and Werner awoke to find their father and brothers gone they complained to Maria.

"But we wanted to go, too, Tante Maria. When will they come back?"

"I suppose they will come back this afternoon for lunch. Would you two like to help me pick some vegetables in the garden for lunch?"

"No." Werner replied feeling dejected. "I wanted to go with Papa."

"Well, that isn't possible now. We are going to the garden to pick vegetables. We are a family now. Everyone has to put in their share," Maria said sternly, but happily.

Irmgard was confused. "What do you mean *we* are a family now, Tante Maria?"

Maria did not think before she spoke. "When your Papa and I get married, I am going to be your mother." The words had slipped out before she realized what she had said.

"You can't marry Papa." Irmgard said defiantly. "You are our *aunt*. You and Papa can't get *married*." Irmgard looked startled and confused.

Maria smiled at Irmgard, "I'm not really your aunt, Irmgardchen. Let's talk about this later. Your Papa can tell you all about it when he is ready. I want to make a special dinner for your Papa and your brothers tonight. You can help me! They have to leave tomorrow on the train."

"Tomorrow? Not tomorrow!" whined Werner.

"Yes, tomorrow. Now brush your hair and let's get going."

Maria, Irmgard and Werner walked to the garden that they had been tending together for nearly three months. The cool morning gave way to a very hot mid-morning and before long the three were sweating in the hot sun. Maria felt irritable, especially since the children spent most of the time chasing flying insects, digging in the dirt, and watching birds. By the time they were ready to head back home she was quite bedraggled and they were filthy. She was happy, but she had not slept well and it was so hot.

Werner and Irmgard followed Maria into the kitchen where she set the vegetables near the sink and wiped her brow with the back of her hand. Werner and Irmgard asked for a drink of water and she gave each a glass. Irmgard went to wash her hands in the bathroom. Werner remained in the kitchen and spied a candy jar that he had not seen before.

"I'm hungry." Werner said. "Look! There is candy up there. Can I have a piece of hard candy from that jar, Tante Maria?

"No. It will spoil your appetite."

"No, it won't. I'll still be hungry even if I have a whole handful of candies!" Werner said in a cheery voice.

"The answer is no. And don't ask again. Go clean up. Wash your hands and face before your father gets back."

Werner did as he was told although he took his sweet time getting about his business. Werner, however, was not at all pleased with Tante Maria's response to the candy request. He scowled to himself and thought a few pieces of candy wouldn't spoil *his* appetite! He waited until Maria went into the bathroom to clean up. He sneaked into the kitchen, climbed on the counter, and reached into the candy dish. Just then Irmgard walked into the kitchen.

"Look what I found!" he said just above a whisper to his sister as he dropped the hard candy into her hand.

"Wow!" She popped one in her mouth and then crunched the sweetness between her teeth.

"Let's go outside on the steps. Come on!" Werner tittered gleefully as he headed toward the door. Irmgard grabbed the rest of the candy before heading outside.

The two children found a comfortable place to sit on the steps about five meters from the house. Irmgard piled the candy haphazardly near her and handed Werner a piece each time she took another.

For a while the two sucked and chomped without saying anything. Then Irmgard moved the candy to one side of her mouth to speak.

"What flavor is yours?"

"I don't know." Werner opened his mouth and stuck out his tongue. "Aahh mah tah ath reth ath yorth?" he asked.

"What did you say?" Irmgard asked. "You have to move the candy over there so I can understand you." Irmgard pointed to his right cheek and Werner repeated his question. "Is my tongue as red as yours?" Irmgard stuck out her tongue and tried to look at it herself. They both started to giggle. "No, yours is green! Really green!" Irmgard said through her laughter.

"What are you doing?" Maria startled the two giggling children. "You little thieves! That was my candy. You have eaten all my candy. Why, you. . ." She grabbed the children by the arm and pulled them into the house. "Don't you ever take anything that is not yours!" she stammered and swatted each on the backside. "There will be no supper for you tonight! I am ashamed of both of you. No supper, do you hear me?" Werner wore a pained look and cowered. Irmgard started to cry. Neither one had been hurt but they were devastated by the humiliation. Werner shuddered. No adult had ever punished him in such a manner and he did not know what to do with the emotions that overcame him.

"I'm sorry, Tante Maria." Irmgard spoke through her tears. "Werner and I . . . we didn't know . . ."

"You knew very well those candies did not belong to you. Werner?"

"I'm sorry, very sorry, Tante Maria. But I didn't do it."

"What? You think you can lie to me? I don't want you in the house now. I am so angry. Outside with you both. Now!"

The children turned and hurried out of the house, nearly stumbling over one another. When they got out the door Ernst, Karl-Heinz and Ernstchen were just approaching the house and the children spotted them on the street.

"Papa! Papa!" Irmgard and Werner ran to their father and cried, "Tante Maria told us to get out of the house. She is really mad. She hit us." Werner tried to explain. "Tante Maria is being really mean to us. She hit me right here like this!" Werner spanked himself and howled afterward.

"She won't even let us eat dinner tonight." Irmgard stated with a pout. She knew how to affect her father by crying so she squeezed the tears from her eyes and spoke through trembling lips, "And I am really hungry, too!" Ernst bent over to comfort both children and they milked every ounce of sympathy from their father. After they had stopped crying he said, "You'll be able to eat dinner. I'll just see what happened. You can stay out here with your brothers for a little while. Don't worry. Everything will be fine."

Ernst was very good at comforting his children and even before he had entered the house Werner and Ernstchen had started a silly game of swatting at each other. Ernst could hear laughter as he entered the house to look for Maria. He found her in the kitchen. Maria was busy preparing dinner and had set the table for four.

"What happened? Why are Irmgard and Werner so upset?" Ernst was angry, but he did not want to say anything rash until he had the whole story.

"Those rascals stole all my candy when I told them they could not have any. I was saving it for a special occasion. I know they are upset, but they have to learn to respect what I say. You let them get away with everything, Ernst, and I won't have them stealing as long as they are living under my roof. The only way they will learn is if there are consequences."

Ernst's ears burned red but he knew things would go better if he turned on the charm instead of demonstrating that he was angry. "Two pieces of *candy*? All this for a few pieces of candy! Maria, they are only little children. They are just babies. They weren't stealing. They can't understand these things. How can you call this stealing?"

"Ernst, you can make excuses for them all day, but they live with me and I have rules in my house. There is no snacking and no *stealing*. When the rules are broken, there are consequences. I am not going to change the rules just because you are here to make excuses for them today."

Ernst felt the hair on the nape of his neck stand on end and he stiffened. "Is it true that you punished them with your hand?"

Maria looked at him directly. "Yes. Stealing must be punished."

Ernst was shocked. He had never raised a hand to his children. "Why have you only set four places at the table?" Ernst was furious, but kept his voice calm and steady.

"The children have full stomachs. There is no reason to serve them supper tonight. Maybe then they will remember to respect others."

Maria's words stung. He replied sternly, "These are my children and they will not go hungry if I have anything to say about it. Set two more places at the table."

"Well Ernst, you are in my house and you don't have anything to say about it."

"The children will apologize to you, Maria, but you will set the table for *six*."

Maria gave him a furious look, but she backed down when she saw how upset he was.

Ernst went outside and told Irmgard and Werner in no uncertain terms that they were to apologize to Tante Maria and to promise never to take anything that belonged to her without her permission. Irmgard and Werner went into the kitchen and apologized as their father had told them. Maria's response was stiff but pleasant.

At dinner that evening Maria and Ernst avoided each other's glance. Karl-Heinz and Ernstchen were talkative. Werner and Irmgard had difficulty swallowing their meal, but their father told them to eat every morsel on their plates. That evening Maria and Ernst kept their distance until one of the children woke up and vomited. Maria flashed a victorious glance at Ernst who shelved the look in his mind for future reference. At least he didn't have to clean up the mess.

On Saturday morning Maria sent the four children off to play outside after breakfast and she cornered Ernst who was packing the washed clothing into a bag for Karl-Heinz and into another for himself and Ernstchen.

"So, are you going to talk to me before you leave or not?"

Ernst put down the shirt he had in his hand and took a deep breath. "I appreciate all the work you have done for my family and for me — the laundry, the cooking, the discipline; you really have been wonderful to the children. But I cannot come here anymore. I can't watch you try to be a stepmother to my children or a wife to me." Maria stared at Ernst, dumbfounded. Ernst went back to his packing. "They can go to live with their grandmother in Hanover, or I will find a boarding school near Potsdam. Maybe they could go to Schlaborn, just north of Hohenelse. The NSV will help to make the arrangements. I'll expect you to send the children to me in Potsdam at the end of the month." Ernst spoke firmly and without faltering.

Maria backed against the wall and stood there speechless. He dared not look at her. After several moments of silence he heard her mutter in anger, "Papa knows best." She turned and went to her bedroom. Ernst could hear her crying, but he did not go to her. His mind was made up.

Several hours later Ernst, Heinz, and Ernstchen said goodbye to Irmgard, Werner and Tante Maria. For the children it was the end of vacation and the end of what had been the happiest moments of their year. For a few minutes they all stood out in front of the house talking and jumping and having a good time.

"Ay, *caramba*." Ernst snapped in Spanish. "I forgot something important in the kitchen. Tante Maria, would you come inside and help me find it?" Ernst did not enjoy lengthy goodbyes, and he knew that this parting could be difficult, but he felt it was necessary. It was likely this would be the last time he would see Maria and he did not want to leave on bad terms. Maria loved him and cared for his young children very much. Maria followed him into the kitchen somewhat bewildered.

"What is it, Ernst? What did you . . .?" There on the kitchen table was a beautiful rose and a sealed note.

"Where did you find this . . .?" Maria began.

Ernst slipped a hand on either side of Maria's neck and drew her to him and smiled. "Maria, you are a rose. A perfect rose." He kissed her warmly and passionately. She encircled him with her arms and went limp. Ernst pulled away gently so he was inches from her face. "If I were sure I was going to stay in Germany, I would want to marry you, Maria. But I want to go home."

"I can wait, Ernst. You will change your mind," she said encouragingly, but her eyes were wet with tears.

Ernst lifted her chin with his right hand. "If I do, you will be the first to know. Send the children to me in Potsdam. I'll make arrangements from there. Thank you, Maria. I will not forget you." He kissed her and walked to the front door.

Maria was stricken to the core. She let him go without another word.

"Are you ready boys?" Ernst called as he left the house.

"Yes, Papa."

"*Auf wiedersehen*, Heinz. *Auf wiedersehen*, Ernstchen. *Auf wiedersehen*, Papa. Come back soon!" Irmgard and Werner waved frantically from the front step. Ernst and his boys turned to wave to Irmgard and Werner who started jumping up and down in front of the house. Maria was nowhere in sight. Ernst imagined that she was still in the kitchen reading his note to her.

"Beautiful Maria. Endearing Maria. Sensible Maria. *Tante* Maria. I am sorry. My heart will always be in Quito."[18]

A week later, on Thursday, August 26, 1943 Ernst, Inge, and Lenchen were sipping coffee and eating apple strudel in Potsdam. Ernst had turned thirty-six the day before and they were celebrating. Their conversation was anything but celebratory.

"It was an amazing sight to see the air attack from Potsdam on Tuesday. The bombings are too close for my liking." Ernst said. "Lenchen, you should move out of Berlin. I think it is getting too dangerous."

"You must be kidding, Ernst. I am happy where I am. You can't predict where a bomb will fall anyway. If everyone keeps moving out of Berlin . . . then what? Are we all going to move to the countryside and starve in a hovel?" Lenchen waved off the preoccupied look of her brother and changed the subject. She had plenty to tell about her job and living at the Wosatkas. She worried about Bio and still had no news of his whereabouts.

Inge shrugged when Ernst asked how things were going at the hospital. "What do you expect? We are at war. Things are bad." Inge had not had any news from Carl either. She seemed rather upbeat hosting the small gathering at her apartment, but her demeanor had changed somewhat. She seemed older, crankier without her husband around. Getting together for coffee made the separations between family members seem less painful. *At least we have each other*, Ernst thought.

Ernst told Inge and Lenchen about the fantastic vacation he had spent with the children in Burg Kreuzen. He talked about the children and the silly things they had done. Inge and Lenchen followed his news as if it were their own. Any news that was happy news was welcome. Ernst also explained that things had become uncomfortable with Maria and, after talking to his mother-in-law, he had decided to move the children to the children's home in Schlaborn so he could see them more often. The NSV was making the arrangements. He expected the children to arrive in three days, on Sunday. Just then there was a knock at the door.

"I wonder who that could be," Inge mumbled as she went to the door. It was a warm day and the man in uniform at the door was sweating profusely.

"Guten Tag, Frau Contag. I have news about your husband. May I come in?"

"Yes, of course. Please. Come in." Ernst and Lenchen stood up and walked into the next room to get a good look at the man. He was in his thirties, but had an older man's voice. "He has news about Carl," Inge said rather flatly.

Ernst introduced himself and his sister.

"A pleasure to meet you both. It is an honor really, to meet Herr Contag's brother and sister as well as his wife. You must be the South Americans," he said, offering his hand first to Ernst and then to Lenchen. "Your brother told us all about the American-German diplomatic exchange. What a story that was!" The excitement in his voice was brief. He lowered his eyes and spoke to Inge.

"I am afraid I am not the bearer of good news, Frau Contag. I think it would be a good idea for everyone to sit down."

Inge stiffened as she motioned for him to move to the table. "Please sit here. Would you like a cup of coffee? It is my brother-in-law's birthday," Inge said anxiously.

"Thank you very much, but I would prefer a glass of water." The man took out his handkerchief and mopped his brow before he took a seat. "It is a very warm day."

Lenchen brought the man a glass of water and he tried not to gulp it down. Ernst offered him a cigarette, which he declined respectfully.

"Three weeks ago I was in Sicily with your husband, Frau Contag. We were on the east side of the island, just outside the city of Catania on the Ionian Sea. We were in the same artillery regiment. God, it was beautiful there at the foot of Mt. Etna. We were right on the Simeto River. We had been fighting Allied forces for three weeks in Sicily. The Americans came in from the South and West, the British forces from the South and East. We did quite well and held our ground— for a time. The younger recruits, who had been so idealistic when we arrived in Sicily, were really scared and started making a big fuss one day. Your husband decided to tell them these fantastic stories to calm them down. He was great! No matter what some might say, we were all really scared. Every day we wondered if it was going to be our day to live or die. Some of the troops were going crazy," he said with a sigh.

"Whenever we could, we asked your husband to tell us another story about South America. A gang of us stuck to your husband like glue because, when he started telling stories about growing up in Ecuador, it kept us fellows thinking about different things, fantasies, you know. The stories kept us from dwelling on the battle. One young artillery soldier told me he felt braver when he heard the gunner's stories. That's what we called your husband sometimes. Gunner Contag. Anyway, this young fellow would gather up a crowd of ten or fifteen men by yelling, 'Get the gunner; it is story time.' He was about seventeen or eighteen years old. Maybe he was younger. He told me he wanted to write home and tell his mother he would be leaving after the war for South America. He planned to live with the Indians and hunt tapir." Ernst wanted to smile at these words but he didn't. The man in uniform was perspiring and wiped his brow again.

The man looked at Ernst and Lenchen, "Your brother told the best stories about the strangest places we had ever heard of. His stories were better than the ones I'd read by Karl May when I was young![19] He told us about your father's brewery and how your father chased a high society French woman once and hit her in the head with an umbrella. He gave all the details and acted things out for us. We laughed so hard when he stood up and did an impression of your father chasing the High Society woman. . . her name was Branchez or Granché or something like that."

Ernst nodded, "Yes, Madame Granger. She was the wife of a Frenchman who founded a brewery near our home in Quito."[20]

"Yes, yes. He told us about how he went hunting for huge, hairy anteaters and for rodents the size of dogs! What fantastic stories he told us. If it had not been for Herr Contag, I think we would all have gone crazy." The man in uniform shifted his weight in the chair.

"August 5, 1943. I won't forget that day as long as I live." The soldier took a deep breath and sighed heavily. "Herr Contag was telling us a story about a worker at the brewery in Quito who was really upset. The fellow was so mad that he tried to poison the beer with chewing tobacco. Herr Contag said that the entire brew was contaminated so they had to open the vat and let the beer run through the streets of Quito like a river. You should have seen us boys pretending to scoop up imaginary beer in our helmets. We drank our *street* brew and laughed until our sides ached!"[21] The man looked as though he were about to cry.

"That was in Cuenca, not Quito," Lenchen corrected the man rather absentmindedly. "But it doesn't matter."

"Yes, ma'am. Herr Contag was just about to tell us about hunting a puma in the jungle when my superior officer asked me to move a vehicle for him. He stood there wanting to listen, too. That is why he asked me to take the vehicle away. I wanted to hear the story so I jumped up quickly and went as fast as I could to park the vehicle where he told me. I parked it and turned around and it was all over. When I got back . . ." the man in uniform mopped his brow and his voice grew thin and it cracked. "Everyone was dead. Everyone. Everyone except for me." He stared at the three of them wide-eyed before dropping his gaze to the table top and repeating, "Everyone except for me."

No one said anything for quite a while. Then the man in uniform continued just above a whisper. "The government sends out notices . . . in the mail." The man raised his eyes to meet Ernst's. "But I wanted you to know first-hand how important Herr Contag was to us. We were all proud to serve with him. He was a true hero."

Inge rose abruptly from the table and spoke. "Thank you, sir. Ernst, will you show the gentleman out." She disappeared into the kitchen and Lenchen followed her. Inge's abruptness startled the man in uniform and he apologized to Ernst.

"I am sorry, Herr Contag, but I thought it would be better if I came to tell you. When my brother was killed they just —"

"We appreciate your stopping by," Ernst said with a wan smile. "I know how hard this must be for you, too."

The man opened the door and walked out shaking his head. "He was a good man, your brother. A fine gunner. A good man."

Ernst closed the door and suddenly heard sobbing from the kitchen. Inge was doubled over and Lenchen was patting her back gently. Inge was having great difficulty breathing through her sobs.

"It's all my fault. I've killed him. He never wanted to go. I made him go." She sobbed, "He wasn't even German! *Gefallen für Gross-Deutschland.*[22] He wasn't even German!"

NOTES TO CHAPTER SIX

[1] Brandenburgishes Landeshauptarchiv.

[2] 1943 Pocket Calendar

[3] 1943 Pocket Calendar.

[4] The "Postparbuch" was an account book issued by the German Reichspost office. It was similar to a bankbook, but the account was held at the post office and not at a bank. The most curious thing about Ernst Contag's account is that he only deposited 600 RM in the fall of 1942, which he withdrew regularly until there were only five Reichsmark left in the account on December 12. He did not make another deposit for over a year. In January of 1944 he resumed making deposits and withdrawals until his final withdrawal made on January 19, 1945. He still had 770 RM in the account, which, it seems, was never closed out.

[5] The message in German was:

> *Wehrbezirkskommando Ausland teilt Ihnen mit, daß nach Entscheid das Oberkommandos der Wehrmacht die aus Amerika zurückgekehrten Reichsdeutschen, die sich unter Eidesleistung verpflichten mußten, für die Dauer des gegenwärtigen Krieges keine Waffen zu tragen, nicht zum Wehrdienst herangezogen werden. Sie werde daher - auch bei freiwilliger Meldung - nicht einberufen.*

Beiliegende Erklärung ist ggf. unterschreiben zurückzusenden.

[6] *Mihija* is an endearing expression commonly used in relation to females in Ecuadorian families. Ernst had made a second deposit of 300 Reichsmark to his account on September 16, but by the middle of October it was obvious that he could not keep his promise to Irmgard. His debt to Inge and his mother-in-law was growing. He could not make another deposit to his account. He withdrew 100 RM on November 6, 1942 in Hanover to give to his mother-in-law for Werner's expenses. A month later, on December 10, 1942, he made a withdrawal of 15 RM from the Reichspost account. Only five Reichsmark remained. There would be no Christmas trip to visit his children.

[7] Of course, I am from Quito, Ecuador.

[8] Foreign-born German

[9] Greet God. Good Morning. Two common greetings in Germany.

[10] Arroyo del Rio. President of Ecuador when the Contag family left.

[11] Danzig is the city that is now known as Gdansk, Poland.

[12] Margarete (Tante Grete) Schmidt Contag was born August 20, 1888 in Tietzow/Nauen and died in 1980 in Berlin. She was the wife of Bruno Contag, born in 1885 in Lichtenberg. According to Eckart Contag, "she was a woman with a warm heart and helpful to everyone." Bruno Contag was an insurance actuary who later on founded a pension group for retired German Press agents. The house they lived in was bombed during the war and they had several addresses in Berlin after the war. Letter written on January 1, 2000 to K.E. Contag.

[13] Employment receipt for May 12. *Interresengemeinschaft Farbenindustrie Aktiengesellschaft, Verkaufstelle Danzig; Verkaufskontor.* On May 12 Ernst was issued a voucher/receipt for his wages for work during the first two weeks of May at the I. G. Farbenindustrie. His gross pay was 281 RM, but netted only 258.58 RM after the required improvement compensation tax (2.78 RM), Reich insurance (7.87 RM), unemployment insurance (4.95 RM), and superannuation funds (6.90 RM) were deducted.

[14] School for Arts and Professions.

[15] *Siegreicher Abschluss der Kämpfe um Kreta.* Pocket Calendar 1943.

[16] The spa is known as Bad Kreuzen, the village as Burg Kreuzen. The fortress was built in 900 A.D. The village, located on the scenic Danube in modern Austria, is over 500 years old.

[17] *The three Marys* refers to a waterfall on the road from Quito to Santo Domingo de los Colorados in Ecuador. The area is subtropical.

[18] Maria Renaud lived at 47 Velser Street in Nuremberg. According to Myriam Maldonado de Contag, Maria Renaud continued to write Ernesto Contag in Quito for three decades after he left Germany. Maria's letters, considered too private to keep, were disposed of shortly after Ernesto Contag's death.

[19] Karl May was a successful nineteenth-century German author who wrote fantastic adventure stories without visiting the places he wrote about.

[20] Mr. (Enrique) Maulme and a Frenchman by the name of Granger founded the brewery "Maulme & Granger" in 1890 and construction on a brewery began at the end of Rocafuerte Street in the area called "Mama-cuchara" or "Mother-spoon" where the force of the river would provide the necessary hydro-electric

energy. The project was never brought to fruition and they never produced beer at that location. Years later the machinery was sold to varied interests, leaving only the pipes that would have carried the water from the Machángara River to the turbines, as a visible reminder of a business gone awry. This information is a translation from a private Contag document titled "Algo sobre las Cervecerias en el Ecuador" that Ernesto Contag had kept until his death. The document is incomplete and anonymous. Ernesto Contag or another brewery enthusiast could have written the document around 1950.

[21] From a taped conversation between Ernesto Contag and his son, Carlos [Karl-Heinz], in Caracas, Venezuela in 1985.

[22] Fallen for Greater Germany. The sentence was stamped on letters and postcards that had to be *returned to sender* when a soldier died while on military duty.

CHAPTER SEVEN

AIR RAID!

POTSDAM, 1943

Ernst paced back and forth in the apartment. He scanned the information in his pocket calendar for the end of August. Each day read, "No communication from Nuremberg." The children were supposed to have arrived in Rheinsberg on Sunday, August 29. He had waited at the station with Ernstchen. Nothing. To make matters worse he had been unable to get through to Nuremberg by telephone. Communication was down. The children were unaccounted for. Carl was dead. Berlin was under attack by air. *How ironic*, thought Ernst, *Greater Germany is planning to celebrate the annual Reichsparteitag in two days.*[1] *What is there to celebrate?*

Upset, he went downstairs to pay Frau von Kauffungen the rent for July and August, and left for work. In the streetcar he worried a hole right through his trouser pocket. "*Carajo*," he swore under his breath and muttered to himself, *"What a world we live in. What a world for children!"* He couldn't help but imagine his children dodging bullets from the low-flying planes that had, on occasion, forced trains to halt, spewing frightened passengers in every direction. He shivered with disgust. At noon he called Rheinsberg and learned the children had arrived safely that morning. "Thank God," he told the man on the other end of the line. He couldn't think of another place that was more remote or tranquil than the boarding school Hohenelse-Schlaborn. Finally he could sleep a night without worrying so much about the children.

On Wednesday and Friday Berlin was bombed again. He watched the bombing from outside Frau von Kauffungen's home. "*Que carajo,*" he swore under his breath. "*What a waste of human energy and ingenuity.*" The destruction depressed him. More destruction was inevitable in spite of the strength of the German military. "A blitzkrieg like this would have been unthinkable in Ecuador at any time in history. But not here." Ernst swatted at the air in front of him in disgust. "Pfff. My life in Quito was never easy, but it was not fraught with worries like these. . . separation, . . . isolation. . . destructive air raids . . . train bombings . . . fear." *Death.* The unthinkable crossed his mind, but he was too superstitious to pronounce the word. He vowed to spend every weekend with Ernstchen, Irmgard and Werner.

On September 18 Ernst made a final trip to Nuremberg. Ernst surprised Maria at her home and for several hours it seemed that the two had never quarreled. By dinnertime on Saturday evening Ernst started to withdraw into himself.

"What is wrong, Ernst?" Maria asked.

"I have lost count." Ernst said shaking his head. "Berlin has been bombed nearly eighty times, but I have lost count. The radio communiqués in Berlin call the strikes 'nuisance attacks.'" He scoffed and covered his mouth with his hand and then rubbed his aching forehead. His face was strained.

"When we arrived in Germany I thought everything was going to be fine. I would get a job and a place to live with the children. Seeing Carl and Inge and Tante Grete, Onkel Bruno, you know, I thought everything was going to be fine. Now, I am not so sure. I've had this bad dream. I keep wondering about the, uh, the 'you-know-what.' No one wants to talk about it. I don't want to talk about it. You know it isn't a good thing to talk about it."

"Don't be so superstitious, Ernst. Talking about what *could* happen doesn't mean those things *will* happen."

"The nightmare I had a week ago. " Ernst sighed deeply. "It was horrible."

"It was just a dream," Maria offered some consolation. "Do you want to tell me what happened?"

Ernst sighed heavily and let his chin fall to his chest. " I was on a train with my children. It was a bright, sunny day. At least that is what we saw outside the windows. We were all on the train, Heinz, Werner, Irmgard, Ernstchen and I. The children were talking and laughing, everyone having a good time. But something felt wrong, sort of eerie to me. So I stood up to look around. Suddenly, the train stopped with a jerk and everything went black. I heard machine gun fire all around me but I couldn't see anything. Tuca, tuca, tuca, tuca. . . Real fast. I couldn't see anything so I started to feel around with my hands, like this." Ernst used his hands as though he was a blind man and he pretended to touch invisible objects in front of him. "I couldn't feel anything on the train seats so I tried to call out to the children over the gunfire. The words were caught in my throat and I couldn't speak. I couldn't even open my mouth and I panicked. I touched my mouth and my lips were swollen shut. I tried to yell and pull my lips apart but I couldn't, so I moved forward blindly trying to find the children. I was crying and I felt hot and wet all over. I stumbled over things so I reached down to move them. There were bodies everywhere in front of me, heavy as lead. Then I heard Irmgard call me. "Papa... Papa... I'm over here. Where are you?" I tried to find her with my hands, but I kept bumping into body parts, but the limbs weren't heavy anymore. They were smooth and lightweight, like the pumice stone we find in the Andes. It looks heavy, but you can pick up a really big rock. Body parts were everywhere. I was frantic. I kept throwing the limbs here and there looking for Irmgard. I heard the children calling me, "Papa... Papa..." I kept stumbling in the dark. There were more limbs. Arms and legs. I pushed them aside and kept looking. Then there was a flash of light and I saw a face looking at me, inches away. Right here. Right in front of me. The eyes were open and the face had swollen lips. Big and purple and swollen. I didn't recognize who it was. I stared at the face and it frightened me. I looked away but just outside the window there were hundreds of faces just like it. All of them lined up against the window. All of them with swollen lips. It was horrible. I woke up in a sweat."

"What an awful nightmare, Ernst!"

"Yes. It was. *Horripilante*.[2] I shiver every time I think of it. At first I worried about the children, but then I thought, what if something happens to me and the children are all alone... orphans!"

"Nothing is going to happen to you, Ernst. But you are right. No one can predict the future. You can't worry about those things. They are out of your control. It's just an emotional reaction—the nightmare, I mean. The children are near you now in Potsdam and you can see them every weekend. It is not unusual to have nightmares about this sort of thing."

The two sat quietly until Maria spoke in a soft, gentle voice.

"I miss the children, but you were right to move them. You need them to be near you."

Ernst sighed and shook his head, perspiring, then sighed deeply and said, "I don't know when I'll come back to Nuremberg."

Maria lowered her eyes. "When I read your note a few weeks ago I didn't expect you were ever coming back to Nuremberg, Ernst. But now I know that isn't true. I am here when you decide to come back and for as long as you want to stay."

"You know, Maria, when I boarded the steamer in Guayaquil I had no idea what I would find for us in Germany. Irmgard and Werner have grown to love Germany, and soon Werner will not remember much about Ecuador. He is losing his ability to speak Spanish. Irmgard too. She is proud to be a little German girl. Her mother would have been happy to see her this way." Ernst smiled at Maria and relaxed a little.

Maria smiled, too, but she lowered her eyes as Ernst continued and eventually she looked away and wiped a tear.

"They will all be German children if we are here much longer. Heinz is adapting quite well and he seems happy no matter where he is. The Rümler family is very kind to him. Ernstchen is the one who learns and adapts the fastest, but he fights change at every turn. He is a lot like I am in that way. We resist change on the inside, not as much on the outside. Ernstchen wants to go back to Quito. He still remembers. I still don't know what we will do. I am not sure Ecuador will even take us back. When we were blacklisted it was as though we had to leave forever. I didn't believe it possible then, but now I am not so sure. Perhaps after the war . . . maybe we won't be able to leave. Who knows what will happen? Nobody knows what will happen."

Maria garnered her strength and spoke, "I want you to bring the children back here so I can see them. I don't know when it might be possible, but I miss them, Ernst. Even my mother misses them. I think she wants to be Oma to Irmgard and Werner. She loves them so much, you know, as much as I love them."

Ernst was apparently not listening to her, "Do you know that I have lived in Germany more than a year and I have not yet traveled to where my wife—" Ernst choked on the words, "—was born? Hamburg. . . the Blankenese. Irmgard told me. She must have been a very special woman, your Elisabeth Dreier." Maria moved away from him.

"I am sorry, Maria. I didn't mean to—"

"Sometimes you are cruel, Ernst. It doesn't matter," she said rather dejectedly. "I am still going to make plans for our future. Why don't you bring the children here next summer so we can have a family reunion."

Ernst smiled. "That is a wonderful idea, Maria. It will be like coming home." On Sunday night, September 1943, they said good-bye and Ernst returned to Potsdam. Neither suspected that these deeply moving moments together would be their last.

A month later on a clear October evening Karl-Heinz stretched out on his bed in the Rümler home, sore after helping to harvest the last of the potatoes and other vegetables he had sown with the Rümlers in the spring and early summer. Frau Rümler had insisted that he bury the carrots in sand in the basement so they would have food in the winter. The stored vegetables would have to get them through the winter months along with the government ration cards. He did not mind working with the vegetables, and he even enjoyed the smell of dirt mixed with fresh vegetables that wafted up from the basement. It had taken him a good ten minutes to clean the dirt and sand from under his fingernails. Still, he always enjoyed wringing his damp hands and watching the stream of mud fall into the sink. He had washed until water dripping from his hands ran clear. Karl-Heinz was the only *man* in the house so the lifting, digging, and burying often fell to him. He rolled his head back and forth on the pillow stretching the muscles that ran down his neck and upper back. It was still early evening, but he was tired so he curled onto his left side and shut his eyes. Karl-Heinz wondered when his Papa would come and visit. After muttering a prayer to himself he drifted off to sleep.

A train whistle was blowing. He was in the house in Quito, pitch dark, the noise deafening. The house was rocking and he ran to the threshold of the bedroom door and froze with a hand on either side of the half-meter thick walls. "Earthquake! Earthquake! Everyone outside!" He turned and started to run but his feet were like lead. Mother's china was trembling in the cabinet. He could hardly breathe.

"Air raid! Karl-Heinz! Air raid!" Frau Rümler was shaking him and screaming at him. He came to. The air raid alarm was blasting in Kassel.

Karl-Heinz pulled on his trousers, slipped into his shoes with lightning speed, and ran with Uli and Frau Rümler to the government bunker in the park across the street from the house. He could hear the defense shots go into the sky. He was panting and sweating when he got there. Once inside the cavity of the earth mound, others who were already inside hushed him. Uli repeated a sentence to herself just above a whisper. "If we can hear the bombs, we are safe. If we can hear the bombs we are safe."

The bombing continued for fifteen endless minutes. Karl-Heinz stood stiff, not wanting to breath. The noise was deafening and frightening even in the shelter. A tall woman next to him had covered her mouth with her palms. Karl-Heinz could see her eyes widen as he heard bombs fall. She shuddered as he did each time another bomb whistled and fell. Karl-Heinz had seen holes where bombs had been dropped before in Kassel and he wondered to himself whether they really were safe in the bunker or not. *In an earthquake*, he thought, *you are not safe anywhere but outside*. He wanted to run outside. He wanted to run away. Run and hide. Instead, he tried to slow his breathing and concentrate. He shivered. The bombs started exploding so often it was hard to distinguish one explosion from another. Each bomb made him cringe. There were hundreds of bombs. Karl-Heinz was stunned. How could so many bombs fall at once? He felt like he was at the base of a giant waterfall. He couldn't even count them. He imagined there must be thousands of bombs and explosions. One woman fell to her knees and wept.

Uli had her knitting and pulled it from a bag. She started in seriously and Karl-Heinz could see that she was really nervous. There had been two bombings in Kassel at the end of July and another on October 3, nineteen days earlier. Tonight the bombs were too close for comfort and one after the other shook them even there, seven meters deep. When the sirens finally fell silent the sealed door to the bunker was opened. When the people ahead of them emerged through the door they heard cries and screams. They witnessed devastation they had never imagined possible, fires that lit up the sky, smoke everywhere. It was as light as day and there was debris in the street. Some stood stunned and had to be pushed out of the way. The windows in all the buildings surrounding the park had shattered. The atmosphere was eerie, the air thick with smoke.

Uli screamed, "Mutti, *unser Haus brennt!*" Frau Rümler gasped and shrieked as she turned to look at her house. "The second story is on fire. Uli! Karl-Heinz! Hurry. The house... the house is burning. Run." Karl-Heinz heard her wail as he passed her, "Oh no... No...!" Karl-Heinz was the first to arrive at the house, but he wasn't sure what to do when he got there and stood a moment looking with disbelief at the flames that licked at the sky from the bathroom and the dining room.

Neighbors whose houses were not aflame helped them put out the fire with sand throughout the night and into the morning hours. The Kassel skyline burned brightly beneath the thick dark cloud above and it was not hard to see where the bombs left their mark. The house was a terrible mess. The yard was a terrible mess. Scorched linens were pulled from the bedrooms and tossed in the yard below. Karl-Heinz helped Uli move furniture and household items away from the area where the bombs had fallen. They tried to collect anything that looked salvageable.

Two phosphorous bombs had hit the house and there were flare-ups for a week. The smoke from the smoldering ashes was suffocating, but Frau Rümler was determined to stay in the house and kept cleaning as though somehow cleaning would make the house more livable. There really was nowhere else to go. In fact, they were far better off than many who did not have shelter or a place to prepare food. Frau Rümler wondered how soon it would be before others had to move in with them. The government was quick to find homes for the homeless.

At night the house was cold, the wind blowing in from different areas, the smell of smoke throughout the city choking them, but they wore more clothing to bed and Karl-Heinz made a joke of it saying that it was still warmer in the bedrooms than sleeping with the window open in Quito. Five days after the British air attack, fires still burned and smoke haze kept them from seeing the stars or the clouds. There was no electricity, no running water. No one ventured too far from the house. It was not safe. The main business and shopping district between the Fulda River and the Königsplatz had been flattened, not one building left standing. The neighbors said that some people wandered in the streets wondering what to do first and not really doing anything. It was rumored that entire families had been lost. The bombing had paralyzed the city. Fear had paralyzed them all.

It was several days after the bombing before the true extent of the devastation became known. Thousands of bombs had been dropped on Kassel. Buildings, bridges, houses— everything had been destroyed. Some said the city was completely destroyed. Others said that nearly 6000 were dead or missing after the October 22 attack. Many people had nowhere to live. Few seemed to be in their right mind. Everyone knew someone who had been found dead. Tragedy was everywhere and on everyone's mind.

The Hitler Youth organized a clean-up crew and troops arrived in the city with pick axes and shovels. There was rubble everywhere and it seemed to many that the clean-up efforts were going to be fruitless. Henschel Gemein was destroyed. The houses on Friedrichsplatz were destroyed and burned. The train station, the hospital, the hotels, the government building on Wilhelms Street, the post office, the churches, the streets, were all in ruins. When it was determined later on that the Hindenberg School was too damaged to reopen after the bombing, a welfare official came to the Rümler house and told Karl-Heinz he was going to be moved to another town nearby where school was still in session.

"Have there been many bombings there?" Karl-Heinz asked the official.

"It is a small town. Korbach hasn't been bombed and I don't expect it will." Karl-Heinz agreed to the move enthusiastically. He was tired of going to bed wondering if he would be alive in the morning. Kassel gave him the jitters. "I will go. Will you let my father know where I am?"

"Yes," the official assured him. "He will be informed."

In November Karl-Heinz said good-bye to Frau Rümler and Uli, climbed in a truck with his belongings, and left for the sleepy town of Korbach less than 30 kilometers from Kassel. It was a new beginning for him, but the look on Frau Rümler's face had nearly caused him to change his mind. Her eyes looked so sad. Uli was visibly upset as well. They had been through so much together and now he was abandoning them. "I'll come back to visit you," Karl-Heinz said reassuringly. "I bet you'll have the house fixed by then, too."

Just outside Kassel the war stopped. The bare, harvested hills turned to lush pine forest-covered mountains. The area was dotted with small farming communities and fields. There was a peaceful town with a red fieldstone church and lovely, painted houses. Black birds flew restlessly in the sky, but the land beneath was undisturbed and at peace. Karl-Heinz imagined that in good times cows would wander through the valleys and graze near the lake or river that he thought might be nearby. As clouds moved in, the small, forested mountains took on a dark hue and he dreamed it was spring and he could run through the hills picking berries or looking for mushrooms in the forest.

The truck hit a pothole and he bounced hard. Karl-Heinz began to feel anxious and gnawed nervously on his lip. He was about to meet his new family in Korbach and wondered what they might be like. Soon the terrain changed and all the small towns started to look the same, sleepy and peaceful. Still, he wondered what Korbach would be like and what his schoolmates would try to do to him.

When they arrived at the edge of a good-sized town he was surprised. The town looked peaceful and clean. A stark contrast from the smoldering rubble he had left in Kassel. People were going about their business as though nothing were going on elsewhere, as though the war was not less than an hour away. He was absolutely amazed how these Germans kept going without appearing to have a care in the world when a city only twenty-five kilometers away smelled of sulphur and lay in ruins. Everything seemed so disconnected. Everyone was so isolated. It was very strange.

Karl-Heinz was one of four foreign-born Germans moved to Korbach that month. One of them was a girl named Vicky who seemed rather talkative at first glance but Karl-Heinz did not go over to talk to her. Her shoes were shined, and her socks had fallen down to her ankles and had wrinkled under her arch. He listened to what she was saying to another foreign-born German and decided that Vicky must be from Luxembourg or Belgium from the names of the places she was talking about.

Vicky was selected first and she went to the Behler's house. The NSV representative introduced Karl-Heinz to Herr Renner, a large man with a full face, round-framed glasses, a mustache and a double chin, who greeted Karl-Heinz by shaking his hand. The NSV representative told him that Herr Renner was an upstanding citizen of the Reich who worked with city government. The two men stood and spoke for a few minutes near the train station before Herr Renner patted Karl-Heinz on the shoulder and said, "Come, Karl-Heinz. It is time to go home for lunch. The house is not far, only about five blocks from here. Can you manage your bags?"

"Yes, Herr Renner." He picked up his briefcase and small suitcase, and caught up to Herr Renner who was walking at a comfortable pace down the street.

"Korbach is a lot smaller than Kassel," Karl-Heinz said trying to make small talk.

"Yes, it is," Herr Renner answered without going into detail. "But it is in better shape. We could see Kassel burning from here after the attack."

Karl-Heinz looked around. Just like in Hohenelse and Kassel the houses were freestanding. There were a few short stone walls surrounding the gardens, but none of the homes was surrounded by tall walls topped with barbed wire and broken glass as the freestanding houses were in Quito. The town had a comfortable feeling and Karl-Heinz felt safe. He took a deep breath.

"That is our house there." Herr Renner pointed with his good hand. Karl-Heinz had noticed that Herr Renner favored one hand over the other.

The house was a whitewashed two-story with dormer windows that jutted through the roof. The two-chimney house was beautiful and impressive. "Look, there is my daughter, Helga. She must be a little older than you are, Karl-Heinz. You must be what... thirteen... fourteen?"

"I turned thirteen in July, Herr Renner."

"Yes, then she is almost two years older than you are. Our son, Eckelhard, is a soldier in the German army. We are very proud of him. You will have his room while you stay with us. Oma is in the guest room."

"Yes, sir."

"You'll have chores to do. My wife, Heinriette, will tell you what is expected."

"Yes, sir." Should I call her Frau Renner or Tante Hein . . . ri . . . ette?" Karl-Heinz stumbled over the name trying to imitate Herr Renner's pronunciation.

Karl-Heinz could tell that Herr Renner was not a man prone to excessive smiling or chatting with children, but he detected a grin when he heard Karl-Heinz stutter through the question. He cleared his throat and answered, "I should think she would like it very much if you called her Tante Hennie. But you can ask her."

"Yes sir, Herr Renner."

Helga spotted her father and the young boy approaching. She waved at her father, and went around to the back door. Karl-Heinz supposed that Helga had gone to tell her mother they were outside. Frau Renner appeared at the door in an apron and spoke.

"Well, you are finally here!" she stated as though they had dallied along the way.

Karl-Heinz juggled his briefcase and suitcase and stuck out his hand to greet Frau Renner. He bowed somewhat like his father did whenever he met a woman. *Es freut mich sehr Sie kennen zu lernen, Frau Renner, . . .* "[3] *"Fraülein Helga . . ."* Frau Renner shook his hand and responded accordingly. Helga added a giggle.

Herr Renner handed his wife a sheet of paper with Karl-Heinz's information on it.

"So. . . Karl-Heinz. . . Contag is it? Welcome. Helga will show you to your room. You can clean up and join us at the table in a few minutes."

"Thank you, Frau Renner."

Karl-Heinz followed Helga up the stairs. "Your room is here. The bathroom is down the hall. Grandmother's room is there."

"Thank you, Fraülein Helga." Helga snickered at his formality and said, "You can call me Helga."

"Thank you, Helga."

The first few weeks at the Renner house were very uncomfortable. Karl-Heinz was given chores, none of which were too difficult, but he missed the rapport he had with the Rümlers. He had new duties and seldom spoke with the family. He shined the family shoes once a week. He fed the pig and twenty chickens every day. This was his favorite job. He cleaned the ashes out of the stove. He kept his room clean and helped prepare vegetables for cooking. Tante Hennie was a good cook and could do much with very little. They didn't seem to lack anything important and the house stayed warmer than the bombed house in Kassel. He got along well with Tante Hennie and Helga, and although he interacted very little with Herr Renner, he believed him to be a good man. He saw even less of Helga's infirm grandmother who was bedridden in another upstairs bedroom.

Karl-Heinz began his studies at the Alte Landesschule in Korbach a few weeks after he arrived and he wrote his first in-class composition on Thursday, December 2, 1943,[4] a first-person narrative about Forest Ranger Hopp who told a story about his lost dog, Krambambuli. Karl-Heinz was proud of his creativity and his penmanship. He had had a little trouble with his new pen and ink, but since he was more interested in writing the story than worrying about the writing equipment, he wrote nearly five full pages. On the way home from school he repeated the dog's name over and over. "Krambambuli, come here; go on, fetch the stick Krambambuli; good dog Krambambuli." It was a terrific sounding name for a dog.

When the composition was returned the following week, his enthusiasm for storytelling in his new school waned. The instructor returned the writing sample with numerous corrections about vocabulary and grammar and three stern comments: *Use the ink blotter. Poor, improve.*

On January 13, 1944 he wrote his second composition and turned it in to the instructor. Once again he felt exuberant when he wrote about "Das war einer feiner Tag,"[4] but imagined the instructor would make the customary humiliating comments about his mistakes.

When he finished his outdoor chores after school, Karl Heinz sat down at the kitchen table to help Frau Renner in the kitchen peel potatoes.

"We turned in our second composition today," Karl-Heinz offered, hoping to strike up a conversation. "I was supposed to write about something happy. I did, but I don't think the instructor will like it much," he told Mrs. Renner glumly.

"Why such a long face, Karl-Heinz?"

"I don't know."

"Bring that bucket of potatoes over here, wash them, and put a few on the table, Karl-Heinz," Frau Renner said. The routine was the same as usual, but she felt obligated to repeat the words anyway. "Well, what did you write about?" she asked.

"A hunting trip with my father . . . before we left Ecuador."

Frau Renner pulled her apron off the hook, pulled it over her head, and secured the ties around her waist. "It has been almost two years since you were in Ecuador, Karl-Heinz. I don't know why you continue to think about that place. Do you really think you can still remember the things that happened there well enough?"

"Oh, yes!" he answered with great enthusiasm. He had hoped she would ask him about the composition. "When I can't sleep at night I try to think about things we used to do as a family. It keeps me from thinking about what happened at Kassel. I often think about that hunting trip, because the jungle was so different from Quito and I remember it so well. We were near Santo

Domingo de los Colorados in the forest and everything was so strange, ... the people, the plants, the animals. My father shot two monkeys and we ate them!" The words were rushing out of Karl-Heinz's mouth.

Frau Renner screwed up her face in astonishment. "You ate monkeys! The instructor will think that was pretty awful, I bet."

"I could tell you about the trip," Karl-Heinz suggested. "That way I can check on the words I used. There were a few things I did not know how to say ... exactly," Heinz offered hopefully.

Frau Renner turned and sat down at the kitchen table across from him. She was not one to spend the afternoon chatting over tea when there was work to be done. "I suppose that would be all right, Karl-Heinz. Tell me about the trip while you peel these vegetables for supper." She pushed the vegetables toward him. "Keep the skins thin."

"Yes, of course. This is how I started the composition. *It was late morning when my brother Ernstchen and I climbed into the back seat of the red Ford behind the driver my father had hired for the hunting trip.*' Papa does not know how to drive so we didn't have a car. Not many people have cars in Quito so he really didn't have to learn how to drive. Oh, Irmgard and Werner had to stay at home; they were too young to go with us."

"You don't have to tell me exactly what you wrote. Just the story. I'll ask if I need explanations or if I need to correct a word." Frau Renner brushed a loose shock of hair into place with the back of her hand.

"All right. Ernstchen and I loved to ride in the red Ford whenever we went anywhere. Our favorite street to travel on was Bolívar Street, named after the Great Liberator, because it was very, very steep and you always felt like you were flying off the back seat if the driver went really fast. It had cobble stones and it was very bumpy like this." Karl-Heinz demonstrated by jiggling up and down in his chair. He had a wild look about him and it was clear that he was enjoying the moment.

"Karl Heinz, did you write about that, too, or just about the hunting trip?"

"Well," he shrugged and looked a little sheepish, "I had to tell how we got out of Quito. But I didn't put in the jiggling or all the extra stuff I told you." He snickered. Seeing Frau Renner's serious face, he continued the story with a bit more decorum, although he felt as though he could burst with excitement as he told each detail. "I was not sure whether we went east or west over the Andes. I can't remember now which I wrote in the composition either." Karl-Heinz hesitated and then continued, "Papa wanted to hunt near *Santo Domingo de los Colorados and. . .*"

"Karl Heinz. That is not German. It is a city or an area?"

"*Santo Domingo de los Colorados* means. . . Saint Dominic of the red Indians, or something like that. It is the name of a town where the Colorado . . . the red Indians live. They wear striped cloth wrapped around them from the waist to the knee, and the men put a red plant substance called *achiote* in their hair. They paint their faces and their bodies with black and red paint made from herbs. It makes their hair stick out like this." Heinz held both hands flat against the top of his head as a demonstration. "It is a bit like a personal umbrella because their hair is combed straight out over their eyes. You can see them from a distance because their hair is bright red!"

Frau Renner looked to see if Karl-Heinz was kidding her, but he looked serious so she shook her head and encouraged him to continue, "So you went to hunt where these. . . painted Indians live?"

"Not exactly. We stopped before we got there, but it was in that direction. In a jungle."

Frau Renner nodded and continued peeling potatoes while she listened now somewhat interested. Karl Heinz loved to tell stories and he thought that Frau Renner was beginning to enjoy listening to him. Still, she didn't want to make him think that she was enjoying the entertainment.

"Keep the skins very thin, Karl-Heinz," she said curtly.

"I will, Tante Hennie. As I was saying, the car left Quito and we headed for the mountains and climbed, climbed, climbed. When we got to the top we could see there was a deep green valley in front of us. The road was bumpy and washed out a bit, so it was sort of scary when we got to a turn in the road. Every once in a while you could spot a small farm with a few cows and some crops, mostly corn. Above the road you could see uninhabited peaks, not snowcapped because it was too warm, but peaks covered in trees and vines. Quito sits in a valley between the two Andean ranges and we had to climb the mountains. . . to the west, I think, to be able to descend to the jungle where Papa wanted to hunt. It was so steep that when we were riding in the car my ears kept popping and Ernstchen kept holding his nose and puffing out his cheeks to make them pop faster. . . like this!" Karl-Heinz plugged his nose and filled his cheeks with air.

"Did you put that in your composition, Karl-Heinz?" Mrs. Renner scowled before putting some of the peeled potatoes into water.

"No, but it was funny remembering how Ernstchen did that." Karl-Heinz chuckled. "The trip was very exciting because it looked like the trees and the rocks were hanging on for their lives on the vertical slopes. I kept thinking that a rock or tree might fall down on the Ford and push us into the valley hundreds or maybe a thousand meters below. The road was so narrow I don't think that in most places two cars could pass each other. It was pretty dangerous and Papa said that some cars and trucks, even buses, had slipped off the road into the green jungle below."

Frau Renner looked up at him and let one eyebrow rise a little. "So it is warm in Quito?"

"Oh, no," Karl-Heinz answered, now a bit irritated with having to interrupt his story. "Quito is up so high in the mountains that it is always cool. That is what was so interesting about *this* trip. The plant life started to change as we descended from the highest point about an hour or so outside Quito. When we started to go down the mountain on the other side, the ground changed. It was covered with vines and gigantic green leaves. The trees were shorter than in Quito, and they were also covered with small-leafed vines. It was a real jungle. Monkeys live there and there are lots of tropical birds. All sorts of birds. Everything looked really green and wet. When we came around a corner hugging the mountain I saw a . . ." Karl-Heinz hunted for the word in German and scratched his head. "Water falling from way up high. . . what is that called in German?"

"*Wasserfall*," suggested Mrs. Renner snidely. It wasn't the most difficult word and she thought he was trying to get her to participate more in the conversation than she really wanted to.

"Yes. Papa said the thin waterfalls were called 'Las Tres Marías' or the 'Three Marys.' From very high up the water fell meters and meters, splashing against dark rocks called *laja* stone. It is sort of like slate, I think. The water ran into the rocky streams below the road. I have not seen any rocky streams here in Germany like those rocky streams in Ecuador. There was a mountain stream in Burg Kreuzen that reminded me of it. My family was there for a holiday last year."

"I see. So you were not as high in the mountains. The temperature must have changed, too." Frau Renner said, getting her ward back into the story.

"The temperature started changing and the humidity did too. That is why I remember it as such a beautiful day. There were bamboo trees and lots of red-leafed plants. Ferns even grew out of the rocks. We stopped for a few minutes," Karl-Heinz lowered his head and said with embarrassment, ". . . uh, to go to the bathroom, . . . and I was surprised to see how wet everything was. . . from the humidity, I mean." He chuckled before continuing. "The ground was muddy near the dirt and cobblestone road.

There were yellow, white, red and lavender flowering bushes. It was a bright sunny day so we could see everything for kilometers and kilometers."

"Did you ever get to go hunting or did you just look at the flowers?" Mrs. Renner asked, trying to hurry the story along a bit.

Karl-Heinz sighed at being interrupted again. "Yes. And when we passed a pig hanging at the side of the road, my father..."

"A pig hanging on the side of the road?" asked Frau Renner, quite stupefied.

"Yes. That is a common sight. They hang the pig up, disembowel it, rub it with *achiote*, the same stuff the Indians put in their hair, and roast it. They sell the meat right there on the road."

When Frau Renner did not make a comment Karl-Heinz continued with his story. "My father pointed out where he wanted the driver to turn. We turned where the pig was hanging and crossed over the rocky creek we had seen from up above. Just beyond the rocky creek it was much warmer, and there were palm trees, poinsettia trees, and tall grasses. We were heading beyond the village of Tandapi to an area where we saw large fields of banana plants."

"How can you remember the name of that village, Karl-Heinz? There must have been many along the way."

"No. Not many people live there. I remember Tandapi because we stopped there to buy some *cocadas*, a coconut candy. In Tandapi *burros*, uh... donkeys... were being loaded with bananas and one of the local villagers had a monkey on his shoulder. Ernstchen kept telling Papa he wanted to take a monkey home with us. Papa just laughed and pointed to his gun like he'd rather shoot it than carry it around on his shoulder."

"That is awful. Did you buy some bananas to eat?" asked Frau Renner.

"No, Papa said that those bananas were going to be used for pig food. There were hundreds of green bananas, piles of bananas, maybe there were thousands of bananas right there. I sure would like to see that pile of bananas today! I'd eat a whole wheelbarrow full and get myself a stomach ache!"

"What an exaggeration. But I do think you would have a lot of help with that wheelbarrow full if they were ripe bananas, Karl-Heinz." Mrs. Renner smiled. "Anyway, where did you go after buying the coconut candy?" She wondered now with genuine curiosity.

"We followed the Toachi River. That is the name of the rocky stream I was talking about. We passed a few bamboo shacks and drove over rolling hills until the driver turned off the road and crossed another rocky stream on the right side." Karl-Heinz looked sheepish as he continued. "We all took another bathroom break because it was so bumpy that Ernstchen couldn't... that's when I saw how well armed my father was. He wore a special holster on his belt. My father loves guns. He told me that he bought a few guns last year in January. He keeps them in his apartment in Potsdam."

"They could come in handy, I suppose," Frau Renner added without much interest.

"Oh, he can't really use them. He signed a paper saying he wouldn't use them. He just keeps them around to show off, I think." Karl-Heinz answered.

"So you went hunting right there by the stream?" Mrs. Renner was starting to look frustrated. She stood up and went to the stove.

"No. There was a small farmhouse... you would call it a shack... and a fellow looked out of his pane-less window at us. I remember he was wearing a big hat. Papa greeted him and we went in the house. It was already getting dark."

"What time was it then?" asked Mrs. Renner.

"It was just after six in the afternoon. The sun sets at the same time each day in Ecuador, not like here in Germany.

Ernstchen and I had supper and lay down on mats to sleep. We were tired and our ears were ringing from coming down the mountain. I think it was the first time I ever slept without any covers. It was so warm there. In Quito it is always quite cold at night. You can see your breath."

"Yes, you mentioned that. So your father didn't hunt that day?" Frau Renner inquired.

"No, we woke up late the next morning and Papa and the man were already gone. His wife gave us some coffee and bananas for breakfast and Ernstchen and I went out to play at the edge of the jungle. Pretty soon we heard some shots. Nearly an hour later my father, some Indians, and the wrinkled man who lived on the farm walked out of the jungle. Papa had shot two monkeys, a large bird and a *Dios te dé*!

"What's that, Karl Heinz? The last thing you said. . . What had he shot?"

"I did not know what to call it in my composition either. It was a . . . *Dios te dé*.[5] That's the sound the bird makes when it calls out. Like this, '*Dios te dé. Dios te dé.*'" Karl Heinz mimicked the bird's *rat-tat-tat call*. "It is a big bird with a large, curved beak almost as big as its body." He demonstrated the size and curvature of the beak with his hands. "Do you know the name in German?"

"No," Frau Renner answered, "but you should have described the bird in German in your composition instead of using . . . whatever it was you said."

"*Dios te dé*. It means, May God grant you that."

"That is an odd name for a bird. Did you eat that, too?" she asked rather shocked.

"We did not eat the *Dios te de*." Karl-Heinz picked up another vegetable and started peeling it and frowned pensively. "I suppose I should have described it in my composition, though."

Frau Renner chopped the peeled vegetables into pieces for soup. "So, they cooked the monkeys and you ate them. What did the monkey meat taste like?" She turned up her nose at the notion.

"It was good. I can't say exactly what it tasted like, but it was a lot like beef. That was a terrific day. I was so proud of my Papa," Karl-Heinz said with a smile.

Helga appeared at the doorway. "Did your brother eat the monkey meat, too? You said he wanted a live monkey. How could he eat a dead monkey?"

"I didn't know you were listening, Helga. Of course he ate the monkey meat. In Ecuador people eat a lot of different things. . . *cuis* in the mountains. . . they are furry creatures like rabbits that have tiny little ears that hide in their fur. On the coast the people eat big land lizards called iguanas. The iguanas sometimes grow this big!" Karl-Heinz stretched his hands apart nearly a meter. He enjoyed making Helga squirm a little.

Helga turned up her nose. "That is awful! Lizard eaters! I bet monkey meat stinks." Helga mocked him ever so slightly. "I wouldn't eat a monkey, ever!"

Helga was just about to turn around when her father entered the house.

"Guten Tag," was all he said.

"Guten Tag," Helga, Frau Renner and Karl-Heinz chimed in unison.

"You just missed Karl-Heinz's story about eating monkeys and lizards in Ecuador, Papa."

Herr Renner shuffled through the kitchen without hesitation, but he spoke as he went toward the stairs. "I don't want stories about foreign places told in my home. You are in Greater Germany, Karl-Heinz. You don't need to go on about things that happened to you years ago. "

"Yes, sir," Karl-Heinz said nervously as he cleaned up his work area.

Frau Renner stood and put the peeled potatoes in a pot. She took a deep breath before she turned to Karl-Heinz and said softly, "That was a good story, Karl-Heinz. I hope the instructor likes it, too. We won't be talking about it again, though." There was genuine compassion in her voice.

"I understand, Tante Hennie," Karl-Heinz answered respectfully, but he felt he had been dealt a blow to the stomach. *What could be so harmful about talking about the past*, he wondered silently. Just before he turned to leave the room he asked, "Is there anything else you would like me to do, Tante Hennie?"

"Not until the potatoes are cooked, Karl-Heinz," she answered.

Karl-Heinz went outside to watch the pig eat. He eyed the pig's barley dinner with jealousy. It was not that he was particularly hungry, but the boiled barley smell had filled the kitchen when he arrived home from school and it had reminded him of the warm barley he had eaten with brown sugar shavings in Quito. Pig food was great, he thought to himself. He held a one-sided conversation about Quito with the pig who sniffed and grunted in response.

When Karl-Heinz received his corrected composition the following week the instructor's notes said, "interesting," but he had deducted a good number of points for penmanship and error correction. Karl-Heinz found the instructor's preference for neatness over creativity uninspiring so he did not report to Frau Renner about the composition grade. He did not think she would be interested anyway. Instead he reported his frustration to the pig that afternoon after school.

"What do you want to know? Snort, snort. Can't talk about it, right? Snort, snort. I don't want you to write about it either. Snort, snort, snort," he said mockingly.

Except for the frustration of being an adolescent without a past he could talk about, school days were actually quite routine for Karl-Heinz in Korbach. The English teacher, Herr Hinterich, and the Latin teacher, Herr Frosh, taught his favorite classes. He disliked the mathematics teacher who pulled his cheek to discipline him.

Karl-Heinz celebrated his fourteenth birthday on July 25, 1944. The Renners did not make a big deal about the birthday. Secretly he had hoped they would have given him gifts and sung songs like he heard some people did in some families. He shrugged off the day and expected nothing. Mrs. Renner did make a cake, though, and afterward he felt much more like a real member of the family.

After his birthday Karl-Heinz noticed two changes in the activities of the German Youth group in Korbach. One was increased pressure to join the military ranks as soldiers. The other was a heightened disregard for other people's property by the youth leaders. The German Youth leaders were only a few years older than he was, and they encouraged the younger boys, who ranged in age from eight to fourteen, to take risks. One time, they told them to steal apples. The leaders tried to show how powerful they were by getting the boys to do whatever they asked of them even if the boys would not have done the deed on their own. The first time that the leaders told them to steal apples, Karl-Heinz and a few others did not join the boys who filled their bellies. Karl-Heinz felt bad that they couldn't do anything about the theft by their comrades either. Dissension was not permitted. But he also felt a little uncomfortable when he did not follow orders to the letter.

Karl-Heinz marched with the other boys in the German Youth and he even learned to sing songs like, "*Wenn die Soldaten durch die Stadt marchieren, stehen die Mädchen an die Fenster und die Türen*,"[6] which he belted out proudly in his voice that was always just a little off key. But when the fourteen-, fifteen-, and sixteen-year old boys from his school were corralled in the theater and strongly encouraged to join the proud ranks of the military, he was keenly aware that only three hands of the one hundred boys in the theater volunteered for military duty. He did not care if the girls stood at the windows and doors to wave him off like they waved to the soldiers in the song. He had no plans to volunteer for military duty at fourteen. Everyone he knew said fourteen was too young.

Shortly thereafter the war arrived in Korbach.

On Sunday morning, May 5, 1944, several precautionary air raid alarms sounded in Korbach. But it was a beautiful, sunny day and Karl-Heinz went behind the house to polish the family shoes. It was peaceful in the backyard. The chickens were noisy and the pig snorted about, but it was still peaceful. Bushes and beautiful shade trees, now empty of their leaves, surrounded the Renner's backyard. The back door was in full sun and he felt the delicious warmth on his back. Startled, Karl-Heinz jumped to his feet. He looked into the sky and saw nearly twenty planes zooming toward him like bees from a beehive. One sent out a marker. In a breath Karl-Heinz dropped the brush and the shoe he was polishing, and dashed into the kitchen screaming, "*Sie geben Rauchzeichen, sofort in den Keller.*"[12] Helga and Frau Renner followed on his heels to the cellar. Within moments Herr Renner rushed out of the bathroom and down the staircase holding his unfastened trousers with his good hand. The first bomb landed before the older man's feet reached the basement floor.

The noise overhead was deafening and Karl-Heinz watched Helga cover her ears instinctively with her hands. He saw Herr Renner protect his head instinctively. Karl-Heinz could feel his heart pounding. He remembered what Uli said and tried to calm down by repeating her words: "You are all right if you can hear the planes and the bombs." All of a sudden an intense pressure drained the breath from Karl-Heinz and his stomach muscles gripped in a panic. The impact had bounced him a third of a meter into the air. He watched his feet leave the floor and land in the midst of shattered glass. He ran his hands over his trousers and his shirt as though he were checking to see if he was all right. There was a baked roll near his shoe and he picked it up. The bread and rolls Frau Renner had baked on Saturday had tumbled into the cellar's center from the shelf where they had been stored. The apple strudel had tipped over, too. The carrots and potatoes and the pile of sand looked untouched. He looked at the Renners.

Frau Renner yelled frantically, "*Gott in Himmel!* Where did the bomb hit? Karl-Heinz, go look out that window!" Chards of glass underfoot, he walked toward the empty window frame, climbed up on a wooden box, and peered at the neighbor's house.

"Their house is half gone! That must have been what made us bounce. Our house is fine." Karl-Heinz shuddered. "But there is a lot of stuff that will have to be cleared out of the yard." Helga started to complain loudly, "My ears hurt and I can't hear. I can't hear anything."

Karl-Heinz gave her a strange look. He could hear the sirens.

Herr Renner turned to Karl-Heinz and motioned to him. "Go ahead, Karl-Heinz. Go on up."

"But the sirens are still blowing, Herr Renner," Karl-Heinz said, amazed at the request.

"Go on. There aren't any more planes."

He felt numb and shuddered. He was convinced that the house had avoided a direct hit but still he was wary as he approached the top of the stairs. He peered around the kitchen floor. Things were lying everywhere in the kitchen. The floor was a mess. He looked up and he could see blue sky. It was then that he realized a bomb had hit their house. He could barely breathe but he called down to Herr Renner, "Our house has been hit."

When they emerged, Frau Renner pushed a piece of the second-story bathtub in the dirt with her right shoe. Karl-Heinz could see she was trembling. She took in a deep breath and looked at her husband and said matter-of-factly, "The tub has been blown to bits. The bomb landed in our filled bathtub and blew it to bits. Look!"

Helga emerged and stood dumbfounded, and Karl-Heinz could see that she had been crying. "Helga," he asked, "are you all right?" But Helga could not hear him and cried out loud, "I can't hear anything! Something is wrong! I can't hear anything!"

The family walked around the house in a daze. The house was so damaged they could no longer live in it. The chickens and pig had vanished. Half the house was blown to bits. Helga watched as her father broke down in tears. She did not remember ever seeing her father cry. She stopped crying and went to be with her father. It was a terrible tragedy.

When he regained his composure, Herr Renner surveyed the damage with Karl-Heinz and discovered that two bombs, not one, had hit the house. One had fallen into the basement under the pantry. There was a deep hole under the cement. He turned to his wife and said, "Hennie, if we had been on the other side of the cellar, we would have been killed. If the bomb had landed a couple of meters closer, we would all be dead. And if Karl-Heinz hadn't come running through the kitchen like he did…" He signed heavily, "My God, look at this house."

Frau Renner turned to Karl-Heinz and said, "You saved our lives, Karl-Heinz!"

On September 25, 1944 at two o'clock in the afternoon there was an attack by the British Air Force on the Korbach Lelbach-Rhena train station just five blocks from the Renners' house. A few people were wounded and one man was killed in what the German radio now called one of the routine terror attacks by Anglo-American forces. Fear began to infest everyday living in Korbach as it had in Kassel not too long before, and Karl-Heinz was not immune to its effects.

The Renner home after the bombing in Korbach on November 5, 1944.

Karl Heinz had not seen his father or his family for months and after the railroad line had been attacked he was convinced that a visit from his father would now be unlikely. To relax at night, he started to daydream more about the happy times he had spent with family and friends in Quito. Thinking about his life in Quito helped to balance the fear he had at night. He kept his thoughts to himself when he reminisced about picnics in El Tingo, hikes in the Andes, swimming trips to the reservoir above the house on the Rocafuerte. His daydreams were vivid but the words to describe his thoughts no longer came easily in Spanish. His boyhood language was fading.

On Wednesday, October 20, 1944, Karl-Heinz finished his composition entitled "Ärger und Freuden im Herbst"[7] with the following words:

> The boy was a good help to his aging grandfather. He had learned all the ins and outs of the forest since he had often gone out with his grandfather to hunt deer and rabbits. He had learned to shoot well at an early age. When the boy became a young man he inherited the old woodsman's house, and he became a great woodsman, too.

He was not inspired enough to put heart and soul into the composition about the boy and the old woodsman. He was delighted when the time to write expired. He had made a meager effort, and it was finished.

When he left the school building around noon, it was still a cool, cloudless day. The sun was warm on Karl-Heinz's face and hands and he relaxed by the time he and a schoolmate were a block from school. Werner Meyer usually walked most of the way home with him and Karl-Heinz enjoyed his friend's quick wit. They usually talked about the other girls and boys in their class or about the teachers. Today was no different. Werner had a complaint about the girl who sat two rows behind him in class.

"She walked right by me today," Werner said with a grimace. "I held my breath as long as I could, but when I couldn't hold it any longer I took in a deep breath and . . . whew. . . the stench was still there! It was really bad today, too."

Karl-Heinz laughed behind his hand and wiped at his nose as though he could smell the girl's stinky feet right there on the street. "She has smelly feet, but she sure knows her history! She knows all the answers in class!"

"She still has the stinkiest feet in town, no matter what she knows about history. It would smell better if she wore two dead skunks on her feet as slippers instead of those smelly, old shoes she wears!"

Karl-Heinz laughed again. "I don't think they wash her socks but once a week. The smell gets worse and worse each day. I bet she smells all right on Sunday, don't you think?"

"Not unless they wash her shoes too," Werner argued before heading toward his house. "See you tomorrow, Karl-Heinz."

"See you, Werner." Karl-Heinz had just turned for home when the sirens went off. *Air raid!,* he said to himself as he sprinted toward the Renner home. He took a short cut through a neighbor's yard and headed to the cellar for safety. Helga and Frau Renner were already there.

Karl-Heinz imagined that the clear sky made the Lelbach-Rhena train station and the nearby bridge easy targets for the two low-flying planes overhead. They must have aimed their gunfire at the area surrounding the train station because he could hear the machine guns as though they were right on top of him. He scratched his head, closed his eyes and prayed.

When the all clear was sounded, Karl-Heinz, Helga, and Frau Renner emerged from their cellar. Frau Renner suggested that the two curious teens not go looking for trouble. They would find out soon enough what had happened at the train station.

Karl-Heinz learned the following day before classes began that a few of the school children who commuted to his school from Usseln and Willingen had panicked during the terror attack and had run for cover under a bridge outside of town. Two fourteen-year old boys from his class, Christian Saure and Helmut Wilke, and a thirteen-year old from Usslen had run under the railroad bridge to hide from the strafing.[9]

"They shot his feet off," one of the schoolboys said, wrinkling his nose. "He bled to death."

Karl-Heinz could feel his stomach turn. "Whose feet were shot off?"

"Christian's. Christian Saure from our class. Someone said another boy from our class was hit in the face and the hip, but he isn't dead. I don't know which boy yet. But can you imagine? They shot Christian's feet off. Good God! It's awful."

"Don't talk about it then," said another boy.

Karl-Heinz tried not to imagine what his classmate had gone through, but when he looked at his own feet he started feeling more than a little queasy. He tried to calm his own fears about being shot by repeating what he had witnessed soon after he arrived in Germany: "There was a soldier who came to my school in Hohenelse and he said that he didn't even know that he was shot in the leg until he saw the blood ooze through his boot. He destroyed six tanks before he realized what happened. I mean, before he realized that he had been shot. He even wore badges on his sleeve to prove that he had blown up six tanks." The other boys listened to the words but he could tell they were as uncomfortable as he was.

School days were never quite the same after the strafing. None of the children who had traveled to school by train returned to their classrooms in Korbach. The instructors told the students in Korbach that other arrangements had been made for their education in the villages where they lived. The empty chairs at school were a constant reminder that each one of them was an easy target. The classmate who survived being shot in the face and the hip didn't return to class either. Karl-Heinz and a few other boys went to visit him and encouraged him to come back to school when he was feeling better, but he didn't. School no longer seemed as important as surviving did, and they were not surprised that he did not want to return. Korbach was no longer the safe haven Karl-Heinz had believed it to be.

In October the daily radio announcements from Berlin indicated that the German army had been victorious on several fronts,[10] especially against the Russians, and against the British and Americans in Italy. Karl-Heinz could only imagine these faraway places that had exotic names. He was not particularly interested in the announcements. Sometimes, at the end of the announcement there was some information about possible losses or trouble spots for Germany. There was never any specific information. One day he heard that the British had hit Stuttgart. Another day there was an assault on Nuremberg. Terror planes from the United States had hit Regensberg. Aachen had also been under fire and on October 22 the report indicated that there had been hand-to-hand combat in the streets of that city.[11] Arms and munitions were being distributed to the Cologne regiment of the People's Army because, it seemed, they would have occasion to use them. Low-flying aircraft continued their attacks against the civilian population in different areas like they had in Korbach. The war was everywhere. It wasn't safe anywhere.

No matter how hard Karl-Heinz tried to ignore the news about the bombings and the terror planes, he worried about his family and what might happen to them. He wondered about Maria Renaud in Nuremberg, his grandparents in Hannover, and whether the hotel where they stayed in Stuttgart in 1942 had been bombed. He wondered if the spa at Burg Kreuzen had become a target; it had been a place of such peace and joy for him. The lack of information about his family made each mention of terror attacks more irritating and annoying. Christian Saure had been the victim of a terror attack. He hadn't planned to die that day. Karl-Heinz found himself looking to the sky for low-flying planes as he walked home from school. He practiced running fast and pretended he was diving for cover. The new slogan that people were repeating at school, "*Achtung! fest anhalten*," did not provide any feeling of comfort. The slogan "Hold tight, Hold tight, and once again, Hold tight!" made him feel as though, with each repetition, he was losing his grip on who he was.

One day Frau Renner asked him to go to the edge of town to bring in a spooked horse that a woman was going to keep near her house.

"The horse is afraid of shadows. No one can do anything with it. You are good with animals. Do you think you could bring the horse in?"

"Sure," Karl-Heinz shrugged. He felt compassion for the horse. *That poor animal feels as jumpy as I do,* he thought to himself as he walked to the edge of Korbach. Karl-Heinz was not afraid of the horse and did not have trouble walking him into town. *You just have to understand the animal's fears,* he thought, *like I do.*

Karl-Heinz knew that his father did not know they had been living in the Schmaltz's basement since the May bombing so he wrote the Schmaltz's address on a sheet of paper from his composition book and stuck it on the front door of the Renners' uninhabitable house. He greeted the neighbors and he walked to the Capitol Theatre for the Youth Film hour. The first warning siren sounded at quarter past eleven and the scheduled film hour had to be cancelled. He dashed through the streets scouring the sky for planes, the hair at the nape of his neck standing on end. *I'll dodge through here, roll there, hide over there, slip through that narrow passage, and take cover under there...*

When he arrived at the Schmaltz's house he was ecstatic to see his father in the basement.

"Papa!" he yelled over the siren.

"Just in time for an air raid, Heinz... and at the beginning of Holy Week!" Ernst received his son with a warm hug.

The two families huddled in the basement while low-flying planes attacked the Lelbach-Rhena train station. Karl-Heinz could never get used to the feeling of panic whenever the sirens went off, but he felt safer with his father at his side. Ernst seemed somewhat immune to fear and gave off an air of carefree confidence. Karl-Heinz imagined that Berlin had been hit regularly and that his father no longer got too upset whenever an alarm sounded. The truth was that it was just the opposite, however. Ernst felt the pangs of fear each time the warnings sounded.

Will my children be orphaned? The thought paralyzed him, but he never allowed others to see how the sirens affected him.

When they came out of the cellar after the all clear, Frau Renner and Helga went to the kitchen. There was an extra mouth to feed. Ernst and Karl-Heinz stood outside.

"I spoke with Frau Renner before you returned from the theater this morning. I was shocked to see the house on Bergstrasse. What a shame! I told her that I thought you should come back with me to Potsdam."

"Really? That would be terrific!" His excitement faded. "But there are more air raids in Berlin and Potsdam than here, right?"

"You can't imagine how many! There are air raids all the time. You won't recognize Berlin or Potsdam," his father answered. "Sometimes I wonder if there will be an apartment to go home to. Many people have already been forced to leave to find housing."

"Then I don't want to go, Papa. Not ye,." Karl-Heinz answered. "It is pretty calm here, and I have friends. I feel safer here. I don't think the Allies care too much about this little town. Besides, I have earned a lot of medals with the German Youth. Look!" Karl-Heinz pulled out his medals and showed them to his father with great pride.

"Impressive!" his father said. "Potsdam isn't the same place you remember, Heinz. Since January there have been many attacks. The street cars don't run anymore and it is hard to get around,"[15] Ernst said, without mentioning anything about the new order to extend defense training to five to twelve-year old children, issued at the end of February and that boys born in 1929 and in 1930, like his son, had already been called to serve.[16] "You have had lots of opportunities here in Korbach. The Renners treat you very well, too. Perhaps you are right to want to stay. You might not like my cooking in Potsdam. I am only good at frying potatoes."

"I hope you don't fry them in castor oil," Karl-Heinz said remembering the meal he had had with his father in Potsdam.

"Cod liver oil, when I can get it," his father offered half-jokingly.

Karl-Heinz shrugged. "What could I do at your apartment in Potsdam, Papa? I wouldn't have any friends there. I don't know anyone. There is nothing I can do. I don't want to see more bombings. I am happy here and I can help the Renners. Now that things are getting back to normal in Korbach, I am glad to stay. Of course, I want to be with you, Ernstchen, Irmgard and Werner, but not when there are so many attacks and bombings." Karl-Heinz shook his head and spoke clearly. "No. I want to stay here until things get back to normal in Potsdam and Berlin. Then I will go there if you want me to." Ernst agreed.

That evening Helga went to sleep in her parents' room and Ernst slept in the room with his son. The next morning Karl-Heinz awoke to his father's snoring. He slipped out of the room, washed and dressed. It was an important day for him and he did not want to miss any of it. His father dragged himself out of bed around seven. Frau Renner did not have to prepare breakfast since everyone planned to eat heartily at the special celebration after the confirmation ceremony at the church. The service was scheduled for eight o'clock, but the air raid sirens kept them all at home with a postponement until nine.

They walked to the church. When the parishioners and confirmants were seated in the pews, Pastor Hohmann began the ceremony. He seemed nervous and everyone was aware that another interruption was probable. Around 9:30 the first warning alarm went off and Pastor Hohmann began to read the names of the confirmants as quickly as he could.[17] Parents got restless and Karl-Heinz sensed that others were trying to decide whether to stay in the church or to run outside. The church could be an easy target, but the area outside the church did not offer good shelter from strafing. Each confirmant rushed up to receive the certificate. Before Pastor Hohmann had finished the list of 100 names the full alarm sounded and planes could be heard overhead.

There were hundreds of people in the church and no one knew quite where to run. Some decided to stay put and dove under the pews, but the Renners, Ernst and Karl-Heinz ran from the church. Ernst and Karl-Heinz hit the ground two meters from each other when one plane flew low overhead. Karl-Heinz squeezed his eyes shut and prayed aloud, "Please God. Don't let them shoot us. Don't let them shoot us." When his father stood up Karl-Heinz rushed over to help him brush the dirt off his suit coat and trousers. Ernst grabbed his son and they headed for better shelter. Eventually they made it back to the basement room where they spent the entire afternoon. When they emerged late that afternoon they learned that the railroad tracks between Berndorf and Twiste had been severely damaged. Ernst made the necessary arrangements to return to Berlin and confirmation day had come to an end without a celebration. For dinner that evening the Renners, Karl-Heinz, and Ernst ate the bread and special cake that Frau Renner had prepared to take to the church.

"At least I got the certificate," Karl-Heinz said rather dejectedly after supper. "I am glad you could come. I am sorry we couldn't have a celebration."

"Just being with you was celebration enough, Heinz. And you'll never forget today!" Ernst hugged his son, shook the Renners' hands and left for Berlin.

Karl-Heinz expected after the brief air raid on Palm Sunday that Holy Week would be calm. He was wrong. The days following his father's departure were filled with chaos. Hundreds of German soldiers marched into Korbach and local residents were told to stay in their basements. Karl-Heinz was truly scared. Now it looked as though a battle would take place right outside their door. The Renner family stayed in the basement for twenty-four hours wondering what would happen. When the noise of the soldiers subsided, the Renners, Karl-Heinz, and many of the their neighbors emerged from their cellars to find the streets empty of soldiers and deathly quiet. There had not been any fighting, but parts of uniforms were scattered throughout the city as though the soldiers had undressed and dropped anything that would identify them as soldiers in the street.

Frau Renner saw the uniforms and weapons strewn in the street and she called to Karl-Heinz.

"Quick, Karl-Heinz. Throw out your uniform and all the medals from the German Youth. Throw them in the bushes behind the house. Do it right now."

"But... why, Tante Hennie? I earned them. They are mine. I don't want to throw them out." Karl-Heinz was confused and growing angrier as he thought about tossing his medals into the yard behind the Schmaltz's house.

"Don't argue. We have to get rid of anything that might put our family in danger. Throw them in the bushes. Now! Get your hunting knife, too. Can't you see that is why the German soldiers had abandoned their uniforms and their weapons? If the Americans or the British find out that you were in the German Youth, there could be trouble for you. You might be considered dangerous. I don't know. Just get rid of all of it. Do it now!"

Frau Renner had never been more adamant than at that moment and there was going to be no argument. Karl-Heinz stomped out of the house and, reluctantly, threw his prize possessions into the bushes behind the house. The uniform, the leather straps, the medals, the knife, everything flew to its new home in the dirt. "I'll remember where they are," he mumbled to himself as he kicked at the dirt a little.

On Maundy Thursday the first tank arrived at the edge of town. When Karl-Heinz saw a tank, he ran inside to tell Frau

Renner. "Tante Hennie, the Americans are in Korbach. I saw a tank." She answered with a demand. "Hurry! Tell the others." By the time they were in the basement, the machine gun firing began.

"Why are they shooting, Tante Hennie?"

"They are clearing the streets. They may shoot people who stay in the street or those who try to fight them. I don't know. We will be safe here." Frau Renner did not look confident but Karl-Heinz tried to believe her words. He could hear the tanks on the street. The chatter of rounds from the machine guns made him tremble.

Finally, when the noise subsided, the residents were called out of their homes and basements. The traffic of American tanks, jeeps and soldiers blocked Bahnhofstrasse just in front of the Schmaltz home. American soldiers had begun to secure the area by checking homes and telling the residents to come out and line up in front of their homes. Karl-Heinz, Helga, the Renners, and the Schmaltz's stood in front of the Schmaltz's house. At least a hundred neighbors lined Bahnhofstrasse. One soldier told them in German that all uniforms, helmets, weapons of any sort, and radios were to be collected and turned over to them. Some of the Americans tossed half-smoked cigarettes into the streets from their perch on top of tanks or from vehicles. One landed near a dead man lying in the street. Karl-Heinz's stomach turned as he saw two Germans who were standing nearby a tank near the dead man pick up the cigarettes and smoke them. He did not sleep comfortably that night.

On the morning of Good Friday Frau Renner sent Karl-Heinz out with a wheelbarrow. He worked steadily clearing the neighborhood of anything the Americans might consider suspicious including uniforms and helmets discarded by the German soldiers a few days earlier. Frau Renner had made it clear to him that it would be dangerous to do otherwise and he complied with the request. He enjoyed the work since it gave him a chance to look at the tanks and the Americans who were busy making the town theirs.

Early Easter morning two American soldiers came to the Renner house. They were armed. Karl-Heinz was unaware that Herr Renner was gone. One of the soldiers spoke to Frau Renner.

"Pistols?"

"*Nein. Kein pistols,*" Frau Renner answered shaking her head.

"Radio?" he asked.

"*Nein. Kein Radio,*" she said.

"*Schnaps?*" he demanded.

"*Nein. Kein schnaps,*" She answered uncomfortably.

"Eggs, then. Eggs!" His comrade repeated the demand in German, "*Eier, Eier!*"

"*Kein Eier.*" Frau Renner responded honestly, now quite afraid. Karl-Heinz wanted to protect her so he translated the words into English for the soldiers. "No eggs here." The soldiers looked at each other and shrugged. The blond soldier told the family to wait. They watched the Americans walk toward the neighbor's house, jump over the fence, and enter through the door. Five minutes later they returned with four duck eggs.

"*Eier,*" the soldier said proudly. "You cook *Eier.*" Frau Renner nodded.

The two soldiers, Helga, Karl-Heinz and Frau Renner all went to the eating area of their small apartment in the Schmaltz's house. Karl-Heinz watched as the dark-haired American soldier tried to tell Frau Renner that he did not want the duck eggs boiled or scrambled. He wanted the eggs cracked into a pan and not turned over. Karl-Heinz followed his gestures and explained what the soldier wanted in German to Tante Hennie. She thought it was odd, but agreed to make them according to his wishes.

It was an extremely uncomfortable situation. The two American soldiers sat down, and put their pistols right in front of them on the table. One of the barrels pointed directly at Karl-Heinz so he moved slightly to the side and then stood still as a statue while Frau Renner fried the eggs. The dark-haired soldier scowled and pointed at Karl-Heinz's waist and demanded. "What is that? Why are you wearing that?"

Karl-Heinz looked down and saw that the American was pointing at his belt buckle that had the words *Blut und Ehre* on it. He felt the color rise in his face and he swallowed hard. Tante Hennie looked as though she were about to gasp, but she did not utter anything. She bit at her lower lip a little. Karl-Heinz had not thought to throw out his belt with his other things. He said what came first to mind holding up his trousers with two hands as though they were about to fall off. "Only one *Gürtel*,"[18] he announced in a mixture of English and German. The Americans laughed at his word for belt, repeating "Girdle" to each other. The Americans were far more at ease than Helga, Frau Renner or Karl-Heinz.

The dark-haired American soldier pulled out a billfold, opened it, and put two photographs on the table next to his pistol. "Family" he said with pride, " My family." Karl-Heinz felt obligated to look so he moved closer to the table to view the pictures, keeping his hands behind him. There were two small, smiling children dressed as rabbits with long ears. Karl-Heinz smiled broadly and nodded to Helga to look at the photographs. The children looked quite adorable dressed as rabbits, sitting in what looked like a metal wagon pulled by their mother. The American tried to explain something about the pictures, but neither Karl-Heinz nor Helga could quite make out what he was saying and he gave up.[19] An air of warmth emanated from the American with the photographs, but Karl-Heinz, Helga, and Frau Renner felt odd with the soldier's attempt to be friendly.

Frau Renner served the soldiers and they ate the eggs quickly. As long as the Americans were in the kitchen and he was wearing his German Youth belt, Karl-Heinz felt nervous and uncomfortable. When the two men left, everyone in the house breathed a sigh of relief. Tante Hennie found an old belt for Karl-Heinz. The belt was far too large for him, and the end with the holes in it hung below the middle of his thigh. But he did not want to take any more chances with the Americans.

The American soldiers had confiscated their means of communicating with the world outside Korbach. There was no way to find out what was happening to his family in Potsdam or anywhere else because no one had a radio and there was no mail service. With no means of connecting with his family, Karl-Heinz turned his thoughts to the Renner family and his immediate situation. His main preoccupation was the fate of Herr Renner, who had worked for the German government. One afternoon he decided to go to American Military Headquarters in Korbach and testify about Herr Renner being a good man. He approached a soldier and told him that he was a South American boy living with the Renners. "Herr Renner is a good man," he said in halting English. A soldier asked him his address which he gave.

The next day there was a knock at the door of Schmaltz's house. Frau Renner came downstairs and told Karl-Heinz that there was an American soldier looking for him.

Karl-Heinz went outside and approached the armed soldier with trepidation.

"So, you are the boy from South America," the soldier said in Spanish.

"*Yawohl*. . . Sí" Karl-Heinz stammered from German to Spanish. "Karl-Heinz Contag Ziehe *von Quito, Eqvateur*."

"Well, what are you doing here in Korbach?" the soldier inquired.

"*Mein Vater. . . mein. . .*" he mumbled trying to find the words in Spanish. "I am from Puerto Rico. Do you understand that?"

"Puerto Rico, Sí, sí." Karl-Heinz responded enthusiastically with native-sounding Spanish. Finally, he thought, his Spanish could be useful. . . if he could only remember the words! He wanted to tell the American soldier that his father was blacklisted in Ecuador, that they had been put on a ship to Portugal, and on a train to Germany. He wanted to tell the American soldier from Puerto Rico that he hoped to be reunited with his family as soon as possible. The ideas ran through his mind but none of the words came in any language but German. He started several times with *"Mein Vater. . ."* but he couldn't remember the simple word for father in Spanish. He was dumbfounded. Spanish seemed entirely erased from his memory. He searched desperately for the words.

The man continued in Spanish with a reassuring voice. *"No te preocupes.* I am not going to hurt you or anything. I just came to get some information about you. Have you lived in Germany long?" The American had taken his frustration for nervousness, but Karl-Heinz could not explain that either.

"Sí," he responded and held up three fingers, *"Drei Jahre."*

"Three years?" the soldier guessed and Karl-Heinz confirmed the translation with a nod of his head. "Did you live in Ecuador before you came to Germany?" Karl-Heinz nodded and answered "Sí" to both questions.

"Were you born in Ecuador?"

"Sí. En Quito. Eleven *years* in Quito." Karl-Heinz responded in Spanish using the word for *years* he had heard the soldier say in Spanish earlier.

". . . and you have forgotten how to speak Spanish in just three years?" the soldier asked him, seeing that he understood the questions in Spanish and could speak a few words at least.

Heinz shrugged, "Sí."

"Are you here alone in Korbach?"

"Sí. . . *Mein Vater. . ."* The words still did not come in Spanish. Karl-Heinz was frustrated with himself. The soldier was clearly trying to find out more information about him, but he could not offer anything significant in Spanish.

"Well, I don't understand why you can't speak Spanish when you understand every word I say. How old are you?"

Karl-Heinz said "fourteen" in Spanish.

"Do you speak English?" the soldier asked him.

"A little. I was learning English in school." Karl-Heinz responded in English, now feeling quite ridiculous.

"Are you having problems in Korbach? Is that why you went to headquarters yesterday?" the soldier asked in Spanish.

"No," he shook his head. Karl-Heinz answered in English. "I say Herr Renner . . . good man."

"Well, that is what they told me you said. There was no misunderstanding then. Do you want to tell me something else?" the soldier asked, somewhat indifferent to the boy's plight.

"Sí. . ." but the words were not there. After several attempts Karl-Heinz said dejectedly, "No, no more Spanish. I don't remember."

The American soldier nodded and walked away. Karl-Heinz did not know what to think about the encounter. He felt like a fool. He wondered if he had done Herr Renner or himself a favor by making contact with the Americans. And he was flabbergasted that he could not even think of the simple word in Spanish for father. He went inside and sat on his bed.

When Helga asked him what the soldier wanted, he shrugged. "Nothing really. I couldn't even talk to him. I have forgotten all my Spanish. I can understand when he speaks, but I can't speak Spanish any more."

That evening Karl-Heinz asked Frau Renner a question. "Now that the Americans are here, how will my father come and get me?"

Frau Renner looked him directly in the eye and said sympathetically, "I don't know, Karl-Heinz. We'll just have to wait and see."

More than six months went by without a word about his family. One day in September Werner Meyer's uncle asked Karl-Heinz if he wanted to open a vehicle repair shop with him.

"You are fifteen now and should start an apprenticeship."

"I don't know anything about fixing vehicles," he said honestly.

What he really wanted was to be reunited with his family, not start a business in a town that he planned to leave as soon as he learned where his family was. He wanted to start school again somewhere, or begin working, but not without his family. Everything was so up in the air during the occupation. He had no news about his family or what his future would bring. Everything in Korbach was at a standstill. It was very unsettling. The Renners treated him much more like family than they had at the beginning, but they were not his *real* family. He awoke each day with the illusion that he might receive news from his father and snuggled into bed each evening disillusioned. *Could my father be dead?* he wondered. When he closed his eyes he prayed a simple prayer. *Please God, keep my family safe. Let me go to be with them. Amen.*

One afternoon in September, he returned home to find a letter on the table addressed to him at Bergstrasse 1. The envelope was already open. Frau Renner answered the question he had on his face, "It came that way."

Karl-Heinz unfolded the paper and read the message. The handwritten letter was from his grandmother in Hannover.[20]

Dear Heinzchen,

I send my warmest and kindest greetings to you, my dear grandson.

I am delighted that you are safe. I thank God that after all this time we have finally located you! No one knew where you were or how to find you. We were all so worried about you. Your father and I were desperate to find you. I am very pleased to learn that you are safe in Korbach.

I know that you must be wondering about your family. I have received word that your family left the Berlin area for Ecuador some months ago. There was no way to let you know about their departure.

Do not let this news upset you, Heinzchen. It will take some time, but someday you and I will follow.

Be good, my dearest Heinzchen. I will write again soon.

Your Oma

Karl-Heinz slammed the opened letter on the table and walked out of the tiny apartment. He stood outside and looked at the cloudy sky above him. He could not believe what he had read. His family had left Germany without him. They were alive! But they had abandoned him and he was alone!

NOTES TO CHAPTER SEVEN

[1] The annual celebration scheduled in honor of the NSDAP was to be held on September 2, 1943. The "Sieg des Glaubens" or "Victory of the Beliefs" was listed in E. Contag's 1943 pocket calendar under National Holidays.

[2] Terrifying.

[3] I am very pleased to make your acquaintance, Frau Renner.

[4] The compositions were recovered in a restoration of the house years after the war. The school papers were returned to C. H. Contag in 1985. The topics covered in the booklet range from essays on the German air force and classical literary topics to an essay on a Sunday outing in Quito.

[5] *Dios te dé* is a toucan.

[6] "When the soldiers march through the city the girls and women stand at the windows and the doors." The song continues with an imitation of the noises made by drums and cymbals in a parade:"A dee dum a da dum und bloss hat der chinderasa chinderasasa."

[7] "Anger and Joy in Autumn."

[8] C. H. Contag interview. The story is corroborated in the Alte Landesschule School (ALS) Newsletter in K. Heuser's accounts,

"Zum 'Opfertod' Korbacher Gymnasiasten im Zweiten Weltkrieg," and "ALS-Schüler Opfer von Tiefflieger-Angriffen," and also in Ursula Hassenpflug's "Nachtrag zu '50 Jahre nach Kriegsende.'" (Heft 1, 1995) in *KLOSTER glöckchen. Nachrichten rür die Mitglieder des Vereins ehemaliger Korbacher Gymnasiasten*. II. Sixty-second year. Korbach, August 1995.

[9] C.H. Contag interview. Corroborated in *New York Times* publications of communiqués from Berlin October 21-31, 1944.

[10] Berlin communiqué transcribed in the *New York Times*.

[11] *You can see them spit smoke! Quick, to the cellar!* " He was referring to the sirens that were screaming, not to smoke emitted from the low-flying planes that were approaching on the horizon. His words are quoted in a letter from Helga (Renner) Emde to Kimberly Contag written on November 30, 1998.

[12] C. H. Contag interview. Corroborated in Erich Amert's account "Fliegeralarm beendete den Konfirmationsgottesdient" published in honor of the 50th Anniversary after the War's end. "Nachtrag zu '50 Jahre nach Kriegsende.'" Korbach, 1995. p. 62, 63.

[13] Irmgard (Contag) Jaunzems. Videotaped conversation in Colorado, 1996.

[14] C.H. Contag interview. Corroborated in "Fliegeralarm beendete den Konfirmationsgottesdient" published in honor of the 50th Anniversary after the War's end. "Nachtrag zu '50 Jahre nach Kriegsende.'" Korbach, 1995. p. 62, 63.

[15] Hermann, Peter, et. al. *Potsdam und das Jahr 1945*. Potsdam-Museum. 1995. p. 7.

[16] Hermann, Peter, et. al. *Potsdam und das Jahr 1945*. Potsdam-Museum. 1995. p. 7.

[17] C.H. Contag interview. Corroborated in "Fliegeralarm beendete den Konfirmationsgottesdient" published in honor of the 50th Anniversary after the War's end. "Nachtrag zu '50 Jahre nach Kriegsende.'" Korbach, 1995. p. 62, 63.

[18] Belt. The German word "gürtel" sounds like girdle, a woman's undergarment, in English.

[19] The American soldier was probably trying to explain that his children were dressed in costumes for Easter.

[20] C.H. Contag interview.

CHAPTER EIGHT

RÉFUGIÉ POLITIQUE

BEAUNE-LA ROLANDE, FRANCE, 1945

"Papa, do you think that Werner and Tante Lenchen will be back in Quito for Christmas?" Ernstchen asked, leaning over the edge of his top bunk in the drafty refugee barracks.

"I don't know, Ernstchen. It depends on many different things... but it is certainly possible they *could* arrive in Quito by Christmas," Ernst said reassuringly. "They have been gone a few weeks already. It probably took a couple of days to get to the ship, nine days to cross the ocean and then, who knows how much time it will take them after Werner is seen by a doctor in the United States. Then they have to get their fare paid to return to Ecuador from New York. That could take some time... perhaps another month or so..." Ernst was ruminating over the facts of Werner and Lenchen's departure on the ship of infirm refugees to the Americas.

"Will Werner get better in Quito? Will he get strong again?" Irmgard asked with a worried look from the bottom bunk, her teeth chattering.

"Why, of course, he will, Irmgardchen!" Ernst pulled her sweater around her neck and snuggled closer to her. "He will be strong again. He just needs to eat a big bunch of bananas and . . . well, he needs to get more vitamins from different foods." Ernst hesitated before he continued. Any talk of specific foods just made their empty stomachs ache all the more. "Then he will be strong enough to walk again. He'll be able to run and jump and chase you around. I bet that by the time we get back to Quito, Werner will be able to climb up the Pichincha mountain and swing from tree branches."

Irmgard smiled at her father, crouched uncomfortably on the bottom bunk, and asked, "Do you remember, Papa, the day I thought we'd lost Werner?" She giggled. "One minute he was sitting next to me at the table and the next minute he was gone! Remember? We couldn't find him for the longest time!" Irmgard sat up to finish her story. "It was the day we had wine to drink because there wasn't anything else. Don't you remember, Papa?"

"No, Irmgard. Tell me the story again," her father answered, letting her finish what had become her favorite story since they arrived at the French refugee camp.

"I found him curled up underneath the table. He must have wilted after drinking the wine and slipped between us to the floor. He was sleeping there and I thought he had disappeared. Poof! Just like that he reappeared under the table. It was just like magic, wasn't it, Papa?"

"You are such a silly girl," Ernst said before kissing her gently on the forehead. "You mean he fell asleep. He didn't wilt. Flowers wilt. Little brothers don't." Ernst laughed and pulled the blanket up toward Irmgard's face. "Now roll over, and I'll rub your back a little, so you can go to sleep."

"Thanks, Papa. I am still a little bit cold," she said as she rolled over. Ernst pushed her braids to one side and rubbed her back gently. There were so few comforts at the camp in Beaune-la-Rolande. To compensate Ernst made the nightly back rub and bedtime story a camp tradition.

"Start your story, Papa. I am listening," Ernstchen said from the top bunk. He delighted in his father's nightly stories. It was the time of day when their father focused exclusively on his children, the best part of the day for the family that had been reduced to three.

"Do you two remember the San Francisco church in Quito?"

"Sure, I do," piped Ernstchen; "It was at the bottom of Rocafuerte Street. We passed by it all the time on the way to school. Why?"

"Well, not too long after the Spaniards arrived in Quito they decided to build a European-like city and they needed a church. So, they started building a church on that site at the foot of the Guagua Pichincha. There was an Indian who had been commissioned to build the atrium for the church, but he just couldn't get it finished on time, and the people who had asked him to build it threatened him. They said they were going to put him in prison!"

"Couldn't he get some other people to help him build it faster?" Irmgard asked.

"He probably tried, but it was a very big job and he needed many people to help him finish. The people in charge told him that it had to be finished before the sun rose the next morning or he would be arrested! The sun went down that night and the Indian still didn't know what to do about his problem, so he asked God to help him. He got down on his knees and he prayed and prayed and prayed. Then, after he ate a little potato soup for supper, he decided to go back to the church where he planned to work until he was taken prisoner at dawn."

"I would have run away and gone into the mountains," Ernstchen commented. "He was a fool to go back to the church and wait for those people to arrest him."

"Well, he went to the church wrapped in a large cape to keep him warm in the cool mountain air and started to work with the stones that he was to use for the atrium. Just then a tall, thin man dressed in red approached him. He had a long, thin nose and a very pointy chin that stuck out sharply. His eyes were piercing, and the Indian shivered in fear. But the man got very close to the Indian and whispered like this." Ernst leaned close to Irmgard whose eyes broadened and she tried to shrink beneath the blanket that covered her.

"I can't hear you, Papa," Ernstchen said. "Tell me, too." Ernst stood and repeated the nasty look he had given his daughter before saying in a loud whisper, "The scary man in red said, 'Don't be afraid, my good man. My name is Lucífero. I have come to help you finish the atrium before the first ray of daylight breaks on the horizon.'"

"It was the devil, Papa, wasn't it? Lucífero was the devil!" Ernstchen whispered back loudly enough for his sister to hear.

"No, Ernstchen. Papa just said Lucífero. Lucífero was not the devil! Right, Papa?"

"Ernstchen is right, Irmgard, because, . . . " Ernst strained his voice a little, " the next thing the man said was, 'My only requirement is this. If I finish the atrium for you, your soul is mine for eternity.'"

"Oh," said Irmgard taken aback. Her father was good at telling scary stories and she was duly frightened.

"The Indian spoke. He said, 'I accept your offer. But there is one condition to our agreement. If the last stone is not placed before matins begins, our contract is null and void.' The devilish man agreed, and the Indian signed the pact. Suddenly, thousands of tiny goblins and miniature devils started working on the atrium. Their hands were everywhere, and they worked without complaint or even taking the shortest rest. It was nearly four o'clock in the morning and the atrium was nearly finished! The poor Indian's Christian soul was doomed."

"He must have been really afraid! He never should have made that pact!" Ernstchen suggested from the top bunk.

"You are right, Ernstchen. He should not have agreed to the pact. He was in luck that night, though. Although the little devils and goblins had worked tirelessly, they had forgotten to place one little stone. One stone had been left out, and the atrium was not complete when the first Ave Maria began. The Indian's soul was safe!"

"Hurrah!" Irmgard offered, delighted. "He was lucky."

"Yes, he was." Ernst agreed. "Old cranky Lucífero and his little helpers disappeared into the early morning fog. After the Indian told his story to the parishioners they decided to put in a special hallway where the devil could pass but could not enter the sanctuary of the church. I guess that no one has ever seen Lucífero again near the atrium of San Francisco."

"I bet God helped the Indian by keeping the last stone out of the wall." Irmgard said from behind the covers. "Remember what you said, Papa? The Indian prayed and prayed and prayed. I think that is what kept him from losing his soul. It was a good thing he prayed first, isn't it?"

"Yes it was," Ernst answered. "Now you two go to sleep. Say a prayer for your brothers, Werner and Heinz."

"When will Heinz come, Papa?" Ernstchen asked.

"Soon. Maybe he'll come sooner if you say a special prayer. It would be nice if he could be here for Christmas, wouldn't it! Now, that would be a very special Christmas present. We just have to be patient," Ernst said before patting his son on the shoulder.

"Good night, Papa," Irmgard said. "I'll say lots of special prayers for Werner to get better and for Heinz to come to France before Christmas."

"He won't like it here when he comes, though," Ernstchen mumbled before rolling over.

"Yes, he will, because he will be with his family," Irmgard said with defiance.

"Right. He'll love the delicious carrots we have every day and sleeping in these comfy, wooden bunk beds, too," Ernstchen said leaning over the bunk to make a face at his sister.

"Never mind, you two. Go to sleep." Ernst pulled aside the large blanket that had been hung between his family and the next family of refugees, and walked out the barracks door. It had already been dark for some time since it was November, and the sun set quite early in the evening at this time of year. He sighed and looked up at the sky.

"At least we still see the same stars, Heinz," Ernst mumbled to himself. "I am doing everything I can think of to find you."

There was no reason to walk too far from the barracks even though he would have liked to have crawled under the barbed wire wrapped haphazardly to discourage refugees from leaving the camp, and make his way to Korbach to hunt for his son. "Heinz, Heinz, Heinz. . .where are you now? We are waiting for you. I will not leave without you," Ernst said in a whisper as he paced back and forth in front of his barracks.

Nearly six weeks had passed since he had sent the letter to Frau Renner requesting that she send Karl Heinz to France. He had nearly memorized its contents since there was little to do at the camp. He closed his eyes and recalled the letter that he had written in the refugee camp on the edge of Paris.

Frau G. Renner
Korbach (Bez. Kassel)
Hindenburg str 5
October 14, 1945, Paris
Dear Frau Renner:
We have been here for more than eight weeks in a camp in Paris as we are waiting for a transport ship that will take us

to South America. My sister, three of my children, and I began our journey to Paris on May 22. I mailed letters to Karl Heinz when I was in Margdeburg and in Erfurt, letters that, I assume, never arrived. If they had, then Karl Heinz would have followed me here. When we arrived in Brussels I went to the British Missions to try to arrange for Karl Heinz to be granted permission to come to Paris. When we arrived in Paris we were told we would be shipped out right away, so all the plans were put on hold. It was a set back. Later I learned that we would be held over in France and I went directly to British Missions again to try to arrange for permission to bring Karl Heinz here to Paris and they agreed to allow it. There are no Ecuadorian diplomats here, and we may be delayed yet a while longer. It is my hope that in the meantime Karl Heinz will come. Since Karl Heinz can no longer attend school in Korbach, I think it would be best for him to travel with me so we can be a family again.

Once Karl Heinz makes the adjustment to being in Ecuador he can get on with his studies. It will be a good thing for all of the children to have proper nourishment for their physical development. Wernerchen, for example, suffers from severe leg pain that doesn't allow him to walk well. It was not possible to have doctors examine him when we were still there and the doctors here can't figure out what is wrong with him. He has been x-rayed, his blood tested, etc. In any case, we will be happy when we are once again in Quito with its bright mountain sunshine and a proper diet.

We will all be overjoyed when our life in this camp in finally over. The food here really leaves much to be desired. The camp called Luna Park is in the neighborhood of the Arch of Triumph. It will be closed down next week. At that time we will be transferred to another camp about 80 km from here. Thank God we have a friend from Ecuador in Paris. Dr.

> Luis Jaramillo has been very helpful with everything. Should Karl Heinz arrive and we are no longer in Paris, he should go directly to Dr. Jaramillo's office on the third floor at 27 Tronchet Street. The telephone number is ANJ 5254.
>
> We were given official word that we will sail the first week of November on the steam ship Gripsholm. I am sorry to say that winter will be here soon. The children have some warm clothes and a coat already. Unfortunately, I had to leave my nice warm coat behind in Potsdam because it was too heavy to bring along. We still have lovely summer weather here. It was often times beastly hot here, but I was able to exchange marks and have been able to buy fruit for the children. One kilo of grapes costs about 30 Franks. You can get fruit without ration cards, and bread will be free of charge. Our camp has seen about 700 South Americans. It is in the vicinity of "Bois de Bologne," a forested area where the children can play.
>
> Here in Paris we have seen some really marvelous sights. You can only travel by subway. There are no trams. And here, I must say, absolutely nothing has been destroyed. Hopefully, your little house is still as it was the last time I saw it. May God keep you well.
>
> For me there is some consolation in knowing the Americans occupied your area since occupation by troops from the other side was no laughing matter.
>
> In the meantime, may you all stay healthy. I send each of you my most heartfelt greetings.
>
> Yours,
> Ernest Contag

Ernst rubbed the stubble on his face. What kind of father was he anyway, he asked himself, shaking his head in shame and bewilderment. Two of his children were suffering from hunger in a refugee camp; he knew nothing of Heinz's whereabouts and was helpless to do anything else; Wernerchen was sick, in pain, and in the Americas. He reminded himself not to lose hope.

"*Guten Abend,* Hauptman Contag," a voice said from behind. It was Richard Ashton, a German from Lourenço Marques, Africa who had become an admirer and a friend.

"*Guten Abend*, Sergeant," Ernst said jokingly. "Have the troops gone to bed?"

"Peter fell asleep a while ago. My wife is talking to Frau Berends."

"Oh, are they scheming again?" Ernst asked in jest.

"Not any more than the rest of us, I don't suppose. Any news?"

"Not really. No one knows when the next ship will leave from France. When I spoke with Msr. Boulore at the Ministry of Deportees, Refugees and International Affairs in Paris before Werner and my sister left on the ship, he seemed rather uncertain as to whether the UNRRA[1] would be able to fund another ship soon. In any case, I am ambivalent. I don't know if we should leave on the next ship or starve while we wait until they find my son, Heinz. I have to get him out of Germany. It will not be easy for him if he arrives in France and we are not here. He is only a boy." Ernst shuffled the dirt at his feet.

"You know, Richard, you would think that anyone who worked at the Ministry in a beautiful building like the one Msr. Boulore is in at 66 Foch Street would be able to do almost anything. He should be able to work miracles. You should see that street, Richard. It is the widest street I have ever seen. It is in a pretty fancy area with all those beautiful, large palace-like buildings . . . and I bet the whole area is well guarded, too."

"I'd love to see it, Herr Contag. *Mein Gott.* I'd be glad to get out of here to see anything, to tell the truth. I haven't had any luck with my letters to Africa. My boss in Lourenço Marques hasn't sent a reply to my letters. Not a word. I have written Dieckmann several times. All I know is that the letters don't come back and I don't get an answer either. I don't know what is going on there. Who knows if the ships are even carrying our mail! Maybe they are just dumping the letters over the side into the ocean! Wolinsky and Aals were talking about how frustrated they are, too." Ashton shook his head. "Your young son and your sister were fortunate to be able to leave here so soon. My son, Peter, would have liked to have been in your son's shoes. He would do anything to have a decent meal. The poor little guy is always hungry." Ernst could sense the frustration in his voice.

"Don't worry so much, Richard. Things will work out for all of us. This camp is just like stopping on a stepping-stone in the middle of a rushing river. You have to keep your balance, take it easy, and prepare for the next step. You can't just jump into rushing waters and expect to swim across."

"Pfff. I am not sure there are any stepping-stones across my rushing river, Ernst. You have friends in high places and you still have family and friends in Ecuador. I haven't got that luxury. When we got here I thought that we would only be here for a month, maybe two. Now, I'm not sure if we will be out of here in six months or a year, ... except... maybe on a gurney."

"What a sense of humor you have, Richard. You know that there is always a different option. Ecuador isn't a large country, but there is plenty of room for a family of three like yours. You just keep working on your stepping-stones. If you can't find one in the direction of Africa we'll just have to look for another sturdy stone that crosses the Atlantic."

"Sure. I am just starting to catch a few words in French. Then I could learn Spanish and... What was the Indian language you mentioned?"

"Quechua. You don't need a lot of Quechua, though, and the more French you learn, the easier Spanish will be. *Das stimmt,*"

Ernst added lightheartedly, trying to cut through Ashton's sarcasm and frustration.

"Do you really think that there would be a place for us in Ecuador?"

"Sure. I have good connections in Quito. You said so yourself. So, if things don't work out one way, another will present itself." Ernst stopped and patted the man on the shoulder as though the conversation were finished.

"You don't have to stop pacing, Herr Contag. I'd be glad to accompany you to the end of the barracks and back again several more times."

"Good idea. We have to get our exercise somehow." The two men started toward the back of the barracks in silence. There were several men outside the clapboard barracks next door and Ernst waved at them and tipped his hat ceremoniously before pulling the collar of his jacket tighter around his neck. He continued his conversation with Ashton: "I just keep writing letters in the hope that we can get Heinz out of Germany and then get our passage to the Americas. I just can't leave without him."

"I hate to ask this question, but —"

"Don't." Ernst interrupted. No one was allowed to speak of the possibility of Heinz's death in his presence. "Brigadier Grotin is the one who gives me the most hope. The other French officers shrug me off, but he listens to me and takes notes. He promised to try to find Heinz. If anyone can find my son, he can."

"Your son is in the American sector, isn't he?" Ashton asked apologetically realizing the guilt and impotence Herr Contag must have felt leaving Germany with only three of his four children.

"*Das stimmt.* I haven't been able to contact him since last March. If I could just go and get him!"

"No chance of that," Ashton said matter-of-factly.

"*Nein. Kein möglichkeit,*" Ernst agreed with a heavy sigh. "I wrote my mother-in-law in Hamburg. I don't know if she can do anything." Ernst scratched his head and tugged at the curl that always seemed to fall on his forehead before continuing.

"I have been to the Ecuadorian Legation on Laborde Street in Paris, to the Intergovernmental Committee on the Champs Elysees, and I have even been to the Police Prefecture on the island with the Notre Dame cathedral to talk to people who might be able to help us find Heinz.[2] Every time . . . I seem to hit a dead end. Everyone suspects that he cannot be found because, well, they think that Heinz is—

"Things will turn out, Herr Contag, just as you said. You'll see. You can't lose hope. None of us can."

Ernst straightened and smiled. "Of course, we can't, Richard. Say, how about a game of chess in the morning."

"Sure, if you can get the board away from Stocker and Pfeiffer."

"No problem. I'll send them off to see Camp Captain Josse for something. As barracks leader, there is always a complaint or a problem that I can get the others to attend to. Captain Josse just loves to hear them complain," Ernst added ironically.[3]

" Maybe you could put in a good word for me!"

"I'll do that, Richard. Your wife must be waiting for you. Don't keep the good woman waiting." Ernst hoped Ashton would leave him to his musings.

"No, sir, I won't. Chess in the morning, then. *Gute Nacht*, Hauptmann Contag." Richard Ashton smiled and disappeared into the barracks. Ernst was alone again with his thoughts. He had never imagined that the Americans could have been so close when he left Heinz in Korbach in March more than seven months earlier. He shook his head and leaned against the barracks wall.

"I wish I had a cigarette, or a banana," he said with a huff. The food at the camp was miserable. Sliced carrots everyday. If he weren't so disgusted with the carrots he might actually complain about being limited to one meager meal of carrots a day.

They were all on starvation rations. Water, coffee, a slice of bread and a few carrots, a few more carrots, and . . . a few more sliced carrots served on metal plates each day. No milk for the children. No fruit. No other vegetables. Nothing else. Just carrots and a slice of bread. Most of the internees already had carrotitis and it was just a matter of time before all of them had it or starved to death by refusing to eat the dreaded carrots.[4] When a few of the internees from his barracks turned up their noses at the slice of cow's udder they had been served a month earlier, Ernst encouraged them to eat it. If the babies ate rice riddled with mouse droppings, the adults could swallow cow's udder. In Ecuador it was common to eat such things. *God, what a dreadful place this was!*

Ernst had been somewhat surprised that no one fought over the cow's udder slices. Another internee commented that even if they had wanted to fight for a larger slice, no one had the energy. The lack of a varied diet after the long walk from Berlin to Paris had weakened Werner so much that he became partially paralyzed. Starvation rations had weakened all of them, but little Werner had suffered the most. *Thank God for the Red Cross, UNRRA employees and the generous people along the refugee trail who helped us,* Ernst thought.

The decision to leave Germany had also been a decision for survival. Soon after Ernst left Heinz in Korbach he learned that over seventy-five percent of Berlin had been destroyed in three weeks of bombing, and that the Americans had taken Kassel. Heavy bombers and hundreds of Mustang fighters had laid Berlin and the rail lines to waste. Tens of thousands of Berliners were dead. Tens of thousands had left the city ruins as refugees.

The attacks from the air and from the ground had been unrelenting. When the Mosquito bombers made attacks on the city, the German FLAK returned devastating blows to the Allied air power from the ground. The Allies retaliated with thousands of planes, heavy bombers and Mustang fighters that dropped thousands of tons of explosives on the city.⁵ Seventy-five percent of Berlin lay in ruins. Travelers told him that smoke could be seen easily from Potsdam as it rose high in the sky over Berlin.

He had arrived at the outskirts of Potsdam after Easter and was met by a line of wooden, horse-drawn carts, each filled with refugees and their belongings. Refugees fleeing for safety overran Potsdam. To make matters worse, common citizens in Potsdam had been outfitted for civil defense and one hundred and ten fifteen-year-old boys had *volunteered* for military service.⁶ Holy Week had been a disaster for Germany.

Ernst went to his small apartment and repacked his travel bag. He packed anything he did not think he could do without. "You don't know if your things will be here when you come home anymore," he said aloud to himself. He stuck his important papers and documents into his breast pocket next to his pocket calendars for 1942, 1943, and 1944. The documents made his jacket stick out oddly, but he didn't care. The most important document was his military release. The document from the Division in Charge of Foreign-born Germans was absolutely crucial to his family's survival. The civilian defense force, called the Volkssturm or Peoples' Army, had been ordered to defend all German cities and villages under penalty of death. His documentation released him from being drafted into and from participating voluntarily in either military defense group. He hoped that he would have time to pull the document from his pocket before a crazy bunch of Nazis decided to hang him or shoot him for not defending the city. It was an absurd situation. The Nazis were paranoid and on a collision course with death. To be safe, before he left for Hohenelse-Schlaborn, he buried the guns he had bought for hunting in the forests outside Potsdam in the ground beneath a neighbor's pantry. The Russian army was approaching from the west and he did not want to put himself in peril, should he be found armed upon his return.

Ernst walked toward the train station where he hoped to find transportation of some kind. The atmosphere in Potsdam had turned ugly and Ernst cringed as he saw youths and small children being trained and armed for street combat. Frau Kauffungen had mentioned to him that food was getting scarce and people were scrambling to get whatever they could before… heaven forbid, things got worse.

Ernst's first priority was to see his children. When he could not get transportation at the station, he walked out of the city and headed north to Hohenelse-Schlaborn. He would certainly be safer in the rural areas than in Potsdam.

It took several days to get to Rheinsberg, sleeping where he could and eating when he was able. The tranquility of the trip to Rheinsberg was unnerving after witnessing the damage done to the Berlin area. The cool, misty air was fresh with the smell of pine, and winter had begun to lift its cloak from the dense forests between Rheinsberg and Hohenelse-Schlaborn.

Ernst went to Schlaborn-house to get Werner and Irmgard. The walk along the rocky road through the forest was peaceful and refreshing. It was hard for Ernst to imagine the war ever getting to a rural area of Germany like this forested area of Mark Brandenburg. For the first time in days he felt happy and safe. He whistled as he walked and imitated the birds in the trees above.

As he approached the Schlaborn-house at the end of the winding road, he saw that all the children were dressed for the weather and were playing noisily in the area in front of the horse barn.

"Papa," Irmgard cried in amazement when she saw her father. "Look, Wernerchen, Papa is here!" Irmgard ran to her father and he bent over to embrace her. She was dressed in a dark sweater over a pink dress that was just a little large, and her long braids hung nearly to her waist on either side. Werner was not far behind his sister and he joined the embrace by hopping up and down next to his father saying, "My turn, my turn." His hair had been trimmed recently and it made him look thinner than the last time his father had seen him. Several other children followed the two Contag children to watch the reunion. All of them recognized Herr Contag since he visited the school quite often.

"Papa, are you coming with us?" Werner asked excitedly.

"Why, where are you going? To Rheinsberg for an outing?" Ernst asked innocently.

"Fraülein Linde said they are going to take us by train to Denmark in a few days. She said Denmark is far away," an older, blond boy said from a distance. "My mother doesn't know they are taking us there. She will be really mad when she comes and sees that we are gone."

"Denmark?" Ernst said, puzzled. "Where is this Fraülein Linde?" The children followed their father toward the large house that served as their school and home.

"Then can I show you where all the dead fish are, Papa?" Werner asked. He pointed away from the house to the lake and said, "A plane dropped a bomb in the lake and there were lots of dead fish around it. Boy, was it stinky around here!"

"A bomb in the lake?" Ernst asked, incredulous.

"It made us all really sad to see the dead fish," Irmgard added with a pout. "I cried when I saw them."

Ernst was trying to pay attention, but he was upset by the tales the children were telling. He spotted a woman at the door of the Schlaborn house and headed toward her.

"All right, children. I see your teacher. After I talk to her we'll go on a little walk. You two go with the other children. I'll find you in a few minutes."

"I want to stay with you, Papa. We can go with you to talk to Fraülein Linde. Please, Papa, we want to stay with you." Several other children also tagged along and Ernst decided that it was futile to try to free himself of the curious grade schoolers.

Ernst introduced himself. "It is a pleasure to meet you, Fraülein. I am Ernst Contag. What has happened to Frau Stahnke?"

"She left on February 28. I am her replacement. My name is Margot Linde, Herr Contag; it is a pleasure to meet you. Frau Stahnke didn't tell anyone that she was leaving and it was really quite a scandal. Fraülein Prochel and Herr Hüging think that she went west. Fraülein Prochel said that she was quite nervous about her family. There is such a fear of the Russians making their way here, you know..."

"Yes, yes," Ernst added trying to hurry her on. He really wanted to know about the decision to move the children. "Fraülein Linde, I am most concerned about moving the children. Is what the children say true?"

"Yes. The headmaster has made arrangements for the schoolchildren to be moved to Denmark. There are ninety-nine children left here in Hohenelse-Schlaborn: forty-nine grade schoolers, twenty-seven in the middle school, and twenty-three in the upper grades. We will go too, of course." Fraülein Linde did not seemed pleased about the idea.

"I was not informed of any move."

Fraülein Linde lowered her voice and spoke directly to Ernst. "No one has been informed. You know that it is impossible to contact the parents of these children. She smiled at the children surrounding Ernst and continued in a louder voice, "There is a train that will take the school children to Denmark where we will all be very safe. We leave in a few days. Frau Stahnke can give you more details if you need them. *Guten Tag*, Herr Contag."

Ernst was taken aback. "I will take Irmgard and Werner with me for the day. We are going to visit my son at Hohenelse. Is that all right?"

"Of course. We will expect them just before the dinner hour, Herr Contag. I don't like to have the children out after dark."

"I will have them here long before dusk, Fraülein, as I must get back to Rheinsberg before dark. Again, it is my pleasure..."

Ernst bowed ever so slightly and took his leave. He was perplexed. *Denmark. My God. Denmark?* He shook his head in disbelief. Heinz was in Korbach and his three younger children were about to be sent along with their schoolteachers to Denmark. *Am I to be entirely alone? For how long? How soon before I see my children again? How will I gather them up again?*

Werner pranced along the dirt path in front of his father. Irmgard followed her brother, but her steps were not nearly as frolicking. She hated the idea of going to Denmark and didn't want her father to get the wrong idea that she was at all happy about it.

The path followed the lake and Irmgard had not been on it since December when the entire group of Schlaborn children had gone out on Christmas Eve in search of a Christmas tree. *That was a happier day,* she thought. The snow had glistened under the bright, moonlit sky and they had wandered the path at dusk with lanterns in search of the perfect Christmas tree. Schoolteacher Bernhardt Hüging and some of the older boys from Hohenelse had met them in the forest and the boys cut down a good-sized pine tree that they helped pull back to the school on a sled. Irmgard remembered that night as the best moment of her days at Schlaborn school. When they arrived back at the house they were sent to wash. Later, when they came downstairs, there were treats for the children, a decorated tree, and they sang Christmas songs in the warmth of the hearth. Irmgard smiled to herself. *That was divine!* When she remembered where she was she began to fret about the trip. *I won't go,* she thought. *I just won't go.*

Irmgard wanted to stomp as she followed the path. It had been too muddy to walk on it earlier, but the pine needles on the path kept her shoes from touching the wetness. It didn't make much sense to stomp, though. The needles would have cushioned the noise. She dreaded having to leave the place she had called home since she left Tante Maria's house in October, about eighteen months earlier.

"Papa, I don't want to go to Denmark with the school. We should be together. We are a family."

"You will be safer in Denmark. The war is coming closer to us. Remember the fish in the lake? It is getting dangerous here in Germany. Denmark will be safer for you," Ernst argued unconvinced.

"What about you, Papa? Will *you* be safe if the war comes closer? What will happen to us if something happens to you? Who will find us in Denmark?"

Werner stopped and turned to see what his sister was whining about.

Ernst reassured her, "Nothing will happen to me, Irmgard. Look, I came here today, didn't I? I'll come for you in Denmark, too. When the fighting stops, I'll come and get you and we will be a family again."

"We'd be safer with you, Papa. We'd be a lot safer with you. You can't let them take us to Denmark. It is so far away. Let us go with you."

"I don't think that is a very good idea, Irmgard. It just isn't safe."

Irmgard started to cry. "I don't care if we have to die. I don't want to be alone. I'm scared. I just want to be with you." She had lost all sense of composure and was weeping uncontrollably.

Ernst stopped and shook his head. He looked at Werner who had come to hold his hand. Werner looked scared. "Papa, are we going to die like the fish?"

Ernst was overcome by his son's question. He resisted an overwhelming urge to cry. His children were so young, their eyes so full of uncertainty and fear. He ran his hand through his hair and worried it a bit before answering.

"*Pobrecitos*," he said in Spanish. "Come here, Irmgard. You two listen to me. I will protect you always. You know that I will make the best decision for you and your brothers. You will never be alone in Denmark, Irmgard. Your brothers will be with you. And I will be with you, too. Don't you always keep thoughts of me in your head and your heart?"

Irmgard was distraught and pulled on her father's arm. "Papa! You want us to go to Denmark instead of staying with you!" She was shrieking in the middle of the quiet pine forest, "I don't want to go. I don't want to go to Denmark on the train! I don't want to be alone with all the children and no Papa. I want us to be with you. I want us to be a family." She wiped her fiery, teary eyes with the back of her hand and slumped. "I just want us to be a family!"

Ernst started walking toward Hohenelse without saying a word. The children followed him. Irmgard continued to cry. Werner walked along the path, confused. He held out his hand to Irmgard and tried to comfort her. "It will be all right, Irmgard. I will protect you." Ernst remembered that when he heard his young son's reassuring words, he shook with emotion and had to wipe silent tears from his face.

"Herr Contag, your daughter is asking for you in the barracks," Señora Suárez startled him from his reminiscing. "I think she has had a nightmare."

"Gracias, señora." Ernst turned and followed the woman back inside the barracks. Maria Suárez was the only refugee he knew at Beaune-La Rolande camp who really had no place to go. She was truly a woman without a family and without a country. Carlos Rueger, Wanda Aouraters, Dr. Koebig, Helena Pohl, and Carlos Passow planned to go to Brazil. Adolfo Neunteufel hoped to go to Paraguay. The Wiens thought they might end up in Rio Negro, Argentina.[7] Some were returning to their homelands. Others were trying to set down new roots where they could find jobs and a fresh start.

Ernst entered the barracks and sat on the bunk next to his daughter. Irmgard's hair was wet and she shivered. "Papa, I had a bad dream."

Ernst's deep voice comforted her. "Here, Irmgard. I saved something for you from my last visit in Paris with Consul Lasso Plaza.[8] This will make you feel better." Ernst handed her a piece of hard candy from a small makeshift table they had near the bed.

"It was a train bombing in my dream and I was scared. The planes came through and I couldn't find any place to go. They started shooting... I was so scared... then, when I was waiting for them to find you outside, I started thinking about my friends at the Schlaborn school, Papa, the ones who died on the train. They must have been terribly frightened, too. All my little friends . . . gone forever. Do you think they are in heaven?" Irmgard sobbed.

"You shouldn't think about such terrible things. Shhhhh. Of course they are all in heaven. I bet they are all dancing and singing together in heaven."

"But their parents miss them, don't they, Papa?"

"You shouldn't think about sad things when you go to bed, Irmgard. Try to think about happy things. Think about . . . playing games with your friends here. What is that game you play with Herr Neunteufel?"

"*Schinken klopfen*." Irmgard giggled. "I like to watch the boys play because they can never guess who ran up behind them and swatted them on the backside."

"There. Think about that. Don't giggle too loudly. I will see you in the morning."

"Papa. I could think about being home for Christmas. Do you think that we could be home for Christmas?"

"As soon as Heinz arrives at the camp, we will rush right out the door and head for home, if we can. Maybe we could be home by Christmas, but Easter is more likely. It is already the end of November. It would be fun to be home for Easter, though."

"All right, Papa. Maybe for Christmas. Maybe for Easter." Irmgard said as she rolled over. "Will you be happy then, Papa?"

"Yes. I'll be happy when Heinz gets here and we are a family again. Now go to sleep."

Irmgard had never seen her father so distraught as he had been since they left Germany without her brother. No one ever really said anything about it, but she knew that her father worried whether Heinz was still alive. He spent many hours each day writing letters to government officials. He tried to learn as much French and English as he could so he could get information and talk to different officials. On a bad day her father would sit with his head in his hands behind the blanket of their assigned bunk area. Irmgard sometimes found him there, alone, just thinking. On a good day her father played chess with the others and told stories about growing up in Ecuador. He was a terrific storyteller and he often entertained people in the barracks with his stories. Since his visit to Paris at the end of October, however, he had grown sullen and more withdrawn. Irmgard and Ernstchen knew that he was worried about leaving Heinz behind or not finding out what had happened to him. She tried to think of Neunteufel and the game. Eventually, she fell asleep.

A short time later Ernst decided to turn in. He was exhausted and it had been dark for hours, but he couldn't sleep. Irmgard's nightmare about the bombing of the train carrying her classmates to Denmark had set him off. He shook his head as he paced back and forth in the barracks from their quarters near the door to the wood stove at the center of the barracks.

Their last weeks in Potsdam had been difficult enough with the worries he had about Heinz in Korbach. The Berlin area had endured air attacks for more than two years, but the thousands of tons of bombs dropped the last three weeks of March had left the city a smoldering, smelly morgue. With Europe's wonder-city reduced to dust and with the war's front so close, Ernst decided to make secret plans to take his children and flee the area as soon as it was safe to do so.

Reports of dead refugees kept surfacing among the living, and Ernst hesitated to take his children anywhere until he felt it was prudent to do so. He suspected he would have to wait until Germany's surrender. However, waiting for the end to come was nearly as perilous as leaving and risking death on the road.

During the first two weeks in April their food reserves had grown thin. It no longer made any sense to stand in line with ration cards. Looting had become a matter of survival for everyone, especially after the bombing of Potsdam on April 14.[9] Ernst and Ernstchen still had to take the risk of going outside regularly to scavenge for food. They spent a good number of hours doing so each day. One day, Ernst and his eleven-year old son returned to the apartment with their clothes covered in jam from a jam factory that had been blown up. The two Contags had followed the trail of jam-takers to the factory. When they arrived, scores of people were scooping up jam into buckets, aprons, hats, and anything they could carry. It was sticky business but no one cared. The factory had been demolished and there was no use in ignoring the tasty jam that oozed from the containers.

Ernst remembered how they all had made fun of being hungry. They were sitting around the table when Werner put on a hopeful face and asked, "Is there any jam left?" The thought of eating potatoes fried in cod liver oil again must have been turning his stomach.

"Just the dab that is stuck on my pant leg after the last washing," Ernst responded jokingly.

"Where? Where?" Ernstchen asked, feigning excitement. His son had dropped to the floor on all four legs and said, "Maybe I can suck it off, Papa, before Werner can get at it."

Ernst remembered lifting his knee and pointing at the hem of his trousers. "Just there . . . look, you can almost see it between the threads. Quick, Ernstchen, . . . before any one else gets it."

Ernstchen furrowed his brow and pretended to pluck tasty tidbits from his father's trouser leg. He smacked his lips. "Mmmmmm," he said, lifting his eyebrows and smiling at Werner, "*Es schmecht gut!*"

"It's not funny," Werner had countered gloomily before slumping into a chair. "I am really hungry and I won't eat potatoes and that horrible tasting oil again. . . ever. Werner put the potato on the table with precision and stated with a grin, "I guess I am not hungry. Someone else will have to peel this potato."

"Why Wernerchen, I am surprised," Ernst remembered saying. "Your brother and I have collected some special spices to make a delicious meal for you today, and you don't want to eat it?"

Werner was not sure how to respond. He knew that there would be nothing on the table other than potatoes, but the smell of the oil made him feel sick. "What kind of special spices did you find?" he said, pretending to be interested. The daily argument about potatoes had become a game for him and a test of his father's patience.

"Well, you'll have to see what special spices we have! Ernstchen, bring the handkerchief." Inside the folds were several tiny leaves and a slice of cabbage. Werner looked at the contents and then at his father.

"Mmmmm. Special spices." Werner added with irony before turning up his nose.

When they heard little Werner make such a mockery of their pitiful loot no one had been able to keep from laughing.

It was no different now at the camp. There was no other way to handle the miserable conditions.

Ernst put another stick of wood on the wood stove before walking back to his bunk. The barracks was still quite noisy. There were at least a hundred people there. Some coughed, some snored, a baby was crying, and someone was singing to quiet her.

"Elisabeth," he muttered to himself quietly, "I need help to find Heinz. I feel so helpless here. *Liebling*, please help me stay strong."

He put his head down on the bunk and tried to sleep. The noise in the barracks reminded him of the night British terror fire destroyed the historical residence of Frederick the Great and parts of Potsdam's old city center, including the Garrison Church, which had been transformed into rubble.[5] That night they had spent hours in the basement of a building. Every time there was a let up in the bombing he could hear heavy breathing and cries.

That was the night that Inge's apartment on Schutzenstrasse had been destroyed. Inge had survived the attack and went to live with family. Ernst did not expect to see her again, ever, because by the end of April the war was nearly over in Potsdam and the pandemonium created by the arrival of the Russians forced him to make the decision to leave Germany for good.

They had been surrounded by the enemy and everyone in Potsdam was nervous. The widespread reputation of the Russian soldiers as ruthless had been circulated by Josef Goebbels on the radio and his words had frightened even the most fearless. Ernst had not been an exception. People started talking about defending the area against the advancing "Ivan" and there was pressure for children to take up anything they could carry to battle the invaders. Battle commanders throughout areas still under German control were threatened with death if they did not defend their towns and cities.[10] Germans turned on Germans, and the entire situation had embittered and saddened him.

The Russians entered the city and started going door to door taking whatever they needed. Watches, radios, women. The Russians called out through loudspeakers and demanded that the Germans surrender their weapons and all the food they had in their homes and deliver it to them. He would never forget the look of fear on his neighbors' faces as they took all their possessions outside. Some took wheelbarrows loaded full of goods. The entire situation was dismal, but it made him angry. He remembered saying aloud, "I don't care if they kill me, but I have children, and they are not to starve as long as I live."

Shortly after that the Russians approached their building like ants going from house to house. He had very little time, but hid what food he could before the Russians made it up the stairs to the third floor. When three Russian soldiers knocked loudly at the apartment door, he had tried to shoo his children aside. Instead, they had stood around him as though trying to protect him from certain evil. The soldiers demanded the surrender of weapons, food, and watches. He had pointed out an alarm clock that he had taken with him on business trips. The soldier said, "Niet, niet! Uhr! Uhr!" The youngest of the three soldiers lifted his jacket sleeve and it looked as though he had nearly fifty watches on his arms, each next to the other. He remembered trying to undo his watch without any facial expression whatsoever. He had not wanted to cause any trouble for himself or his children. His children were too important.

Several hours later Ernst heard his neighbors in the street. Someone was screaming. He rushed outside. A woman from the apartment above theirs had thrown herself to her death. He knew what the Russians had sought in her apartment, and it made him sick to his stomach to see the dead woman there on the street after the violent attack. The following day he agreed to keep the neighbor girl, a fifteen year old, in his apartment, dressed as a younger child. "If there is a knock at the door, he had told the two girls, curl up small and cover yourselves with that blanket. We don't want the soldiers to know how old you are." Potsdam was a city without able men and boys. They had been made to take part in the war machine.

Ernst remembered praying for the war to end and for the madness to stop. His young children had witnessed more devastation and human humiliation than he thought they could stand. As soon as the war was over officially, he went with his family to the Russian authorities in Potsdam to get some papers to let him take his family out of Germany.

"I need papers to take my family out of Germany. We are not Germans. We are South Americans," he had told the short man at the desk. The man had round glasses that made him look rather astute.

"Why do you want to leave?" he had asked.

"My children and I were born in Quito, Ecuador, and we want to go back home," he explained. The Russian had taken out an old map to look for the country of Ecuador, but he could not locate it on the map.

"I have never heard of such a place," he said.

"It is in South America. On the coast, the Pacific coast."

"No such place. No such place on my map," the man had repeated with a scoff. "No papers."

"Of course there is such a country," he had told the man, "Ecuador is located between Colombia and Peru in the middle of the Andes, toward the north and west. The capital is Quito. The Americans took us out of Ecuador in 1942 for an exchange and now we want to go home."

The man behind the desk had turned the map around. "See. No Quito. No Ecuador."

It was true. His map had no such country. Ernst remembered how strange the encounter had been, and he shook off a shiver thinking what might have happened had the general in the back room not appeared in time. It was a miracle from heaven. The general opened the door and asked the officer behind the desk to explain the problem. After a brief discussion, the general gave the desk clerk a strange look. Then he returned to his room and brought out a different, newer map.

"Of course, there is such a country. Yours is a worthless map," Ernst had imagined the translation of the Russian words he heard from the general. After a long wait he had left the building with *walking* papers.

Walking papers. There wasn't a more appropriate name for them, Ernst decided. With the exception of a few short jaunts on a train or in a horse-drawn cart, they had walked from Berlin to Paris, France. First they walked to Potsdam to pick up his sister, Lenchen, whom he had to beg to leave with them, and then the five of them on May 22. They walked for weeks and weeks, pushing a wheelbarrow from Berlin to Paris along what was left of the damaged railroad tracks.

The memory of the interminable journey along the shattered railroad tracks was not a pleasant one for Ernst. The blisters, the hunger and thirst were the least of the problems they had encountered, it seemed. He had worried about his children making the long trip on foot, but it had really been the hardest on his sister, Lenchen, and on little Werner. Lenchen hobbled uncomfortably with her crippled hip. Werner needed constant help. His growing muscles ached from a lack of nutrition, and Ernst had only been able to carry him intermittently on the journey. Ernstchen and Irmgard helped to push the wheelbarrow with the family's things in it, but they, too, had tired easily on the uneven terrain and under the terrible strain of the devastating situation in which they found themselves.

The trail of refugees heading toward France was long, and the assistance offered by the Red Cross and some caring townsfolk had been the key to their survival. They had needed water, food, and a place to rest undisturbed. They had walked in the chilling rain, in the heat of the summer sun, and had slept under both turbulent and star-filled skies. Ernst repeated one phrase in Spanish each evening before falling asleep surrounded by his children, "Elisabeth... you are my guiding light. *Guíanos a casa.*"

Ernst arose early in the morning with the cries of a small child in the barracks. Hunger pangs started early each day. Ernst and his children dressed and went to the general washroom, a short walk from the barracks. It was a glorious, crisp morning and Ernst imagined that, if he were living in the town of Beaune-La-Rolande about 300 meters away, he would have taken in the fresh air with a smile. As it was, the chill cut through his weathered clothing and made him shiver. *It is going to be a long, cold winter*, he thought.

Around ten thirty he met Richard Ashton for a game of chess. There were no chairs in the barracks so each sat on a bottom bunk. In early autumn many would have liked to have played chess outdoors, but it was not inviting without any chairs to sit on. Most internees spent the day in the barracks, going out only to use the washroom and toilet, or to participate in forced exercise, or to help out in the kitchen with food preparation when it was their turn. Ernst moved the bishop carefully on the board that teetered slightly on the makeshift table between himself and his African friend.

Ashton was in better spirits than he had been the night before and he joked about beating Ernst at chess. Ernst said nothing but shrugged a little and said, "We'll see, sergeant, we'll see."

He preferred false humility to being a braggart. It was his style and often he could bluff his way through things and come out on top.

Fifteen men and women from the barracks gathered around for the match and young Peter Ashton, who was about the age of Ernstchen, and the two Contag children played a game with pebbles on the floor nearby. Everyone had to while away the hours before mealtime and chess or playing with pebbles was as good a way as most. A few feet from the game Gerhard Hartgring, a Dutchman who had also befriended Ernst had begun to rail against Europe in general and was just explaining how it might be best if they just set the whole continent on fire.[11]

"*Das Schach,*" Ernst said to Richard Ashton. He never gloated over his battles; his face was wrought with serious thought. His chess game had improved significantly since he arrived at the Beaune-La Rolande camp, but he never let on that he thought the game was won. Ashton struggled forward on the bunk and stared pensively at the board.

"*Attention . . . Monsieur* Contag. *Approchez vous,*" a French guard barked from the barracks door. Ernst stood and walked toward the door. Ernstchen and Irmgard followed him. After their reunion in Potsdam the children had always felt insecure about officials and guards speaking to their father. They feared that their father could be taken from them at any moment. As long as they could see their father, they felt safe and secure.

"Stay here, children," Ernst said, walking toward the soldier.

"What do you think he wants, Papa?" Ernstchen asked already finding it hard to let his father go on ahead alone.

"No idea. Stay with your sister."

A second guard arrived at the door and a third as well. Ernst, who seldom felt panic-stricken, slowed his steps and tried to imagine what the interruption was all about.

"Msr. Contag. Something has arrived for you," the guard said. "You will be needed outside."

As he reached the doorway a third guard tossed a brown leather briefcase at Ernst's feet and it caused a cloud of dust to rise from the floor.

"Pick it up, Msr. Contag," the guard said harshly.

Ernst crumbled over the briefcase and started to cry. "Heinz?" he whispered through his tears as he turned the familiar briefcase around in his hands. He turned to the others in the barracks and called out as loud as he could in a broken voice, "Heinz! Heinz!" The barracks were filled with silence and expectation. No one moved.

The straps of the briefcase were unlatched and there were school papers inside. Then a look of panic crossed his face and he turned toward the guards.

"*C'est tout?* Is this all there is?" he asked frantically in French. "*C'est tout?*" Ernst asked pointedly before heading through the guards at the door. "*C'est tout?*"

The guards, Irmgard, Werner, the Ashtons, and nearly the entire inhabitants of the barracks followed him outside wondering whether the briefcase meant tragedy or joy.

"C'est tout? C'est tout?" he called out with a sense of confusion on his face.

Two guards approached him and said, "Come with us, Msr. Contag. This way." They led him toward the guardhouse at the entrance of the camp. It was on the side of the camp opposite the railroad tracks. Ernst thought this unusual, but could think of nothing but solving the dilemma of his son.

Ernst searched the guarded area with his eyes. *There is nothing unusual here. Where did the briefcase come from? Where is Heinz? Who found the briefcase I bought in Quito and gave to Heinz for school? Where is Brigadier Grotin? Is Heinz alive? Is this all they found? A briefcase . . . just a leather briefcase?* Ernst's thoughts were like bullets leaving a machine gun.

Just then he spotted a man he recognized on the other side of the gate. It was a familiar face. He stopped dead in his tracks.

It was the French officer who had promised to search for his son. He stood there alone. Ernst felt the blood drain from his face.

When the gate opened the French officer made a move to enter but stopped short of entering. He nodded his head and put his hand on his chest before extending it forward toward Ernst. A tall, fifteen-year old boy walked to the center of the open gate from behind the guardhouse. "Papa."

"Heinz!" Ernst called as he rushed toward the gate. Two guards stopped him and told him to wait. Heinz walked straight into his father's arms. The entire barracks stood and watched. Suddenly there was a roar of clapping and cheers. The cheers brought out hundreds of others from nearby barracks. Gerda Ashton saw that Ernst wept as he held his grown son.

Irmgard and Ernstchen had not seen their brother for more than two years. While Karl-Heinz hugged Irmgard and Ernstchen individually, Ernst put his hand to his lips and then his heart and mouthed the words, "*Merci, Msr. Brigadier. Merci pour mon fil. Merci pour mon fil*, Heinz." The man outside the guarded fence nodded with a gesture of mutual respect and left the gate for the town.

Gerda Ashton wondered if the officer had also been overcome with emotion as many of the internees had. People around her wept as though one of their own had been found.

"Papa, this is a happy day," Irmgard said. "We are a family again!"

More than a hundred internees looked on. Karl-Heinz was speechless.

"Come on, son. Now that you are here, we can start for home," Ernst said, clapping his son on the back, in the middle of the crowd. "Now we can all go home together." The crowd cheered.

When they went into the barracks Irmgard and Ernstchen started making room for their brother's things.

"I can't believe it," Ernst said, shaking his head.

"We all want to hear his story, Herr Contag," one of the women called out.

"Let the poor boy get settled," another woman called from her bunk, "then he can tell us how he got here. Wasn't he in the American sector?"

"Don't pry," called out another.

"Who's prying?" said the woman on her bunk. "We have all been waiting for this boy. He is just like family."

Ernst said, "Heinz, these are our new friends." Then he addressed the others, "He can tell his story later. Right now we just want some time to be a family."

There was a brief hush in the barracks before the noise reached its customary level.

Ernst clapped his grown son on the shoulder. "*Mein Gott*, we are so glad you are here, Heinz."

"Yes," Irmgard said brightly. "Now we can go home for Christmas . . . or Easter."

"I hope this camp is better than the one I was in at Luna Park in Paris," Karl-Heinz said emphatically. "I was there for a week and the food was terrible. I couldn't touch it. I'm famished."

Ernst, Ernstchen and Irmgard looked at each other furtively while Karl-Heinz spoke, but no one said a word.

"At least the bunks aren't five high like at that camp. I was terrified there. I didn't speak a word of French and they told me I couldn't speak any German. They said my name was Carlos, not Karl-Heinz." Karl-Heinz's voice was filled with excitement. "One French officer told me, 'It says here you are Ecuadorian. Speak Spanish.'" Heinz imitated the officer's gruff voice before continuing with his own. "But I couldn't. I couldn't speak a word of Spanish. So I didn't talk to anybody. I just drank wine and fell asleep in my bunk the first night. You couldn't even look at the food without getting sick. I just didn't eat. I couldn't."

"You look terrific, Heinz," Ernst observed. It must have been all right in the American sector. You don't look like you have suffered too much."

"How long have you been here?" Heinz asked. "I got a letter from Oma and I thought you were already in Ecuador. I was pretty mad about that letter, you know. And you didn't write or send for me or anything!"

"Papa tried to find you," Irmgard piped up, defending her father. "Papa wrote letters! He mailed them but you didn't get them. We wanted to go to get you, but we couldn't."

Ernstchen sat down on the bottom bunk. "We walked from Berlin to Paris. We have been here at this camp since the middle of September," he explained.[12]

Karl-Heinz was shocked. "More than two months! Well, I am glad you are still here! I was worried when I got to Luna Park transit camp in Paris. When I arrived no one talked to me for days. Then a man who spoke a little German and a little English came over to me and said that he knew you, Papa. He told me that you had been at Luna Park for a short time. 'Long enough to blink an eye,' is what he said. When I asked him where you were, he didn't know, but he thought that you were still in France somewhere." Karl-Heinz imitated the man's deep voice, "'He was here overnight in October. He had the bunk above me. Said something about a sick son and a camp south of Paris.' I thought I would have to try to find you. That made my head swim . . . what a crazy idea that was. . . because I can't even speak French. It was another four days before the Frenchman you saw at the gate told me that he would take me to you. He had the crazy idea of sending in the leather briefcase."

"He was an angel sent from heaven," Ernst muttered aloud. "*Gott sei Dank*. Thank God for the French officer. Do you want to unpack your things, Heinz?"

"I don't have much, Papa," Heinz shrugged. "My school papers . . . a few clothes. There isn't much with the bombing and the move and . . . I had to throw out my medals and everything! Mrs. Renner was afraid. Do you know what?" Heinz asked just above a whisper. "I left Germany in the back of an ambulance and without any papers!"

"*Wirklich*? Without papers? You must tell us how they got you out of Germany, Heinz. It must be quite a story!" Ernst said encouragingly. "Are the Renners all right?"

"Yes, but they are still living at the Schmaltz's house near the train station. The Rümler women are fine, too. I stayed with them before being transported to Paris. She kept me out of that Polish camp they wanted to put me in!"

"Potsdam was destroyed," Irmgard interrupted, "but Papa still found a way to celebrate my birthday. Papa went to a banker friend and traded his best suit so he could buy me a birthday cake! He brought me the biggest lilac bouquet you have ever seen with white and purple flowers! It was really beautiful!" Irmgard was enthusiastic.

"Yeah . . . and if you held the bouquet in front of your eyes you didn't have to see the rubble in the streets or the hungry people walking around looking for a way to get away from the Russians," Ernstchen offered with a sneer.

"Ernstchen," Ernst chided, "let your brother tell us more about how he got out of Korbach."

Heinz smiled and began. "A few weeks ago there was a knock at the house. I was in the kitchen peeling a potato when Tante Hinnie called me to the front door. I saw two French soldiers and Tante Hinnie said they had come for me. I was scared, really scared. Tante Hinnie looked pretty upset, too. I couldn't understand what they were saying so she had to translate for me. They had a sheet of paper in French and they showed it to her. She spoke some French and could understand the soldiers. She said, 'These men have come to take you out of Germany, Karl Heinz. They say they have special transport papers for you.'[13] When I asked her where they were going to take me, the soldiers said they couldn't tell me. Mrs. Renner didn't want me to go with them, but I thought I might be able to find you or go back to Ecuador where I thought you were already. So, I told her that I wanted to take the chance and I wanted to go. She wanted me to leave later on with Oma Dreier, but I didn't want to wait that long. I wanted to go right away. I did not want to finish my schooling and get a job in Germany where I was going to be all alone. I wanted to be with my family and I told her so. Then she agreed to let me go," Karl-Heinz breathed a celebratory sigh of relief before continuing his story.

"The soldiers told her to have me ready for transport to Kassel in the morning. I guess they were going to put me in a Polish camp in Kassel until they could take me out of Germany, so I was really scared. I was nervous, and I told her I didn't want to go to the camp where they were planning to take me. I was afraid I would never get out of there. So, I asked Tante Hinnie if she could try to make arrangements for me to stay with the Rümlers in Kassel until I was transported out of Germany. She agreed and I left for Kassel the next morning with my briefcase and my small bag. I was sad to leave the Renners, but I wanted to follow you and go home."

"Did you stay with the Rümler women in Kassel, then?" Ernst asked.

"I was so thankful that Frau Rümler let me stay with them for three days. I was so afraid of that Polish camp. She was my salvation, Papa! She and Uli were always so kind to me, and they kept me out of that camp. They are very good women. I had missed them more than I thought. It was great to see them again! Uli and I went for a walk through the streets and talked. They couldn't believe how tall I was," Karl-Heinz said with a smile.

"You have grown really tall, Heinz, but I am catching up," Ernstchen said standing between the bunks.

"You are a giant compared to two years ago!" Heinz responded with a finger to his brother's midsection.

"I'd be even taller if I had some good food to eat," Ernstchen added all puffed up.

"So you were in Kassel with the Rümlers. . ." Ernst urged him to continue.

"Yes. Uli was terrific, but they didn't have any food at their house. I guess food is really scarce. They told me that if I wanted food I would have to go to one of the centers where they served food. I didn't want to go alone, so I just went without eating. It was all right. Uli and I went for a long walk later on and I didn't get too hungry. I was amazed how little had really been rebuilt since the October bombing in 1943. Kassel was still just rubble even after two years. That surprised me since we didn't see much bombing in Korbach . . . just the Renner's house and another one nearby. Korbach wasn't destroyed at all really . . . ," Heinz mused.

"Uli and her mother were wonderful!" he continued. "For three days we talked and talked and talked."

"What about Mr. Rümler?" Ernst asked, knowing that Mr. Rümler had been an officer.

"That's strange. No one mentioned Mr. Rümler, so I don't know if he was killed or if he came back after the war." Heinz shrugged. "I don't know what happened to him."

"It was so hard to leave the Rümlers again that last day, because no one knew where I was going to end up. I was scared and they were frightened for me, too. Uli and I just cried together before I had to leave. That was really hard," Heinz said as he nodded matter-of-factly.

"Where did they take you from Kassel, Heinz?" Ernst asked.

"A few French soldiers picked me up and took me to a secret location in Kassel where three other people and I were loaded into the back of an ambulance. They shut the door and I thought it was the end of us. We rode for hours and hours. It seemed like we were going to be in that ambulance forever. It was cold and sort of stuffy in the box and no one said one word to the other. You couldn't see anything and no one said anything. I was really uncomfortable then. I don't even know why no one spoke. I think they must have been as terrified as I was." Karl-Heinz expected his father to interrupt, but he seemed lost in thought. He continued his story.

"When the ambulance stopped and they opened the door I asked a woman where we were. She told me that we were in Paris. It looked like a warehouse district or something. There were five buildings, lousy food, . . . some bread, wine and mush served in metal dishes that I thought would turn my stomach inside out. You know what, though? There wasn't a barbed wire fence surrounding the camp like there is here. Boy, when I saw that this camp was so well guarded with rolls of barbed wire, I wasn't sure I wanted to go through the gate. If I hadn't seen you amongst the men, Papa, I would never have crossed the entrance willingly. What a fright that fence gave me! How did you ever get stuck here?"

"It isn't as easy to leave as you might think, Heinz." Ernst decided not to explain anything about their experience at the Luna-Park Paris Transit Center, run by the Ministry of Prisoners, Deportees and Refugees and the French Repatriation Military Mission. It didn't really matter now that it was an annex Transit Center for aliens who were trying to be repatriated or reassigned new homes in different countries. Heinz was finally a part of the family again. Now he would pin his hopes on the UNRRA organization that had put together money to help refugees and deportees get home. He explained that they had put all of their effort into getting Tante Lenchen and Werner out. They were four of thousands of refugees at the camp in Beaune-La Rolande. Everyone wanted to get out.

Karl-Heinz looked at his brother's hands. "How did you get so yellow?" he asked. "What did you do? Jump in a bucket of paint?" he snickered.

"*Karottitis*. It happens when you eat too many carrots. Look. Everyone here has it... just about," Ernstchen explained. "But it doesn't kill you or anything. Just makes your nails and skin look sort of dirty all the time..."

Karl-Heinz hesitated before he started speaking. The look on the faces surrounding him did not bode well for the food at the camp. "You eat a lot of carrots, then?"

"I'll say," Irmgard answered quickly. "You are lucky, Heinz. We've been eating carrots for more than two months already. I can tell you that when I get out of this camp I am never going to touch a carrot again. Never!"

"I don't mind carrots too much," Karl-Heinz argued.

"Not yet you don't," Ernstchen added. "You'll see. After a few days here you'll never want to see a carrot again."

Ernstchen was right. Karl-Heinz detested the cut carrots that were the mainstay of their diet. He detested the camp, the freezing accommodations, the perpetual illness that seemed to taunt those interned there, and the tediousness of group living at the camp. Except for the night he and several other boys were caught stealing wood outside the camp fence for the wood-burning stove in the barracks, nothing of any great interest occurred until February 7, 1946, the day the Contag family departed the camp at Beaune-La Rolande for the port at Marseilles.

NOTES TO CHAPTER NINE

[1] The United Nations' Relief and Rehabilitation Agency.

[2] Ernst Contag listed the places he visited and the people he talked to in his homemade pocket calendar for 1945 and the first two months of 1946.

[3] Captain Josse signed travel papers for Ernst Contag. Travel documents from Beaune-La Rolande camp dated in October 1945, January and February 1946.

[4] C.H.Contag interview and *Les Camps d'internement du Loiret: Histoire et mémoire 1941-43*. Centre de Recherche et de Documentation sur les camps d'internement et la déportation Juive dan le Loiret, 1996. The book contains images and descriptions of the concentration camps in the Loire valley including the camps at Pithiviers, Beaune-La-Rolande and Jargeau. The camp at Beaune-La-Rolande had been used as a concentration camp for Jewish men, women and children who were taken from the camp to other locations where they were exterminated. A history of the camps was published in David Diamant's book *Le Billet Vert*, Renouveau Edition, 1977. A special Memorial that was destroyed by a storm in 1990 was restored and commemorated in 1991 with the support of the community in Beaune-la-Rolande. The memorial is dedicated to the adults and children who lost their lives. Less is known and recorded about the years that Beaune-la-Rolande served as a camp for political deportees and refugees.

⁵Dettmar, Werner. *Die Zerstörung Kassels im Oktober 1943: Eine Dokumentation.* Germany: Hesse GmbH and Dettmar, 1983.

⁶Hermann, Peter, et. al. *Potsdam und das Jahr 1945.* Potsdam: Potsdam-Museum, 1995.

⁷Ernst Contag pocket calendar 1945-6.

⁸Leonidas Plaza Lasso served as Ecuadorian Consul to France during the repatriation conducted by the United Nations Relief and Rehabilitation Agency. Ernst Contag had known Plaza Lasso in Quito.

⁹Hermann, Peter, et. al. *Potsdam und das Jahr 1945.* Potsdam: Potsdam-Museum, 1995.

¹⁰German radio broadcasts published by the *New York Times* newspaper.

¹¹Richard Ashton wrote two letters to Ernst after he returned to Ecuador. In both letters (July 22 and August 28, 1946) Ashton and his wife, Gerda, plead for his help in getting out of the repatriation camp. According to the letter, Ernst had written them in June promising to help get Ashton a job with a brewery in Quito. Hartgring wrote E. Contag from The Hague on November 19, 1946, and complained of his situation in the Netherlands. W. Contag files.

¹²E. Contag, Jr. medical certification for transport to Beaune-la-Rolande. Ernstchen Contag received medical certification indicating that he was free of all contagious diseases and that he received a yellow fever vaccination. This was issued by R. Brodowsky on September 15, 1945 at the Paris Transit Center Luna-Park, Ministry of Prisoners, Deportees and Refugees and the French Repatriation Military Mission, "Annexe" Transit Center for Aliens.

[13]Transport papers for Carlos Heinz Contag were issued on November 14, 1945 by the Liaison Mission of the French Republic on November 14, 1945. The order was to the 7th U.S. Army Det. G39 and read as follows (translation from the French original):

```
            Routing Order
Carlos Heinz Contag, born on July 1930
in Quito, Ecuador, an Ecuadorian citi-
zen, living in Korbach at Bergstrasse 1.

 -According to a letter from the
 Ministry of the Interior from Octo-
 ber 1, 1945
 -According to an order issued by
 the French Commander in Chief in Ger-
 many /Ref. LR/S Nr. 651/PDR on Octo-
 ber 13, 1945 is authorized to turn
 himself in to the Luna Parc Repa-
 triation Center in Paris where he
 will be retrieved by his father Mr.
 Ernesto Contag.

The authorities and French Military are
required to give him all the assistance
and food he requires for the trip).

                   Jean A. Boucherat
                             Captain
                French Liaison Officer

Seal: Military Government Det. G-39
French Liaison Visa
```

Karl-Heinz arrived in Paris, Luna Park, before November 26, 1945 when he was issued a transit order that would allow him to travel as a political deportee from Paris Auster City to Beaune la Rolande. According to the document, the transport to the camp had to be completed before November 30, 1945.

(The document is translated from the French original and included below).

```
Ministry of Prisoners, Deportes, Refugees.
Ministry of the Interior.
Direction du sevice des Réfugiés

Evacuation or Repatriation 3rd Class
Special BON for Transport
No. 2443 Mousieur Carlos Heinz Contag
Valid until November 30, 1945.

Baggage is limited to 50 kilos per person.
Issued in Paris on November 26, 1945.
```

At the top left corner of the transport document the word "Equateur" is hand-written in ink. Karl-Heinz, now Carlos for all intents and purposes, was again an Ecuadorian citizen, a political deportee, and an international refugee.

CHAPTER NINE

LETTERS FROM EIGHTH AND 51ST

NEW YORK CITY, 1946

It was going to be a long bus ride from New York to Miami, but the Contag children were delighted to be on their way *home* with their father. Ernst had been able to get the money for the bus tickets at the last minute, saving them from being sent back to France. Ernst finally felt successful. His children had grown stronger in New York and Karl Heinz had even learned more English. Now they were on their way back home where they belonged.

Karl Heinz and Erntschen chatted in the seat in front of him and Irmgard slept at his side. As they traveled south the terrain changed from spring to summer and Ernst felt the warmth of the sun against his face. *Keep the sun in your heart*, he murmured to himself, recalling the old German poem. He sighed with a deep sense of satisfaction.

Ernst had packed their belongings the night before and was surprised to see that they had acquired quite a few clothing items while in New York. The Salvation Army and a number of families had been very generous. Nothing meant more to him, though, than the papers and letters he had placed in Karl Heinz's leather satchel that now sat at his feet. He picked up the satchel and undid the leather straps. He leafed through the official internment papers, the medical documents, German bankbooks, and pocket date books that he had carried thoughout his journey after leaving the Berlin area. These documents alone could tell the story of what had happened to them. He had no intention of ever getting rid of them.

A postcard of the Hotel Capitol in New York, date books, letters from Maria Renaud, official documents and personal letters associated with the four years of exile were found amongst Ernst Contag's guarded effects after his death.

Ernst's right hand rested on a bundle of letters tied with a piece of string. He pulled the bundle from the satchel and placed them on his lap. He sorted through them and finally hit upon the one he was looking for. It was the letter he had written to his brother-in-law telling him about their flight from Beaune-La Rolande. He unfolded the letter he had written in February but had not sent because it was in the hotel when he finally had an opportunity to send letters. He had written a separate one with similar information. Nevertheless, he had stashed this letter with the others. He did not know why he had kept it.

Ernst unfolded the letter on hotel stationary and read it with interest.

Hotel Capitol
OPPOSITE MADISON SQUARE GARDEN
51st STREET AT EIGHTH AVENUE
NEW YORK CITY
Telephone Circle 6-3700

New York, February 26, 1946

Señor Don
Hermann Dreier
c/o Vorbeck Inc.
Avenida 24 de Mayo No 70
Quito, Ecuador

My dear Hermann,

It is a true pleasure for me to write you from New York City, U.S.A. as we are delighted to be in the Americas again, finally, after having such a difficult time getting out of the Beaune-La-Rolande repatriation camp in France.¹ I thank God everyday that we were able to get out of that camp!

I hope that my sister Helena and Werner arrived safely in Quito. We have had no information here about them since they left France last year. Please write and tell me if you know where they are and if Wernerchen is in good health again. It has been very difficult for me wondering at every moment if Werner is healthy and safe.

I received your telegram indicating that I should try to arrange for our voyage through the Ecuadorian consulate in Paris. As you can see, I was successful in getting an IOU from Consul Leonidas Plaza Lasso and countersigned by Carlos Peña. It was my understanding that Reinaldo Espinosa would take responsibility for the cost of the voyage on the Gripsholm. He must have arrived in Ecuador some time ago. His address is #287 Roca Street. I will send him a letter requesting his help again. The United Nations Relief and Rehabilitation Agency along with the Ministry of Foreign Relations in Ecuador must be handling the cost of repatriation. I will append my copy of the cablegram that speaks to this information to this letter.

Now I must ask you for another favor, my good brother-in-law. Please ask Reinaldo Espinosa, and the Ecuadorian government, to intervene once again on our behalf. We must guarantee the cost of the return trip from New York to Quito as soon as possible. I look forward to hearing from you directly about this matter since we are only allowed two short months in New York before my family is deported back to France and the repatriation camp. I refuse to think of that unimaginable tragedy for our family.

In the meantime, Heinz, Ernestito and Irmgard are well. I have started speaking Spanish to them again here in New York. Ernestito has maintained a good amount of Spanish, and Heinz, who we must now call Carlos, understands everything, although he does not speak much yet. He spends hours every day trying to translate any document or paper he can get his hands on. He is improving both in English and in Spanish. Irma, like Werner, has retained little or no Spanish at all after our years abroad. It will take her quite some time to learn to speak Spanish again. The children are getting stronger, and they will adapt again when we get back to Quito. I am conducting all of my discussions here in New York in Spanish whenever I can, and the children listen to me when I ask others for any information I can get on Ecuador or South America. English, of course, is quite a challenge for me. I noticed that one official even wrote down Heinz's birthday wrong on our visa based on my mispronunciation of his birth year which was recorded as 1913 instead of 1930!

The children spend their free time at Central Park while I try to arrange for additional assistance for our stay here and our trip home. The Salvation Army has been a good help to us. I spoke with Heinrich Paul Suhr, pastor of the St. Pauls' Church and the Deutsche Evangelische Lutherans, who works with the Lutheran World Relief Fund. I have been to the Ecuadorian General Consulate on Rockefeller Plaza as well. The children were able to ice skate on the plaza while I stood in line and spoke with representatives. The children had a nice time skating and we met some kind people on the ice after my visit at the Consulate.

It is still quite cold here, but we will not complain ever again about being cold after nearly freezing to death in the French camp. You cannot imagine how we suffered there. We have a nice hotel room here on the third floor at the Hotel Capitol and we eat more regularly than we have in more than a year. There is a cafeteria nearby called Horn and Hardart where the children can put a coin into a slot and they pull out something to eat that they like. They find the strange machines at the cafeteria quite amusing. They enjoy something called "cottage cheese" very much. It is very much like lumpy "quark" that you must remember from your childhood. They are not in school, of course. Heinz went one day but could not understand a word. Since we only expect to be here a short time I agreed to let them stay together in the hotel without going to school. They have already suffered too much.

I would be glad to conduct any business you might need done here in New York. I have found the addresses for the Winchester and Stoeger Arms Companies in the telephone book and also for A. Gusmer, Inc. and a few import/export companies like the Insular Export Company, Import Chemical in Jersey City, Europa Import on 207 E. 84th Street, the Curtiss-Gabaldoni Company, and Import-Export Industries on Rockefeller Plaza.

I have not been able to find out which airline travels to Ecuador. I was given the name of a Miss Norton with the Ardel Travel Bureau whom I will visit next week. As soon as I hear from you I would like to make travel arrangements.

I have learned that Arturo is interned in a Crystal City camp somewhere in the United States. I have a box number, 788, but I am not sure how to contact him yet. I will write him when I get more information.

I send my warmest regards to you, Anita and the girls. Please give my love to my dearest Wernerchen and to my sister, Helena, when you see her. Tell Werner that we will be home very soon. Awaiting your reply,

*Your brother-in-law,
Ernesto Contag*

Ernst folded the letter and opened the response he received from Hermann in March.

AIR MAIL
AEREO

Vorbeck Inc.
IMPORTACION-COMISION-REPRESENTACIONCORREO
AVENIDA 24 DE MAYO No 7o
QUITO-ECUADOR

H/D Quito, 5 March 1946[2]

Señor Don
Ernesto Contag,
a/c. Hotel Capitol,
Eighth Avenue at Fifty First Street,
<u>New York 19- N. Y.</u>

My esteemed Ernesto:

Just now I received your well-crafted letter sent the 26th of last month, and I am happy that all of you have arrived safe and sound in New York.

    Helena and Werner arrived well and are in perfect health. Helena left yesterday for Otavalo with the intention of making an arrangement with the American Jack Sheppard who is interested in employing her as his secretary. He is married to Mary Alvarez whom you must still remember. Helena left for San Rafael located on the banks of the Saint Paul lagoon, where they will come to an agreement about salary, type of work, etc. Helena and Werner have been living in my home together. Now it is just Werner and our daughter Tootsie. The two of them play together very well, even though they end up in big fights quite often. You know that Werner is only two months older than Tootsie, but she is a good head taller than he is. How about that!

    Reinaldo Espinosa did not intervene in any way in regard to the arrangement or costs of your trip on the Gripsholm because right after his arrival he moved to Ambato. Even though the cable from the

Ecuadorian Foreign Relations' minister indicated that the Ecuadorian government would pay the expenses for your family on the Gripsholm, this is not the case, since I had to fill out a complicated document to make good on the incurred debt. The document had to be pre-authorized by the National Contractor, notarized and vouched for by businesses, etc., and guaranteed by Jacobo Vorbeck. This document stated that the entire amount of the voyage, along with an additional 5000 sucre fine was to be paid in full as soon as the North American government demanded the payment.

For the same reason as the one I mentioned above, there is not the least shred of hope of obtaining one cent from the government for your travel expenses from New York to Ecuador. For this reason I wrote this morning to the National Filter Corporation, 147 West 22nd Street, New York 11- N.Y., to make a payment of $800.00 U.S. dollars on your behalf to the Ecuadorian Consulate in New York, since I was unaware of your address until your letter arrived today. The requested payment may not be sent immediately since the National Filter Company only has $300.00 U.S. dollars. In order to complete the required $800.00 U.S. dollars I have asked Bode & Voigt, 31 Union Square, to transfer $550.00 U.S. dollars to the National Filter Company that are still held by them for a commission to La Campana Brewery. What you can do now is make reservations on

Panagra Airlines or Avianca Airlines so that you will not have any delay when the amount due is made available. You can pay the airlines later.

What you can do while you wait for your tickets to become available is to see Mr. E.G. Mueller of the Crown Cork and Seal Co., Inc., at 305 Madison Avenue, New York 17- N.Y. Greet him cordially in my name and urge him to do everything possible to speed up the departure of the CEMCO 50 for La Victoria Brewery, another CEMCO 50 for La Campana Brewery, and the CEM 28 for Orangine Bottling. Also, tell him to send me as soon as possible the blueprint for La Victoria.

You could also visit Mr. H.F. Sittenfeld of the National Filter Corporation, whose address I mentioned before. Greet him warmly, and thank him personally for the lovely records he sent us for Christmas which give us many enjoyable moments at home. I append a letter that was written the day that the records arrived for me and Helge and Jacobo Vorbeck, signed by all of us who know Mr. Sittenfeld personally. Please take this letter to him in person and tell him that we were all together in Helge's home one night until the wee hours of the morning, drinking, dancing and having a terrific time with the records he sent. Urge him again to make every effort possible to see that the bottle washer for the Victoria is shipped. It is needed <u>URGENTLY</u>.

Besides working with Jacobo Vorbeck as his representative, I am also working at La Victoria Brewery as an Assistant Manager as a result of the series of difficulties that occurred on both sides when you were still here.

I must finish this letter quickly since today is Carnival and the Post Office will not be open in the afternoon. Tomorrow I will travel by plane to Guayaquil where I will be for eight days making the arrangements for the railroad to transport two trucks and 25,000 dozen bottles as far as Cajabamba since the road through Babahoyo has been completely washed out by our devastating winter.

If you are able to do so, send me a cable with your date of departure. You can send it to my P.O. Box 54, to Box 577, which is Vorbeck's, or to Box 206, La Victoria Brewery. In each case I would receive the cabled letter immediately.

I send you warm greetings, and greetings from my wife Anita, daughter Tootsie and your son Werner. I hope to be able to greet you personally very soon. As always,

Hermann Dreier[1]

The bus jolted to a halt and a letter fell from Ernst's lap. He picked it up. It was the letter he had written to Maria but had not sent. He had written about the couple in New York that wanted to adopt Irmgard. He thought the news might have broken Maria's heart. He could not send it nor could he toss the letter in the garbage. As he read, his own words triggered a deep sadness and he let his head toss about as he read through tears that welled up in his eyes.

Hotel Capitol
OPPOSITE MADISON SQUARE GARDEN
51st STREET AT EIGHTH AVENUE
NEW YORK CITY
Telephone Circle 6-3700

New York, March 25, 1946[3]

Maria Renaud
Velserstrasse, 47

My dearest Maria,

 I do not know if this letter will reach you. There was no way for me to write you until now, and even now I am cautious about sending letters overseas. You must understand why. Still, I cannot go another day without telling you that we are all safe and that we will soon be on our way home to Quito. We only have a few weeks before our visa expires, but I am confident that we will not be returned to France. My brother-in-law has made every effort to help us find the thousand dollars that we will need for the journey. I don't know how I will ever be able to repay him for his dedication to our return. Without his help and the assistance of the good family Vorbeck and the breweries in Quito we would be returned to the French refugee camp we left in February.

 I will not tell you about the devastating and difficult time we had leaving Germany. I understand that Nuremberg was destroyed and you must have seen and heard plenty of stories of personal tragedy. I will only tell you that after many, many difficult months we were able to leave the repatriation camp at Beaune-La-Rolande for our return to Ecuador. I must tell you that the children were strong and encouraging throughout our trials. I would have lost hope long before our departure if it had not been for their smiles, encouragement, and their belief in me. I am torn. Irmgard sees me still as a hero who will protect her from the evils that we have encountered. I see myself only as a weak father who, with the miraculous help of others, has been able to keep our small family safe. I am no hero.

Last week a childless couple here in New York made an unusual overture to me. They offered to adopt Irmgard and give me $500.00 U.S. dollars for her hair that has grown quite long. We have been in such desperate circumstances... unable to return to Ecuador for lack of funds, fearful of being deported again to France, and facing an uncertain future. I actually considered their offer. You will be appalled by this, I am sure, as I was. We met the Browns at their bakery, which is not too far from our hotel. During the first few weeks of our stay in New York the couple fell in love with Irmgard and I believe they were trying to be kind and generous with their offer to adopt her. Irmgard is very fond of them, too.

Desperate thoughts occur to people in desperate times. I have often wished that I could protect little Irmgard better from the tragedies she witnessed and lived during the past year. She is so young and should never know the cruelties of man. I was tremendously frightened for her safety when the Russians arrived in Potsdam and even in the repatriation camp I made sure her brothers kept an eye on her.

I told the couple from the bakery that I could not let them have my only daughter no matter how desperate we may be now. They told me that, if at the last moment we are to be deported back to France, I should consider making the agreement for Irmgard's sake. No matter how reasonable this arrangement must seem to them, I could not abandon my daughter even to a special, loving couple who would raise her like their own and provide for her better than I may be able to in Ecuador or, God forbid, in France. I would never be able to forgive myself. I suppose that it is out of selfishness that I keep her with me.

    Werner is not with us here in New York. I learned recently from my brother-in-law in Quito that Werner and my sister arrived and both are now healthy. I knew nothing about their whereabouts for six months so I was very relieved to hear this news. Werner became very ill after our long journey on foot from Berlin to Paris, and he left on an earlier refugee ship for the infirm in the company of my sister. Werner will stay with my brother-in-law and his wife in Quito until I return. The months in the repatriation camp were very difficult for me since I knew nothing of Werner and my sister, and Heinz had been left behind in Korbach after we left Germany. We did not know if he was dead or alive and it was not easy for the Location Service of U.N.R.R.A. to find him. A French officer whom I met at the camp took pity on our plight and went to get Heinz himself. I will thank God for his perseverance and kindness the rest of my life. It really was a miracle we were able to leave Europe at all. Many are still in the repatriation camp in France with little hope of ever leaving.

    Enough of the sadness in my life. Our hotel is adjacent to the Capitol Theatre and Greyhound Bus Terminal. We can see the buses leave regularly. The hotel is near many theatres and the children spend countless hours peering through storefront windows that line the streets in this area. We are all amazed by the items that are available for sale in New York City! The famous Fifth Avenue shops are only five minutes walk from our hotel. We often walk up and down the street looking at the people dressed so elegantly and the expensive things in the windows.

The Hotel Capitol rooms are comfortable, but nothing like the fancy Greenbrier Hotel in West Virginia that I told you about after we first met. We have a small, clean room with a vanity and a three-panel mirror that fascinates Irmgard. She can see the side and back of her hair that already reaches her waist, and she likes to sit in front of the mirrors and watch me braid her hair in the morning. I couldn't believe it when a woman on a bus offered us money for her hair. You should have seen Irmgardchen's reaction to cutting and selling her hair!

I am sitting near the lone window in our hotel room that looks over Madison Square Garden. The garden is not in bloom since it is still winter here, but I am sure that when spring arrives in a month or so, the garden will be beautiful and impressive. I should like to take a long walk with you there someday, Maria. Now, of course, seeing you again seems quite unlikely.

When we left Germany, the countryside had just come into full bloom. The horse chestnut trees, linden trees, and spring flowers had already burst into a floral display that stood out in contrast to the terrible devastation all around us. It was our only pleasant memory of the last few weeks in Potsdam.

I do not sleep well at night here. There is street noise and the footboard keeps me from stretching out full length. The radiator under the window spits and gurgles throughout the day and night and I have not yet grown accustomed to its interminable rattle. The only thing that reminds me of home is the decorative moorish-style archways in the lounge that are decorated with colonial-style street lamps like the ones we saw in the narrow streets of Lisbon or on the plazas in Quito.

I have made some progress in getting things in order for our return to Quito. My days in New York are spent with visits to different businesses and welfare agencies. We can still only afford to eat once a day here in New York, but the welfare agencies have been generous in their assistance and we have been very fortunate with the treatment we have received in the United States.

The children keep busy with trips to Central Park. I leave them alone in the morning so I can run errands, but we often eat together at a nearby cafeteria later on in the day. All of us lost many kilos while we were in the camp and we have made every effort to gain some weight back. Even Heinz, who had eaten well before coming to the camp, looked emaciated when we left. Heinz tried to make up for all the lost weight during our nine-day voyage on the Gripsholm Steamer that took us across the Atlantic. The day we arrived at the port in Marseilles there were free doughnuts and coffee for the passengers. Heinz ate doughnuts until he vomited. Then he went back for more. None of our stomachs could hold much anymore. I can laugh about it now. On this voyage he was just as seasick as he was on our first voyage on the Drottningholm, but the nausea didn't matter to him this time. He ate a plate full of spaghetti, vomited over the side and returned to the table to eat more. He was so hungry. Poor thing.

It is odd how things change in a family. Ernestito has become a special companion to me during these past year's trials. He listens to me and often takes the dark side of things so I am forced to brighten his thoughts and lift my own spirits. In this way we balance each other's moods. I cannot imagine how I would have survived this past year without him. He is such a responsible boy for his age. He is becoming a little cynical, though, and he has the humor of a grown man who has lived through torturesome experiences. I am sorry that I cannot give him his childhood back, but I am thankful that he has been able to carry me through when I have needed it most.

> *Dearest Maria, I must ask you to write me when I return to Quito. Do not write me here at this address. If God desires it, we will be leaving New York soon. I will write again with an address where you can write me in Quito. I look forward to getting news about you and learning how you have managed with everything.*
>
> *We have not forgotten you, Maria. I hope you are safe and that soon your life will be in order again. Thoughts of you and your beautiful smile have kept me from despair on many occasions. May God keep you well until I hear from you.*
>
> *Ernst Contag*

Ernst stiffened and pushed his back against the bus seat. He chuckled at his description of not being able to sleep at night. It was true, but it now seemed inappropriate to include in the letter.

He smiled to himself as he once again justified his decisions. Maria was an interesting woman and he had thoroughly enjoyed their time together. Ernst enjoyed the idea of an ongoing romance with Maria through letters. He would have no other responsibility than to respond to them and buy stamps. He would not have to deal with a mother-in-law or taking orders and he would not have to worry about Maria checking up on his behavior or disciplining his children. There was an ocean between them. He turned away the nagging pain of loneliness. He was, after all, going back to Elizabeth. He folded the letter and retuned it to the satchel.

The next piece of paper was the note he had scribbled on a sheet of paper before transferring it to hotel stationary on March 28. It was a short letter he had sent to his brother who, to his surprise, had been interned in Crystal City, Texas throughout the war years.

March 28, 1946

Arturo Contag
P.O. Box 788
Crystal City, Texas

Dear Arturo, Alcirita and children,

I was delighted to find out from the Red Cross where you are staying.* I hope that you are all well in the camp in Texas. I have been told that the accommodations are comfortable. I hope this is so.

I am writing to inform you that if everything goes as planned we will be leaving New York for Ecuador in a few weeks. You should not write me at this address but send any communication to Quito in care of my brother-in-law, Hermann Dreier, who is currently working for the Vorbecks. I will write you from Quito in more detail.

I do not know if Lenchen contacted you about the sad news concerning our brother so I feel that I must tell you. Our dear brother Carl was lost to us on the island of Sicily on August 5, 1943. His wife, Inge, has new accommodations in Potsdam.

Lenchen and Werner are already in Ecuador. Heinz, Ernestito, Irmgard and I will be joining them shortly

God will provide.

Ernesto

Ernst wondered how Arturo and Alcira must have taken Carlos' death and if Lenchen or Hermann had sent the news earlier. There was nothing to be gained by thinking on those things so Ernst tucked the note behind the bundle. The note that followed was one he had written to the Hoeners. The couple had been of great help to them during their stay in New York.

April 1946

Mr. and Mrs. Harold Hoener
43-58 193 Street
Flushing, New York

Dear Elsa and Harold,

 I wanted to send you a short letter thanking you for your friendship and your support during our stay here in New York as we will not have the opportunity to thank you in person. I am so grateful that we met you, Elsa, at the Ardel Travel Bureau, and that you and Harold took such an interest in our welfare and in the happiness of my children. We will always have fine memories of you.

 We leave for Miami in the next few days on one of the Greyhound buses that leave from a street near our hotel. Miss Norton may have already informed you of our departure which she so kindly arranged for us at the last moment. The children are anxious to leave New York, as we will be able to see much of the Atlantic coast as we travel toward Miami, Florida.

 I am looking forward to starting a more regular life back home in Quito. I will turn forty years old a year from August. I can hardly believe it. What do I have to show for my forty years? I have nothing except my family. In times like these, perhaps this is enough.

 Please accept our kindest regards and a special greeting from your Ecuadorian friends,

Ernesto, Carlos, Ernestito, and Irmgard Contag

 Ernst had kept the copy because it had the Hoener's address on it. He barely looked at the letter before tucking it behind the ones he had already read. The one that followed interested him more. He had kept the letter as a memento and had sent a cablegram instead. Their departure had been urgent and the letter had simply not been sent.

Hotel Capitol
OPPOSITE MADISON SQUARE GARDEN
51st STREET AT EIGHTH AVENUE
NEW YORK CITY
Telephone Circle 6-3700

New York, April 1946[5]

Señor Don
Hermann Dreier
c/o Vorbeck Inc.
Avenida 24 de Mayo No 70
Quito, Ecuador

My dear Hermann,

I have just sent you a cablegram announcing our departure. If we had not made the arrangements by this week we would be on our way back to France! Instead we will be leaving for Miami by train where we will stay until we can leave on Panagra Airlines for home. I cannot tell you our arrival date, although I have made a special promise to Irmgard that we will try to be back home for Easter. Miss Norton at the Ardel Travel Bureau has not been able to tell me with absolute certainty how much time we will spend in each Central American country or how long we will be in Bogotá, Colombia before flying to Quito. We had to make open reservations and will take the first flights that become available. Miss Norton has informed me that the trip will take several weeks, so you should not expect to see us much before Holy Week.

The last few weeks here have been difficult for us. Worry, worry, worry. The Office of Immigration has been quite concerned about the delay in our departure for Ecuador and at every moment we fear that something might go wrong and keep us from being able to go home. I will not stop worrying until we step off the plane at the Mariscal Sucre airport.

As I said in the cablegram I will try to contact you from Bogotá so that you will know our approximate arrival date and time. I think that the Consulate will allow us this convenience. I will not arrive with any money, as you might expect, and it would be kind of you to meet us at the airport, and good of dearest Anita to make a meal for us when we arrive. The children are looking forward to seeing their dear uncle and aunt and their beautiful cousins. We will go back to the Contag house to sleep unless, for some reason, this is not possible.

Please tell Jacobo and Helge Vorbeck how thankful we are for their help. I will thank them personally when I arrive, of course. I will be indebted to them and to you, dear Hermann. If you have the opportunity, you might mention to Jacobo that there are a number of very capable people at the camp in France who have not been able to find a way to return to their homeland. My good friend from Lorenço Marques, Africa, Richard Ashton, would be an excellent hire for La Campana or La Victoria, for instance. Please tell Jacobo that if he has a generous heart and pocket, he could help Richard, Gerda, and son Peter Ashton find a home. I can vouch for him, his wife, and son who would all pledge their service to him and any endeavor he chose for them. I will speak to him personally, of course, when I arrive. But it would be marvelous if Jacobo could think about the prospect before I arrive. Tell him that I will take care of the details of the transfer myself.

You are a fine man, Hermann. I am proud to have a brother-in-law such as you. Elisabeth, dear Elisabeth, would be proud to see what you have done for her family.

Please tell Werner that his father, brothers and sister will soon be home. Give my warmest regards to Anita and warm embraces to your two growing daughters.

Ernesto Contag

Ernst realized how obsolete the letter was already. They were not traveling by train but by bus, for instance. He folded the letter and glanced at the Cablegram on his lap. It was the last communication from Hermann.

CABLEGRAM[6]

```
April 1946

Ernesto Contag
Consulado Ecuatoriano,
Bogotá, Colombia

Hermann Dreier
Vorbeck Inc.
Box 206, Quito, Ecuador

Hermann, Anita, Tootsie & Werner await
your arrival on Easter Sunday. Our be-
loved daughter, Betty, is with God, Para-
lytic Fever.
```

Irmgard moved against Ernst's arm and awoke. She looked up and asked, "What are you reading, Papa?" Ernst had not told the children of their little cousin's death.

"I'm just going through some of my papers. Have you looked out the window at the landscape, Irmgard? It is really very pretty." Irmgard straightened up and looked through sleepy eyes out the window.

Ernst wrapped the bundle of letters in string and returned them to the satchel.

"Are we almost there, Papa?"

"Almost where?" Ernst asked with a twinkle in his eye. He expected it would take them nearly two weeks to get to Quito. They would have just a few more hours until they reached Miami, but they were scheduled to take several flights on different days to airports in different countries. He looked on these flights as the final adventure to their four-year exile from Ecuador. Unfortunately, the adventure was not over. The Contags would discover that the welcoming home and life Ernst had been dreaming of was no more than an illusion, and that their return to the Quitus Valley was the beginning of feeling like exiles in a country he had always called home.

NOTES TO CHAPTER NINE

[1]Ernst Contag applied for a transit visa on January 3-5, 1946 in Paris. On January 16, 1946 he completed the application for a transit certification. He circled the date in his calendar and started making plans for the return trip. On January 29 he sent a cablegram to his brother-in-law, Hermann Dreier, asking him for assistance in collecting funds for the February departure. On February 1, 1946 Ernst received a cablegram from Hermann Dreier who sent it from the Foreign Ministry office in Quito. Hermann Dreier suggested that Ernst try to get the expenses for the trip on the Gripsholm from the Ecuadorian government. "*Ministro exterior cabelgrafio ministro Ecuador. Paris procurar pasajes Gripsholm por cuenta gobiernoecuador.* Hermann." On February 2, 1946 the American Foreign Service issued the Contags a transit visa for two months to the United States. The information in this chapter is taken from copies of the original documents kept by Ernst Contag until his death and retained in Werner Contag's files, and from interviews with Carlos Contag and Irmgard (Contag) Jaunzems and written documents submitted by them to the authors.

[2]The original letter was written in Spanish and retained by Werner Contag after his father's death. Hermann Dreier worked for the Vorbecks for a short time during the war after DREICO was closed in 1942. Vorbeck and his sons were Danish immigrants who were good friends of Ernst Contag before he left for Germany in 1942. The Vorbeck family had run the brewery on

24 de mayo street since February 1912 when Enrique E. Vorbeck purchased the brewery from Mariano Ingrate.

³The information in this letter is taken from interviews and correspondence with Irmgard (Contag) Jaunzems and C.H. Contag, 1999-2000, and information in Ernest Contag's pocket calendar 1945-46.

⁴Ernst Contag pocket calendar. Arturo Contag was arrested and detained by a U.S. agent and Ecuadorian officials in Cotocallao, Ecuador during the first week of January 1944. He was neither seen nor heard from again until March 1944 when Arturo's wife, desperate for news about her husband, left with her children on a steam ship for Panama. Arturo was reunited with his family on the ship, although they were transported in separate quarters. This was a twenty-one day voyage for Alcira and her five young children from Guayaquil to New Orleans. The family was bathed with a chemical disinfectant when they arrived in New Orleans and were then taken by train to the Crystal City, Texas internment camp. Arturo's family remained in the internment camp until November 1947. It was impossible for them to make enough money for the return trip. By November 1947 they were a family of eight. US officials encouraged the Contag family to become citizens like many other interned families had done, given the desperate circumstances surrounding repatriation. Alcira and Arturo were interrogated separately on many occasions but always insisted upon returning to Ecuador. The US government agreed to have them repatriated to Ecuador in November 1947, more than two years after the war between Germany and the United States had ended. Alcira Contag unpublished "Recuerdos," October 1998.

⁵C.H. Contag interview. E. Contag pocket calendar 1945-46.

⁶Anna Elizabeth "Betty" Dreier (June 16, 1940-February 22, 1943) died of typhoid fever.

CHAPTER TEN

FOG IN THE QUITUS VALLEY

QUITO, APRIL 1946

Ernst Contag listened to the small airplane's propellers and wondered if it would be able to climb over the tall Andes Mountains surrounding Quito and land safely at the airport. It was morning and they would be able to see Quito from the air as they approached if he could scratch enough of the frost off the small windowpane next to him. He had never seen Quito from the air and he was excited to see his home in the Quitus Valley just beneath the clouds.

The plane shuddered restlessly and Ernst felt himself grasp the seat on which he was sitting.

"It's kind of a rough ride up here, *¿no es cierto?* Ernestito," he said in Spanish, with a forced smile. "You have to pretend you are on horseback going down a mountain."

"It is more like a ride on the back of a donkey!" the boy responded looking a bit pale. "Look at Heinz! He looks as green as he did on the Gripsholm!"

Ernst nodded. He was also queasy and didn't want to pursue the thought. He took a breath, but the air didn't get much past his sternum. He thought about seeing Werner on his feet again. His son had grown so weak in the repatriation camp but Hermann's letters had assured that Werner was strong and healthy again. What a delight to see Hermann, Anita, and Tootsie after four long years.

Just then the plane started to climb again. The plane sputtered and Ernst felt a chill run up his spine. *It won't be long now until we are home*, he thought to himself, nibbling at his lower lip. *I wonder what our old house will look like after all these years?* Ernst shrugged and kept the thought to himself. He had persevered in getting his family home to Quito and he wanted to enjoy the accomplishment. *No need to worry about the unknown, yet*, he mumbled under his breath.

The plane approached Quito. Ernst had never flown into Quito before and the view was breathtaking. He could not close his eyes even as the tip of the mountain appeared to scratch the belly of the plane before dropping precipitously into the deep valley that had belonged to the Indians since ages past. The ride was exhilarating and a little frightening, too. Minutes later the small plane landed and they deplaned on the runway. Ernst stopped at the bottom of the portable steps and took his first deep *Ecuadorian* breath.

"Ahhhh, it smells just like home! You can already imagine the smell of burning eucalyptus, can't you?" he asked the children.

"It doesn't smell like home to me," Irmgard said, obstinately, shaking her head. "I think pine trees smell like home. It sort of smells like Bogotá here. Sort of stinky."

Irmgard, who was usually cheerful and easy-going, had started to act out of character when they arrived in Central America. She couldn't understand the Spanish spoken around her and she had begun to play the part of an unwilling participant in their return home. She spoke more about Germany and its lakes and pine trees than about their accommodations in New York City or the endless suffering she had endured in the French camp.

"It's not much of an airport for an *international* airport," Ernstchen said, interrupting his father's thoughts. "We will be back in our house soon and none of this will matter, will it, Papa?"

"No, none of it will matter, Ernstchen. We are home."

"I am just glad we are on the ground again," Karl-Heinz sighed, getting his color back.

Ernst went to immigration first and handed the official his paper work issued by the Embassies in New York and Colombia. The immigration official went off to speak briefly with a supervisor, but there was not much delay before the Contags were allowed to pass through to customs. The customs official rummaged through their baggage and waved them on. Neither official had said much and neither welcomed the family back to Ecuador.

The baggage handlers and taxi drivers near the exit of the small airport building surrounded Ernst, but he declined their services politely. He couldn't pay them. It felt strange to be so much taller than everyone else. For the first time in his life he felt a certain uneasiness surrounded by so many men who did not look like he did. He was shocked that being back amongst Ecuadorians felt so uncomfortable and strange. Ernst guided his children to the door where he saw his brother-in-law Hermann standing stiffly a good two heads taller than anyone near him.

"*Bienvenidos*," he said in Spanish with a grin. Ernst embraced his brother-in-law and clapped him firmly on the back.

"*Por fin!*" Ernst responded, "Four years have passed, dear brother-in-law, four long years! And here we are! Finally!" Ernst sighed with relief. Hermann Dreier greeted each nephew and niece separately. He spoke first in Spanish.

"Wait until your Tante Anita gets a look at you, Heinz. You will tower over her! You've grown so tall! You are nearly a full-grown man! And look at you!" Hermann held his hand out to Ernstchen. "Can you be little Ernestito? You are almost big enough to wear your father's suit jacket! What a good-looking boy you've turned out to be. You are a little thin, but a few good meals will take care of that."

The boys smiled at their uncle and nodded their heads in agreement. Hermann Dreier turned to Irmgard who was still standing close to her father. Hermann's voice softened, "And Irmgard, you are quite the young lady! Let's see . . . you must be ten years old already! Tootsie and Werner will be so surprised to see all of you!" Irmgard looked at her uncle with suspicion. She could not understand him.

"Come on. I have a car waiting," Hermann said before leading the Contag family to the parking area outside the small, unassuming airport building.

When the Contags were seated in the back seat of the car, Hermann turned and said proudly, "We have fanesca today! Anita decided to make the traditional Easter fanesca for you, Ernesto. She remembered how much you like fanesca."

"How nice," Ernst said politely before adding emphatically, "*Dios mio*, it is great to be home."

The drive from the airport to the center of Quito was a noisy one. The road had potholes and the streets of cobblestones made the Ford bounce and sputter. More than a half hour later the car pulled up and parked in front of several houses. The street was still full of people and the car caused a bit of a stir amongst the neighbors who watched as the *gringos* unloaded their things and themselves. Ernst helped the children place their belongings onto the small curb in front of the house and before they could pick up the last bag Ernst heard a scream of joy from within the white-washed house.

"Papa! Tootsie, come look!" the nine-year old called out. "Tante Anita, look who is here! Papa! Papa is here! Irmgard! My brothers are here! Papa! You're here!" Werner wanted to jump into his father's arms, but he was too big. He hugged his father around the waist. Irmgard kissed her little brother while he was still wrapped around his father's midsection. Ernestito rubbed his brother's hair and smiled from ear to ear. "So, Uncle Hermann says you might be able to run faster than I can. I'll give you a good run for your money!" Ernstchen laughed.

Werner greeted Irmgard and Ernstchen with a hug and then gave Heinz a strange look and said, "Heinz! You are so tall! You look different now." Heinz hugged his brother warmly, but the two of them stood staring at each other as though the other were the stranger. It had been more than three years since they had seen each other.

"You look different, Werner. You are not a baby anymore. You grew up a lot in three years," Heinz said with a smile as he patted Werner on the shoulder.

"And I can speak Spanish again, too!" he piped up.

"Has it really been that long since you have seen each other?" Anita's voice was high above the others. She emerged from the front door with a broad smile and clapped her hands together just over her heart before hustling out to hug her niece and nephews. "Three years?"

"Yes, I suppose it has been that long," Ernst answered Hermann's wife who was busy going from child to child with embraces that enveloped them entirely. "The last time we were together as a family was in Burg Kreuzen, the summer of 1943."

"That is unbelievable," Anita said almost in anger. "Come in off the street, Ernesto." Anita put her arms around Heinz's back. "Heinz! I can't believe how much you have changed! You are a grown man already. When you left you were just a little boy!"

Anita was a small woman but she was the life and soul of the Dreier family in Ernst's eyes. She had always been gentle and kind with the children, especially with Heinz, and she made sure that there was something in everyone's stomach, no matter how tight their budget was.

The Dreier house was comfortable and seemed lavish compared to the Contags' dwellings in the last year. Ernst was not surprised that his brother-in-law was doing well but a small voice inside had to remind him not to feel jealous.

"Look at all of you!" Anita beamed. "What a beautiful sight to see you all together! Tootsie, look at how much your cousins have grown! I bet you can barely recognize them!"

None of the children said anything. As far as the returning Contag children were concerned, Tootsie was a stranger. And Spanish did not come easily.

"Take your things into the children's bedroom for now, Ernesto. It is nearly dinnertime and there isn't room elsewhere. Werner, show your father the room where you and Tootsie sleep. Show them where the bathroom is so they can wash."

"Yes, Tante Anita. Come on Irmgard. *Hände waschen. Hände waschen*," Werner said rubbing his hands together. "This way to the bathroom, please." Werner was all puffed up and proud to show his family around the house where he had been living for more than half a year. Ernst smiled to see his son's sense of humor and strength had returned.

At dinner the conversation centered around the Contag's three-week trip from New York, the bombing of Oma Dreier's house, Werner's recuperation from partial paralysis, business deals in New York, and bowls of colorful fanesca that cooled slightly each time a spoon dipped in for another bite.

"The fanesca is delicious, Tante Anita. Just as I remember it!" Ernestito said enthusiastically. His older brother nodded in agreement.

"I don't remember it," Irmgard muttered, as she tasted another spoonful, "but it does taste very good, Tante Anita." Irmgard spoke in German and she was polite, but she felt very much out of her element. Something was wrong and she couldn't put her finger on it. She pushed a few green peas onto her fork and lifted them to her mouth. The fanesca was a tasty but odd-looking dish. She stared at her bowl and studied it like a scientist. She discerned corn, peas, potatoes, onions, whitish bean-like things that her aunt had told her were *porotos*, brownish flat beans that Tante Anita had called lentils, fish, and hard-boiled eggs that were crumbled on top for decoration. The fanesca also had a nutty smell mixed with a pungent garlic odor that seemed quite pleasant and still somewhat odd. She hunted for the small, crunchy tidbits that she thought were bits of peanuts and chased them around in her mouth before crunching them between her teeth. *What a change from eating carrots in France!*

Ernst ate slowly and savored his meal, punctuating each swallow with a question or a remark. They had been out of the country for more than four years and he had a lot of catching up to do.

"I learned in Bogotá that we have a new president in Ecuador!" Ernst said to Hermann before lifting a heavy spoonful to his mouth.

"There was a popular revolt on May 28, 1944. Arroyo del Rio was out of a job right after that. Ex-president Velasco Ibarra was given a hero's welcome when he came out of exile; you should have seen the reception! Velasco Ibarra came in with a bang and a lot of leftist notions. To the surprise of everyone, he threw out the Constitution last year. In another odd turn of events he discredited the leftist politicians who supported him in the first place and called for a new Constitutional Assembly. That was three weeks ago or so, right Anita?"[1]

"Yes, I think so, Hermann."

"He has named Mariano Suárez Veintimilla to head his new Assembly. Now it looks like there will be a swing to the right. Suárez Veintimilla is no leftist, you know." Hermann expected a response from Ernst, but Ernst merely nodded his head in agreement and continued chewing.

"I heard a rumor just last week that ex-president Arroyo del Rio has taken to writing a justification of his whole administration. That will be quite a feat!" Hermann said before lifting another mouthful to his lips.

"I'd say," Ernst agreed enthusiastically. "I don't know how he'll justify signing away half of our territory to Peru. I can't imagine any one in their right mind would touch that rubbish here in Ecuador. It will be interesting with Velasco Ibarra back in the presidential palace, though. I can't say I am disappointed to see Arroyo del Rio out. He sold us to the Americans. No offense, Anita."

Anita nodded silently. "We don't talk much about those days, Ernesto. Let God be the judge."

"The atmosphere for Germans isn't any better now than it was four years ago, Ernesto. Privately, people are kind and personable, but publicly, and for political reasons, Germans have become pariahs. I am fortunate to have a job. It hasn't been easy," Hermann explained.

"Oh, I can't believe that!" Ernst straightened in his chair and brushed off the idea with a wave. "Since when has the average Ecuadorian had anything to say about international politics? They don't even read!"

"I wouldn't jump to conclusions, Ernst. The atmosphere is quite hostile toward all things German. The newspapers printed all sorts of sordid details about Germany and the journalists have turned us into Enemy Number One and the North Americans into heroes. Why do you think I am working with the Vorbecks and trying to make a go with the American REO trucks? I am lucky to have a job that pays and food to put on the table!"

"It can't really be all that bad, Hermann," Ernst countered flippantly. "You are doing all right. Look at your lovely home!"

Hermann shrugged unwilling to make a battle out of the discussion. Ernst would have ample evidence of his own in a few short weeks.

Hermann turned to Heinz and smiled broadly and said in German, "Heinz, how would you like to come to work for me? I could use someone who can type and file papers in the REO truck operation. Your father said you were translating things from English to German and Spanish when you were at the Hotel Capitol in New York. There is a typing course that starts next week downtown. I talked to the director last week and he said you could start right away. What do you think?"

Heinz beamed with pride. Uncle Hermann had asked him outright and he was excited about making the decision himself. "When do I start?" he asked, slapping his hands on his thighs as though ready to begin a new project immediately.

Hermann chuckled and then put on a stern business face. "You have got to learn to type first. . . then we will talk."

Ernst gave his son an agreeable nod and turned to Anita to ask a question. "Will my sister be back soon? What news does she have about her husband?"

"No news. When she left us to work for Dr. Sheppard she was pretty upset about the mail service. I guess it takes about five weeks to get a letter from South America to Germany. Not knowing what has happened to him in the Russian sector is the toughest part, I think."

"The Russians are nasty, crusty fellows. There is no telling what kind of facility he might be in over there. The Russian soldiers we came into contact with in Potsdam and Berlin . . . well, my stories about those days won't do for dinner conversation." Ernst waved off the bad memories. He hesitated and then added, "It won't be easy to bring him back to Ecuador either."

"She won't give up." Anita said. "She does what she sets her mind to."

Ernst shrugged and rubbed his forehead, pensively. "True. It is a strange situation, Anita. They were together six weeks and apart for four years. I don't know. It's not my business to say anything, but... I wonder whether we'll ever see him again. I don't know what to think about it."

"It is a tragic situation for your sister, Ernesto. You will have to do what you can to help her," Hermann added.

"Of course," Ernst said, only half committed. "We'll see what effect her letter-writing campaign has. When we know where Bio is and what we can do about it, then we can put two and two together."

After dinner Hermann offered Ernst some cognac, which he accepted gladly. The liquor burned his throat and he smiled through the pain and shivered. It had been quite a while since he had enjoyed the sting of cognac going down his throat. Hermann and Ernst sat down in the living room area to talk. Ernst asked about others in his situation, but Hermann told him that few who left in 1942 had returned. He had no news of Arturo or his family, Walter Detken, or any of the others.

"What about the Mikette children?" Ernst asked.

Hermann shook his head. "No one knows. No one knows anything yet."

Irmgard followed Tante Anita into the bedroom that Tootsie shared with Werner. While Anita started packing up Werner's clothing, Irmgard looked around the room and spotted a lovely doll. She toyed with the doll's skirt a while before saying anything.

"I had to leave *my* doll in Germany," Irmgard announced abruptly in German. "She was almost half as big as I was... well,... half as big as I was when I was seven anyway. I am a lot bigger now." Irmgard walked over to her aunt and turned so she could speak directly to her face. "Tante Anita, she had a pretty white blouse and a full skirt and she had a long braid that went around her head like this." Irmgard circled her own head with one of her long braids. "I even had a soft wool jacket for her when it got cold outside. She was the most beautiful doll you have ever seen! We were like sisters!" Irmgard cast her gaze downward and she thrust out a pouty lower lip. "I had to leave her there."

"It sounds like she was a pretty special doll," Tante Anita said. "I bet you miss her."

"I sure do. Some other girl probably has her now or. . . maybe she was blown to bits or something," Irmgard was milking her aunt for more sympathy and Anita knew it. She just listened to Irmgard speak.

"Ernstchen had a harmonica from Uncle Carl and Tante Inge. He couldn't bring that along either. Tante Lenchen got to bring a lot of her things, though. . . Papa couldn't talk her out of it and he had to carry it all the way from Berlin to Paris!"

"Yes, I know. Your Tante Lenchen stayed here for a while with Werner. I saw what she brought along, and she told us about the long walk from Berlin. I am sure you all would have liked to have brought more things. You'll be able to get a few things eventually, after your father has a job. Then, perhaps, you can get a new doll." Anita smiled sweetly at her niece.

"I might be too grown up for dolls by then," Irmgard said. "I am almost eleven years old already. I don't think I'll be getting anything soon." She hestitated and then sucked in her lower lip. "Last year Papa traded his best suit for a cake for me, and he brought me a bunch of lilacs. It was very nice of him to do that for me, don't you think?" Irmgard asked, trying to win her approval.

Anita Dreier nodded and touched her nieces' shoulder. "Very nice. You have a birthday coming up again soon, too, don't you, Irmgard?"

"Yes. In four weeks!" she said proudly.

Anita would have liked to suggest that Irmgard might get a doll for her birthday, but it seemed unlikely her father would be able to spend money on things that were not absolutely necessary. He would have his hands full with the abandoned house. Anita had gone on Saturday before Holy Week to get the house on Rocafuerte street ready for the Contags' arrival. She had cleaned the empty house as well as she could and purchased five straw mats and heavy wool blankets for Ernst and the children so they could stay warm at night in the cool mountain air. The empty house was a pretty depressing sight. She had wanted everything to be nice and comfortable for their return, but it was not possible. There wasn't anything else she could do.

Anita had urged Hermann to do anything he could to help Ernesto's family. The decision to help fund the return trip was a moral decision, not an economic one. The thirty thousand sucres that was required for their return trip was an unbelievable amount of money for anyone in Ecuador. She doubted that Ernesto could ever repay such a sum or even make a dent in it, for that matter. The cost of the two legs of the trip in dollars was $ 1,800.00 for Ernesto's family. Anita had written her mother in the United States about the extraordinary cost, and her mother was aghast. The average annual income for a U.S. citizen was only $2,500.00. To think that an Ecuadorian could pay nearly $2000.00 U.S. on an Ecuadorian salary was unthinkable. She could practically feed a family of four on 20 sucres or the equivalent of a dollar and a quarter U.S. per week. Salaries in Ecuador were commensurate with the cost of living. Ernesto had four children to raise. It was unimaginable to expect him to pay back the debt, except perhaps over the long term. This thought was quite worrisome. The government might come after her own family for the debt.[2]

Hermann had never discussed the option of not helping the Contags in any way they could. He and Anita were united in their effort to help Ernesto and the children get back to Ecuador. The Contag Dreier children were their only family on Hermann's side, and family was most important.

"There it is... all packed," Anita said to Irmgard. "Are you ready to go home?"

"I guess so," Irmgard said quietly. "Do you think Tootsie would mind if I gave her doll a hug?"

"No, of course not. Tootsie would think that was just fine. Go on. Give her a hug."

Irmgard waited until her aunt was out the door before she picked up the doll. "I wish you could come home with me. I would take really good care of you." She hugged the doll and put her back on the bed, fanned her skirt out on the blanket, and went out into the living room where her father was sitting with her Uncle Hermann.

Irmgard thought she remembered the house on the Rocafuerte. It was a castle on the mountain. At least that was how she remembered it. When she first started school in Nuremberg she had fantasized about seeing all the things that they had left there. There was a glass train that belonged to her older brother, Heinz. It was one of her favorite things even though she had never held it in her hands. Now she was old enough to hold it. She would be old enough to wear the roller skates that Heinz had used when he was young. She hoped that the skates would fit her. There was the Doodlebug scooter that she had dreamed would be hers one day. She imagined herself on the scooter, speeding past her brothers on the street.

When her uncle finished a sentence, Irmgard interrupted in German, "Werner is all packed, Papa. We can go home now."

Uncle Hermann had made arrangements for a car to take the Contags home. When it arrived, the Dreiers helped them carry out their baggage. The wirey Ecuadorian driver placed the baggage in the trunk with care. They had very few things. Tante Anita handed Ernst a bundle of foodstuffs. "Just to get you started, Ernst," she said kindly. "It is pretty bare over there," she whispered in his ear.

"You are very generous, Anita. I don't know what we would do without your help. I am sure everything will be fine."

As Ernst and his four children climbed into the car, Hermann and Anita looked at each other and understood each other's thoughts. It was clear that Ernst and the children had unrealistic expectations about their new life in Quito. Disappointment and disillusion were certain to follow.

The Contag house was a good distance from Hermann's home, and the children peered curiously out the car windows trying to remember the streets they had once called home. Ernst chatted with the driver and made comments about the buildings that seemed no worse for the wear during his four-year absence. When the car passed the penitentiary on their way up the Rocafuerte, Ernst recognized many people and he felt his spirits rise. *Home!*

Every face their father recognized was the face of a stranger to Irmgard. Irmgard got a funny feeling in her stomach and she felt a lump in her throat. She bit at her lower lip but smiled nervously at her brothers who were anxious to get out of the car.

The paint on the wooden gate entrance was peeling and there was a bit of garbage and dirt blown up against it. Ernst stepped out of the car and they unloaded their things into the street. From behind him they heard a woman call out gruffly in Spanish, "Juanita. Come look. The *gringos* have returned!" Ernst turned and greeted the woman with a nod of his head and a smile. He looked up to a second story window and saw Juanita appear.

"Señor don Ernesto. . ." was all she said politely but enthusiastically.

"Niña. . .I see all my old friends are still here!" Ernst responded as he kicked the garbage toward the street and turned the key in the gate.

Ernst pushed hard on the dilapidated wood that needed a coat of paint and entered. The children followed. Heinz and Ernestito were excited to be home. They would have dashed up the stone stairs if their father had not called them to help carry the baggage and bundle of goods that Anita had sent along. Irmgard entered with some trepidation and looked around.

"*Chispas*," Ernesto said as he looked up toward the house from the bottom of the stone stairway. The grassy areas above were overgrown. The house looked abandoned and in need of care.

Heinz and Ernstchen headed up the stairway first. Werner and Irmgard went up three or four stairs and turned to their father for a sign to continue. "Well, go on up," Ernst said encouragingly.

The higher Heinz and Ernestito climbed, the stronger the feeling of being an intruder in their own home. Many of the plants that Heinz remembered had died in their absence. The beautiful lilac bush that his grandmother had planted nearly a half-century earlier was now an icon of the haunting neglect that saddened Heinz as he approached the main entrance on the first floor. "Go on up to the top floor, Heinz. We want to go in that door," he heard his father call from behind.

At least one window was broken at the back of the house and there was a dank smell about the place. "Grandma Gertrude's rose bush is still here, Papa," Heinz said with a little excitement from hill behind the house. "It needs a little pruning, but it is still here."

The door on the second floor led into the living area. Heinz pushed it open and it swung noisily on its hinges. The floorboards creaked under his step. It was dark and it took his eyes a moment to adjust.

"Where is the table?" Heinz asked with panic before stepping into the middle of the long, empty room. "Where is all the furniture?" He put down the bundle he was carrying on the floor and stepped hastily into the bedrooms. Ernstchen followed on his heels. There they saw five rolled, woven straw mats. Heinz vaguely remembered Indians selling them in the open market place at San Roque. He cocked his head and stared at the mats and pile of llama wool blankets on the bare floor. Ernstchen screwed up his face as though trying to understand where he was and what the mats and blankets were doing there against the wall.

"We've been robbed, Papa! We've been robbed," Ernstchen yelled from the bedroom doorway. He walked back into the living area and called out again, "All the thieves left was Beethoven," he said pointing at the eerie portrait that still hung on the wall of the dining area. The portrait of Beethoven hung at an unusual slant, the eyes all the more menacing for the lack of light in the room. "They could have taken that hideous portrait instead of all our things!"

Irmgard started to cry. "I want to go back to Germany, Papa. I want to go back home. We could live with Oma Dreier after she fixes her house, don't you think? This isn't my house. I don't remember living here like this. There isn't even a chair to sit on. This is worse than the French camp, Papito! At least there we had beds to sleep on."

"Nothing is worse than that camp," her father responded with determination. "We were just gone a long time and people came to get our things. They didn't know we were coming back," he explained as he lost his composure. He was just as angry as the children to find everything gone, but did not want to startle them. He just shook his head and took a deep breath. The ray of evening sunlight dimmed in the bedrooms and he walked across the floor to look out toward Rocafuerte street from the bedroom window.

From his perch at the bedroom window he heard the children whining as they went from room to room. "It is bare in here, too," Ernestito said going into the second bedroom. "All our things are all gone." His voice echoed against the bare walls and the wooden floors. "Everything... everything is gone."

"I don't want to live here." Irmgard pouted. "I had such pretty things in Germany. I had a bed, . . . and a pretty doll. . . lots of pretty things. Now I am going to sleep on that thing . . . on the floor?" She pointed a finger at the pile of straw mats and let the tears fall onto the bare floorboards.

Ernst straightened and turned for the kitchen. *There is no use in complaining*, he thought. "My God. Look at this," he muttered under his breath with frustration. The cupboards were bare. Anita had left a pot for boiling water and some wood where the cook stove used to stand. He put the bundle of foodstuffs that Anita had prepared for them on the floor in what used to be the kitchen. "Thank God for Anita and Hermann," he muttered to himself trying to keep a stiff upper lip.

"Heinz, Ernestito, come here," Ernst urged. The two boys peered into the outdoor cooking area where their father stood. "We need to make this place habitable. Heinz, before it gets completely dark I want you to look around and see if there is *anything* we can use *anywhere* in the house for a shelf or a table or something. Ernestito, take a look at the water system and the bathroom. See what condition it is in. We will have to hunt for some scraps of paper. There won't be any up there, I don't suppose. Check the water pump, too."

Ernst sighed deeply and continued. "Ernestito, do you remember the woman across the street who makes blasting powder?" The boy nodded. "Tell her you need a few matches to start a fire in the morning. Tell her the house is empty. I'll pay her back for the matches when I can. She'll be agreeable. Now, off with you both. The sun will set soon."

"All right, Papa," the boys said in unison.

"And, Heinz?"

"Yes, Papa."

Ernst stood speechless and stared at the bare room in front of him. "I don't know," he shook his head. "I . . . I don't know. Go ahead. See what you can find."

―――

At six-thirty the sun had already dropped behind the mountains surrounding Quito and it was pitch black in the house. Ernst lit several candles that Anita had sent using the matches from the neighbor. He had decided to wait to build a fire until the next morning. Ernst dripped some candle wax onto the thick windowsill in the front bedroom and stuck the candle on top of it. He lit another one in the window of the living room area. The four Contag children sat outside on one of the stone walls beside the house and watched the flame flicker on the sill. The air was cool and fresh. The majority of the city was blanketed in darkness.

"Papa, what does Quito mean?" Werner asked in German.

Ernst smiled in the darkness and relaxed. "The name, Quito, comes from the name of a warrior Indian, Quitumbe, who settled at the bottom of this hill."[3]

"What kind of Indian?" Werner asked as a wind gust sent a chill up his spine. He inched closer to his brother.

"His tribe was called the Quitus. The Quitus lived in large huts with stone and adobe walls topped with a straw roof," Ernst answered knowledgeably.

"How do you know?" Irmgard asked, pulling the sweater about her neck.

"Oh... we learned a lot of history in school when I was a child. The Quitus loved their village in the valley so much that they fought fiercely against all the other invading tribes from the coast. They even had a special guard dog whose name was Ashco who helped to defend their village. They spoke Quechua and they called all dogs "Ashco" in reverence to that first great guard dog, Ashco."

"Are the Indians across the street Quitus, too, Papa?" Werner asked, keeping his father's attention.

"They are descendants of the Quitus and the Incas who came later."

"Dios mio," Ernst said looking to the sky. "Look up, Werner. The Quitus worshipped the sun, the moon, the stars, the mountains and the rivers. They prayed to the sun and the moon and built temples on the Panecillo, the Cayambe, El Quinche, and on San Juan hill so their crops would grow and they would lead good lives."

"When did the Incas come then, Papa? Were they Indians, too?" Irmgard asked.

"Yes. The Incas traveled north from deep in Peru. They didn't come to this area until the fifteenth century, about a hundred years before the Spaniards arrived in the valley. An Inca called Túpac Yapanqui and hundreds of thousands of Inca warriors led a march to the villages in this beautiful valley. After many bloody battles they raised the fortress of Ingapirca which is near Cuenca where I was born, and the fortresses of Pumapungo and Tambo Blanco."

"Those are funny sounding names," Irmgard said with a giggle. "Pumapungo... Tambo Blanco. That sounds really funny!"

"Yes, I suppose it does sound funny to you, Irmgard. But soon you will know a great deal about the Incas and their language," Ernst continued.

"Years later the great Inca, Huaynacápac, fell in love with the valley of the Quitus. He ordered the slaughter of anyone who resisted him and his people. Tens of thousands who tried to keep him out of the valley were beheaded at Yaguacocha. They called it Blood Lake."

"I don't want to hear any more about that, Papa," Irmgard complained. "Just tell us the nice things, all right?"

"All right, Irmgardchen. No more tragic history," her father said with a smile. "I wish I had a cigarette." Ernst heaved a sigh.

"I don't care about the bloody stuff. It is a good story. Tell us some more about that great Inca warrior, Papa." Ernstchen urged.

"As I was saying, Ernstchen, Huaynacápac was a powerful leader. He loved the valley of the Quitus so much that he transformed the village into the main city of his empire. He made Quito more important to the great Inca civilization than Cuzco, the traditional center of the Inca Empire. This made many people very angry. Those who are descendants of the great Incas never forgave Huaynacápac for this betrayal and they have been trying to steal Ecuadorian territory ever since. They are all thieves."

Heinz interrupted, "I remember my school teacher telling me that the great Inca you are talking about ordered his people to build roads and paths from here all the way to Cuzco! That is a long, long way, isn't it Papa."

"It certainly is."

"I remember some things I learned from Señor Callecas when I was at the German School before we left for Germany. The Incas could record history using cords and knots of different sizes and colors, too. The Inca Empire was supposed to have been very advanced for Indian civilizations."

"The Inca had a marvelous empire and Huaynacápac was very proud of Quito and the advancements that took place right here in the valley."

"So why are the Indians not respected now, Papa?" Ernestito asked, remembering his childhood in Quito.

"That question is hard to answer, Ernestito. Things changed, attitudes changed... everything changed, I suppose. Everything changed after the Spaniards arrived," Ernst said with his customary shrug.

"How did the Spaniards change things?" Werner asked.

"Some years before the Spaniards arrived, the great Inca Huaynacápac fell ill so he decided to leave his beloved Inca kingdom to his two sons, Huáscar and Atahualpa. Atahualpa received the northern territory, including Quito. Huaynacápac left Huáscar the empire that was ruled from Cuzco. But the two sons were not happy with the arrangement and they formed armies and fought because each wanted to rule the entire empire, not just half."

"They were really greedy," Irmgard offered.

"Yes, they were. Their greed became their greatest weakness. When the Spaniards arrived, the brothers were still set against each other. The Spaniards took advantage of the brother's rift, and were able to defeat the great Incas by siding with one and not the other."

Ernst sat quietly with his children until Ernstchen interrupted. "That doesn't explain why the Indians are not respected now, Papa."

"The descendants of the great Inca and the other tribes in South America were not respected by the Spaniards. The Indian traditions, their religion, their regard for nature was considered bad, pagan, not Christian."

"Just like the Jews weren't respected by the Nazis," Heinz said under his breath.

"But the Indians who live around here are Christian, right Papa?" Irmgard asked, trying to understand.

"Yes. Many of them are Christian."

"So, why don't they get respect now that they are Christian like the rest of us?" Werner asked.

"Like I said, Werner. That is a hard question to answer. Well, I think it is bedtime. Let's go inside. I am getting cold."

Ernst helped the children unroll the Otavaleño straw mats and covered them with blankets. The children squirmed, fully dressed, on their mats and snuggled under the heavy wool blankets. The floor beneath them was cold and Werner complained.

"I am cold, Papa. I don't like this at all. The floor is going to be really cold for sleeping," he said shivering.

"Why don't you move closer to Irmgard? We'll put one blanket underneath the two of you and the other one on top. That way you'll both be nice and warm."

"If there were a lantern in here I bet I could see my breath! I can't tell with just that candlelight," Ernestito said from his straw mat.

"Good night, children. Papa is tired, too."

"Good night, Papa," the four children chimed together.

Before Heinz fell asleep he heard the guards call out from each of the five corners of the penitentiary below, "Uno... dos. .. tres... cuatro... cinco..." *Now that is a sound I haven't forgotten!* Heinz thought, ... *I wish I had a pillow.* He drifted off to sleep.

The night was still and silent and they were all exhausted. Ernst draped his llama wool blanket around his shoulders and went back outside to sit until he felt tired enough to sleep. *Pobrecitos*, he whispered quietly to himself. *Where is the silver lining? When will things get easier?*

Ernst felt the wind blow a thick fog down the slope of the mountain into the valley. By morning it would be as thick as potato *loucro*.

——

Weeks later Ernst woke up on the same straw mat he had first slept on the night of April 21, 1946. He sat up in the cold room and looked out across the half-meter thick windowsill.

Dense fog kept him from seeing across the street or even into the small dirt patio. His back ached and he rubbed it gently before stretching and shivering in the brisk morning air. He slipped on his shoes, smoothed his hair back, and stumbled upstairs to the open-air kitchen on the second floor.

He started the eucalyptus wood on fire. It would take a good half hour before he could heat any water. The mountainside was still and quiet. He walked outside and up the stairs to the bathroom. *It is unusual not to be awakened by the blasts at the quarry across the street,* he thought. *It must be too early or perhaps the workers have decided to wait until the fog lifts a little.* He had planned to hunt rabbits before heading back into Quito to inquire about employment, but there was no reason to go out now until the fog burned off. Later on he would have to send Ernestito and Heinz out to hunt. Hunting was the best way to put food on the table.

Ernst went into the dining room. There were three guns there on the floor. "Good old friends," he muttered. He had bought two old army rifles, a shotgun and ammunition with money a friend had given him. The boys were thrilled with their rifles at first. Ernestito loved the hunt and he needed no encouragement. Heinz, on the other hand, did not have his heart in killing animals. A week earlier Heinz and Ernestito had gone out to hunt and Heinz had shot a deer. The Indians who had gone along as guides had slit the deer's throat and opened it up to remove the heart and the meat that the Contag boys would take back to Quito. According to Ernestito, the Indians had offered the heart to the successful hunter, as was part of their tradition or religion, and had expected Heinz to drink the warm blood that oozed from the animal's heart. Heinz had refused to drink it, swooned, and stumbled as he turned and fled. The next day Heinz returned home. He had spent the night under a rock and had walked back alone. Heinz had milled about in an unhappy fog for two or three days after that.

Ernst went outside to stoke the fire and he rubbed his hands together over it. The warmth and the smell of eucalyptus wood were pleasant. The familiar, pungent odor meant he was home. He closed his eyes and thought to himself. Home didn't feel quite right anymore. Quito was as strange a city as Lisbon or Potsdam or Nuremberg to him. The people, the buildings, the mountains looked the same, but he no longer saw Quito with the same eyes. After weeks of wandering the streets trying to decide what was different, he finally came to the conclusion that he was the one who had changed, not Quito or the Quiteños. He was not just four years older; his understanding of the world and his place in it had changed. He had left Quito as an "enemy of humanity" and returned as a "political refugee." He had become an unwanted man who didn't really belong anywhere.

Ernst opened his eyes and squinted in the smoke that stung his nostrils. It was time to wash and get dressed for another day of hunting for work. He had had no luck finding suitable employment in Quito and things were getting desperate in the house. He had spoken with many of his friends and business associates, including the Vorbecks who, though friendly, did not have a job for him. Some offered him some money to buy a few things. He had accepted.

Just then Heinz appeared at the doorway.

"*Guten morgen*, Papa."

"*Guten morgen*."

"So, what is on the list of things to do today?"

"You and Ernestito should go hunting when the fog clears. Maybe you can get a rabbit or two. I have a morning meeting with Gustavo Vásconez[4] who has a large hacienda near Pifo."

"Oh," Heinz said trying to figure out what the meeting might concern.

"I knew Vásconez as a young man. He has become quite successful. Vásconez studied in England, France and Switzerland in his youth and he has made a name for himself in the public eye as a writer and as a politician. At least that is what people are saying... Vásconez has a hacienda. There is a possibility I could work for him as a manager. He is an absentee landlord and needs someone to run things."

"I thought you were going to find a job in Quito. If you go to Pifo what will we do?"

"You'll stay here. There is an Italian man by the name of Giacomette who is married to a German woman. They have been looking for a place to live and they could live here and help you when I am out on the hacienda. The rent would pay for things. Do you think you could hold things together, Heinz?"

Heinz shrugged. "I guess so... don't you think we could go with you to the hacienda, Papa?"

"I don't know. If I get the job I'll go alone first. Then, maybe after your typewriting course is finished, you can come out to the farm. By then things could work out, perhaps. You would have to wait until I sent word... that is, if I get the job."

"You'll get the job, Papa," Heinz said.

The second week of June Ernst made final preparations for his journey to the Vásconez hacienda outside Pifo. He had purchased a number of items that Gustavo Vásconez had requested for the farm. He organized the butter churn, wire, tubes, hammers, nails, brushes, gasoline, and batteries into one area behind the gate and the food items that he planned to take along into another. He had several heads of red cabbage, radishes, and a few other things that would make the trip easily and store well in the mountain air on the hacienda. The items would be loaded the following morning onto a truck that would take him and his family to Pifo. From there the hacienda was only accessible on horseback, and the items would have to be carried by the burros and horses that belonged to the Vásconez hacienda. The majordomo was to meet him in Pifo and they would load the things with the help of some of the Indians from the huasipungo.⁵

The Giacomettes had moved into the lower part of the Contag house a few days earlier and Ernst thought that the couple seemed pleasant enough. Giacomette's wife was outside hanging up clothes as he climbed the stairs to the second floor. He greeted her and tipped his hat. Everything now seemed to be in order for the day and he decided to walk to the post office to mail several letters he had written by candlelight the night before. One was addressed to his friend Richard Ashton at the French repatriation camp in Beaune-la-Rolande, the other was addressed to Maria Renaud in Nuremberg, the last one to his mother-in-law in Hanover.

When he returned from the Post Office he heard Irmgard crying on the steps and rushed up to ask what had happened.

"I am sorry, Papa," Irmgard said in Spanish, gulping down a sob. "I am really sorry I burned the new shiny pot you bought. I didn't mean to do it. It looks so easy when the Indian women cook rice. I thought I could do it. Just rice and water. It looked so easy!" she said with her face in her hands. Irmgard had been slowly replacing German with Spanish when she realized that they would not be returning to what she remembered as home.

When she settled down enough to hear him, her father consoled her, "Its just a pot, Irmgard. Let me see it. Maybe we can clean it and use it again."

"Heinz said it was too burned, Papa, but you can look at it," she said, still gasping for air. Ernst inspected the pot but it had been scorched and no matter how much he cleaned it, the pot would never be the same... shiny or new.

"Next time let Heinz help you with the rice. He can teach you how to cook while I am gone. Then you will be an expert. Perhaps Blanca won't have to do all the cooking then. Stop thinking about the pot. Tomorrow we are going to go to El Tingo to swim. I want to spend the day with my precious daughter before I have to leave for Pifo.

The following morning, the Contag's gathered their swimming suits and rode to El Tingo, a tiny village with a swimming pool. It lay to the east and five hundred meters lower than the capitol city. It was more than an hour ride in the back of the truck, but they still arrived in plenty of time to swim several hours before dusk. Heinz met a young girl named Rose Möler at the pool who had come to El Tingo with her grandmother. She was about the same age as Heinz and half German. She lived with her Ecuadorian grandmother and widowed father in a charming village called El Guápulo. Heinz introduced himself as "Carlos" and they spoke in a mixture of German and Spanish since her grandmother was Ecuadorian and listened in on their conversation.

Rose was attractive and kind. Her grandmother did nothing to impede in the budding friendship between Rose and Heinz. She even told Ernst that Heinz was welcome to visit them at their home in El Guápulo on a weekend after school started. Ernst was surprised at the encouragement on the grandmother's part, but as she was sincere, he agreed to allow the visit that would require an overnight stay and a lengthy bus ride for his son. If he wanted to visit Rose in October or November he would not discourage it. Heinz was nearly sixteen years old and he had expressed very little interest in girls. Even when Ernst had encouraged Heinz to get to know the daughter of a German woman friend of his, Heinz didn't seem to know what to do about things. The German woman, who declared she knew Hitler personally, had tried to woo Ernst with some success. She was tall and attractive. Heinz, however, had never grown fond of the daughter. The two had been civil to one another, but little else had come of the meeting. It was time, Ernst thought, that Heinz got to know a girl and learned to enjoy the good things in life.

Ernst said good-bye to his children who left that evening. He stayed in El Tingo that night and waited for the manager to arrive from Pifo where they would load the horses and mules with heavy packs. Ernst did not return to Quito for six weeks.

Fog surrounds Ernst Contag and his traveling companions on a slippery mountain road outside of Quito, Ecuador.

"My Papa! Papa is home from the farm!" Werner announced from first story window.

Ernst looked exhausted, but happy to see his children who met him at the top of the first set of stairs.

"You are home! You are home!" Irmgard exclaimed.

"How's my big girl?" Ernst asked, hugging her.

"Fine now that you are here," she answered with a smile.

"I've come for a visit."

Heinz and Ernestito appeared on the patio. "Vásconez has plenty of room out there for all of us. What do you think about spending a few months with me out there after you finish your class?"

"Terrific! Sure! Let's go! When do we leave," he heard the children say one after the other.

On a dark July morning the Contag children arrived in the small village of Pifo. They had a large radio, a battery, four mattresses and some luggage. Several men met them. The one in charge greeted them and ordered the Indians who accompanied him to load the Contags' belongings. Besides the pack animals, there were two mules that carried a large metal milk can on either side, donkeys and a large mule named Filpo.

"Señor Contag! You can ride Filpo. You think you handle mule and radio, sir?" the majordomo asked Heinz in Spanish.

"Sí," he answered proudly, and added in a friendly tone, "This is a Zenith Radio. It is the best American radio available. Someone else should carry the battery for my father."

"Yes, sir," the man responded. "Careful, sir. He ornery mule. Filpo killed man once . . . throw him."

The warning did not make Heinz feel very comfortable. The majordomo's tone was respectful, but there was something about the way he had said the words that gave Heinz an eerie feeling. The majordomo seemed to have a mean streak. He did not wear the traditional Indian clothing, but it was obvious that he was also Indian. Heinz was somewhat surprised to hear him bully the barefoot Indian men who were packing the animals.

Ernestito, Irmgard and Werner each rode a small donkey. It was quite an adventure for them and the four Contags were very excited. They rode up and down the Andean hillsides in a long train of horses and pack donkeys. About a half hour into the ride the Zenith radio slipped out of Heinz's grasp and fell to the ground. Heinz heard gasps from the others behind him. Two barefoot Indians rushed to lift the radio back into his arms. Embarrassed, shocked, and terrified that he had ruined the radio, Heinz held on tightly and stared ahead without saying a word.

When the path allowed them to do so, Ernestito and Werner rode up closer to their brother and Ernestito asked, "Do you think it still works?"

"Hope so." Heinz took a deep breath. "If not, I hope I can fix it."

"Werner could do a better job than you on that radio," Ernestito said with a chuckle. "He is plenty better than you at fixing things with wires. You had better pray it still works."

"I did already. It isn't like I tried to drop the radio or anything," Heinz said sheepishly.

"Your mule wasn't stumbling or anything," Werner said. "Were you sleeping, or what?"

"Never mind," Heinz said with a scowl. "This thing is heavy," he balanced it again in front of him. "You probably shouldn't ride so close to Filpo. Filpo killed a man once. Go on. Move back."

Heinz could see where the hacienda property began. Its form was circular with crops outlining the farm property and animals and buildings near the center. Horses, cows, sheep and young lambs grazed in open areas that looked unfenced. Indians dotted the fields. The hacienda was a perfect picture of tranquility from his perspective: the Antesana mountain on one side of the valley, the foothills on the other, and a peaceful valley of fields in the middle.

About an hour after leaving Pifo they arrived at the whitewashed farmhouse at the center of the valley, a rather large mud house with walls that were a meter thick, few windows and a door. The Indians who handled the milk cans unloaded their things and put them in the house. Ernestito spotted their father out near the thatched huts. He waved and received another wave in reply. Ernestito was curious about the huts and went to investigate one of them on his way to greet his father. Heinz, Irmgard and Werner followed.

The hut nearest the dirt road that served as an entrance had a few guinea pigs and chickens running around near it and three dusty-faced, barefoot children dressed in crudely made clothing that seemed a little too big or too small for the child that wore it.

The children moved away from Ernestito and it surprised him that they might be frightened of him.

"I just want to look in the hut," he said in Spanish. The three small children stood motionless and watched him try to peer into the darkness beyond the small opening in the mud hut covered with thatch. The thatch was thick and he could not see anything but a bare dirt floor within.

"There isn't anything in that hut that I could see," Ernestito told Heinz. "It sort of looks like our house on the Rocafuerte the day we arrived. They must just sleep in there on the bare ground. It was pretty dark, though, they might have had some mats rolled up somewhere. Did you see how afraid those little Indian children were of me."

"Well, you are sort of scary-looking," Heinz said screwing up his face and crossing his eyes.

Werner ran to meet his father. "Papa, we got to ride on a donkey from Pifo. I rode all by myself!" Werner hugged his father.

Irmgard smiled and kissed him, too. "It is wonderful to see you, Papa. I am so glad you sent for us."

"They don't understand you, Ernestito," Ernst said patting his son on the shoulder. "They don't speak Spanish, so they didn't know what you were going to do. Some of the adults speak a little Spanish, but most of them only understand Quechua."

"They looked scared, though, Papa. I wasn't going to hurt them. I just wanted to look into the hut," Ernestito explained.

"They are afraid of you because you are the son of a white manager. Out here the Indians are trained with the gun and the whip. This is a *huasipungo* and the rules are different here. That's what Gustavo Vásconez told me when he hired me. He handed me a gun and a whip and told me to use them if there was any trouble. There was no room to disagree with him, but I have had better luck with them by not using either." Ernst motioned for his children to follow him back to the farmhouse.

"You can't live under a gun like we did in that camp in France without knowing what it feels like to be threatened. Vásconez owns these Indians. Owns them because they came with the land. They work for a wage, but for no reason at all they can lose everything. If a cow or a sheep dies, his majordomo says, 'Deduct it from their wages or punish them. That is the way it is out here.' That is why they are afraid of you. You represent authority."

"That doesn't seem fair, taking away the money they earned or punishing them when a cow dies, does it Papa?" Heinz said. "Sometimes cows just die. No one has to do anything to make them die. They can get sick and die, just like people. It isn't fair." Irmgard and Ernstchen agreed.

Several weeks after they arrived a calf died. There were flat parasites in the calf's liver. Ernst did not know how long it had been since the calf had died and he thought it best to have the carcass buried. He asked several Indians to dig a hole and they rolled the calf in and buried the calf where it lay. The majordomo swore and kicked at the dirt. "Someone will pay for this death. Someone will pay."

"It died from liver disease," Heinz argued. "No one killed it."

"No matter, señorito. Someone pays. Dead calf . . . someone pays," he answered in Spanish with a heavy indigenous accent. "Señor Vásconez want all animals live. Bring money. Señor Vásconez not be happy, no sir. Someone pay."

The next morning Ernst went out into the field where the women of the huasipungo had hobbled the cows' forelegs and milked the cows where they stood. "*Arekua changuwe*," he repeated in a loud voice to the Indian women who were milking the cows. It was an order in Quechua to get the women to milk each of the three teats well. They had orders to leave the fourth teat alone so that there was enough milk for the cow's growing calf. The women nodded in agreement and kept milking.

Ernst returned from field upset. "Indians dug up that calf to eat it." He shook his head in front of his children. "Hope they don't get sick. Could mean trouble for the farm if they get sick."

"Why did they dig up the calf, Papa?" Werner asked.

"Hungry. If they have to pay for the natural death of the calf, I suppose they thought they should at least get something in exchange. So . . . now they have diseased meat." He waved off the thought. "The Indians who helped bury it should have discouraged them. I can't do anything about it now. Come with me to the creamery, Ernestito. I need some breakfast."

Ernst walked with his son and complained. "The Jew who buys and sells the milk in Pifo is complaining about us. He told the majordomo we are drinking too much milk and that is why production is down. Unbelievable. That drunkard doesn't know how to produce milk. All he knows how to do is drink and make a mockery of his wife. He is worthless as a majordomo. Besides, those cows can't produce much milk on what they eat out here. It is no wonder to me that they can only produce a few pints a day. I don't know what the majordomo wants me to do. Vásconez won't be happy, though, if he hears production is down. The majordomo will blame it on me."

"We can drink more water, Papa," Irmgard suggested. "Then we won't drink as much milk."

"You will drink the milk you want, children. I won't have my children starve themselves just because a drunk thinks that they are too much bother for him. He can just put up with it. If he goes after us about the milk, I will inform Vásconez about his drinking. The man has no respect for life or limb. He beats his wife for no reason at all. He threatens the Indians. Damn him."

"Papa!" Irmgard said with surprise.

"All right. Let's get breakfast. I have to go into Pifo to get a tractor today. You need to carry back some water for us today. Take a few Indian women to help you. I will be home by suppertime. I'll have the women make you some *loucro* for supper. They will probably bring it to the house the same time as usual."

"Tell them to make it with corn and potatoes only, Papa," Irmgard said. "I don't want any of that calf meat."

"Good idea."

That evening they enjoyed a delicious meal of corn and potato soup with fried eggs that two of the women brought for the Contags. It was clear that the Indians respected and liked Ernesto Contag. He did not disrespect them like the others in roles of authority.

Within a week Vásconez came for a visit. The majordomo, Ernst, and the children were at the farmhouse to meet him. Heinz had expected to like Vásconez. He was high society, though, and soon Heinz found himself looking for reasons to dislike the absentee landlord. It didn't take long. The Indians of the huasipungo despised Vásconez for what he represented and feared him for the power he had over their lives. Heinz could see the feigned humility in their faces. But whatever they felt for Vásconez, it was far kinder than what they felt for his majordomo.

When the majordomo ordered the prettiest girl on the huasipungo to carry his recently deposited feces to the simple latrine behind the farmhouse, Heinz knew he could never admire men who oppressed others in this way. His own father used the latrine. Heinz used the latrine. He didn't see why the majordomo couldn't use the latrine like all the others. It wasn't private—just whitewashed mud walls that opened to the sky—but he thought it arrogant and demeaning of men with power to ask a teenage beauty to carry the smelly deposit to the dugout and clean out the metal chamber pot with water. After Heinz's treatment in Germany and France, "high society" attitudes made his stomach turn. He wondered what other indignations men like these were capable of.

Living on the *hacienda* had been a godsend for the Contag children and their father. There was no refrigeration, no electricity, no restrictions, no classes, no important responsibilities, no Giacomettes. For four months they recovered the freedoms they had lost after their deportation and exile, and they reveled in the joys of living worry-free and unburdened on the hacienda. Heinz and Ernestito learned to work with the animals. Heinz became an expert with the lasso and he had no fear of his mule, Filpo, who seemed to respect him like no other man on the farm. Werner and Irmgard spent hours playing with the ropes that the Indian rope maker made by slapping meters of cowhide against his shin and weaving the wide straps into a rope. They created unique games that they taught their older brothers. They had tried to trap a menacing fox without success. They learned to take care of the different animals. It was a happy time for the children and their father, although not without the pain of learning how to get along as a family again.

Ernst and Ernestito had grown very close in Europe, and were nearly inseparable. Heinz was old enough and confident enough not to need his father's approval. Irmgard, the only girl, won her father's attentiveness with ease. It was Irmgard who noticed how difficult the adjustment to life with Papa was for Werner and tried to mother him. This made matters worse for Werner, who became obstinate and belligerent whenever his father was nearby. Ernst, disturbed by the countless injustices he was made part of, withdrew from all of them, turned inward, and became more and more agitated concerning his managerial position on the farm and less interested in his children. For this reason, it was difficult when the children had to leave their father and the life of freedom on the farm for the constraints of living in Quito under the watchful eyes of the Giacomettes, and the difficulties of returning to the Ecuadorian classroom.

In September the Contag children returned to the city to get ready for school. Heinz planned to work for his Uncle Hermann after school. All of them would have to work to return to Spanish after speaking German on the hacienda. Ernst hoped they would adjust quickly to school and life in Quito.

Ernst completed the orders that Vásconez had left for him. He had a road built in the form of a cross. He hired road workers and stone layers. He had the *zanja* completed. He had doors built and cobblestones laid in the hallway of the main house. He made improvements to the Pilapamba canal and installed the equipment for making cheese. He plowed the highlands with the tractor they had purchased, and had the Indians sow the new fields. He and several others built a lean-to for the calves. Production was up and all seemed well.

Ernst spent Christmas alone at the hacienda. Shortly after Three Kings' Day, Vásconez came to the farm. He refused to pay Ernst what they had agreed upon and they argued in a gentlemanly fashion. Ernst quit. He returned empty handed to Quito. There would be no Christmas presents for the children this year.

When Ernst arrived at the house his children were still in school. He greeted Giacomette's wife and went upstairs to the second floor where he kept the few things that he owned. There, on the mattress on the floor, were three letters addressed to him.[6] He opened the first one with trepidation. It was from a man he had met at the camp in Beaune-la-Rolande.

Ernst, Irmgard, Werner and Karl Heinz Contag pose for the camera at their home in Quito, c. 1948.

He had never written to Gerhardt Hartgring and was surprised to see a letter from him. Ernst stood next to the window and held the thin paper at a slant so he could read the handwriting without picking up the shadow of the letters that bled through from the backside.

November 19, 1946

GHA Hartgring
Lekstraat 139 The Hague
Holland

Esteemed Herr Contag,

I hope that you have begun your first letter to me and have written that you are still fine. Everything is fine here for me, and I cannot complain. I have been in Holland for four weeks already but I can't get used to it. I am terribly upset that I have no friends. It is cold here and you can see the ice on the canal in the city. How are things going for your sister? Is she still on a quest? Did the children get home in good health? You must write me all about it because I am very curious how things have been going for you.

I am working for a British bank as a bookkeeper and I like the work. But I don't like the place. Perhaps you still remember that I keep a keg of gunpowder around for Europe just in case... and maybe I'll need it. I am still furious. Tell me something about Ecuador, and Quito, because I am so interested in learning what life is like there. Maybe someday I can visit you when I am no longer in Holland.

Every once in a while I think about the camp in Paris. Thank God we got out of there! I just got a letter from a South American today. It came from Argentina from the boss of a female friend of mine. I have not heard from the others. I hope that you will be an exception and won't forget me. That would make me very happy. Now I must end my letter.

Warmest Greetings to you and your family.

Gerhardt
Your friend in Holland,

I hope I hear from you soon.

Hartgring had been a sarcastic man from the first day they met and the letter reflected his personality well. Hartgring was no better off than Ernst. He was also a man without a home, without a country, without a future. It was depressing to see that Hartgring was in a similar situation. They had all had such high hopes of good lives. They had all counted on the outside world making up for the years they had suffered as unwilling participants in the Nazi regime.

Ernst looked at the other envelopes. One had been sent in July, the other in August. They were both sent by his friend, Richard Ashton, whom he had promised to help upon his return to Ecuador. Then he had held high hopes for the future. Now he felt guilt and a sense of impotence as he sliced open the envelopes mailed from the French camp and removed the thin pages covered in blue ink from margin to margin. *Ashton . . . still at the camp*! He sighed and read first the handwritten message in the margin. The short message was handwritten by Richard's wife, Gerda.

Dear Mr. Contag
I would be very happy if we could all see each other again. It would be good for Peter if he could start a new life near your children. We send our most heartfelt greetings.

The numbers on our passports: Titre de voyage

(Gerda Ashton) No. 462
Richard A. and Peter A. No. 460

Beneath it was the letter from his friend, Richard. From Gerda's carefully written note it was clear that the Ashtons still held out hope that he could do something to get them out of the repatriation camp. Ernst sighed heavily, remembering how devastating and difficult the time had been at the camp and how his children had suffered. He read the letter slowly.

Beaune la Rolande, July 22, 1946

Ashton Richard
Brewery-Engineer

E. Contag
Quito, Ecuador Casilla 54

Dear Mr. Contag:
Thank you very much for your letter written on June 12; about which I was very happy. I will send a telegram today, dated August 22, which should arrive long before this letter does. This is what it contains:

> *I am still at Beaune. Arrange the best contract possible, also immigration. I accept the job la Campana. Send me a response by telegraph and by airmail, (which requires five weeks).*

> *I hope that you will be prudent and clever in getting it done. I am still at the camp: I have*

received two job offers from Argentina, one from the Quilmer Brewery in Buenos Aires; the other is from the Schneider Brewery in Santa Fe. I would prefer to go to Ecuador since I need to find something with greater promise. Besides, the Quilmer-Combine is a non-discriminating factory and not really a brewery anymore.

While I wait every day for a contract from either of these two Breweries, I would also like to get a speedy response from Ecuador. I will wait for two to three weeks for that. Here I am <u>still</u> in this hole of a camp in Beaune la Rolande. They have barely left us two chairs to sit on. As soon as I receive an offer from you, I will write the other breweries. We also hope that everything is going well for you, and that we can embrace each other once again. It is likely that those who remain in the camp will be rounded up again soon. Of the old inmates only Aals, Fonst, Wolinsky, Neves, de Moore, Suarez, Stiftl, Hermann, Pfeiffer, Jims, Isenlhen, and Stocker are still interned here. Captain Josse must dismantle the camp. Becaria is still here too. My wife does Frau Berends' job now because she left on the most recent ship. I while away the time making laundry and hand soap when I should be rolling up my sleeves at the Campana Brewery instead. Take pity on us so that we can get some money together soon, and improve our situation in Paris. Please give our best to your whole family from the three hopeful Africans.

Yours truly,
R. Ashton

"Richard, I did not receive your cable. It was impossible," he mumbled before unfolding the second letter and reading the contents.

August 28, 1946

Richard Ashton
Beaune la Rolande
France (Loiret)
Camp des Étranges

Dear Mr. Contag:

From one day to the next we are waiting for official notification from you whether or not you have received the telegram and letter from us. Perhaps our letters crossed paths in the mail? Please Mr. Contag, write me soon indicating if things can be worked out and how things stand. We can no longer manage a decent life here at the Camp. The camp was closed on August 15. The Russians and the Yugoslavs have been sent to work on farms or in factories. All that is German has also been removed.

Only Foust, Stocker, and Aals are still here with us as "honorary guests." I would like very much if next week I could be at work so I could put my family's anxieties to rest. Now perhaps you will understand why we are so desperate and are waiting impatiently for some word from you about whether I can go to Ecuador to work at the brewery or not. I have not heard from Argentina. If the Brewery job does not work out, it would be great if we could start something up together with your funds. For now I am making camp laundry and bathroom soap, which I could also do where you live.

Perhaps you have found someone who can send us travel funds.

You can see, I will do anything in my power to move on from here. I have just learned that my previous boss in Africa is a Jew, and my permission to enter the country depended on him. I am afraid that I may be condemned to live as a common laborer in France.

My wife, Peter and I send our greetings to your children and to your sister,

R. Ashton

In the margins there was a note from Gerda:

Dear Mr. Contag!

My husband has sent you greetings on my behalf, but I also want to write you a few words of my own. You must certainly know that during the last few weeks every time we build castles in the air we think of you. Thank God we can still hold fast to our hopes and dreams. It has been the only way to survive these last few weeks. Ecuador has been our only glimmer of hope for a future. Peter, in particular, lives to see your children. Now we can only wait and see what the future will bring for us. We are all healthy and we can all work. Wishing you and your children the best.

Yours truly,
Gerda Ashton

Ernst folded the letters and placed them lovingly in the box where he kept his family's pictures. He stood and decided to go downtown. He wanted to be surrounded by people, by the noise of chattering friends.

Ernst went to see his old friends at La Victoria. He raised a glass of beer to his lips and said aloud, "I raise a toast to my good friends. To the good people at the camp at Beaune-la-Rolande! May they find a castle or the stone to build one wherever they are now."

The men around him cheered and drank with him, oblivious to the significance of the toast. Ernst put one hand in an empty pocket and sat down. The noise around him faded as he found himself lost in thought. He stared out the window over 24 de Mayo Street. Under his breath he mumbled, "There are no castles to be built in the Valley of the Quitus. God be with us."

NOTES TO CHAPTER TEN

[1]Arroyo del Rio was allowed to leave Ecuador for exile in Colombia. His fellow countrymen mocked him. Ironically, Arroyo del Rio complained that he too had been deprived of his rights as a citizen.

Velasco Ibarra was president from 1944-1947. After the May 28, 1944 revolution, Velasco Ibarra returned to Ecuador and was given a hero's welcome. But he overturned the Basic Charter of 1945 after March 1946, and prepared a new Constitution. His defense Minister led a coup against him in 1947. *Historia contemporanea*, p. 477.

[2]Hermann Dreier paid at least $800 U.S. of his own money toward the return trip. Ernesto did not inform his children of this debt. Werner Contag and his wife, Myriam Maldonado de Contag, reimbursed Hermann Dreier years later for much of the unpaid debt.

[3]The legend is common knowledge amongst Quiteño children. There is a version of the legend included in the Ecuadorian third grade primer.

[4]Gustavo Vásconez was born in 1911. He studied in England, France and Switzerland. He was the government undersecretary and provincial advisor for the Pichincha. He was the Ambassador to the Holy See and served as Ambassador in Colombia. He was president of the Ecuadorian Ateneo and Grupo América.

He published four novels, and a biography of Juan Montalvo. *Maravilloso ECUADOR*. Quito and Barcelona: Círculo de Lectores, 1978, p. 220.

[5] A *huasipungo* is a group of indentured Indian families that "belong to the land" and the landowner.

[6] W. Contag files. Ernesto Contag kept all three letters until his death. The letters are translated from the originals written in German.

EPILOGUE

ERNST CONTAG ZIEHE (1910-1985)

Sr. don Ernesto Contag, as he was known in Quito, sold imported typewriters and collectible guns. Except for the documents, letters and photographs he saved in the house he shared with his sister Lenchen Contag de Beate, he had very little to show for years of work. He lived comfortably with day-to-day earnings, worrying only that his international agreements with exporting companies might be taken over by someone more ambitious than he was. He visited his children and their families in the United States, Ecuador and Venezuela, and died in his son Werner's arms after suffering an aneurism. He lies in peace in the German cemetery in Quito next to Elisabeth, his dear wife of seven years, his son Ernst, and his mother-in-law Cecilie Dreier.

KARL-HEINZ CONTAG (1930-)

After completing a veterinary degree from La Universidad Central in Quito, Dr. Karl-Heinz (Carlos) Contag received a scholarship and continued his graduate studies at Iowa State Unviersity in Ames where he met his wife, Ann Schwermann. He taught at universities in Quito, Ecuador, Iowa and Minnesota during his career and practiced veterinary medicine in New Ulm, Minnesota, for over thirty-five years. He retired from veterinary practice in 1997 after suffering a stroke. Carlos and his wife raised five children who live in the United States and work in the global community.

ERNST CONTAG, JR. (1933-1984)

Ernst traveled to Germany to study brew making after finishing high school in Quito. When he returned to Ecuador, he was employed as a brew master in a malt factory in Latacunga. He was an avid hunter and fisherman. After years in the Andes, he moved his family to the subtropical forest just outside the city of Santo Domingo de los Colorados where he and his wife Mucki ran a world-class restaurant with a small zoo and floral gardens until his death from pancreatic cancer in 1984. Of their four children, two live in Ecuador, one in Chile and one in Alaska.

IRMGARD (CONTAG) JAUNZEMS (1935-)

Irmgard worked for her father until she left for new opportunities in the United States in the 1960s. She met her Latvian husband Juris Jaunzems while living in California and working as a trilingual secretary. They have three children who live and work in Oregon. Although Irmgard remembers Germany fondly, she has never returned to Europe. Since her arrival in the United States, she has visited Ecuador only once.

WERNER CONTAG (1936- 1998)

Werner completed an engineering degree in Quito and worked for NASA in Ecuador. In 1965 he took his family to California where he studied business. He worked for several companies in the U.S. and South America before founding his own company in Caracas, Venezuela, in 1973. He and his wife Myriam Maldonado de Contag raised their three children in Caracas. When the political climate changed in Venezuela, he moved his family to Palm Coast, Florida. Shortly after they moved into their new home he was diagnosed with cancer and died shortly thereafter. In recent years his children have moved their families to the United States.

ARTURO CONTAG ZIEHE (1907-1987) AND ALCIRA MEJÍA DE CONTAG

Arturo, his wife Alcira and their six children remained in the internment camp in Crystal City, Texas, until the U.S. government found a way to repatriate them to Ecuador in 1947. Their sixth child was born at the camp. After returning to Quito, Arturo founded a successful clothing business called Imán that he ran until his death. Alcira Mejía de Contag lives in Quito and is visited often by her seven living children, twenty-eight grandchildren and their families.

HELENE CONTAG ZIEHE (1912-1993) AND BERNHARDT BEATE

Lenchen was able to help her husband, Bio Beate, return to Ecuador several years after the end of the war. They raised three sons in Quito. On a postcard to her brother Ernst in 1960, she wrote that her husband Bio suffered from the cold since he was never able to replace the warm winter coat the Russians had taken from him.

HERMANN AND ANITA DREIER

Hermann Dreier left his management job at the La Victoria Brewery in 1947 and worked in imports and the automotive industry until 1961 when he left Ecuador for the United

States. He and his wife Anita raised four children and lived the rest of their lives in California.

MARIA RENAUD

Maria Renaud never left Germany for South America, but she continued to correspond with Ernst Contag until his death. Her letters, considered too private to share or keep, were destroyed shortly after his death in 1985.

INGE CONTAG BEUTNER

Inge never remarried after Carl Contag's death in 1943. Arturo Contag and his wife Alcira paid her a visit shortly before 1980. According to Alcira Mejía de Contag, Inge still felt the sting of guilt for her husband's death as a soldier.

(ULI) FRAU URSULA KRONE RÜMLER (1926-)

In May 2000, twenty years after Frau Ursula Krone sold her mother's home on Trottstrasse 18 in Kassel, she received a call from the buyer saying that a Mr. Contag was at the house trying to locate "Uli" Rümler. Did she know of anyone by that name? She responded, "No one has called me that for years." When Dr. Carlos Contag's youngest son Ted Contag got on the phone, he said, "My father has been looking for you for over fifty years and we have finally found you! This is a miracle." Ursula Krone is a widow. She lives in Siegburg, Germany near her children and grandchildren. Frau Krone's father survived the war but did not return to the family. Her mother died of brain cancer in 1949.

HELGA RENNER EMDE (1928-)

The Renner family and the Carlos Contag family have had the opportunity to get to know each other over the years. After the death of her parents, Helga continued to correspond with Heinz (Carlos) Contag. Helga and her husband raised two children in Korbach and they rent out the family home that was bombed during the war. Shortly after Dr. Contag and his wife visited the Emdes, they sent their son Jörg to New Ulm, Minnesota, to spend the summer with the Contag family. A few years later Mr. Emde found Karl-Heinz's composition books and papers under rubble in the basement of the old Renner home that they remodeled in the 1980s. The books and papers were returned to the family when Kimberly Contag visited the Renners in 1985.

POLITICAL REFUGEES IN FRANCE

By the time the research for the book began, all ties with families in French camps had been lost. Searches on the Internet were inconclusive. There is no indication that the Richard Ashton family was able to find safe passage to South America, and it is quite possible they were obligated to make their home in France since a return to Africa was impossible.

BLACKLISTED GERMAN ECUADORIAN FAMILIES

At this time no one knows how many of the German Ecuadorians who left Ecuador in 1942 and 1943 returned to South America over the years. Some of the returnees are buried in the German Cemetery in Quito. Many of their children, now grandparents or even great grandparents, have not yet shared their wartime experiences or their recollections of life abroad with their own children or grandchildren. The past continues to be silenced in an effort to bury painful memories and loss, in favor of preserving the joys of the present.

AUTHORS' NOTE

We have not been able to ascertain the whereabouts of young Peter Ashton, the child of German exiles from Lourenço Marquez, Africa, who played in the dirt of the refugee camp (formerly a concentration camp in Beaune-La Rolande, France) with Kimberly's uncle, aunt, and father. Nor do we know the fate of his parents. It is poignant that Kimberly's grandfather saved the letters from his friends at the refugee camp until his death in 1985. We can only speculate why he kept these letters for nearly forty years.

To our knowledge, the only published photographs of the refugee camp at Beaune-La Rolande are included in a book on the concentration camps in Loiret, *Les Camps d'internement du Loiret: Histoire et mémoire*. The Huré family gave Kimberly a copy of this book when she visited the area in May 2000. The Hurés live next door to the site of the internment camp in Beaune-La Rolande. Small children attend school on the site now and they have a memorial garden in memory of the Jewish children who were taken from the camp to their deaths in the gas chambers of Auschwitz in 1942. There is also a large stone memorial that faces the city. Kimberly stood there and wept.

Kimberly's father did not know that Beaune-La Rolande had been a concentration camp before it was used as a repatriation camp at the end of the war, or that many Jewish adults and children who lived in the barracks where he stayed with his family for many cold months in 1945 and 1946 had been put on a train for Drancy and then sent on to the gas chambers of

Auschwitz a few months after his family arrived in Europe in the summer of 1942. We do not know if the adults in the camp knew about the history of the camp or not, but Ernesto Contag did not share this knowledge with his children.

In June 2000 Kimberly and her brother Ted located Ursula Krone, Uli, in Germany. Ursula Krone remembered Karl Heinz as though they had been brother and sister. A half-century had passed without any communication between the two of them. The videotape of *Uli* speaking to Kimberly about her father left him in tears. The two families reconnected as though they were long lost relatives.

In May 2001 Jim and Kimberly and two of Kimberly's brothers returned to Quito with Dr. Carlos Contag. He expected it would be his last trip home and we believe that Kimberly's mother feared he might never return to Minnesota. We understand now why she worried. He shook with excitement as we stood atop the Panecillo and looked down over the immense city of Quito that now filled kilometer after kilometer of the Andean valley. He begged to climb the Inca ruins of Rumicucho near the new monument to the Center of the World and had to be half-carried up its tremendous slope and down again along the dirt path. When we stood atop the abandoned ruins, Carlos let what remained of his fractured eyesight roam the deep valley and the tall mountain range. We stood in silence for what seemed like hours.

"*Déjame aquí nomás*," he said to Kimberly in Spanish. "Just leave me here."

SOURCES

NEWSPAPERS

El Comercio. Quito, Ecuador. January-June 1942

El Mercurio. Cuenca, Ecuador. January-June 1942

El Universo. Guayaquil, Ecuador. January-June 1942

The New York Times, New York. January 1942-January 1947

Stuttgarter Neues Tagblatt 1942

BOOKS AND ARTICLES

Arroyo del Rio, Carlos Alberto. *Por la pendiente del sacrificio*. Guayaquil: Unidad Editorial de la Dirrección Regional de Programas Culturales-Banco Central del Ecuador, 1996.

Connell, Thomas. *America's Japanese Hostages: The World War II Plan for a Japanese Free Latin America*. Westport, Connecticut: Praeger, 2002.

Jacobs, Arthur. *The Prison Called Hohenasperg: An American Boy Betrayed by his Government During World War II*. Florida: Universal Publishers. 1999.

Krammer, Arnold M. "In Splendid Isolation: Enemy Diplomats in World War II." *Prologue*. A Journal of the National Archives. Spring 1985. Vol.17, No. 1, p. 25-43

Lisken, Gunter. *Der Zeitzeuge: Ein Deutsches Schicksal in Südamerika.* Mönchengladbach: Kühlen, 1999.

Riley, Karen Lea. "Schools Behind Barbed Wire: A History of Schooling in the United States Department of Justice Internment Camp at Crystal City, Texas, during World War II, 1942-1946." Ph.D. dissertation University of Texas, Austin, 1996.

"Report of the Axis Diplomats and Nationals at the Greenbrier December 19th,1941 to July 8th, 1942. (201 days stay)." This is an unpublished report made available to the authors by the Greenbrier Hotel historian, Robert S. Conte.

Salvador Lara, Jorge. *Breve Historia Contemporánea del Ecuador.* México. Fondode Cultura Económica, 1994.

The World War Two Experience, The Internment of German-Americans in German-Americans in the World Wars. Vol. IV. Jacobs, Arthur and Joseph E. Fallon, co- editors. Munich: K.G. Saur, 1995.

Tinajero, Fernando. *Itinerario de un acercamiento: Colegio Alemán 1917-1992.*

Quito: Asociación Ecuatoriana-Alemana de Cultura y Educación. 1992.

ELECTRONIC PUBLICATIONS

Internment. Arthur Jacob's web site on internment and relocation of German Americans during World War II is one of the most complete records of internment connections and information. http://www.netzone.com/~ajacobs/rel_int.htm.

NBC Dateline, 1994. The electronic publication of the aired television program is located at http://www.msnbc.com/news/185258.asp?cp1=1.

United Nations Relief and Rehabilitation Agency. The encyclopedic entry is located at http://www.infoplease.com/ce5/ce053348.html.

INTERVIEWS

Dr. and Mrs. C. H. Contag, Minnesota
Hermann Detken, Ecuador
Mr. Hermann Dreier, Jr., California
Helga (Renner) Emde, Germany
Mr. Huré, Beaune-La Rolande
José Antonio Gómez Iturralde, Ecuador
Maria Luisa Flores de Valencia, Ecuador
Irmgard (Contag) Jaunzems, Oregon
Ursula Krone, Germany
Myriam Maldonado de Contag, Florida
Alcira Mejía de Contag, Ecuador
María Mikette, Ecuador
Annette Olbricht, Germany
Pietro and Beti Tosi, Ecuador
Giovanni Tosi, Ecuador
Prof. Willington Paredes Ramírez, Ecuador